WHAT IS AN
Aspen RoadMap?

Aspen RoadMaps™ are comprehensive course outlines that lead you, step by step, through your law school courses—helping you prepare for class and study for exams. With a clean, modern design that is as easy to use as it is visually appealing, you'll be guided from the "big picture" to the details you need to know.

WHAT MAKES THE ASPEN ROADMAP™ FOR EMPLOYMENT DISCRIMINATION SO VALUABLE?

The Aspen RoadMap™ *for Employment Discrimination:*

■ Explains the Civil Rights Act of 1964, with a focus on Title VII and the relevant state law, in clear, straightforward language.

■ Provides definitions and examples throughout to guide you through the terminology of employment discrimination.

■ Provides you with a historical and legal framework with which to better understand the underpinnings of employment discrimination law.

■ Gives complete subject coverage including: the three general theories of liability, individual and systemic disparate treatment discrimination, enforcement of antidiscrimination laws, procedures, and remedies.

■ Includes discussion of the policy bases for antidiscrimination law: weighing its economic—and noneconomic—costs and benefits.

THE PRACTICAL COMPONENTS OF YOUR ASPEN ROADMAP™

■ ***The Casebook Correlation Chart*** helps you match sections of your casebook to this RoadMap™.

■ ***The RoadMap*™ *Capsule Summary,*** cross-referenced to the outline text, provides a "big picture" view anytime you need it.

■ ***Chapter Overviews,*** each no more than two pages long, highlight key concepts.

■ ***Hypotheticals*** are interwoven throughout to help further clarify important concepts.

■ ***Examples***—complete with accompanying analyses—are included in each chapter to provide lively and memorable illustrations of key points.

■ ***Chapter Review Questions***—complete with answers—test and reinforce your knowledge.

■ ***Exam Tips*** help you to target what you need to know, maximize your study time, and do well on exams.

■ ***Sample Exam Questions and Answers*** help you prepare for the final exam.

ASPEN LAW & BUSINESS Educational Division

Dear Student,

Historically, the employer-employee relationship in the United States was described by the "at-will" rule, by which neither party was bound, as by a contract, to any legal commitment whatsoever. The employer could hire or fire at will, and the employee could quit at will. Not hiring someone on the basis of their race or gender was the prerogative of the employer. Anyone who was excluded because of a prospective employer's prejudice had no legal recourse except to seek employment elsewhere. The Civil Rights Act of 1964, the result of the pivotal Civil Rights Movement, was the beginning of the end of these and other forms of employment discrimination.

The Civil Rights Act of 1964, and state laws enacted since the Civil Rights Movement, operate as exceptions to the at-will rule. An employer can still terminate employment for many reasons, but he or she can no longer lawfully terminate an employee on the basis of race, color, sex, religion, national origin, age, or disability. Some states have added further protections that additionally prevent termination of employment on the basis of political affiliation, marital status, or sexual orientation.

Employment Discrimination is a particularly interesting field of law because it reflects not only the relationship between employer and employee, but, more broadly, the generally pendular movement of society toward or away from social reforms in general. It is a measure of society's inclusiveness or exclusiveness, a reflection of the country's demographic changes, its political climate, and its national—and even international—identity.

Your *Employment Discrimination RoadMap*™ will help you to better understand and enjoy the intricacies of the law as well as the broader questions as you prepare for class and for your exam. While nothing can substitute for careful preparation of the assigned materials, your *Aspen RoadMap*™ will give you a clear presentation of the structure of the law, the context in which various issues of employment discrimination arise, and the relationships among the major concepts that form employment discrimination today.

Your *Aspen RoadMap*™ is organized to be used with all the major casebooks. Its many features—clearly written chapters covering all the major topics, chapter summaries, review questions and answers, a comprehensive capsule summary, exam tips, and sample exam questions with answers—will help you to be more prepared for class and exams.

I have practiced, taught, and written about employment discrimination law for many years. And I am still engrossed in it. I hope your *Aspen RoadMap*™ will give you a deeper appreciation for employment discrimination law.

Sincerely,

Michael J. Zimmer

Michael J. Zimmer
Professor of Law

P.S. I welcome your suggestions for making this Aspen RoadMap even more useful. Please write to me at Aspen Law & Business, Educational Publishing, Marketing Department, 1185 Avenue of the Americas, 37th Floor, New York, NY 10036, or e-mail me at zimmermi@shu.edu.

Aspen Publishers, Inc. A **Wolters Kluwer** Company

1185 Avenue of the Americas, New York, NY 10036
www.aspenpublishers.com

Employment Discrimination

Michael J. Zimmer

Professor of Law
Seton Hall University

ASPEN LAW & BUSINESS
A Division of Aspen Publishers, Inc.
Gaithersburg   New York

This publication is designed to provide accurate and authoritative information in regard to the subject matter covered. It is sold with the understanding that the publisher is not engaged in rendering legal, accounting, or other professional services. If legal advice or other professional assistance is required, the services of competent professional person should be sought.

—From a *Declaration of Principles* jointly adopted by a
Committee of the American Bar Association and a
Committee of Publishers and Associations

Library of Congress Cataloging-in-Publication Data

Zimmer, Michael J., 1942-
    Employment discrimination / Michael J. Zimmer.
        p.   cm.—(Roadmap law course outlines)
    Includes index.
    ISBN 0-7355-1247-7
    1. Discrimination in employment—Law and legislation—United
States—Outlines, syllabi, etc.   2. Law students—United States—Examinations—Study
guides.   I. Title.   II. Series.
KF3464.Z9 Z56   2000
344.7301'133—dc21   99-089400

SUMMARY OF CONTENTS

CONTENTS

2 INDIVIDUAL DISPARATE TREATMENT DISCRIMINATION   9

4   SYSTEMIC DISPARATE IMPACT DISCRIMINATION

5

THE INTERRELATION OF THE THEORIES OF DISCRIMINATION   95

6   SPECIAL PROBLEMS OF GENDER DISCRIMINATION   111

9   SPECIAL PROBLEMS OF AGE DISCRIMINATION   153

13 EQUAL PAY FOR EQUAL WORK 209

14 COVERAGE OF THE ANTIDISCRIMINATION STATUTES 223

15   PROCEDURES FOR ENFORCING ANTIDISCRIMINATION LAWS   235

16 JUDICIAL RELIEF   253

CHAPTER OVERVIEW   253

CASEBOOK CORRELATION

Aspen Roadmap	Zimmer, Sullivan, Richards & Calloway **Cases and Materials on Employment Discrimination** (5th ed.)	Estreicher & Harper **Cases and Materials on the Law Governing the Employment Relationship** (2d ed.)	Friedman & Strickler **The Law of Employment Discrimination: Cases and Materials** (4th ed.)	Player, Shoben & Lieberwitz **Employment Discrimination Law: Cases and Materials** (2d ed.)	Smith, Craver & Clark **Employment Discrimination Law: Cases and Materials** (4th ed.)
1. THE BACKGROUND AND POLICY BASES FOR ANTIDISCRIMINATION LAW					
A. The Background for Antidiscrimination Law	1-31, 511-512	3-7, 697-705	1	2-6	1
B. Antidiscrimination Law as an Exception to the At-Will Rule	14-22	585-586, 696-775	1-10	7-21	1-2
C. The Law and Economics Challenge to Antidiscrimination Law	33-61	3-7, 9-16	1-2	2-6	1-86, 111-120
D. Responses to the Libertarian Challenge to Antidiscrimination Law	44-50, 61-82	9-16		2-6	1-86
E. Developing a Personal Policy Perspective Concerning Discrimination	39-41, 61-67	14-16		381	86-94
2. INDIVIDUAL DISPARATE TREATMENT DISCRIMINATION					
A. Antidiscrimination Statutes	85-87, 95-109	17-27	934-947, 979, 1010, 1050	21-27	95-120
B. Individual Disparate Treatment Is Intentional Discrimination	87-95	11, 43-48, 96-98, 159-160, 310-311, 375-376, 392-403, 437-459	86, 127-171, 233	187	121-157
C. There Are Two Recognized Ways to Prove Intent to Discriminate	95-109	47	84-85	179-187	121-126, 133-151
D. Circumstantial Evidence or "Pretext" Cases Showing Intent to Discriminate	109-162	29-30, 37, 105, 137	84-230	187-204	121-151
E. The Three Step *McDonnell Douglas/Burdine* Analysis	109-162	27-38	84-126, 157-158, 172	98-116, 187-204	121-157, 245-248
F. The Background of the Direct Evidence or Mixed Motive Test of Intent	162-197	38-48	127-171	96-103, 179-187, 204-222	149-150
G. The Present Approach to Direct Evidence Cases	197-207	38-48, 513, 533	143-147, 155-157, 244	213-215	149-150
H. The Relationship Between the Circumstantial and Direct Evidence Approaches to Individual Disparate Treatment Discrimination	197-207	38-48	120, 157-158, 984	213-215	149-150

Aspen Roadmap	Zimmer, Sullivan, Richards & Calloway **Cases and Materials on Employment Discrimination** (5th ed.)	Estreicher & Harper **Cases and Materials on the Law Governing the Employment Relationship** (2d ed.)	Friedman & Strickler **The Law of Employment Discrimination: Cases and Materials** (4th ed.)	Player, Shoben & Lieberwitz **Employment Discrimination Law: Cases and Materials** (2d ed.)	Smith, Craver & Clark **Employment Discrimination Law: Cases and Materials** (4th ed.)
I. The Collapse of the Existing Order and the Emergence of a New Approach	197-207	35-38, 46-50, 381-384, 837-840	84-85		
3. SYSTEMIC DISPARATE TREATMENT DISCRIMINATION					
A. Policy or Practice of Intentional Discrimination	209-210	50-74, 145-146, 176, 182, 839-840	278, 305-307, 320, 327	229	157-181
B. Establishing a Prima Facie Case	210-222, 316-360	50-63, 72-74, 207-209, 225-276	1108-1233	82-92, 150-178	248-266, 345-358, 486-492
C. Formal Policies of Discrimination					
D. Patterns and Practices of Discrimination	223-270	50-63, 72-74	320-356	222-243	157-181
E. Using Statistical Evidence to Prove Systemic Disparate Treatment Discrimination	223-270	63-72, 392-403	333-356	234-243, 301-303	220-229
F. Defenses to Disparate Treatment Cases	270-360	29, 32-34, 61-62, 72-74	172	482-483, 688-691	443-457
G. Bona Fide Occupational Qualifications	287-316	297-324, 384-392	172-202, 506-510	116-150, 482-483	665-676
H. The Defense Against Individual's Remedies	232-233, 270-287	61-62, 72-74	172-202	187, 190, 201, 627	157-181
4. SYSTEMIC DISPARATE IMPACT DISCRIMINATION					
A. The Disparate Impact Concept	361-362	74-78	230	244	220-229
B. A Brief Background	362-385	74-78, 83-85, 98-111	230-235, 250-263	244-252, 270-279, 287-304	181-195, 203-210
C. The Present Statutory Structure of Disparate Impact Discrimination	385-386	107-111	235	177-178, 189, 201, 276-277, 296-304, 627, 636	203-204
D. The Prima Facie Showing of an Employment Practice Causing Impact	386-421	50-75, 78-111	236-249	279-287	210-235
E. Defendant's Rebuttal	421-446, 454-482	111-142, 166-206, 649-653	263-320	177-178, 252-270, 305-322	195-210, 273-295, 477-486
F. Alternative Employment Practice Surrebuttal	446-454	107-111	172	277, 587, 600	207, 247
G. The Same Decision Defense to Limit Individual's Remedies		61-62, 72-74	233-234, 263-278	746	905-915
H. Procedures and Remedies	1072-1074	46-50, 382, 439	720-722, 916, 923-925, 1029-1032	26, 267, 737, 754, 758	950-954

Aspen Roadmap	Zimmer, Sullivan, Richards & Calloway **Cases and Materials on Employment Discrimination** (5th ed.)	Estreicher & Harper **Cases and Materials on the Law Governing the Employment Relationship** (2d ed.)	Friedman & Strickler **The Law of Employment Discrimination: Cases and Materials** (4th ed.)	Player, Shoben & Lieberwitz **Employment Discrimination Law: Cases and Materials** (2d ed.)	Smith, Craver & Clark **Employment Discrimination Law: Cases and Materials** (4th ed.)
I. Disparate Impact in Other Antidiscrimination Statutes	480-482	50, 335	865-867	39-40, 267, 499, 626	676-689
5. THE INTERRELATION OF THE THEORIES OF DISCRIMINATION					
A. The Differences Between the Three Theories of Discrimination	484-486	27-142	230, 234, 243-246, 328-329	229	443-457
B. The Relationship Between the Two Systemic Theories	486-500	27-142	230, 234, 243-246, 328-329	251	157-235
C. The Relationship Between the Systemic Theories and Individual Disparate Treatment Discrimination	500-505	27-142	230, 234, 243-246, 328-329	229	157-235
6. SPECIAL PROBLEMS OF GENDER DISCRIMINATION					
A. The Four Special Gender Discrimination Problems	521	277-278	398-510	375-535	318-320
B. Pregnancy	522-548	288-297	400-403, 411-435	92-96, 118, 128-141, 148, 349-357, 503-519	384-414, 495-504
C. Sexual Harassment	548-613	324-337	435-475	358-366, 375-390	420-438
D. Grooming and Dress Codes	613-624	310-311	403-410	110-115, 324-334	414-420
E. Sexual Orientation	624-640	159-160, 802-803	486-506	388-390, 520-535	438-443, 218-524
7. SPECIAL PROBLEMS OF RELIGIOUS DISCRIMINATION					
A. The Four Special Problems of Religious Discrimination	651	468	357-358	536-539	296-318
B. The Duty to Accommodate Employee's Religious Practices	651-673	469-481	357-387	149, 538-555	296-318
C. Title VII's Exemptions for Employers to Discriminate Because of Religion	673-678	481-487, 492-493	61-79, 371, 374	117, 555-566	296-318
D. The Constitutionality of Title VII's Treatment of Religion	678-691	481-493	61-83	562-563	492-494

Aspen Roadmap	Zimmer, Sullivan, Richards & Calloway **Cases and Materials on Employment Discrimination** (5th ed.)	Estreicher & Harper **Cases and Materials on the Law Governing the Employment Relationship** (2d ed.)	Friedman & Strickler **The Law of Employment Discrimination: Cases and Materials** (4th ed.)	Player, Shoben & Lieberwitz **Employment Discrimination Law: Cases and Materials** (2d ed.)	Smith, Craver & Clark **Employment Discrimination Law: Cases and Materials** (4th ed.)
C. The Scope of §1981 Protection	133-134, 195	151-165, 875-879	848-867	38-40	545-576
D. 42 U.S.C. §1983	193-197	160-161	868-893	41-42	504-524
E. 42 U.S.C. §1985(c)	193-197	879-885	894-909	38-44	545-552
12. DISABILITY DISCRIMINATION					
A. The Broad Scope of the Americans with Disabilities Act	737-742	437-440	1033-1034	37-38, 567	711-716
B. Individual Disparate Treatment Case of Disability Discrimination	742-881	441-463	1034-1063, 1082-1107	37-38, 117-118, 567-569, 571-606	698-711
C. The Other Theories of Discrimination	897-919	439-463	1063-1082	35-36, 569, 602, 606-614	495-504
D. Special Disability Discrimination Problems	881-918	159-160, 459-460, 802-803	1048-1049, 1054-1057	593-606	711-712
13. EQUAL PAY FOR EQUAL WORK					
A. Gender Discrimination in Compensation	640-641	337-373	398-400, 931-933	32, 421, 448	601-602
B. The Equal Pay Act	640-645	337-342, 345-351, 364-373	398-403, 475-485, 934-940	31-32, 392-420	345-374, 593-643, 781, 967-976
C. Using Title VII to Attack Gender-Based Wage Discrimination	645-650	342-373	940-969	421-463	320-345, 374-384, 781
14. COVERAGE OF THE ANTIDISCRIMINATION STATUTES					
A. Coverage Issues Are Important to Scope of Application	512-521	151-165	26-60	49	237-238
B. Title VII of the Civil Rights Act of 1964	512-521	48-50, 827-874	25-83	49-73	237-245
C. Age Discrimination in Employment Act of 1967	515-521	374-375, 378-379, 384	970-973, 1032	27, 615	658-697
D. Reconstruction Civil Rights Statutes	124-133, 517	151-165	848-909	38-44	504-524, 545-576
E. Americans with Disabilities Act	918-924	449-450, 460	1033-1063	37, 568	711-716
F. The Equal Pay Act	640-650	337-348, 352-357, 363-365	931-969	21, 31-32, 413-419	643-658
15. PROCEDURES FOR ENFORCING ANTIDISCRIMINATION LAWS					
A. The Scope of Antidiscrimination Procedures	927-929	822-827	511	74-75, 694-695, 704-705	747
B. Private Enforcement of Title VII	929-994	822-852	511-571	75-77, 313-314, 695-738	748-774

Aspen Roadmap	Zimmer, Sullivan, Richards & Calloway **Cases and Materials on Employment Discrimination** (5th ed.)	Estreicher & Harper **Cases and Materials on the Law Governing the Employment Relationship** (2d ed.)	Friedman & Strickler **The Law of Employment Discrimination: Cases and Materials** (4th ed.)	Player, Shoben & Lieberwitz **Employment Discrimination Law: Cases and Materials** (2d ed.)	Smith, Craver & Clark **Employment Discrimination Law: Cases and Materials** (4th ed.)
C. Private Class Actions	994-1007	853-859	571-576, 612-660	738-740	774-777
D. Public Government Enforcement	1007-1010	665-685	581-597	719-736	761-768, 830-851
E. Title VII Suit Against Governmental Employers	920-924, 1012-1017	665-696, 776-803	604-611	77-78, 174-175, 570-571	797-830
F. The Relationship Between Public and Private Suit	1010-1012	665-685	597-603	736	769-780
G. Settling and Arbitrating Discrimination Suits	1017-1035	627-649	576-580	740-742	790-795, 861-881
16. JUDICIAL RELIEF					
A. The Scope of Judicial Relief	1037-1038	48-50	661-847	751, 754-755	237-238, 737-746
B. Full Relief for Individual Victims of Discrimination	1038-1087	48-50	661-726	175, 743-747	861-966
C. Types of Remedies in Individual Cases	1113-1129	48-50, 649-653, 859-874	661-813	268, 314-315, 381, 475-476, 747-789	676-684, 905-976
D. Relief for Systemic Discrimination	1087-1113	166-206, 207-225	813-847	174-175, 748-750	851-859, 882-905

CAPSULE SUMMARY

To maximize the usefulness of this Capsule Summary, the focus of discussion reflects the importance of material that is especially helpful for exam preparation. Thus, some levels of the outline that are discussed in the main text are not discussed here, since—while they provide important background material—they are less significant once the reader begins to prepare for the exam.

1 THE BACKGROUND AND POLICY BASES FOR ANTIDISCRIMINATION LAW

A. THE BACKGROUND FOR ANTIDISCRIMINATION LAW

At common law, "at will" employment was presumed. That meant either party could terminate the relationship for good reason, bad reason, or no reason at all.

B. ANTIDISCRIMINATION LAW AS AN EXCEPTION TO THE AT-WILL RULE

The main focus of employment discrimination law is Title VII of the Civil Rights Act of 1964, the Age Discrimination in Employment Act of 1967, and the Americans with Disabilities Act of 1990. Many employment discrimination courses also cover the Equal Pay Act of 1963 as well as two provisions—42 U.S.C. §§1981 and 1983—that survive from the civil rights legislation passed in the Reconstruction era after the Civil War.

The effect of such antidiscrimination legislation is to create an exception to the at-will rule established at common law. Thus, the proper statement of the at-will rule is now that an employer may terminate an employee for good reason, bad reason, or no reason but the employer may not take action against an employee because of discrimination on the basis of race, color, religion, national origin, or sex under Title VII, age under the Age Discrimination in Employment Act, or disability under the Americans with Disabilities Act.

C. THE LAW AND ECONOMICS CHALLENGE TO ANTIDISCRIMINATION LAW

The law and economics movement has challenged antidiscrimination law by claiming that law is not an appropriate means to end what is acknowledged to be the wrong of discrimination.

1. Law Is Not Necessary to Redress Discrimination

John Locke claimed that we all own our own labor and that freedom to contract that labor is an essential human value. The role of law should be limited to the protection of the freedom of contract. The common law of fraud, force, and incompetence is as far as law should go because these laws protect the market.

2. "Rational" Profit Maximization

To be **"rational,"** as neoclassical economists use the term, means to act to maximize economic profits. Over time, as employers skim the best of the majority workers, it will become rational for employers, even those with a taste for discrimination against members of minority groups, to begin to hire minority group members because they will be better workers than the majority group members still in the pool of people looking for work.

3. The Discrimination That Persists Is Rational

The discrimination that persists when the free market operates is "rational," with rational meaning that it leads to profit maximization for the employer that discriminates.

D. RESPONSES TO THE LIBERTARIAN CHALLENGE TO ANTIDISCRIMINATION LAW

1. The Economic Answers

The most significant response to the libertarian position that a free labor market will drive out most discrimination is history. From an economic perspective, the persistence of discrimination reveals an imperfection in the market.

2. Non-Economic Costs of Discrimination

Social policy as established in law can look to values other than the economic dimension of various preferences of workers and employers and can conclude that the preference for discrimination is not to be valued while the preference against discrimination will be enforced through the law.

E. DEVELOPING A PERSONAL POLICY PERSPECTIVE CONCERNING DISCRIMINATION

To best study employment discrimination law, you should try to make your own judgments about the persistence of discrimination and its causes.

 2   INDIVIDUAL DISPARATE TREATMENT DISCRIMINATION

A. ANTIDISCRIMINATION STATUTES

Title VII of the 1964 Civil Rights Act, the Age Discrimination in Employment Act of 1967, the Americans with Disabilities Act of 1990, and the Equal Pay Act all prohibit discrimination in employment. Several statutes survive from the First Reconstruction, especially 42 U.S.C. §1981.

B. INDIVIDUAL DISPARATE TREATMENT IS INTENTIONAL DISCRIMINATION

The courts have developed more or less uniform rules for dealing with disparate treatment claims brought by individuals, without regard to the statutory source of the claim.

"Disparate treatment" . . . is the most easily understood type of discrimination. The employer simply treats some people less favorably than others because of their race, color, religion [or other protected characteristic]. **Proof of discriminatory motive is critical,** although it can in some situations be inferred from the mere fact of differences in treatment. Teamsters v. United States, 431 U.S. 324, 335 n.15 (1977).

1. Stereotyping

While the intent or the motivation to discriminate is seen as the essence of individual disparate treatment discrimination, the Supreme Court has also focused on **stereotyping** as a form of intentional discrimination.

C. THERE ARE TWO RECOGNIZED WAYS TO PROVE INTENT TO DISCRIMINATE

The Supreme Court has recognized two methods to prove individual disparate treatment discrimination. One relies on "direct" evidence of intent and the other on "circumstantial evidence" that supports drawing an inference of discriminatory intent.

D. CIRCUMSTANTIAL EVIDENCE OF "PRETEXT" CASES SHOWING INTENT TO DISCRIMINATE

Most individual disparate treatment cases are analyzed using the **circumstantial evidence** method of proving discrimination. The circumstantial evidence approach is based on the assumption that it may sometimes be reasonable for a factfinder, looking at all the evidence in the record, to draw an inference that discrimination is the real reason for the employer's action, even when the evidence does not include direct evidence—a "smoking gun" statement—of the employer's intent to discriminate.

E. THE THREE-STEP *MCDONNELL DOUGLAS/BURDINE* ANALYSIS

In *McDonnell Douglas,* the Court established a three-step analysis of an individual disparate treatment case based on circumstantial evidence, involving **plaintiff's prima facie case, defendant's rebuttal,** and the third, surrebuttal step of plaintiff proving **pretext.**

1. Plaintiff's Prima Facie Case

    a. The four parts of a prima facie case

        i. **Racial minority**

        ii. **Qualified**

        iii. **Rejection**

        iv. **Job remained open**

    b. Limiting the scope of circumstantial evidence. *Hazen Paper* held that evidence of a correlation between age and pension eligibility did not support a finding of age discrimination.

    c. The consequences of establishing a prima facie case. The establishment of a prima facie case creates a rebuttable presumption in favor of the plaintiff.

2. Employer's Rebuttal

The second step in a *McDonnell Douglas/Burdine* case requires the employer to rebut the inference of discrimination based on the prima facie showing of intent to discriminate by showing a *legitimate nondiscriminatory reason* for its action. In *Burdine,* the Court clarified the significance of this rebuttal burden by finding that the employer must do more than introduce evidence sufficient to raise a question of fact so that a reasonable factfinder could find that it was the actual reason for the decision. Since *Hazen Paper,* the reason need only be one that plaintiff cannot challenge as discriminatory.

3. Plaintiff's Showing of Pretext

The third step in the *McDonnell Douglas/Burdine* analysis gives the plaintiff a chance to show that the reasons advanced by the employer were a **"pretext," hiding the employer's true discriminatory motivation.** In St. Mary's Honor Ctr. v. Hicks, 509 U.S. 502 (1993), the Court held that a finding of pretext, in the sense that the employer's proffered reason was not the true reason for its actions, did not justify finding as a matter of law that the employer had discriminated against the plaintiff. A finding of Title VII liability must be based on a finding of the ultimate question of "whether [the] plaintiff has proven 'that the defendant intentionally discriminated against [him] because of his race.'" *Hicks.*

4. Level of Showing

The plaintiff bears the burden of proving that but for discrimination the adverse action would not have been taken against her.

F. THE BACKGROUND OF THE DIRECT EVIDENCE OR MIXED MOTIVE TEST OF INTENT

After years of development of the circumstantial evidence approach to proving individual disparate treatment discrimination, the Supreme Court's decision in *Price Waterhouse* became the basis for the development of a separate approach for proving intentional discrimination because most courts have followed Justice O'Connor's concurring opinion, which with the plurality opinion made a majority.

G. THE PRESENT APPROACH TO DIRECT EVIDENCE CASES

Unlike the circumstantial evidence cases, *Price Waterhouse* involved statements by the employer that revealed an intent by the employer to discriminate or at least reliance upon stereotypical thinking about the plaintiff because she was a woman.

As a result of the amendments added to Title VII by the 1991 Civil Rights Act, *Price Waterhouse* **direct evidence** cases involve two steps, the plaintiff's prima facie case followed by the employer's affirmative defense.

1. The Prima Facie Showing of "a Motivating Factor"

Section 703(m) now provides that "an unlawful employment practice is established when the complaining party demonstrates that race, color, religion, sex, or national origin was a **motivating factor** for any employment practice, **even though other factors also motivated the practice.**"

2. The Same Decision Defense to Full Remedies

Congress changed the consequences of the employer successfully carrying its *Price Waterhouse* rebuttal burden of proving the same decision defense from a defense to liability to a limitation on remedies. According to

§706(g)(2)(B), where the **employer can prove that it "would have taken the same action in the absence of the impermissible motivating factor,"** the court can only order declaratory or injunctive relief (other than reinstatement or backpay) plus attorney's fees.

H.   THE RELATIONSHIP BETWEEN THE CIRCUMSTANTIAL AND DIRECT EVIDENCE APPROACHES TO INDIVIDUAL DISPARATE TREATMENT DISCRIMINATION

Given two separate methods of proving individual disparate treatment discrimination, it is necessary to find the boundary that divides the two approaches.

1.   Only One of the Two Approaches Applies to a Case

While a plaintiff could claim both approaches in any case, the trial judge must decide which of the two methods is applicable before sending the case to the jury.

2.   *McDonnell Douglas/Burdine* Is the Default Approach

In deciding which approach applies, first decide if the *Price Waterhouse* direct evidence approach applies, and, if not, then the *McDonnell Douglas/Burdine* approach applies as the default position.

3.   The Existence of "Direct Evidence" Is the Boundary Between Circumstantial and Direct Evidence Cases

The lower courts have taken several different positions as to what evidence is sufficiently direct to trigger the use of the *Price Waterhouse* direct evidence method of proving individual disparate treatment discrimination.

a.   The two different definitions of what is direct evidence.   In Harris v. Shelby County Board of Education, 99 F.3d 1078 (11th Cir. 1996), the court adopted the classical definition of direct evidence as "evidence, which if believed, proves the existence of the fact in issue without an inference or presumption." In contrast, in Deneen v. Northwest Airlines, 132 F.3d 431 (8th Cir. 1998), the court defined direct evidence as evidence that supports an inference of discrimination. Direct evidence "demonstrates a specific link between the alleged discriminatory animus and the challenged decision, sufficient to support a finding by a reasonable factfinder that an illegitimate criterion actually motivated the employer's decision." This approach is sometimes called the **"circumstantial-plus"** approach to the threshold for the use of the *Price Waterhouse* approach because it requires that "circumstantial evidence must be tied directly to the alleged discriminatory animus."

I.   THE COLLAPSE OF THE EXISTING ORDER AND THE EMERGENCE OF A NEW APPROACH

There has been much criticism of the *McDonnell Douglas/Burdine* approach and some for maintaining two separate approaches to proof of individual disparate treatment discrimination. There have been several alternative approaches suggested.

1. **Applying the 1991 Civil Rights Act Provisions to All Individual Disparate Treatment Cases**

   Since §§703(m) and 707(g)(2)(B) already apply to *Price Waterhouse* direct evidence cases, these same provisions could easily be read to apply to *McDonnell Douglas/Burdine* circumstantial evidence cases as well.

   a. **"A motivating factor" test for all cases.** The burden on plaintiff in the first instance would be lowered from having to prove that the protected characteristic was the "determinative influence" to the lesser level of "a motivating factor."

   b. **Same decision limit on remedies for all cases.** If plaintiff establishes a prima facie case, defendant would have a new affirmative defense under §706(g)(2)(B) not previously available under the *McDonnell Douglas/Burdine* approach to try to limit full remedies by proving it would have made the same decision even if it had not considered plaintiff's prohibited characteristic in making the decision.

2. **A Gravitational Move Toward a Unified Approach**

   The lower courts may be moving toward a unified approach to individual disparate treatment cases, even without saying so by collapsing the application of the two methods into one.

3. **The Traditional Approach to General Litigation**

   Some courts are simply deciding to review the record to determine whether there is sufficient evidence of whatever kind to support drawing the inference of discrimination.

 SYSTEMIC DISPARATE TREATMENT DISCRIMINATION

A. POLICY OR PRACTICE OF INTENTIONAL DISCRIMINATION

The broadest definition or theory of discrimination is **systemic disparate treatment discrimination.** It is a system of discrimination, that is, a **formal policy** or a **general practice** of an employer to discriminate on a basis prohibited by an antidiscrimination statute.

The plaintiff can establish a prima facie case of systemic disparate treatment using one of two different paths. First, the plaintiff may demonstrate that the employer has an announced, formal policy of discrimination. Second, failing proof of a formal policy, a plaintiff may nevertheless establish that the employer's pattern of employment decisions, its general practice, reveals that a de facto policy of disparate treatment exists.

B. ESTABLISHING A PRIMA FACIE CASE

Systemic disparate treatment discrimination can be proved in two ways—a formal policy of the employer that discriminates, or a practice of discrimination showed by the pattern of the employer's decisions.

C. FORMAL POLICIES OF DISCRIMINATION

The first way to establish a prima facie case of systemic disparate treatment is to prove that a formal, typically written, policy of discrimination exists.

1. The Employer Admits the Policy

Since the BFOQ defense is tied to a formal policy of discrimination, the employer trying to defend a policy based on the BFOQ defense may admit the existence of a formal policy of discrimination.

a. Voluntary affirmative action. A "reverse" discrimination Title VII plaintiff carries the burden of persuasion to prove that a voluntary affirmative action plan of the employer violates the Title VII standards. There are much stricter standards if equal protection under the Constitution is the basis for the claim.

i. The Title VII standards for affirmative action. The Supreme Court has upheld the use of race and gender by an employer under Title VII attack where the employer was acting pursuant to a voluntary affirmative action plan that meets certain standards.

(a) The burden of persuasion is on the plaintiff.

(b) The standards for using affirmative action.

(1) The purpose is to break patterns of discrimination. Affirmative action will be upheld if the plan is designed to "break down old patterns of racial segregation and hierarchy." In another statement, the Court said the intent of the plan must be to "eliminate a manifest racial balance."

(2) The plan does not unnecessarily trammel the rights of majority workers. The second element necessary to uphold an affirmative plan from attack under Title VII is that the "plan does not unnecessarily trammel" the interests of the white employees.

(3) The plan must be temporary. A third element is that "the plan is a temporary measure; it is not intended to maintain racial balance, but simply to eliminate a manifest racial balance."

ii. Affirmative action and the Constitution. The Supreme Court has declared that the use of any race classification by a governmental actor that is challenged in an equal protection case must satisfy strict scrutiny. In contrast, it has yet to decide what level of scrutiny applies to the use of affirmative action to aid women.

The strict scrutiny standard of equal protection applied to all racial classifications imposes the burden of persuasion on the governmental employer to justify the classification by proving that it furthers a compelling government interest and that it is narrowly tailored to serve only that interest.

(a) A compelling governmental interest. So far, a limited list of interests has been found to be compelling enough to satisfy strict scrutiny.

(1) Remedy to defendant's discrimination.

(2) Remedy present effects of past discrimination. There is authority that remedying the present effects of past discrimination is a compelling governmental interest.

(3) Diversity. It is not clear whether diversity is a compelling governmental interest justifying affirmative action.

(4) Remedying societal discrimination is *not* a compelling governmental interest. A governmental actor's attempt to cure the effects of societal discrimination that is not attributable to its actions that are discriminatory is not a compelling state interest.

(b) Narrowly tailored remedy. If the defendant is successful in arguing that its use of affirmative action serves a compelling governmental interest, it then must prove that its use is narrowly tailored to that interest.

(1) The remedy must serve only the compelling interest. The use of a racial classification must serve only the compelling interest that justifies its use and it cannot serve interests other than the articulated compelling interest.

(2) The plan does not unnecessarily trammel the rights of the majority. It appears that this aspect of the narrowly tailored requirement is shared with Title VII's approach to affirmative action.

2. The Policy Is Shown by Inference

The other situation where formal policies of discrimination may exist involve situations where the nature of the classification is not always immediately clear but requires some deciphering.

D. PATTERNS AND PRACTICES OF DISCRIMINATION

Even if no formal, announced policy of discrimination can be proved to exist, a systemic disparate treatment case can still be established if the plaintiff can prove that the practices the employer follows reveal an intent on the part of the employer to discriminate.

1. The Comparison of the Workforce and the Labor Pool

The comparison of the statistics of the employer's workforce versus the labor pool is the key to making out a practice of systemic disparate treatment discrimination.

2. "Gross and Longlasting Disparity" or the "Inexorable Zero"

This is the level of showing necessary to draw the inference that the employer has a practice of discriminating.

3. The Employer's Post-Act Workforce

The employer's **workforce** can be established by taking a "snapshot" of the racial representation of the employer's workers in the target jobs on the day the lawsuit is commenced. That snapshot then must be refined by subtracting all the employees hired before the Act applied to the employer.

4. The Qualified Labor Pool

To make out a systemic disparate treatment case, the plaintiff must also show that, given their availability in a **qualified labor pool,** so many fewer women or minority group members are working for the employer than would be expected that it is possible to conclude that a "gross and longlasting disparity" exists between the employer's workforce and the labor pool from which workers are selected.

    a. The probability theory underpinning statistical evidence. Statistical evidence can support a finding that the employer has a practice of discriminating because of probability theory: If there is no discrimination, then over time the employer's workforce should resemble the racial, ethnic and gender composition of the population from which it hires its employees.

5. Anecdotal Evidence Supports the Inference of Discrimination

Fact witnesses telling about the employer's treatment of them can bolster the statistical evidence.

E. USING STATISTICAL EVIDENCE TO PROVE SYSTEMIC DISPARATE TREATMENT DISCRIMINATION

The comparison of the statistics of the employer's workforce versus the labor pool is the key.

1. The Employer's Observed Post-Act Workforce

Only employment decisions made after the effective date of the antidiscrimination statute at issue may be used for the comparison.

2. The Qualified Labor Pool

The job qualifications and the geographic area from which the employer would draw employees but for discrimination are the two elements to establishing the qualified labor pool.

a. Qualifications. In *Teamsters* and *Hazelwood,* the Court differentiated between two different kinds of jobs and the labor pools that would be appropriate for each.

i. Unskilled or low-skilled jobs. Where the employer's workforce involves unskilled or low-skilled workers, the general population may be used as the qualified labor pool to be compared with the makeup of the employer's workforce.

ii. Skilled jobs. When special qualifications are required to fill particular jobs, comparisons to the general population (rather than to the smaller group of individuals who possess the necessary qualifications) may have little probative value.

b. Geographic labor pool. The second basis for manipulation of the labor market statistics is the geographic area used for the comparison. As to racial and national origin groups, rather extreme patterns of residential segregation make the choice of geographic area outcome determinative in many cases. In contrast, the residential patterns of men and women appear to be more or less evenly distributed.

3. Sources of Qualified Labor Pool Statistics

There are a number of potential ways to find the statistics to show the pool of qualified workers and the geographic area in which the employer would look for employees, absent discrimination.

a. The employer's own workforce as a labor pool. If two groups of the employer's workforce share skills but the representation of protected workers is much higher in one group than in the group that is the focus of the case, the one group can be used as the qualified labor pool.

b.   Applicants for employer's jobs.   After the employer's own employees with skills similar to the skills required in the jobs in question, the next closest labor pool would be the pool of applicants for work with the employer. Those people have shown they are interested in working for the employer and they are likely to meet the minimal qualifications the employer has announced for its jobs.

c.   Labor market statistics.   The labor market is the pool of potential workers with the special skills that would qualify them to work at the job in question.

4.   Sophisticated Statistical Techniques

The **probability assumption stated in Teamsters v. United States, 431 U.S. at 339-340 n. 20**—that "absent explanation, it is ordinarily expected that non-discriminatory hiring practices will in time result in a work force more or less representative of the racial and ethnic composition of the population in the community from which employees are hired"—is the basis for the use of sophisticated statistical techniques to prove systemic disparate treatment discrimination.

a.   A statistical expert report establishes a prima facie case.   A prima facie case of systemic disparate treatment is established if a witness, qualifed as a statistical expert, presents a statistical report that concludes that race, gender, or another protected characteristic was a **statistically significant** factor explaining the difference between the employer's treatment of black and white workers. Such a report will fail to establish a prima facie case only if the trial court determines that it is "so incomplete as to be inadmissible as irrelevant." While there could be many variations on the type of statistical technique used, all are based on the probability assumption that is the basis of the science of statistics.

    i.   The null hypothesis.   All statistical studies start with the statement of the null hypothesis. The **null hypothesis** is a statement made at the outset of the study saying what the study will test to be true or false. The null hypothesis is stated as the converse of what the study is expected to find.

    ii.   Expected probability.   Once the null hypothesis is stated, the expert then decides what probability to expect. In a study dealing with employment discrimination, the probability would be set by the representation of women or minority group members in the qualified labor pool. All of the manipulation to establish the qualified labor pool, which is a legal rather than a statistical question, is done in order to set the probability number because that number is the key to the comparison between the employer's workforce and the labor pool.

iii. **Level of confidence.** Statisticians choose a **level of confidence** in deciding whether the null hypothesis should be accepted or rejected. They typically set the risk at 5%. This means that there is a 5% chance that an innocent employer will be found liable. It also means that there is something like a 50% chance that a guilty employer will be found not liable.

iv. **Accepting or rejecting the null hypothesis.** The key question is whether the data could occur by chance or whether the variable set by the null hypothesis is a factor that explains the outcome. In the employment discrimination example, the null hypothesis— that race is not a factor—would be accepted if the outcome of the probability study could be explained by chance more than 5% of the time. Correspondingly, **if the particular statistical technique shows that these outcomes would occur by chance less than 5% of the time, then the null hypotheses—that race is not a factor—would be rejected.** Based on the rejection of the null hypothesis, it is then reasonable and logical to conclude that race was a factor. Such a showing establishes a prima facie case of systemic disparate treatment discrimination.

v. **Choosing the type of statistical study.** Statisticians have available a number of techniques that can be useful to prove systemic discrimination, including binomial distribution and multiple regression.

F. DEFENSES TO DISPARATE TREATMENT CASES

There are two ways to defend a systemic disparate treatment case.

1. Rebutting the Inference of Discriminatory Intent

A prima facie case can be undermined and overcome through rebuttal.

a. **Rebutting a formal policy case.** In a prima facie case based on a formal policy of discrimination, the defendant can argue that in fact no such policy exists or that the policy that does exist is not discriminatory.

b. **Rebutting a practice case.** Where the prima facie case is based on a showing of practice of systemic disparate treatment, the employer can rebut the evidence plaintiff relies upon by challenging the statistics plaintiff uses or by challenging the inference of discrimination that is based on those statistics.

i. **Rebut the inference of discrimination.** Even if plaintiff's statistics hold up, employers can try to rebut plaintiff's case by challenging the inference that the employer intended to discriminate. The argument is that the defendant has not acted with the intent to discriminate unless it acted at least in part " **'because of,' not merely 'in spite of,'** its adverse effects upon a particular group."

2. Establish a Bona Fide Occupational Qualification

G. BONA FIDE OCCUPATIONAL QUALIFICATIONS

Title VII and the ADEA include **bona fide occupational qualification (BFOQ)** defenses to systemic disparate treatment cases. Thus, §703(h) of Title VII provides that "it shall not be an unlawful employment practice for an employer to hire and employ employees . . . on the basis of religion, sex, or national origin in those certain instances where religion, sex, or national origin is a bona fide occupational qualification reasonably necessary to the normal operation of that particular business or enterprise." The BFOQ defense is available as to **religion, sex, national origin, and, through the ADEA, age** but **not** to disparate treatment where the claim is discrimination **because of race or color.** The BFOQ defense involves two steps.

1. The Qualification Must Be Necessary to the Essence of the Business

2. Either No Person in Excluded Group Can Do the Job or It Is Impractical to Determine Who Can Do It

The second step of the BFOQ is for the employer to prove one of two different tests.

a. No member of the protected group can perform the job. The first alternative to the second step in proving the BFOQ defense is for the employer to prove that it had reasonable cause to believe that no one in the excluded group can perform the functions of the job in question safely and efficiently.

b. Highly impractical to determine qualifications on individualized basis. The second subpart to the second step of the BFOQ test requires the employer to show that sex, national origin, religion, or age was a legitimate proxy for the job qualifications because it is "impossible or highly impractical" to determine on an individualized basis whether workers in that excluded category could safely perform the job in question.

H. THE DEFENSE AGAINST INDIVIDUAL'S REMEDIES

Systemic disparate treatment discrimination typically affects many workers and applicants. Establishing a systemic disparate treatment case, therefore, creates a presumption of relief to those workers or applicants. To preclude relief to any of the affected individuals, the employer carries the burden of proving that it would have made the same decision as to that person, even if it had not engaged in a practice of systemic disparate treatment discrimination. While this is not a defense to the liability of the employer for its discrimination, it is a defense to the provision of full remedies to all affected individuals.

 4 SYSTEMIC DISPARATE IMPACT DISCIRMINATION

A. THE DISPARATE IMPACT CONCEPT

Disparate impact discrimination "involve[s] employment practices that are facially neutral in their treatment of different groups but that in fact fall more harshly on one group than another and cannot be justified by business necessity. **Proof of discriminatory motive . . . is not required** under a disparate impact theory." Teamsters v. United States, 324 U.S. at 336 n.15 (1977).

B. A BRIEF BACKGROUND

The disparate impact theory was created in Griggs v. Duke Power Co. in 1971, with a three-step litigation structure developed for the theory in Albemarle Paper Co. v. Moody. In 1989, Wards Cove v. Atonio substantially cut back on the theory, particularly by redefining business necessity and by putting the burden of persuasion for the entire case on the plaintiff. The Civil Rights Act of 1991 amended Title VII to create a new statutory-based version of disparate impact law that is used today.

C. The Present Statutory Structure of Disparate Impact Discrimination

The Civil Rights Act of 1991 amended Title VII to add a new §703(k), which for the first time includes the term "disparate impact" in Title VII and sets forth a structure for deciding disparate impact cases.

D. The Prima Facie Showing of an Employment Practice Causing Impact

A prima facie case based on disparate impact is established if "a complaining party [plaintiff] demonstrates [by carrying the burden of persuasion] that [an employer] uses a **particular employment practice that causes a disparate impact** on the basis of race, color, religion, sex, or national origin." §703(k)(1)(A)(i).

1. A Particular Employment Practice

A broad array of employer policies and practices have been found to be employer practices subject to disparate impact analysis, including short form **IQ tests and educational prerequisites, height and weight prerequisites,** and **rules** excluding people who were **in methadone maintenance programs.** "[D]isparate impact analysis is in principle no less applicable to **subjective employment** criteria than to objective or standardized tests." Watson v. Fort Worth Bank & Trust, 487 U.S. 977 (1988).

There are **five exceptions** to the requirement that plaintiff point to a particular employment practice in order to make out a prima facie case of systemic disparate impact discrimination.

a. **The "bottom line" exception.** While maintaining the general rule that disparate impact must focus on particular employment practices, §703(k)(1)(B)(i) adds an exception that allows the plaintiff to use **"bottom line" statistics** to establish a prima facie case of disparate impact discrimination.

b. **No impact defense.** The employer can escape the business necessity defense by proving that its use of the practice does not cause an impact.

c. **The exception for rules prohibiting drug use.** The 1991 Act added an exception limiting the use of disparate impact discrimination to attack employer rules barring the illegal use of drugs.

d. **The passivity exception.** A lower court has recognized that employer passivity or inaction is not an employment practice subject to disparate impact attack.

e. **The fringe benefits exception.** A lower court has found that changes in fringe benefits do not trigger disparate impact attack.

2. **The Employer's Use of the Practice**

Section 703(k)(1)(A)(i) requires plaintiff to prove that the employer "uses a particular employment practice that causes a disparate impact" but does not say that the employer's use of the practice must cause impact. **The 1991 Act appears to allow the plaintiff to use national data or data derived from the use of the challenged practice by other employers to prove a prima facie case of impact.** The employer can then use data from its own use of the practice to escape liability by proving that its use does not cause an impact.

3. **Amount of Impact**

In its disparate impact decisions, the Supreme Court has used an **"eyeballing the numbers"** approach to determine whether the impact was sufficient to support a disparate impact case.

4. **The Impact Is Adverse**

The issue of adverseness has arisen in several cases involving national origin discrimination claims by bilingual employees concerning the use of languages other than English. The courts have found that plaintiffs failed to make out a prima facie case of disparate impact because the challenged policy had an impact but that impact was found not to be adverse to them.

5. **The Impact Is to a Protected Group**

Title VII protects all persons against employment discrimination because of race, color, sex, religion, and national origin. That protection extends to disparate treatment discrimination **but it is not clear that disparate impact theory is available to whites or males.**

E. **Defendant's Rebuttal**

There are **five different responses** potentially open to an employer **to rebut** a prima facie case of disparate impact discrimination. Two have their source in the Civil Rights Act of 1991 and the other three are found in Title VII as originally enacted.

1. **The Employer's Use Does Not Cause the Impact**

Section 703(k)(1)(A)(i) states the general rule that "a complaining party demonstrates that a respondent uses a particular employment practice that causes a disparate impact," with "demonstrate" being separately defined in §701(l) as "meets the burdens of production and persuasion." Section 703(k)(1)(B)(ii), however, appears to create an affirmative defense that imposes on the employer the burden of persuasion to prove that "a specific employment practice does not cause the disparate impact."

2. **Business Necessity and Job Relatedness**

If the plaintiff is successful in establishing a prima facie case and the efforts of the employer to rebut it fail, the next affirmative defense available to the employer is §701(k)(1)(A)(i). It requires the **employer to prove "that the challenged practice is job related for the position in question and consistent with business necessity."**

This language is significant in three ways. **First,** it replaces the *Wards Cove* language about reasoned review of the employer's justification for the challenged practice. Congress rejected the Court's view that the practice need not be "essential" or "indispensable" and returned to the notion of **business** *necessity.*

Second, the new section makes it clear that the **burden** on the employer on these issues is one of **persuasion.**

Third, the plain meaning of the section requires the *employer* to demonstrate *both* that the challenged practice is (1) job related for the position involved and (2) justified by business necessity. Job relatedness is a narrower, more difficult, justification than business necessity. To prove something is job related the employer must prove that the practice affects the performance of the employee on the particular job that she performs. Business necessity is broader in that it may take into account factors not directly related to employee performance on a particular job. Requiring both should make this a difficult defense to prove.

3. Professionally Developed Tests

Title VII as originally enacted included §703(h), which provides an exception to liability for "an employer to give and to act upon the results of any **professionally developed ability test** provided that such test, its administration or action upon the results is not designed, intended, or used to discriminate because of race, color, religion, sex, or national origin." This is an affirmative defense, with the employer carrying the burden of persuasion to prove the test is valid.

a. Defining a "test." Those employment practices that are deemed to be "tests" must be validated pursuant to professional test validation standards. Presumably all paper-and-pencil tests must be validated. Use of a "performance assessment center," which is a simulation of important elements of a job, is a test to be validated.

b. The professional test validation standards. The professional test standards set forth a complex system for validating tests.

    i. Job analysis. The standards start with the requirement that, before any test is used, the job for which it will be used must be analyzed to determine the nature of the skills, knowledge, etc., entailed in doing it.

    ii. Two methods of validation. There are two methods of validating tests. If content validation is accepted, there is a greater chance that the test will be found valid.

        (a) Criterion-related validation. This method of validation is a controlled experiment. The employer administers the tests to a sample of applicants, hires all of them and then, after the workers have been on the job for a while, evaluates their work performance using trained evaluators and standard scoring measures. A statistical technique called the correlation coefficient is then used to compare the test scores with the job performance scores to determine whether the test is valid.

        (b) Content validation. This technique of test validation involves the construction of a test that is actually a sample of the job the employee will hold. If the test is a good sample of what workers who get the job will do, then it is valid.

        (c) Differential validation and race test scores. New §703(1) added by the 1991 Act prohibits employers from adjusting test scores by race.

4. Bona Fide Seniority System

Bona fide seniority systems are sheltered by §703(h) from attack based on the disparate impact theory: **"an otherwise neutral, legitimate seniority**

system does not become unlawful under Title VII simply because it may perpetuate pre-Act discrimination. Congress did not intend to make it illegal for employees with vested seniority rights to continue to exercise those rights, even at the expense of pre-Act discriminatees." Teamsters v. United States, 431 U.S. 324 (1977).

a. **Collective bargaining agreement seniority systems.**   Only union-bargained seniority systems fall within the exception.

b. **The traditional component of seniority systems test.**   The employer must prove that the challenged policy is in fact a traditional component of a system of seniority.

c. **Seniority systems with their "genesis in discrimination."**   In *Teamsters,* the Court recognized that §703(h) does not shelter seniority systems that were the product of an intention to discriminate.

5. **Bona Fide Merit and Piecework System**

Finally, §703(h) provides an exception to disparate impact liability for bona fide merit systems or systems "which measure[] earnings by quantity or quality of production . . . provided that such differences are not the result of an intention to discriminate because of race, color, religion, sex, or national origin."

F. **ALTERNATIVE EMPLOYMENT PRACTICE SURREBUTTAL**

Section 703(k)(1)(A)(ii) defines the third, surrebuttal stage of a disparate impact case as involving the plaintiff proving the existence of an **alternative employment practice** that the employer refuses to adopt: "the complaining party makes the demonstration described in subparagraph (C) with respect to an alternative employment practice and the respondent refuses to adopt such alternative employment practice." The statute requires definitions of what constitutes an "alternative employment practice" and of what "refuses to adopt" means.

1. **Defining "Alternative Employment Practice"**

Section 703(k)(1)(A)(ii) replaces the idea of "pretext" with "alternative employment practice." That would appear to eliminate the state of mind of the employer as an issue in the surrebuttal stage of disparate impact analysis. That leaves the content of the concept as the showing of a less discriminatory alternative. **Alternative employment practices are "alternative policies with lesser discriminatory effects that would be comparably as effective at serving the employer's identified business needs."**

2. **The Employer's Refusal to Adopt the Alternative**

The statutory language requires the plaintiff to show that the employer "refuses to adopt" the alterative practice. **"Refuses"** seems to mean more than the mere failure to use the alternative practice. The **employer must**

somehow be aware of the existence of the alternative practice and have made the conscious decision not to adopt it. "Refuses" also suggests that the refusal is a continuing one.

3. The Alternative Employment Practice as an Independent Cause of Action

The plain meaning of §703(k)(1)(A) creates an independent cause of action if the individual plaintiff proves that an alternative practice to the one plaintiff was affected by exists and the employer refuses to adopt it.

G. THE SAME DECISION DEFENSE TO LIMIT INDIVIDUAL'S REMEDIES

The employer can escape liability to individual class members by proving that, as to each individual, it had not discriminated.

H. PROCEDURES AND REMEDIES

While Congress codified disparate impact law in the Civil Rights Act of 1991, disparate impact was excluded from the right to jury trial and the opportunity to seek compensatory and punitive damages, which rights were added for claims of intentional discrimination.

I. DISPARATE IMPACT IN OTHER ANTIDISCRIMINATION STATUTES

Since the enactment of the Civil Rights Act of 1991, disparate impact discrimination has been codified in Title VII, which is modeled somewhat on the disparate impact provisions in §102(b)(3) of the Americans with Disabilities Act. Section 42 U.S.C. §1981, however, has been construed as not including the disparate impact theory of discrimination. Whether disparate impact discrimination is incorporated within the Age Discrimination in Employment Act is yet to be definitively determined.

 THE INTERRELATION OF THE THEORIES OF DISCRIMINATION

A. THE DIFFERENCES BETWEEN THE THREE THEORIES OF DISCRIMINATION

The three main theories that apply in antidiscrimination statutes all derive from different definitions of the term "discrimination."

1. Systemic Disparate Treatment Discrimination

The broadest definition of discrimination is systemic disparate treatment discrimination because **any policy or general practice that is discrimina-**

tory is systemic disparate treatment discrimination. **The key element in a systemic disparate treatment case is the intent of the employer to discriminate** because of a characteristic prohibited by an antidiscrimination statute. Intent to discriminate to support a systemic disparate treatment case can be proven by showing a formal policy of discrimination or a practice of discrimination.

a. **Formal policies of discrimination.** Once a formal policy is shown to exist, in writing or admitted by the employer, intent to discriminate is established.

b. **The defenses to a formal policy case.** If the employer cannot rebut the existence of the policy or the inference that it is a policy of discrimination, only two defenses are available.

 i. **Bona fide occupational qualification.** The BFOQ defense applies to religion, sex, and national origin, but not to race or color discrimination.

 ii. **Voluntary affirmative action.** The affirmative action plan applies only where historic victims of discrimination are aided.

 iii. **Defenses that do not apply.** Business necessity and the lack of an adverse impact are *not* defenses to a formal policy of discrimination.

c. **Practice of discrimination.** Even without a formal policy of discrimination, systemic disparate treatment can be shown by evidence, both statistical and anecdotal, that the employer as a general matter treats employees or applicants differently because of their race, gender, or other characteristic protected against discrimination.

 i. **No affirmative defense to a practice case.** The employer's only defense is to rebut the evidence supporting plaintiff's prima facie case or the inference that it acted "because of" rather than "in spite of" the discriminatory impact.

2. **Systemic Disparate Impact**

In contrast to systemic disparate treatment with its key being the employer's intent to discriminate, systemic disparate impact does not require proof of intent to discriminate. Instead, its focus is on employer practices that weigh more heavily on a protected group than on the majority.

a. **Plaintiff's prima facie case. The key to systemic disparate impact discrimination is plaintiff's proof that the employer uses an employment practice that causes disparate impact** because of race, color, religion, sex, or national origin.

b. **Defendant's rebuttal.** There are five possible defenses to a prima facie case of systemic disparate treatment.

    i. **Employer's use does not cause impact.** If plaintiff establishes impact using data not connected with the employer, the employer bears the burden of proving its use caused no impact.

    ii. **Business necessity and job relatedness.** The employer bears the burden of proving its practice is job-related for the position in question and consistent with business necessity.

    iii. **Professionally developed test.** The employer bears the burden of proving that the test it used was validated by professional test standards.

    iv. **Bona fide seniority system.** The employer bears the burden of proving that the challenged practice is a traditional component of a bona fide seniority system.

    v. **Bona fide merit or piecework system.** The employer bears the burden of proving that the challenged practice is a bona fide merit or piecework system.

  c. **Plaintiff's alternative practice surrebuttal.** Even if the defendant carries its burden of proving one of the defenses, plaintiff can still prevail by proving that an alternative employment practice exists and the employer refuses to adopt it.

3. **Individual Disparate Treatment Discrimination**

Individual disparate treatment discrimination focuses on the treatment by the employer of individual employees or applicants. The key in individual disparate treatment cases is the intent to discriminate. Intent to discriminate to support an individual disparate treatment case can be established through direct or circumstantial evidence.

  a. **Direct evidence of intent.** Direct evidence of intent, such as an admission by the employer that it discriminated or in some courts "circumstantial-plus" evidence, establishes a prima facie case of individual disparate treatment discrimination. Liability attaches when the finder of fact finds that race, gender, etc., was **"a motivating factor"** in the decision of the employer that plaintiff challenges.

    i. **Defense to a direct evidence case.** In addition to attempting to rebut the evidence establishing plaintiff's case, defendant can limit full remedies to the plaintiff by proving an affirmative defense upon which it carries the burden of persuasion that it would have made the same decision even if it had not relied on an impermissible factor such as race or gender.

  b. **Circumstantial evidence of intent.** If there is no direct evidence establishing intent to discriminate, a case of individual disparate treatment can still be established through circumstantial evidence sufficient to support an inference that the employer acted with an intent to discriminate. There is sufficient evidence when plaintiff has shown that the most likely nondiscriminatory reasons for the employer's action did not apply to the plaintiff.

   i. **Defendant's rebuttal.**   The employer can rebut the plaintiff's prima facie case by introducing evidence sufficient to raise an issue of fact that a reason other than discrimination motivated the employer.

   ii. **Plaintiff's surrebuttal.**   The final step requires plaintiff to carry its burden of persuasion to prove that the employer's intent to discriminate was the **determinative factor** in its decision. It can do this with the evidence used to establish the prima facie case, evidence that the employer's reason is a pretext, and other evidence.

   iii. **No same decision defense.**   Unlike a case based on direct evidence, there is no same decision affirmative defense available to the employer in an individual disparate treatment case based on circumstantial evidence.

B. THE RELATIONSHIP BETWEEN THE TWO SYSTEMIC THEORIES

Both systemic theories focus on the general policies and practices of an employer that affect many employees and applicants.

1. Plaintiffs Prefer Systemic Disparate Treatment

Because of the availability of a jury and of compensatory and punitive damages, plaintiffs prefer to bring systemic disparate treatment claims.

2. Both Systemic Theories Do Not Always Apply

While the Court in *Teamsters* said that, "Either theory may, of course, be applied to a particular set of facts," it is not always true that both systemic disparate treatment and systemic disparate impact cases apply to any particular case.

   a. **The disparate impact theory is not used in formal policy cases.** Plaintiffs have little incentive to use systemic disparate impact when both systemic theories apply because of the advantages in remedies available in systemic disparate treatment cases.

   b. **The scope of disparate impact theory is more limited than for disparate treatment.**   The Civil Rights Act of 1991 requires plaintiff to try to prove the impact of each specific employment practice being challenged. But §703(k)(1)(B) creates an exception allowing the use of "bottom line" statistics of the employer's workforce "if the complaining party can demonstrate to the court that the elements of a respondent's decisionmaking process are not capable of separation for analysis."

3. Where Both Disparate Treatment and Disparate Impact Theories Apply

Both systemic disparate treatment cases based on proof of an employer practice of discriminating and systemic disparate impact actions require proof of disparate impact. When both apply to the same case, two issues of the relationship between the theories are raised.

a. Less impact esablishes disparate impact than disparate treatment. The kind of "gross and longlasting disparity" showing necessary to draw the inference of intent to discriminate in a systemic disparate treatment requires a showing of a more substantial amount of impact than the "substantial impact" necessary to support a disparate impact case.

b. Defending disparate treatment claims can concede disparate impact claims. Even where plaintiff only brings a systemic disparate treatment case, the employer's defense strategy to that charge may concede a prima facie case of disparate impact discrimination. In trying to explain away the inference of intent to discriminate, the employer may point to one or more employment practices it uses that produce the impact. That may show that the employer lacked the intent to discriminate because it made its decisions despite rather than because of the impact. But it would operate as a concession that those practices caused a disparate impact. Once a prima facie case of disparate impact discrimination is established, the employer can escape liability only by proving that "the challenged practice is job-related for the position in question and consistent with business necessity" or is justified by one of the §703(h) defenses.

C. THE RELATIONSHIP BETWEEN THE TWO SYSTEMIC THEORIES AND INDIVIDUAL DISPARATE TREATMENT DISCRIMINATION

The relationship between systemic disparate treatment and systemic disparate impact on one hand and individual disparate treatment on the other has two aspects, depending on whether the systemic case is successful or not.

1. A Successful Systemic Case

Where a systemic disparate treatment or a systemic disparate impact case is successful and the action has been certified as a class action, all members of the class affected by the employer's discrimination are presumed to be entitled to relief.

2. An Unsuccessful Systemic Case

Where a class action claiming a systemic theory of discrimination fails, that does not cut off the right of individuals within the class from pursuing their own claims of individual disparate treatment discrimination.

C A P S U L E   S U M M A R Y

6 SPECIAL PROBLEMS OF GENDER DISCRIMINATION

A. THE FOUR SPECIAL GENDER DISCRIMINATION PROBLEMS

There are four special problems that arise in gender discrimination—**pregnancy, sexual harassment, grooming and dress codes,** and **sexual orientation.**

B. PREGNANCY

Originally, Title VII was construed such that discrimination because of pregnancy was not sex discrimination. Congress amended Title VII in the Pregnancy Discrimination Act of 1978 (PDA) to prohibit pregnancy discrimination in employment.

1. The Pregnancy Discrimination Act

There are two clauses in the PDA. The first defines "sex" to include "pregnancy," but it has a second clause providing that women affected by pregnancy "shall be treated the same for all employment-related purposes, including receipt of benefits under fringe benefit programs, as other persons not so affected but similar in their ability or inability to work."

2. The Effect of the PDA on the Main Theories of Discrimination

a. **Individual disparate treatment.** While there is a split of authority, equal treatment should mean that the employer treats the pregnant employee in the same way it treats another employee similarly situated in terms of the ability to work but who was not pregnant.

b. **Formal pregnancy policies are systemic disparate treatment.** Whether a formal classification of pregnancy violates the PDA depends on whether the classification serves to treat pregnancy less favorably or more favorably than other similar situations.

   i. **Formal policies treating pregnancy less favorably.** The use of formal pregnancy classifications that treat pregnancy less favorably than other similar situations is systemic disparate treatment discrimination.

   ii. **Formal policies treating pregnancy more favorably.** The equal treatment clause of §701(k) does not forbid employers from giving special preference for pregnancy benefits since it sets a floor prohibiting less favorable treatment.

c. **Systemic disparate impact.** Since the second clause of the PDA appears to set an equal treatment test of discrimination, disparate impact analysis may not be available as to pregnancy. But an employer practice that has disparate impact on pregnancy may be attacked if it also has a disparate impact on women.

C. SEXUAL HARASSMENT

There are three elements to a sexual harassment case. **First, the harassment must be either quid pro quo or hostile environment harassment. Second, the harassment must be because of sex** (or other characteristic protected by Title VII). **Third, employer liability must be established by showing the harassing supervisor to have been aided in his harassment by his authority as a supervisor because a tangible employment action was taken against the employee or by showing the employer was negligent in that it knew or should have known of the harassment by a supervisor or by co-workers and failed to correct it.**

1. Harassment Is Either Quid Pro Quo or Hostile Environment Harassment

The first step in establishing a case of sexual harassment is to decide whether the case is a quid pro quo or a hostile environment case.

a. Quid pro quo sexual harassment.   The essence of quid pro quo harassment is that the employee is threatened by a supervisor, "sex or your job," and the alleged sexual advances are unwelcome.

b. Hostile environment harassment.   Where sexual relations between a supervisor and a subordinate are not involved, a hostile environment case can be made out when the workplace is permeated with "discriminatory intimidation, ridicule, and insult."

   i. Severe or pervasive to alter employment conditions.   To make out hostile environment harassment, the harassment must be sufficiently severe or pervasive to alter the conditions of the victim's employment and create an abusive working environment.

   ii. All relevant circumstances test.   In deciding whether there is a hostile environment, it is necessary to look at all the circumstances.

   iii. Objective and subjective harassment.   The harassment must be both subjectively abusive to the plaintiff and objectively abusive to a reasonable person in the position of the plaintiff.

c. The boundary between quid pro quo and hostile environment harassment.   Quid pro quo harassment occurs when a supervisor threatens an employee's job if she does not have sex with him. If she gives in to his demands or if she refuses and the supervisor acts on the threat, it is a quid pro quo case. If, however, she refuses and the supervisor does not take the action he threatened, it is a hostile environment case.

2. **The Harassment Must Be Because of Sex**

Harassment violates Title VII only when the plaintiff proves that the harassment was because of sex by one of the following scenarios:

a. **Male-female quid pro quo harassment.** In quid pro quo cases, the inference that the harassment is because of sex is "easy to draw in most male-female harassment situations, because the challenged conduct typically involves explicit or implicit proposals of sexual activity; it is reasonable to assume those proposals would not have been made to someone of the same sex."

b. **Homosexual quid pro quo harrassment.** Where the harasser is seeking homosexual sex, that also establishes that the harassment was because of sex. "The same chain of inference would be available to a plaintiff alleging same-sex harassment, if there were credible evidence that the harasser was homosexual."

c. **Hostile environment harassment not motivated by sexual desire.** Harassment not motivated by sexual desire still violates Title VII where the harassment was because of sex.

d. **Harassment because of race, color, religion, national origin also violates Title VII.** Title VII's protection against harassment is not limited to harassment because of sex: "a work environment abusive to employees because of their race, gender, religion, or national origin offends Title VII's broad rule of workplace equality."

3. **Employer Responsibility for Harassment**

A plaintiff need not show that she suffered economic, tangible, or psychological harm from the harassment to make out a case of harassment. But the failure of plaintiff to prove a tangible employment action was taken against her raises an affirmative defense to employer liability where a supervisor is the harasser.

a. **A broad general rule of employer vicarious liability.** An employer is subject to vicarious liability to a victimized employee for an actionable hostile environment created by a supervisor with immediate (or successively higher) authority over the employee.

b. **The supervisor takes a tangible employment action against victim.** Where it is shown that a supervisor has taken a tangible employment action against a victim of sexual harassment, the employer is liable to the victim.

   i. **Tangible employment action.** "A tangible employment action constitutes a significant change in employment status, such as hiring, firing, failing to promote, reassignment with significantly different responsibilities, or a decision causing a significant change in benefits.''

c. **The supervisor does not take a tangible employment action.** When no tangible employment action is taken, a defending employer may raise an affirmative defense to liability or damages, subject to proof by a preponderance of evidence. The defense comprises two necessary elements: (a) that the employer exercised reasonable care to prevent and correct promptly any sexually harassing behavior, and (b) that the plaintiff employee unreasonably failed to take advantage of any preventive or corrective opportunities provided by the employer or to avoid harm otherwise.

d. **Co-worker hostile environment harassment.** Where the harasser or harassers are not in a supervisory position over the victim of the harassment, the case is treated as a hostile environment case, even if demands are made for sexual relations. That is because co-workers typically lack the power to threaten the job of the victim. Employer liability for co-worker harassment is limited to situations where the ''employer is negligent with respect to sexual harassment if it knew or should have known about the conduct and failed to stop it.''

D. GROOMING AND DRESS CODES

An exception has been created from Title VII's proscription of formal policies of discrimination for employers who implement and use gender explicit dress and grooming codes.

E. SEXUAL ORIENTATION

Title VII has so far been held not to protect employees against discrimination because of homosexuality, transexuality, or bisexuality. Sexual harassment is the one area in which Title VII has provided some protection. Thus, same-sex harassment was found to violate Title VII where the plaintiff can prove that the harassment was because of sex.

 7   SPECIAL PROBLEMS OF RELIGIOUS DISCRIMINATION

A. THE FOUR SPECIAL PROBLEMS OF RELIGIOUS DISCRIMINATION

Title VII treats religions specially in three ways and that special treatment raises the fourth special problem, the constitutionality of that treatment under the Free Exercise and Establishment Clause of the First Amendment.

B. THE DUTY TO ACCOMMODATE EMPLOYEES' RELIGIOUS PRACTICES

Section 701(j) of Title VII imposes a reasonable accommodation duty on employers through its definition of "religion." "The term 'religion' includes all aspects of religious observance and practice, as well as belief, unless an employer demonstrates that he is unable to reasonably accommodate to an employee's or prospective employee's religious observance or practice without undue hardship on the conduct of the employer's business."

1. The Contrast with Disparate Treatment and Disparate Impact

The duty to accommodate does not prohibit the employer taking religion into account as does disparate treatment but requires the employer to take the religious beliefs and practices of individuals into account.

2. The Structure of a §703(j) Case

There are **four elements** a plaintiff must prove **to establish a prima facie case of failure to accommodate** and the employer's rebuttal may be made on either of two possible grounds.

a. The prima facie accommodations case.

   i.   **A sincere religious belief.**   Plaintiff must prove that his religious belief is sincere. Religious belief is broadly defined and is hard to rebut. The fact that plaintiff's belief evolved over time or even changed does not necessarily undermine the finding of sincerity.

   ii. **The belief conflicts with employer's rule.**

   iii. **The employer knew of conflict.**   An employer need have "only enough information about an employee's religious needs to permit the employer to understand the existence of a conflict between the employee's religious practices and the employer's job requirements."

   iv. **The employer did not satisfy plaintiff's belief.**   The plaintiff must prove that, whether or not the employer took any action to attempt to accommodate the plaintiff, the employer did not satisfy plaintiff's needs.

b. The employer's rebuttal burden.   Proof of a prima facie case shifts the burden of persuasion to the employer to demonstrate either that it made an accommodation that was reasonable or that any accommodation that would meet the employee's needs would be an undue burden on the employer's business.

   i.   **An accommodation that is reasonable need not fully accommodate the employee's belief.**   Once the employer has "reasonably accommodated the employee's religious needs, the statutory inquiry is at an end. The employer need not further show that each of the employee's alternative accommodations would result in undue hardship."

ii. **Any cost over a de minimis cost is an undue hardship.** Only if the employer fails to offer the employee any accommodation or the accommodation offered fails to be found reasonable, does the issue of undue hardship arise. An accommodation that satisfies plaintiff's needs is an undue hardship if it requires the employer "to bear more than a de minimis cost."

C. TITLE VII'S EXEMPTIONS FOR EMPLOYERS TO DISCRIMINATE BECAUSE OF RELIGION

There are three statutory grounds that allow an employer to discriminate because of religion:

1. The Religious Employer Exemption

Churches and other religious institutions are exempt for Title VII's proscription of religious discrimination.

2. The Religious Curriculum Exemption

A school may hire employees of a particular religion if the school's curriculum is directed toward the propagation of a particular religion.

3. The Bona Fide Occupational Qualification

Religion is one basis upon which a bona fide occupational qualification can be based. See Chapter 3.G.

D. THE CONSTITUTIONALITY OF TITLE VII'S TREATMENT OF RELIGION

The First Amendment of the Constitution provides: "Congress shall make no law respecting an establishment of religion, or prohibiting the free exercise thereof." Because Title VII is a statute enacted by Congress that concerns religion, there are two First Amendment issues involving Title VII's treatment of religion based on the religion clauses of the First Amendment.

1. Section 703's Duty Not to Discriminate and the Free Exercise Clauses

While §702 exempts religious institutions from the proscription of religious discrimination in employment, the basic antidiscrimination provision, §703, applies to discrimination by religious employers because of race, color, national origin, and sex. Section 703 violates the Free Exercise Clause by interfering with a religious organization's ability to fill core positions necessary to carry out the mission of the organization and it violates the

Establishment Clause because the enforcement of §703 entangles the government in the operations of religions.

2. **Section 702's Religious Institutions Exemption and the Establishment Clause**

The special treatment §702(a) gives to religious organizations and §703(e)(2) gives to schools that use their curricula to propagate religion to discriminate in favor of members of their own religion do not violate the Establishment Clause of the First Amendment.

3. **Section 701(j)'s Accommodation Duty and the Establishment Clause**

The question whether the duty of an employer to reasonably accommodate the religious practices and beliefs of employees required by §701(j) violates the Establishment Clause has not been finally decided by the Supreme Court. But, it seems likely that §701(j) would be found constitutional.

8   SPECIAL PROBLEMS OF NATIONAL ORIGIN AND ALIENAGE DISCRIMINATION

A. THE SPECIAL PROBLEMS OF NATIONAL ORIGIN AND ALIENAGE DISCRIMINATION

Difficult definitional problems result from the interaction of national origin, alienage, ancestry, and race. First, Title VII prohibits national origin discrimination but not alienage discrimination. Second, 42 U.S.C. §1981 prohibits discrimination because of "ancestry or ethnic characteristics," race, and alienage but not because of national origin. Third, in addition to prohibiting discrimination because of national origin, the Immigration Reform and Control Act of 1986 (IRCA) prohibits discrimination by employers against aliens who are "lawfully admitted for permanent residence."

B. ALIENAGE DISCRIMINATION IS NOT PROHIBITED BY TITLE VII

1. **Title VII's Prohibition of National Origin Discrimination Does Not Prohibit Discrimination Based on Alienage**

National origin is not the same as citizenship. Congressman Roosevelt said that National origin "means the country from which you or your forbears came. . . . You may come from Poland, Czechoslovakia, England, France, or any other country."

2. **Disparate Treatment and Disparate Impact Theories Do Apply to National Origin Discrimination**

It is possible, therefore, that alienage discrimination may violate the disparate impact theory of national origin discrimination.

C. **42 U.S.C. §1981 Prohibits Race, Ancestry, and Ethnic but Not National Origin Discrimination**

Looking back to the meaning of race at the time after the Civil War was just over, the Court found that "Congress intended to protect from discrimination identifiable classes of persons who are subjected to intentional discrimination solely because of their ancestry or ethnic characteristics. Such discrimination is racial discrimination that Congress intended §1981 to forbid, whether or not it would be classified as racial in terms of modern scientific theory." St. Francis College v. Al-Kharaji, 481 U.S. 604 (1987).

1. **Section 1981 Prohibits Alienage Discrimination**

Since the 1991 Civil Rights Act, §1981 prohibits alienage discrimination by public and private employers.

D. **THE IMMIGRATION REFORM AND CONTROL ACT PROHIBITS ALIENAGE AND NATIONAL ORIGIN DISCRIMINATION**

Section 102 of the Immigration Reform and Control Act of 1986 makes it an "unfair immigration-related employment practice" to discriminate because of a person's "national origin" or protected status. An individual is protected if she is a citizen or national of the United States or an authorized alien.

E. **ACCENT AND LANGUAGE AS NATIONAL ORIGIN DISCRIMINATION**

Speaking English with an accent, not being able to speak English, or speaking languages in addition to English are all potentially related to a person's national origin.

1. **Speaking English with an Accent**

The courts have so far been uncertain whether discrimination because a person speaks English with a foreign accent is disparate treatment because of national origin.

2. **Requiring the Ability to Speak English**

Employer rules requiring the ability to speak English have generally withstood attack under Title VII.

3. **English-Only Rules**

Employer rules requiring bilingual employees to speak English on the job have been upheld because there is no adverseness to the employees.

9 SPECIAL PROBLEMS OF AGE DISCRIMINATION

A. THE FIVE SPECIAL PROBLEMS OF AGE DISCRIMINATION

This chapter addresses the five major issues.

B. THE PROTECTED CLASS

Section 4(a) of the ADEA prohibits discrimination "because of such individual's age." Section 12, however, provides that the protection against discrimination because of age "shall be limited to individuals who are at least 40 years of age." These two provisions interact as follows. "This [statutory] language does not ban discrimination against employees because they are aged 40 or older; it bans discrimination against employees because of their age, but limits the protected class to those who are 40 or older."

1. No Involuntary Retirement Because of Age

The ADEA now protects older workers with no age cap and prevents employers from involuntarily retiring employees because of age. In removing the age cap and in prohibiting mandatory retirement because of age, amendments to the ADEA created exceptions for bona fide executives eligible for a substantial pension and for police and firefighters.

C. INDIVIDUAL DISPARATE TREATMENT DISCRIMINATION

Since the amendments to the *Price Waterhouse* approach were made only to Title VII, it is clear that Congress did not amend the ADEA to include them. But it is also clear Congress did not in any way suggest that these new provisions could not be referred to in the ongoing judicial enforcement of ADEA claims. It is possible, however, that the approaches to individual disparate treatment cases between the two statutes may begin to diverge.

D. THE ADEA AND DISPARATE IMPACT DISCRIMINATION

The Supreme Court has never decided whether or not disparate impact discrimination is available in ADEA actions. There are differences in terms between Title VII and the ADEA that bear on this question.

1. Differences in the ADEA and Title VII Statutes

a. Title VII specifically includes disparate impact discrimination. Until passage of the Civil Rights Act of 1991, neither Title VII nor the ADEA specifically included provision for disparate impact discrimination claims. The 1991 Act amendments to Title VII establish a specific

statutory scheme for disparate impact cases. The 1991 Act did not amend the ADEA in that regard, so the ADEA still does not include specific provision for disparate impact discrimination.

b. ADEA provisions not in Title VII. The ADEA has two provisions, with no correlative Title VII provisions, that emphasize that only discrimination because of age is prohibited—the "good cause" and the "reasonable factors other than age" sections. A practice that causes an impact on older workers is not age specific, so it is "a factor other than age." The question is whether it is "reasonable."

2. The Split in the Circuits

There is a split among the courts of appeals, with most recent decisions finding that the ADEA does not include the disparate impact theory.

E. FRINGE BENEFIT PLANS

Congress has made several amendments to the ADEA dealing with employee fringe benefit plans.

1. Benefits Paid or Cost Incurred Must Be Equal

Congress has adopted the equal cost or equal benefit test for the legality of fringe benefit plans.

2. Pension Plans May Use Age to Establish Eligibility

Section 4(l)(1)(A) now provides that defined benefit pension plans will not violate the ADEA solely because the plan "provides for the attainment of a minimum age as a condition of eligibility for normal or early retirement benefits."

F. DOWNSIZING, REDUCTIONS IN FORCE, AND EARLY RETIREMENT INCENTIVE PLANS

In this era of downsizing and corporate reorganization, employers have devised various means to reduce the number of their employees, which raises two issues:

1. Reductions in Force and Individual Disparate Treatment Cases. Reductions in force involve both a reorganization as well as the discharge of a group of workers. Some lower courts, in dealing with reduction-in-force situations in individual disparate treatment cases, have created a modified form of the *McDonnell Douglas/Burdine* showing required for plaintiff to establish a prima facie case to deal with the problem that no identifiable person took plaintiff's job.

2. Early Retirement Plans

Congress, in the Older Workers Benefit Protection Act of 1990, addressed problems concerning **waiver of ADEA claims** generally as well as the employer use of early retirement plans.

a. **Conditions for waiver of ADEA rights.** There are seven minimum conditions necessary for an effective waiver of all ADEA rights.

b. **Additional conditions for early retirement program waivers.** If the waiver of ADEA rights is part of an early retirement program, §7(f) adds two more requirements extending the time for employees to consider the package and providing information about the impact of the plan on groups of workers.

c. **No "tender back" of benefits necessary to challenge waiver of ADEA rights.** Plaintiffs need not tender back benefits received as part of the waiver of ADEA rights in order to challenge the waiver.

 RETALIATION

A. THE ESSENCE OF RETALIATION

Retaliation is the adverse response of an employer to the actions of its employee who participates in proceedings to remedy employer discrimination or who opposes employer discrimination.

B. STATUTORY AUTHORITY

Title VII, the ADEA and 42 U.S.C. §1981 all prohibit employer retaliation.

C. THE STRUCTURE OF A RETALIATION CASE

There are three basic elements to a retaliation case.

1. Section 704 Protects Applicants, Present and Former Employees

Section 704 applies whether the plaintiff is an applicant or a former or present employee.

2. The Plaintiff Must Show She Engaged in Either Free Access or Opposition Conduct

Two types of employee conduct are protected against employer retaliation—**"free access"** and **"opposition."**

a. **Free access retaliation.** Where the plaintiff can show that she filed a charge of discrimination or otherwise participated in a legal proceeding claiming discrimination, a free access claim is established and her protection will be absolute.

    b. Opposition clause retaliation.   Where the plaintiff cannot make out a free access clause case, she can use the opposition clause, which bars employer retaliation if an employee "has opposed any practice made an unlawful employment practice by this title." Opposition clause cases, because they may involve a very wide array of different kinds of employee behavior, involve a balancing of interests so that some conduct that does oppose an employer's discrimination is nevertheless found not to be protected because it is unreasonable. An employee will be protected if she, in subjective good faith, believes the employer has discriminated and, in objective fact, has a reasonable basis for that belief.

3. The Plaintiff Must Show that the Employer Took Adverse Action Against Her Because of Her Protected Conduct

Where the adverse action occurred reasonably close to the time the employer learned of the employee's protected conduct, then it is easy to conclude that the adverse action was because of that conduct and was, therefore, retaliation. Some courts say that the adverse action must be an "ultimate employment decision."

11 RECONSTRUCTION CIVIL RIGHTS ACTS

A. THE RECONSTRUCTION ERA CIVIL RIGHTS STATUTES

After the Civil War, Congress passed a series of Reconstruction civil rights statutes to protect former slaves from renewed oppression in the states that had made up the Confederacy. Those that survive are 42 U.S.C. §1981, 42 U.S.C. §1983 and 42 U.S.C. §1985(c).

B. THE RELATIONSHIP OF THE RECONSTRUCTION STATUTES AND TITLE VII

Title VII does provide a reasonably comprehensive scheme for the protection against race discrimination. There are four reasons why the Reconstruction era statutes are still useful.

1. Reconstruction Era Statutes May Reach Conduct Exempted from Title VII

The Reconstruction era statutes may be used to attack conduct sheltered by exceptions to Title VII.

2. No Administrative Agency Filing Required

Claimants relying on the Reconstruction statutes can go immediately to court without having to first file their claim with any administrative agency.

3. Statutes of Limitation

One reason to bring an action under one of the Reconstruction era civil rights statutes is if the Title VII period for filing with the administrative agency has run.

4. Remedies

The Reconstruction era statutes do not have the caps on compensatory and punitive damages that Title VII has.

C. THE SCOPE OF §1981 PROTECTION

There are four facets to §1981 that define its scope.

1. "Race" for §1981 Means "Ancestry" or "Ethnic" Background

While the focus of §1981 was race discrimination, "race" had a different meaning in the nineteenth century than today. "Congress intended to protect from discrimination identifiable classes of persons who are subjected to intentional discrimination solely because of their ancestry or ethnic characteristics." Saint Francis College v. Al-Kharaji, 481 U.S. 604 (1987).

a. National origin verses ethnic or ancestral origin. While national origin, which is not protected by §1981, is the country where a person was born, or the country from which his or her ancestors came, ancestry, which is protected, is the ethnic group from which an individual and his or her ancestors are descended.

b. Section 1981 protects whites against race discrimination. Despite the language that every person is entitled to the same protection "as is enjoyed by white citizens," §1981 is applicable to racial discrimination in private employment against white persons.

2. Section 1981 Prohibits Alienage Discrimination

Since the 1991 Act amendments, discrimination is proscribed by §1981 whether the employer is public or private.

3. Sex Discrimination Does Not Violate §1981

Sex discrimination is not prohibited by §1981.

4. Section 1981 Reaches Private and Public Employers

Since §1981 was enacted under §5 of the Fourteenth Amendment, it does reach private contracts, such as private employment.

5. **Section 1981 Prohibits Race Discrimination for the Duration of the Contract Relationship**

The 1991 Civil Rights Act made clear that §1981 applies throughout the term of the contractual relationship.

6. **Only Intentional Discrimination Is Prohibited by §1981**

Since the disparate impact theory does not apply in §1981, only intentional discrimination is prohibited by it.

a. **The *McDonnell Douglas/Burdine* structure applies.** In absence of direct evidence of discrimination, the *McDonnell Douglas/Burdine* structure applies in §1981 cases.

b. **Disparate impact discrimination does not apply.** Only intentional discrimination is prohibited since, "§1981, like the equal protection clause, can be violated only by purposeful discrimination."

D. **42 U.S.C. §1983**

Unlike §1981, which creates a right against race discrimination in contracts, §1983 creates a remedy against state actors for their violation of rights created by the Constitution or other federal laws.

1. **Scope of §1983 Actions.** Since employment discrimination sometimes violates the Constitution, §1983 is available as a cause of action to remedy that violation. While Title VII accords "rights . . . secured by [federal] laws" that theoretically could be protected in a §1983 action, Title VII has been held not to be a federal law that is protected by §1983 since its has its own enforcement and remedial scheme.

2. **The State Actor as Defendant**

Since §1983 applies only to action taken by a person under color of state (not federal) law, the section does not apply to private employers.

E. **42 U.S.C. §1985(c)**

This section is designed to provide a remedy to protect people from conspiracies to deprive them of their civil rights. Section "1985 may not be invoked to redress violations of Title VII," since that might undermine the use of Title VII.

12 DISABILITY DISCRIMINATION

A. THE BROAD SCOPE OF THE AMERICANS WITH DISABILITIES ACT

The Americans with Disabilities Act of 1990, 42 U.S.C. §§12111 et seq., broadly prohibits discrimination against individuals with disabilities, including but not limited to employment discrimination. While the general rule focuses on individual disparate treatment discrimination, the statutory scheme includes five more concepts of "discrimination."

B. INDIVIDUAL DISPARATE TREATMENT CASE OF DISABILITY DISCRIMINATION

The general rule prohibiting discrimination because of disability set forth in §102(a) is cast in terms of individual disparate treatment discrimination.

1. Plaintiff's Prima Facie Case

There are three elements for a plaintiff to prove a prima facie individual disparate treatment case.

a. An individual with a disability. Plaintiff must prove she is an individual with a disability.

   i. A physical or mental impairment that substantially limits a major life activity.

   (a) Physical or mental impairment. The EEOC has defined a broad list of physical and mental impairments and the Supreme Court has added to that list.

   (b) Major life activities. The Supreme Court has indicated that major life activities should be viewed broadly and practically. Major life activities as stated in the ADA regulations include "caring for oneself, performing manual tasks, walking, seeing, hearing, speaking, breathing, learning, and working."

   (c) Substantially limits. The factors in determining whether an individual is "substantially limited" include the nature and severity of the impairment; its duration and its permanent or long-term impact.

   (1) With or without mitigating measures. The EEOC takes the position that "the determination of whether an individual is substantially limited in a major life activity must be made . . . without regard to mitigating measures such as medicines or assistive or prosthetic devices." The lower courts have not accepted the EEOC approach.

    (2) Substantially limiting work. With respect to the major life activity of working, the EEOC has defined "substantially limited" as meaning significantly restricted in the ability to perform either a class of jobs or a broad range of jobs in various classes as compared to the average person having comparable training, skills, and abilities. The inability to perform a single, particular job does not constitute a substantial limitation on the major life activity of working.

ii. A record of impairment. A person who may not now have a disability is nevertheless protected by the ADA if she is discriminated against because she has a record of having a disability.

iii. Regarded as having an impairment. People are within the group of individuals with disabilities protected by the ADA if they are regarded by an employer as having a disability, even if the actual nature of their condition does not satisfy the requirement of "a physical or mental impairment that substantially limits one or more of the major life activities."

b. Qualified individual. A person with a disability within one of the definitions of disability described above must prove that she is "qualified."

i. Essential functions. To be qualified, the individual must be able to perform all the **essential functions** of the job. The ADA does not define "essential functions" but §101(8) does say that, "consideration shall be given to the employer's judgment as to what functions of a job are essential."

ii. Reasonable accommodation as a component of the essential function element. To be qualified, an individual needs to be able to perform the essential functions of the job, but that performance is determined "with or without reasonable accommodation."

    (a) Accommodation. "The employer must be willing to consider making changes in its ordinary work rules, facilities, terms, and conditions in order to enable a disabled individual to work.''

(b) Reasonable accommodation.   To be reasonable, the cost of the accommodation must not be disproportionate to the benefit.

iii. The relationship between the ADA and Social Security disability.   The fact that an ADA plaintiff has claimed total disability for Social Security purposes does not cut off her ADA action.

c. Proving the employer acted because of plaintiff's disability.   If plaintiff proves she is ''a qualified individual with a disability,'' then she must still prove that the employer took its action against her because of her disability. She may use *Price Waterhouse* direct evidence that the employer admitted or conceded it took her disability into account or, where the employer denies that it took disability into account, she may rely on the *McDonnell Douglas/Burdine* circumstantial evidence test to support the factfinder in drawing an inference that the employer acted because of plaintiff's disability.

2. Defenses to Disability Discrimination Claims

In addition to rebutting the facts of plaintiff's prima facie case of individual disparate treatment discrimination, the ADA provides two defenses: undue hardship to the employer and direct threat to others.

a. Undue hardship to the employer.   Where plaintiff claims that she is qualified if the employer makes a reasonable accommodation, §102(b)(5)(A) establishes an undue hardship defense. Factors include the nature and cost of the accommodation needed, the overall financial resources of the facility or facilities involved, the overall financial resources of the covered entity, and the type of operation or operations of the covered entity.

b. Direct threat to others.   ''Direct threat'' is defined as ''a significant risk to the health or safety of others that cannot be eliminated by reasonable accommodation.'' Courts ''should assess the objective reasonableness of the views of health care professionals [on what is a direct threat] without deferring to their individual judgments.''

C. THE OTHER THEORIES OF DISCRIMINATION

In addition to the central focus on individual disparate treatment discrimination, the ADA includes five more theories of discrimination.

1. **Systemic Disparate Treatment Discrimination**

   Formal policies or patterns and practices of discriminating because of disability amount to systemic disparate treatment discrimination.

   a. **Benefit plan exception.** While the ADA prohibits employers from discriminating on the basis of disability in the provision of health care to its employees, the statute does provide an exception from systemic disparate treatment liability so that formal disability classifications are permitted in a benefit plan as long as the plan is not a subterfuge to evade the purposes of the ADA.

2. **Systemic Disparate Impact Discrimination**

   The ADA specifically includes disparate impact as a theory of discrimination so that it is discrimination for an employer to use "qualification standards, employment tests or other selection criteria that screen out . . . an individual with a disability or a class of individuals with disabilities unless the standard, test or other selection criteria . . . is shown to be job-related for the position in question and is consistent with business necessity."

3. **Failure to Reasonably Accommodate a Known Disability**

   While reasonable accommodation can be involved in an individual disparate treatment case, the ADA also creates a separate theory of liability if the employer fails to reasonably accommodate a known disability, with undue hardship as an affirmative defense.

4. **Testing that Causes Impact**

   Section 102(b)(7) requires that "test results accurately reflect the skills, aptitude, or whatever other factor of such applicant or employee that such test purports to measure, rather than reflecting the impaired sensory, manual, or speaking skills of such employee or applicant."

5. **Protected Relationship**

   Section 102(b) protects against discrimination because a person has a relationship with a person with a disability.

D. **SPECIAL DISABILITY DISCRIMINATION PROBLEMS**

   There are a number of provisions that exclude alcohol and drug use rules, various sexuality related conditions, kleptomania, and pyromania from the ADA. The ADA also establishes special rules concerning health examinations.

13   EQUAL PAY FOR EQUAL WORK

A. GENDER DISCRIMINATION IN COMPENSATION

Title VII prohibits sex discrimination and discrimination **in compensation**, so it does generally bear on the problem of sex discrimination in compensation. The **Equal Pay Act deals with** one form of gender discrimination in wages by requiring employers to pay **equal pay for equal work.**

B. THE EQUAL PAY ACT

Plaintiff must show an employer pays different wages to employees of the opposite sex for substantially equal work. That showing shifts the burden of persuasion to the employer to prove one of four affirmative defenses.

1. Plaintiff's Prima Facie Case

To establish a prima facie case, a plaintiff must prove that two workers of opposite sex worked: (1) in the same "establishment"; (2) received unequal pay; (3) "on the basis of sex"; (4) for work that is substantially "equal."

a. **The establishment requirement.** The EPA does not define the term "establishment." The mere existence of physically separate operations is not necessarily fatal to an EPA claim.

b. **Unequal pay.** Comparing the pay of two jobs requires consideration of inflation, fringe benefits, as well as rates of pay.

c. **Equal work.** This issue is central to an EPA case. The EPA only requires equal pay for "equal work on jobs the performance of which requires equal skill, effort, and responsibility, and which are performed under similar working conditions." Equal work, however, has been construed to mean "substantially equal" and not identical. To constitute equal work, there must be a substantial, perhaps predominate, core set of tasks common to both jobs.

d. **On the basis of sex.** Plaintiff must prove that the wage differential is "on the basis of sex." Showing one male and one female who are paid the same suffices since this is not an intent to discriminate element.

2. Defenses to the Prima Facie Case

The defendant in an EPA case may avoid liability by carrying the burden of persuasion of proving one of four statutory exceptions.

a. **"Any other factor than sex."** While there is a long list of factors, the key is that a factor cannot be "other than sex" for EPA purposes if it would violate the disparate treatment definition of discrimination under Title VII. Nevertheless, courts have found it hard to determine whether gender has played a part when compensation is based on the labor market or on economic benefit to the employer.

b. **Seniority system.** To be a system of seniority, it must operate to improve employment rights and benefits as the employees' relative length of employment increases.

c. **Merit systems.** Some courts have required merit systems to involve an organized and structured procedure that enables employers to evaluate workers according to the predetermined criteria.

d. **Incentive systems.** Most incentive pay systems can be characterized as objective and job-related.

C. USING TITLE VII TO ATTACK GENDER-BASED WAGE DISCRIMINATION

The EPA only applies where the content of the work is substantially the same. Therefore, where the jobs at issue are not substantially equal, the only means to redress wage discrimination because of sex is Title VII.

1. The Bennett Amendment Harmonizes the EPA and Title VII

Congress did attempt to harmonize Title VII with the EPA, via the Bennett Amendment to Title VII, which incorporates the four affirmative defenses of the EPA into Title VII gender compensation cases.

2. Title VII Theories of Discrimination in Gender Compensation Cases

Engrafting those four EPA affirmative defenses onto Title VII has lead to a constricted application of Title VII to claims of compensation discrimination because of sex.

a. **Individual disparate treatment.**

i. *McDonnell Douglas/Burdine* **circumstantial evidence cases.** Some lower courts have found that the *McDonnell Douglas/Burdine* approach is unavailable.

b. **Systemic disparate treatment discrimination and comparable worth.** Statistical job evaluation studies and comparable worth statistics alone are insufficient to establish an intent to discriminate required under disparate treatment theory since they are based on labor market differences between the wages of men and women.

c. **Systemic disparate impact.** The disparate impact theory of discrimination does not apply to claims of sex discrimination in compensation.

14 COVERAGE OF THE ANTIDISCRIMINATION STATUTES

A. COVERAGE ISSUES ARE IMPORTANT TO SCOPE OF APPLICATION

Coverage sets a floor below which an antidiscrimination law does not apply.

B. TITLE VII OF THE CIVIL RIGHTS ACT OF 1964

Section 703 makes it unlawful for "an employer" to discriminate against "employees or applicants."

1. An Employer Under Title VII

An **"employer"** within the coverage of Title VII is a "person engaged in an industry affecting commerce who **has fifteen or more** *employees* for each working day in each of twenty or more calendar weeks in the current or preceding calendar year, and any agent of such a person."

a. Counting employees. Employees are counted by the "payroll" method. By looking at who is on the employer's payroll, "all one needs to know is whether the employee started or ended employment during that year and, if so, when. He is counted as an employee for each day working after arrival and before departure."

b. A "person" as "employer." A "person" as an employer means natural persons as well as legal entities acting as individuals. Further, the definition of employer includes individuals, governments, and governmental agencies, political subdivisions, labor unions, partnerships, associations, corporations, legal representatives, mutual companies, joint-stock companies, trusts, unincorporated organizations, trustees, or receivers.

c. An "industry affecting commerce." Congress exercised its power under the Commerce Clause of the Constitution to reach the private sector to the extent that an employer is engaged in "an industry affecting commerce."

d. State and local government employers. In the 1972 amendments to Title VII, Congress expanded the coverage of Title VII to include state and local governmental employers. In doing so, Congress relied on its powers enumerated in both the Commerce Clause in Article I of the Constitution as well as §5 of the Fourteenth Amendment.

e. Federal employment. In the 1972 amendments to Title VII, Congress added a new §717 which extended Title VII to most federal employment but established specialized procedures for the claims of federal employees.

f.   Individual liability of agents.   Section 701(b) defines "employer" to include "any agent" of the employer so that the employer is bound by the acts of its agents. There is a split within the circuits as to whether the agents themselves are individually liable as employers for the discrimination that they cause.

g.   Extraterritorial employment.   Section 701(f) defines "employee" to apply Title VII extraterritorially: "With respect to employment in a foreign country, such term includes an individual who is a citizen of the United States."

2.   An "Employee" Under Title VII

Section 701(f) defines an "employee" as simply an individual employed by an employer but it does not include elected officials.

C.   AGE DISCRIMINATION IN EMPLOYMENT ACT OF 1967

The ADEA makes it unlawful for "an employer" to discriminate against "any individual" because of age, with the protected class of individuals defined as those age 40 or older.

1.   An "Employer" Under the Act

The ADEA coverage provisions mirror Title VII but coverage **requires 20 employees**, not the 15 that satisfies Title VII.

D.   RECONSTRUCTION CIVIL RIGHTS STATUTES

Three civil rights statutes survive from the Reconstruction period following the Civil War and have potential impact on employment discrimination.

1.   42 U.S.C. §1981

42 U.S.C. §1981 prohibits race discrimination in all contracts. Since employment is typically characterized as contractual, §1981 covers all employment. It does not, however, reach the federal government as employer.

2.   42 U.S.C. §1983

Section 1983 creates an action for damages in individuals when their constitutional or other federal rights are violated by someone acting under color of state law.

a.   The "every person" defendant under §1983.   "Every person" includes those individuals acting pursuant to state action, such as employees of state and local government agencies. There is absolute immunity from liability under §1983 for prosecutors and judges. Qualified immunity is available to many others.

        i. **"Under color of law."** "Under color of law" includes actions by defendants "who carry a badge of authority of a state and represent it in some capacity whether they act in accordance with their authority or misuse it."

      b. **42 U.S.C. §1985.** Section 1985 provides a remedy when two or more individuals conspire to deprive another of equal protection or equal privileges and immunities under the law. While all individuals might be conspirators violating the civil rights of others, Title VII rights are not among the rights subject to §1985(3) protection.

E. AMERICANS WITH DISABILITIES ACT

Section 102(a) of the ADA creates the general rule prohibiting discrimination because of disability. **"No covered entity shall discriminate against a qualified individual** with a disability because of the disability."

1. A "Covered Entity" Under the Act

Section 101(2) defines "covered entity" as "any employer, employment agency, labor organization, or joint labor-management committee." The definition of an "employer" under this Act mirrors Title VII, so that a person who employs at least 15 people for each working day for 20 or more weeks a year falls within the purview of the Act.

2. Other "Covered Enti[ties]"

The ADA extends its application beyond employers.

F. THE EQUAL PAY ACT

The Equal Pay Act looks to the Fair Labor Standards Act to determine who is an employer within its coverage.

1. An "Employer" Under the EPA. There are two ways to establish EPA coverage: the **individual test** and the **enterprise test**.

    a. **The individual test.** If the individual plaintiff was "engaged in commerce" or "in the production of goods for commerce," then that person's employer is covered by the Fair Labor Standards Act and the Equal Pay Act.

    b. **The enterprise test.** In 1961, FLSA was amended to create a new basis for coverage that looks to whether the enterprise is engaged in commerce by doing a particular dollar volume of business or was among a list of specific industries where the enterprise had individual employees who were engaged in commerce or in the production of goods for commerce.

    c. **Federal and state employees** are covered.

PROCEDURES FOR ENFORCING ANTIDISCRIMINATION LAWS

A. THE SCOPE OF ANTIDISCRIMINATION PROCEDURES

Title VII created a complex enforcement scheme that generally applies to subsequently enacted federal antidiscrimination statutes.

1. Modern Antidiscrimination Procedure

The civil rights legislation passed in the twentieth century involves complex procedures that require private plaintiffs to first file charges with the EEOC before they can initiate private litigation.

2. Reconstruction Era Civil Rights Statutes

The Reconstruction era civil rights statutes, 42 U.S.C. §§1981 and 1983, do not have a federal agency charged with their enforcement and have no required procedure specific to their application. These statutes are enforced in much the same way as any private suit in civil litigation. The primary procedural issue is the appropriate statute of limitations, with the rule being that all §1981 and §1983 actions are subject to the state statute applicable to "personal injury" actions or the most analogous state statute.

B. PRIVATE ENFORCEMENT OF TITLE VII

Under the Title VII procedures, an individual must meet two preconditions. The procedures are identical for Title VII and the ADA, but there are several minor wrinkles in the ADEA procedures.

1. Filing a Timely Charge

A charge of discrimination must be timely filed with the EEOC.

a. Filing. An individual must file a charge under oath with the EEOC.

b. Timely. The general rule is that the charge must be filed within 180 days "after the alleged unlawful employment practice occurred." That 180-day rule is extended where a state or local antidiscrimination agency exists, so the charge can be filed with the state or local agency and also with the EEOC within 300 days of the alleged violation or "within thirty days after receiving notice that the State or local agency has terminated the proceedings under the State or local law, whichever is earlier."

i. The ADEA wrinkle. While the 180/300-day time period applies in ADEA actions, filing with the state deferral agency is not a prerequisite to filing with the EEOC. Thus, filing with the EEOC within 300 days suffices, though at some point filing with the state agency is necessary.

c.   The time the alleged discrimination occurred.   Section 706(e)(1) requires that the charge be filed within 180/300 days "after the alleged unlawful employment practice occurred." The filing period starts running when the act of discrimination occurs and the employee receives notice of the employer's act.

> **i.   Continuing violation exception.**   A continuing violation can exist if the discrimination is ongoing. It is necessary that what continues is the discrimination and not just its effect.

d.   Timely filing with the EEOC is not jurisdictional.

e.   Grounds to toll the filing of the charge include waiver, estoppel and equitable tolling.

2.   Timely Filing Suit

Filing an EEOC charge is a precondition to filing a Title VII suit in federal or state court. After a charge is filed with the EEOC, the charging party must adhere to procedural requirements.

a.   The EEOC has 180 days.   The charging party must wait a minimum of 180 days from the filing with the EEOC before bringing suit in court unless EEOC procedures are terminated earlier. After 180 days, the charging party can demand a right-to-sue letter from the EEOC.

b.   No time period runs while charge is at EEOC.   The charging party may elect to permit the EEOC's procedures to continue after the 180-day period and still retain the power to demand a right-to-sue letter at any time up until the EEOC has made a determination.

c.   Letting EEOC pursue process.   The EEOC will either bring suit itself, find no reasonable cause and dismiss, or find reasonable cause and attempt conciliation, which, if unsuccessful, leads to a suit by the EEOC or a right-to-sue letter to the charging party.

d.   File lawsuit.   Once the EEOC has notified a charging party that it has terminated its actions, the claimant has 90 days to file suit.

3.   Relationship of the EEOC Charge to Private Suit

There are three questions concerning the relationship of the charge filed with the EEOC and the subsequent lawsuit filed in court.

a.   Proper plaintiffs.   Plaintiffs must have standing in the sense of being aggrieved by the discrimination.

b.   Proper defendants.   A defendant who is sufficiently implicated by

C
A
P
S
U
L
E

S
U
M
M
A
R
Y

the charge on which the action is predicated may be sued under Title VII, even if not named in the charge.

c. **Scope of the suit.** The requirement that the allegations in a judicial complaint filed pursuant to Title VII "may encompass any kind of discrimination like or related to allegations contained in the charge and growing out of such allegations during the pendency of the case before the Commission."

C. PRIVATE CLASS ACTIONS

In order to maintain a Title VII, §1981, or ADA class action suit, Rule 23 of the Federal Rules of Procedure must be satisfied. Moreover, while the ADEA is not technically governed by Rule 23, courts have borrowed from Title VII decisions applying Rule 23 to ADEA cases.

1. Requirements of Rule 23(a)

Rule 23(a) sets forth four requirements which all must be met by the party seeking to maintain the suit as a class (1) *numerosity*, (2) *commonality*, (3) *typicality*, and (4) *adequate representation*. Most of the problems focus on the adequacy of representation. The scope of class actions is limited so that a plaintiff can only represent a class of those similarly situated to herself.

a. **Adequacy of representation.** Adequacy of representation tends to be the focus of most class action questions. This factor focuses on conflicts of interests among named plaintiffs and other class members, the competence of plaintiffs' counsel, and potential collusiveness.

i. There is recent authority that class actions are not available in intentional discrimination cases seeking compensatory and punitive damages.

2. Requirements of Rule 23(b)

Once a suit has met the requirements of Rule 23(a), it still must fall within either Rule 23(b)(2) or (b)(3).

3. The Preclusive Effect of a Class Action

Every class member who does not opt out is bound by a class action judgment. If an employer did not engage in a general pattern or practice of racial discrimination against the certified class of employees, that does not preclude a class member from maintaining an individual claim of racial discrimination against the employer. The filing of a Title VII class action tolls the applicable statute of limitations and thus allows "all members of the putative class to file individual actions in the event that the class certification is denied."

4. Settling Class Actions

Rule 23(e) provides, "[a] class action shall not be dismissed or compromised without the approval of the court, and notice of the proposed dismissal or compromise shall be given to all members of the class in such manner as the court directs."

D. PUBLIC GOVERNMENT ENFORCEMENT

Title VII enforcement by the federal government is largely committed to the EEOC, with the exception of the Attorney General's role in bringing suits against state and local governments.

E. TITLE VII SUIT AGAINST GOVERNMENTAL EMPLOYERS

The Department of Justice, rather than the EEOC, has the authority to sue state and local governments under Title VII.

1. State and Local Government Employment

The Attorney General, not the EEOC, has the power to sue state or local governments under Title VII.

2. Federal Employment

Title VII, the ADEA, and the Rehabilitation Act (adopting ADA remedies, procedures and rights) afford protection to most federal employees against discrimination. The procedures with respect to federal employees differ from the procedures that apply to employees of all other employers.

F. THE RELATIONSHIP BETWEEN PUBLIC AND PRIVATE SUIT

There are two issues concerning the relationship of public and private suits.

1. The Public Suit

When the EEOC files suit on behalf of an individual, the individual loses the right to bring a private cause of action, but may intervene in the EEOC action.

2. The Private Suit

Courts have split on the issue of whether an earlier filed private suit bars the EEOC from filing a public suit on behalf of the individual or whether both suits may proceed concurrently.

G. SETTLING AND ARBITRATING DISCRIMINATION SUITS

Most employment discrimination claims are not litigated but are settled.

1. Knowing Waiver of Discrimination Claims

The Older Workers Benefit Protection Act permits a knowledgeable waiver of ADEA claims so long as minimum conditions are met. That statute has served as a guide for courts attempting to interpret waivers of rights under the other antidiscrimination laws.

2. Settlement by Agreement or by Consent Order

A settlement can be a purely private contract or can be incorporated into a consent order approved by the court.

a. Binding of nonparties. The 1991 Civil Rights Act added §703(n) to Title VII, which binds nonparties to consent settlements when (1) they have been adequately represented by a party or (2) they had actual notice of the threat to their interest and an opportunity to protect themselves.

3. Arbitration

Voluntary agreements to submit actual disputes, including existing discrimination claims, to binding arbitration provide a valuable opportunity for employees and employers to resolve their dispute in a timely and effective manner. The law is unclear whether executory agreements to arbitrate discrimination claims that may occur in the future ought to bar an employee from bringing a lawsuit claiming discrimination.

 16 Judicial Relief

A. THE SCOPE OF JUDICIAL RELIEF

Once a violation of an antidiscrimination statute has been proven, a broad array of equitable and legal relief is available.

B. FULL RELIEF FOR INDIVIDUAL VICTIMS OF DISCRIMINATION

The statutory remedial schemes to redress individual discrimination provide a variety of types of legal and equitable relief, as well as attorney's fees. Courts are to make whole the victim of unlawful discrimination. Additionally, the court is permitted to assess punitive damages.

1. Section 706(g)(2)(B) Exception to Full Relief

The Civil Rights Act of 1991 added an affirmative defense to full relief when the employer carries its burden of proving that it would have made the same decision even if it had not discriminated. If the employer does carry its burden on this same decision defense, then the court "shall not award damages or issue an order requiring any admission, reinstatement, hiring, promotion, or payment" of backpay. But, plaintiff is entitled to declaratory relief, injunctive relief (except for orders of admission, reinstatement, hiring, or promotion), and attorney's fees and costs demonstrated to be directly attributable only to the pursuit of a claim under §703(m).

C. TYPES OF REMEDIES IN INDIVIDUAL CASES

Full equitable and legal remedies are available in discrimination suits.

1. Backpay

Antidiscrimination statutes permit a victim of discrimination to recover the equitable relief of backpay for the income lost due to the employer's unlawful discrimination, which includes all the compensation the victim would have received in the absence of discrimination.

a. Backpay is presumptively awarded to victims of discrimination.

b. Calculation of backpay. The federal antidiscrimination statutes provide little guidance on how to calculate backpay awards.

  i. The backpay period. The beginning date for backpay is generally the date the victim first lost wages due to the unlawful conduct, which may or may not be the same date as the discriminatory act, and it normally ends on the date of judgment. Title VII, but not the ADEA, limits backpay to a period of two years prior to the date of filing the charge with the EEOC.

   (a) Limits on period. There is a two-year limit to backpay prior to the date of filing for Title VII; none for the ADEA.

   (b) After-acquired evidence. An employer can cut off the period for backpay before the date of judgment by proving successful in ending the backpay period because of evidence of the plaintiff's wrongdoing of such severity that the employee would have been terminated on those grounds alone.

c. The duty to mitigate damages. The antidiscrimination statutes require the court to reduce backpay by amounts that were or could have been earned with reasonable diligence from other employment. The employer has the burden of proving that the backpay should be reduced because the plaintiff could have earned more by showing the existence of comparable employment, the amount the plaintiff would have earned, and that the plaintiff's lack of reasonable diligence resulted in the failure to obtain the position.

  i. Burden on employer to prove backpay should be reduced because plaintiff could have mitigated.

  ii. Offering the claimant the previously denied job. The accrual of backpay tolls when the defendant offers plaintiff the job she originally sought, even though she rejected the offer because it did not include retroactive seniority.

    iii. **Fringe benefits.** Plaintiffs must attempt to procure substitute coverage of fringe benefits such as insurance.

  d. **Prejudgment interest.** Prevailing plaintiffs may recover prejudgement interest on their backpay awards.

2. Instatement, Reinstatement, Retroactive Seniority, and Prohibitory Injunction

Equitable relief includes reinstatement, a grant of seniority retroactively, and further injunctive relief.

  a. **Reinstatement and instatement.** The same policy of providing a make-whole remedy underlying the presumption of backpay supports a similar presumption of instatement in a hiring case and reinstatement in a discharge case.

    i. **Rebuttal.** The employer can overcome the presumption by proving that an innocent incumbent holds the job plaintiff would receive, or by proving that there is such hostility and animosity between the plaintiff and the employer that a harmonious working relationship would be impossible.

  b. **Retroactive seniority.** Victims of hiring discrimination are presumed to be entitled to the grant of retroactive seniority under a "rightful place" right to instatement. "Rightful place" means that the victims are hired into the first job opening and then granted seniority retroactive to the date they would have been hired but for employer's discrimination.

  c. **Injunctive relief.** There is a presumption that a guilty defendant will be enjoined from further discrimination.

3. Front Pay

An award of front pay compensates a victim of discrimination for the wages and benefits she will lose even after the judgment date until the victim is reinstated or, if not reinstated, as "the difference (after discounting to present value) between what the plaintiff would have earned in the future had he been reinstated at the time of trial and what he would have earned in the future in his next best employment."

4. Compensatory and Punitive Damages

The availability of compensatory and punitive damages in employment discrimination varies from statute to statute. Both compensatory and punitive damages are available under §1981 and §1983, with several restrictions applying when the employer is a governmental entity. Title VII and Title

I of the ADA allow such damages, but place limits on the amount of these awards where (1) disparate treatment is proven, and and (2) the claim is not recognized under §1981. Compensatory and punitive damages are capped depending upon the number of employees. The caps are: (1) $50,000 for an employer with 100 or fewer employees and (2) $300,000 for an employer with 500 or more employees. The ADEA and the EPA do not permit either type of damages, although both allow liquidated damages, which are essentially double damages for willful violations.

5. Liquidated Damages

The ADEA and the EPA permit recovery of "liquidated damages" if the plaintiff can establish a "willful" violation. Willful means knowledge or reckless disregard of the risk on the part of the employer that its action violated the statute.

6. Lost Wages Under the Equal Pay Act

Lost wages under the EPA are the same as backpay in Title VII.

7. Attorney's Fees

Each antidiscrimination statute, with slight variation, contains a provision allowing an award of attorney's fees and costs to the prevailing party. While a prevailing plaintiff is presumed entitled to attorney's fees, a court may award attorney's fees to a prevailing defendant only upon a finding that the plaintiff's action was frivolous, unreasonable, or without foundation.

a. Prevailing plaintiffs. Absent special circumstances, a prevailing plaintiff is entitled to attorney's fees.

b. Prevailing defendants. Prevailing defendant is entitled to attorney's fees only if plaintiff's action was frivolous, unreasonable or without foundation.

c. It is not always clear who is a "prevailing party."

d. Calculation of attorney's fee.

    i. Calculating the fee. The fee calculation is a two-step process:

        (a) Hours worked times reasonable fee.

        (b) Special circumstances justifying an adjustment.

D. RELIEF FOR SYSTEMIC DISCRIMINATION

Individuals merely must show they are members of the class to gain the presumption. To deny relief to a class member, the employer carries the burden of persuasion to prove that the individual was not discriminated against.

1. **Retroactive Seniority and Backpay**

There is a presumption that individuals affected by sytemic discrimination are entitled to relief.

a. **Individual relief.** Proof of a pattern or practice of discrimination creates a presumption that all employment decisions as to individuals affected by that practice were discriminatory. The defendant has the burden of proving that individuals who have shown themselves to be affected were nevertheless not the victims of discrimination.

b. **Retroactive seniority and nonapplicants.** Individuals who did not apply for the job affected by discrimination carry the burden of proving that they were potential victims of that discrimination.

c. **Backpay.** The potential class of victims are those people rejected because of discriminatory reasons as well as those deterred from applying because of the discrimination. Courts either figure out which of the affected class would have gotten the available jobs but for discrimination or divide the total backpay award and divide it among all the members of the affected class.

d. **Choosing between the individual and class approach.** The individual approach works best with small classes and the class approach works better when the class is so numerous that it would be hard to pick which individuals would have been selected but for discrimination.

2. **Affirmative Action Relief**

Judicially imposed affirmative action relief is a form of classwide relief that requires the employer to take positive action to benefit members of the discriminated class. The use of race is justified as a compelling government interest because it remedies the prior discrimination of the defendant, even if some beneficiaries were not themselves the victims of the employer's discrimination.

THE BACKGROUND AND POLICY BASES FOR ANTIDISCRIMINATION LAW

 CHAPTER OVERVIEW

This chapter reviews the background and policies behind antidiscrimination laws.

- **The Common Law At-Will Rule:** At common law, contract law was the basis for analyzing employment, with a strong presumption that the contract was at will. The at-will rule, which continues as modified, means that either the employer or the employee could terminate the contract at any time for good reason, bad reason, or no reason. The modification added by antidiscrimination statutes is that the employer may act for good reason, bad reason, or no reason, but it can no longer act because of discrimination.

- **The Libertarian Challenge:** Libertarian and some law and economics theorists have challenged the use of law to prohibit discrimination in employment. Letting freedom of contract have full rein in employment would, according to these theorists, result in most discrimination being driven from the market because it is **"irrational,"** that is, not consistent with profit maximization. Since any remaining discrimination is "rational," it leads to profit maximization; antidiscrimination law is not justified and a preference for discrimination is of equal value to a preference against discrimination.

- **The Economics Response:** The basic response from an economics point of view is that discrimination existed before it was prohibited and that it persists even with the enforcement of antidiscrimination law. That persistence shows that the market is imperfect, which imperfection justifies antidiscrimination law, even for neoclassical economists.

1

- **The Non-Economics Response:** More powerful than the economic rebuttal to libertarianism is the rebuttal that law should look to other values in addition to economic freedom in setting social policy. The benefits to discriminators and the burdens to those discriminated against are not limited to bloodless economics but can involve deeply rooted hatreds and the sick need to degrade others on the part of those who discriminate and great pain and injury to the victims of discrimination. Further, cognitive psychology suggests that perpetrators and victims of discrimination may all be victims of our need to categorize sensory input, with such categorization including stereotypical thinking that subconsciously influences perceptions.

- **A Personal Perspective:** In deciding whether antidiscrimination law makes sense to you, it is important to decide the appropriate perspective. Looking at the problem as one of rooting out the behavior of a few idiosyncratic racists or sexists leads to the development of very different doctrine than seeing the problem from the point of view of many innocent victims whose lives are seriously affected for the worse because of a structure of employment relations that operate in ways that harm them.

A.   THE BACKGROUND FOR ANTIDISCRIMINATION LAW

At common law, a presumption was established that, unless otherwise clearly modified by the agreement of the parties, employment was **"at will,"** which meant that either party could terminate the employment relationship at any time for good reason, bad reason or no reason at all.

 # EXAMPLE AND ANALYSIS

Suppose two at-will employees discover that their supervisor has stolen some cash from the employer. One tells the owner and the other says nothing. As at-will employees, the employer can discharge the one employee because he did *not* "rat" on his supervisor and can also discharge the other employee because he *did*. The employer can terminate an at-will employee for any reason it wants to or for no reason, for whimsy.

B.   ANTIDISCRIMINATION LAW AS AN EXCEPTION TO THE AT-WILL RULE

The main focus of employment discrimination law is Title VII of the Civil Rights Act of 1964, the Age Discrimination in Employment Act of 1967, and the Americans with Disabilities Act of 1990. Many employment discrimination courses also cover the Equal Pay Act of 1963 as well as two provisions—42 U.S.C. §§1981 and 1983—that survive from the civil rights legislation passed in the Reconstruction era after the Civil War.

The effect of such antidiscrimination legislation is to create an exception to the at-will rule established at common law. Thus, the proper statement of the at-will rule is now that an employer may terminate an employee for good reason, bad reason, or no reason but the employer may not terminate an employee because of discrimination on the basis of race, color, religion, national origin, or sex under Title VII, age under the Age Discrimination in Employment Act, or disability under the Americans with Disabilities Act.

The study of employment discrimination law is the study of how these different antidiscrimination laws operate as exceptions to the at-will rule.

EXAMPLE AND ANALYSIS

In the example above concerning the two employees fired, one for "ratting" on the supervisor and the other for failing to "rat," neither could challenge the termination under the common law at-will rule. However, either or both might be able to challenge being fired if it is possible to prove that the termination was because of discrimination based on race, sex, or other characteristic protected by antidiscrimination law.

C. THE LAW AND ECONOMICS CHALLENGE TO ANTIDISCRIMINATION LAW

There was broad support for passage of Title VII as part of the civil rights movement of the 1960s and there has been continuing support for expanding antidiscrimination law as seen in the 1990 enactment of the Americans with Disabilities Act and the Civil Rights Act of 1991 that bolstered Title VII. At the state and local level, law continues to be relied on to prohibit discrimination on an expanding list of grounds including marital status, political affiliation and sexual orientation. Nevertheless, there has always been rather pointed criticism at the use of law to end discrimination.

The mainstream debate has not been based on claims that discrimination is morally or ethically acceptable. Instead, the claim is that law is not an appropriate means to end what is acknowledged to be the wrong of discrimination.

The most powerful voice for that view has been that of Professor Richard A. Epstein of the University of Chicago Law School in his book, Forbidden Grounds: The Case Against Employment Discrimination Laws. Echoing the views of Chicago economist Milton Friedman, who opposed the initial enactment of Title VII, Professor Epstein combines laissez-faire economics with libertarian thought to support his conclusion that antidiscrimination laws are not necessary to eliminate discrimination and that they do more harm than good.

1.   Law Is Not Necessary to Redress Discrimination

The starting point of Professor Epstein's book is John Locke's claim that we all own our own labor and that freedom to contract that labor is an essential human value. The role of law should be limited to the protection of the freedom of contract. The common law of fraud, force, and incompetence is as far as law should go because these laws protect the free market.

2.   "Rational" Profit Maximization

Neoclassical economists like Epstein use the term **"rational"** to mean to act to maximize economic profits. With unfettered markets and with all participants acting rationally, a free market best allows for the maximum economic development. Any interference with the market leads to less than optimum economic development. In terms of employment, Professor Epstein supports the at-will rule because it maximizes freedom of contract.

Given free entry of everyone to purchase or sell their labor and to resell whatever that transaction produces, a "person who wishes to discriminate against another for any reason has it in her power only to refuse to do business with him. . . . The victim can *unilaterally* . . . seek out those persons who wish to make the most favorable transactions with him." At a broader level, systemic discrimination against all the members of a particular group should fail as long as members of minority groups are free to seek jobs from those willing to hire them and where at least one person is willing to hire minority group members. Over time, as employers skim the best of the majority workers, it will become rational for employers, even those with a taste for discrimination against members of minority groups, to begin to hire the minority workers who are better workers than the majority group members still in the pool of people looking for work. Employers with a strong taste for discrimination will lose in the competition for good workers to employers who do not discriminate. In the long run, discrimination will end, or at least be reduced to only discrimination that is "rational," that is, justified by its contribution to profit maximization.

3.   The Discrimination That Persists Is Rational

There is uncontroverted evidence that substantial differences in employment outcomes in terms of race and sex continue to exist today. There is also ample contemporary evidence that discrimination is one cause of those different outcomes.

Epstein explains the persistence of discrimination on the ground that much of this discrimination is "rational." He uses the example of an employer piping in music to improve the productivity of workers. It is rational to pick employees that all like the same music, even if that means that the resulting workforce may be homogeneous. In essence, the employer may then use the race of the applicants as a proxy for the kind of music the applicants like, even if not all members of a particular group in fact like that type of music. Epstein's point is that it may be efficient for the employer to use race because it is less costly than other methods of discovering which workers will work well together.

For Epstein, social policy should not ban discrimination because what remains of it is rational and because there are costs associated with governmental interference in the free labor market. There are three main costs that, for Epstein, cause the burdens of antidiscrimination law to outweigh the benefits of proscribing employment discrimination:

a. **Antidiscrimination law is a "tax" that reduces the number of jobs.** Epstein views antidiscrimination laws as a sort of "tax" on employers. By raising the cost of employment, the laws result in lower profits, which translates into an overall reduction in the number of jobs an employer will be able to provide.

b. **The market will concentrate the bigots.** Allowing the free market to operate would allow all the bigots to join together in a small group of employers thereby improving the working conditions for everyone else.

c. **Preferences for discrimination are of equal value with preferences against discrimination.** Freedom of contract really means that society should not rule out of bounds the preferences of people, even if those preferences are along racial or gender lines: "there is no obvious reason why the preferences of any individuals should be excluded in determining the desirability of public regulation." Since Epstein's system proceeds from a value system based exclusively on economics, this last cost associated with antidiscrimination law is merely a reflection of that system: racism or opposition to racism are simply factors entering into the decision-making processes of consumers and providers of labor and so *a priori* they are of equal value in the calculus of establishing social policy.

D. RESPONSES TO THE LIBERTARIAN CHALLENGE TO ANTIDISCRIMINATION LAW

There are responses to the challenge Professor Epstein makes to antidiscrimination law both on economic and social policy grounds.

1. The Economic Answers

The most significant response to the libertarian position that a free labor market will drive out most discrimination is history. The racially segregated South and the system of gender segregation that generally existed before Title VII was passed existed in spite of the free market. Discrimination continues even in the face of antidiscrimination law.

Further, libertarian and law and economics approaches to discrimination have been attacked as not taking into account all the economic factors that are relevant. Professor Richard H. McAdams, in Cooperation and Conflict: The Economics of Group Status Production and Race Discrimination, 108 Harv. L. Rev. 1003, 1007, 1035 (1995), explains why conventional economic analyses of discrimination fails to explain reality. "Perhaps what seems so barren about the application of the economic method . . . is that it seems to require overlooking what many regard as the central realities of race discrimination: discrimination produces for its practitioners a gain beyond the mere avoidance of association, and discrimination victims suffer not just material harm, but also degradation."

Professor John Donohue has studied the effect of antidiscrimination law and concluded that such laws, rather than interfere with the market, actually bolster market forces by which discriminatory employers are driven out of the market. See John J. Donohue III, Is Title VII Efficient? 134 U. Pa. L. Rev. 1411 (1986). Professor Paulette Caldwell claims that antidiscrimination law is economically efficient because it helps to allow individuals to achieve their full economic potential so that, in the long run, business efficiency will be improved by expanding the pool of qualified workers that employers can chose from. See Paulette Caldwell, Reaffirming the Disproportionate Effects Standard of Liability in Title VII Litigation, 46 U. Pitt. L. Rev. 555 (1985).

2. The Non-Economic Costs of Discrimination

The most powerful response to the free market position is to attack the premise that economic value is all that counts. Social policy as established through law can look to values other than economic ones and can conclude that the preference for discrimination is not to be valued while the preference against discrimination will be enforced through the law.

Epstein characterizes the discriminatory rejection of applicants as a bloodless event without any personal pain. For him, rejection is simply the loss of one economic opportunity, making it time to look for another. But the reality is that discrimination involves great hurtfulness to the victims. Professor Mary Becker, in The Law and Economics of Racial Discrimination in Employment Needed in the Nineties: Improved Individual and Structural Remedies for Racial and Sexual Disadvantages in Employment, 79 Geo. L.J. 1659, 1654 (1991), describes the lack of any redeeming value of some discriminator's conduct: "One does not believe that African Americans and women are less than fully human because of an analytically rigorous delineation of subtle differences between them and white men. To the contrary, racism and misogyny are deeply irrational emotions, based on hatred or a lack of empathy for 'the other,' often accompanied by the need to establish one's own importance by denying others' humanity."

In contrast to the consciously racist and sexist description of discrimination described by Professor Becker, cognitive psychology explains much discrimination as being an "unintended consequence" of the need that we all have to categorize our sensory perceptions in order to make sense of the world around us. Professor Linda Hamilton Krieger, in Content of Our Categories: A Cognitive Bias Approach to Discrimination and Equal Employment Opportunity, 47 Stan. L. Rev. 1161, 1187–88 (1995), puts it this way:

> **[S]tereotyping** . . . is simply a form of categorization [of our sensory percep-tions], similar in structure and function to the categorization of natural objects. According to this view, stereotypes, like other categorical structures, are cognitive mechanisms, that *all* people, not just "prejudiced" ones, use to simplify the task of perceiving, processing, and retaining information about people in memory. . . . [O]nce in place, stereotypes bias intergroup judgment and decisionmaking. . . . These biases are *cognitive* rather than *motivational.* They operate absent intent to favor or disfavor members of a particular social group. . . . These biases "sneak up on" the decisionmaker, distorting bit by bit the data upon which his decision is eventually based. . . . Stereotypes, when they function as implicit prototypes or schemas [by which we evaluate each other], operate beyond the reach of decisionmaker self-awareness.

Whether discrimination is the product of conscious decision-making or is an unconscious product of cognitive categorizations, the characteristics for which race and gender are used as proxies are not the sort of neutral factors as are tastes for different types of music. Instead, racial and gender stereotypes frequently operate as negatives, with these negative stereotypes of what all African Americans, all Latinos, all older workers, all women or all persons with a disability are like. The stereotype can be so powerful that the individual is invisible.

E. DEVELOPING A PERSONAL POLICY PERSPECTIVE CONCERNING DISCRIMINATION

Professor Alan Freeman, in Antidiscrimination Law: The View from 1989, The Politics of Law: A Progressive Critique 121, 124–126 (David Kairys ed., rev. ed. 1990), sets out two points of perspective that can be used to look at discrimination and discrimination law.

1. Victim Perspective

Looking at discrimination from the viewpoint of the victim, you see that, "For black Americans [their history] has been one of harsh oppression, exclusion, compulsory reduced status, and of being perceived not as a person but as a derogatory cultural stereotype. Years of oppression have left their mark in the form of identifiable consequences of racism: residential segregation, inadequate education, over representation in the lowest-status jobs, disproportionately low political power, and a disproportionate share in the least and worst of everything valued most in our materialistic society."

2.   Perpetrator Perspective

The other viewpoint is to look at who discriminates, the so-called perpetrator. That perspective is concerned "with rooting out the behaviors of individual bad actors who have engaged in 'prejudicial' discriminatory practices. [The job of antidiscrimination law] is to isolate and punish racial discrimination viewed as an instance of individual badness in an otherwise nondiscriminatory social realm."

Professor Freeman would have us look at discrimination from the perspective of the victims. From that viewpoint, remedying the wrong, the hurt, and the injustice easily move to the highest priority. As you study employment discrimination law, it is important to reflect on your judgment about how much discrimination exists in society today, who is hurt most by it and whether you tend to view discrimination from the perspective of the victims of it or its perpetrators. This will help you to consider whether the courts, in developing legal doctrine, have changed their judgment about these underlying points of perspective and whether that has influenced how antidiscrimination law has developed.

EXAM TIP

Probably few exam questions will ask directly for the background or policy bases of antidiscrimination law. Yet it can be effective in analyzing fact patterns to use policy arguments to support the legal doctrine you develop and apply.

REVIEW QUESTION/ANSWER

Question: Employee Al Abrams, an African American, has worked for his employer, B. Beta Corp., for more than 20 years. His productivity is good and his performance has been recognized by the employer through raises, promotions, and good evaluations over the years. He is then discharged at age 53 and replaced by a much younger person with no experience but who is willing to do Abrams' job for half the money. The new employee, a white woman, rather quickly becomes more productive than Abrams by doing three quarters of the work he had been doing for half the pay. Should Abrams be able to sue Beta Corp?

Answer: Yes. Under the at-will rule, Abrams would not have a cause of action. Title VII of the 1964 Civil Rights Act proscribes race and sex discrimination and the Age Discrimination in Employment Act protects workers over age 40 from discrimination because of their age.

INDIVIDUAL DISPARATE TREATMENT DISCRIMINATION

CHAPTER OVERVIEW

This chapter examines the legal doctrine, called individual disparate treatment, applied in most discrimination cases since most cases involve an individual who challenges an employer's action as discriminatory. The intent or motive of the employer is the key question in individual disparate treatment cases. There are two well established, but mutually exclusive, ways to prove individual disparate treatment discrimination. Given substantial discontent with these two approaches, there appears to be some movement toward a new approach.

- **The Direct Evidence or Mixed Motive Approach:** Price Waterhouse v. Hopkins establishes one approach to the proof of individual disparate treatment discrimination. That approach is triggered by the plaintiff's introduction of direct evidence, that is, evidence that proves the employer's intent to discriminate without the need to draw any inferences or at least evidence directly connected to the decision the plaintiff challenges. Since the 1991 Civil Rights Act amendment, such proof by a plaintiff establishes liability if the factfinder finds that race, gender, etc., was "a motivating factor" in the employer's decision. The employer, however, can limit full remedies by proving that it would have made the same decision even if it had not relied on the discriminatory reason in making its decision.

- **Circumstantial Evidence or Pretext Cases:** The *McDonnell Douglas/Burdine* cases establish the default approach if plaintiff does not have direct evidence to prove a *Price Waterhouse* case. Plaintiff establishes liability under this approach by introducing circumstantial evidence upon which a factfinder can draw an inference of discrimination. There is a three-step analysis, with plaintiff's prima face case easily established, as is the defendant's rebuttal burden of introducing evidence of a reason for its action other than discrimination. The case finally focuses on the third step of determining whether the employer's reason is a pretext and if the employer did act with an intent to discriminate. Plaintiff must convince the factfinder by a preponderance of evidence that the protected trait had "a determinative influence on the outcome" of the employer's decision-making process.

- **Movement Toward a New Approach:** There is much criticism of the existing two approaches to analyzing individual disparate treatment cases. So far no single model has emerged but there is some action among the lower federal courts in that direction.

A. ANTIDISCRIMINATION STATUTES

Beginning in the 1960s, Congress enacted a series of statutes dealing with various aspects of the pervasive problem of discrimination in employment. The core provision is Title VII of the Civil Rights Act of 1964 but other important statutes include the Age Discrimination in Employment Act of 1967 (ADEA), the Americans with Disabilities Act of 1990 (ADA), and the Equal Pay Act (EPA). There are also statutes that survive from the Reconstruction following the Civil War, especially 42 U.S.C. §1981.

1. The Basic Provisions of the Antidiscrimination Statutes

a. **Title VII of the 1964 Civil Rights Act.** Section 703(a) of Title VII sets out the basic prohibition against employment discrimination by making it **"an unlawful employment practice for an employer—(1)** to fail or refuse to hire or to discharge any individual, or otherwise **to discriminate** against any individual with respect to his compensation, terms, conditions, or privileges of employment, **because of such individual's race, color, religion, sex, or national origin,"** to classify his employees or applicants for employment in any way which would deprive or tend to deprive any individual of employment opportunities . . . because of such individual's race, color, religion, sex, or national origin." Section 703.

b. **The Age Discrimination in Employment Act.** The ADEA tracks Title VII's language in §703 but ends each clause with **"because of such individual's age."** "Age," however, is defined only to protect those **at least 40 years of age.**

c. **42 U.S.C. §1981.** This statute—a carryover from the period immediately following the Civil War—provides: **"All persons** within the jurisdiction of the United States **shall have the same right** in every State and Territory **to make and enforce contracts . . . as is enjoyed by white citizens.**

> **d. The Americans with Disabilities Act.** Section 102 provides a general rule that no employer "shall discriminate against a **qualified individual with a disability** because of the disability of such individual." Other sections then elaborate on what §102 means.
>
> **e. Equal Pay Act.** The EPA requires **equal pay for equal work** on jobs the performance of which requires equal skill, effort, and responsibility, and which are performed under similar working conditions.

B. INDIVIDUAL DISPARATE TREATMENT IS INTENTIONAL DISCRIMINATION

Although there are differences in statutory language, the courts have developed more or less uniform rules for dealing with individual disparate treatment claims, without regard to the statutory source of the claim. These cases are called individual disparate treatment cases. Since these cases are the most prevalent claim litigated, the study of discrimination law starts with individual disparate treatment discrimination.

In Hazen Paper Co. v. Biggins, 507 U.S. 604, 610 (1993), an age discrimination case, the court gave an overview of the law of disparate treatment discrimination.

> In a disparate treatment case, liability depends on whether the protected trait (under the ADEA, age) actually motivated the employer's decision. The employer may have relied upon a formal, facially discriminatory policy requiring adverse treatment of employees with that trait. . . . Or the employer may have been motivated by the protected trait on an ad hoc, informal basis. . . . Whatever the employer's decisionmaking process, **a disparate treatment claim cannot succeed unless the employee's protected trait actually played a role in that process and had a determinative influence on the outcome.**

In Patterson v. McLean Credit Union, 491 U.S. 164 (1989), the Court said that the basic approach developed in Title VII cases applies in §1981 cases.

1. Stereotyping

> While the intent or the motivation to discriminate is seen as the essence of individual disparate treatment discrimination, the Supreme Court has also focused on **stereotyping,** that is, acting on negative traits associated with all women, as one form of intentional discrimination. In Price Water-house v. Hopkins, 490 U.S. 228, 251 (1989), the plurality opinion said "as for the legal relevance of sex stereotyping, we are beyond the day when an employer could evaluate employees by assuming or insisting that they matched the stereotype associated with their group." Similarly, in Hazen Paper Co. v. Biggins, 507 U.S. 604, 610 (1993), the Court said that, "Congress' promulgation of the ADEA was prompted by its concern that older workers were being deprived of employment on the basis of inaccurate and stigmatizing stereotypes." The Court then found that, **"It is the very es-**

sence of age discrimination for an older employee to be fired because the employer believes that productivity and competence decline with old age.''

While intent to discriminate or discriminatory motivation may connote a conscious state of mind of the employer, a decision made on the basis of a stereotype is not conscious discrimination. Yet a showing that an employer relied on a negative stereotype in making an employment decision satisfies the intent to discriminate element of an individual disparate treatment discrimination case.

EXAM TIP

Most employment discrimination cases are individual disparate treatment cases and most employment discrimination exams include an individual disparate treatment question.

C.   THERE ARE TWO RECOGNIZED WAYS TO PROVE INTENT TO DISCRIMINATE

The two methods of proving individual disparate treatment discrimination are based on the quotation in International Brotherhood of Teamsters v. United States, 431 U.S. 324, 335 n.15 (1977).

> The employer simply treats some people less favorably than others because of their race, color, religion [or other protected characteristic]. Proof of discriminatory motive is critical, although it can in some situations be inferred from the mere fact of differences in treatment.

Note the tension between two concepts of discrimination—intent or motive to discriminate and unequal treatment—with the synthesis of the two being that proof of unequal treatment can be the basis for drawing an inference about the state of mind of the employer.

 ## EXAMPLE AND ANALYSIS

Plaintiffs, four African-American women, worked in a factory. One day their white supervisor told them to stop production and to start the more arduous task of a general cleanup of the work area. A white co-worker, with little seniority, was excused and another black co-worker was recalled from another department to help with the cleaning. When the workers asked why they had been assigned the cleaning work, the supervisor responded, "Colored folks are hired to clean because they clean better."

Even before considering this "smoking gun" statement by the supervisor, other circumstances showed **unequal treatment:** The African-American workers were assigned the difficult and unpleasant cleaning work, while a white worker was excused without any explanation and an African-American worker was recalled to take her place. Those circumstances would, without more, support a factfinder drawing an inference that the supervisor assigned these workers this cleanup job because of their race. Thus, showing unequal treatment is **circumstantial evidence** of the employer's intent to discriminate because it supports an inference that the reason the workers were assigned the cleanup was that they were African Americans.

Adding the statement of the supervisor was **direct evidence** that his decision in assigning the cleaning was made because of the race of these workers. This statement, "Colored folks . . . clean better," also expresses a stereotype about African Americans. While here stated as a positive, it may, in the supervisor's mind, carry a negative correlative, something along the lines that African Americans are only good at cleaning. Note that the supervisor's basing of his work assignment is intentional discrimination even if the supervisor was not conscious that his action was based on race and even if he actually thought he was being complimentary in stating his reason for the assignment. See Slack v. Havens, 7 F.E.P. 885 (S.D. Cal. 1973), *aff'd as modified,* 522 F.2d 1091 (9th Cir. 1975).

D.   CIRCUMSTANTIAL EVIDENCE OR "PRETEXT" CASES SHOWING INTENT TO DISCRIMINATE

Most individual disparate treatment cases are analyzed using the circumstantial evidence method of proving discrimination. The circumstantial evidence approach is based on the assumption that it is sometimes reasonable for a factfinder, looking at all the evidence in the record, to draw an inference that discrimination is the real reason for the employer's action, even when the evidence does not include direct evidence—a "smoking gun" statement—of the employer's intent to discriminate. As the Court described it in International Brotherhood of Teamsters v. United States, 431 U.S. 324, 335 n.15 (1977), "Proof of discriminatory motive is critical, although it can in some situations be inferred from the mere fact of differences in treatment."

The approach that has developed for analyzing circumstantial evidence cases, however, is not as simple and straightforward as the approach used in general civil litigation that you learned in your civil procedure class. Using that approach would have the finder of fact look at all the evidence in the record and decide whether, based on a preponderance of the evidence, the plaintiff has proved that the action of the employer she challenges was because of her race, gender, or other characteristic protected against discrimination. Instead, the Supreme Court has developed a very complicated, some would say convoluted, way of analyzing individual disparate treatment cases based on circumstantial evidence. This approach, based on a rather long string of cases, is known by two of the most significant cases that established the parameters of the circumstantial evidence approach—the *McDonnell Douglas/Burdine* method—named for McDonnell Douglas v. Green, 411 U.S. 792 (1973), and Texas Dept. of Community Affairs v. Burdine, 450 U.S. 248 (1981).

This method is sometimes called the **"pretext"** method of proving individual disparate treatment discrimination because its original focus was on deciding whether to believe the reason the employer advances to explain its action or instead to find that the employer's reason was a pretext or cover-up for its intentional discrimination. St. Mary's Honor Ctr. v. Hicks, 509 U.S. 502 (1993), emphasized the need for a finding of intent to discriminate, and not just pretext. So, this method is now usually referred to as the circumstantial evidence approach to distinguish it from the *Price Waterhouse* direct evidence method.

 # EXAMPLE AND ANALYSIS

McDonnell Douglas Corp. v. Green, 411 U.S. 792, 802 (1973), involved a former employee who while on layoff had actively engaged in illegal civil rights activities against his employer. When his former job opened up, he applied but was not rehired, with the employer claiming that it did not rehire him because of his illegal conduct aimed at it and not because he was an African American. The record did not include any direct employer statements that the plaintiff's race was involved in the employer's decision not to rehire him. Based on the evidence, the trial court found that the refusal to rehire the plaintiff was based solely on his participation in the illegal demonstrations aimed at the employer. Since "Title VII tolerates no racial discrimination, subtle or otherwise," the Supreme Court ruled that the plaintiff should be given the opportunity to prove that the reason the employer advanced as the basis for its decision was in fact a pretext for discrimination because of his race.

EXAM TIP

In answering a question involving individual disparate treatment, always try to apply both methods of proof that the Supreme Court has created—the *McDonnell Douglas* circumstantial evidence approach as well as the *Price Waterhouse* direct evidence approach.

E. THE THREE-STEP *MCDONNELL DOUGLAS/BURDINE* ANALYSIS

In *McDonnell Douglas,* the Court established a three-step analysis of an individual disparate treatment case based on circumstantial evidence, involving **plaintiff's prima facie case, defendant's rebuttal,** and the third, surrebuttal step of plaintiff proving **pretext.**

1. Plaintiff's Prima Facie Case

In order to escape summary judgment and to have a trial, plaintiff must establish a prima facie case by showing (i) that he belonged to a racial minority; (ii) that he applied and was qualified for a job for which the employer was seeking applicants; (iii) that, despite his qualifications, he was rejected; and (iv) that, after his rejection, the position remained open and the employer continued to seek applicants. The Court failed to make it clear exactly why this showing successfully made out a prima facie case of individual disparate treatment discrimination. In an accompanying footnote, the Court emphasized that the stated approach was fact specific and "not necessarily applicable in every respect to differing factual situations."

Subsequently, in International Brotherhood of Teamsters v. United States, 431 U.S. 324, 358 n.44 (1977), the Court explained why the prima facie showing in *McDonnell Douglas* supported the inference of discrimination: "the alleged discriminatee demonstrated at least that his rejection did not result from the two most common legitimate reasons on which an employer might rely to reject a job applicant: an absolute or relative lack of qualifications or the absence of a vacancy in the job sought. Elimination of these reasons for the refusal to hire is sufficient, absent other explanation, to create an inference that the decision was a discriminatory one." This shows that it is easy to establish a prima facie case since all plaintiff need do is show that the usual nondiscriminatory reasons for an adverse action did not apply to her. Without explanation, that suffices to support an inference that the employer acted with an intent to discriminate because of race.

a. The four parts of a prima facie case

i. Racial minority. In McDonald v. Santa Fe Trail Transp. Co., 427 U.S. 273 (1976), the Court said Title VII prohibited "the discharge of 'any individual' because of 'such individual's race.' Its terms are not limited to discrimination against members of any particular race." Thus, whites, African Americans, Latinos, and members of all other racial groups are protected against employment discrimination because of race.

It follows that women and men are also protected against sex discrimination, members of all national origin groups are protected from national origin discrimination, and members of every

different religion are protected against religious discrimination as
are people who are discriminated against because they are not
members of particular religions.

In addition to Title VII's protection of all workers against race,
color, sex, national origin, and religious discrimination, the
ADEA's protection against age discrimination, and §1981's
protection against race, ancestry, and alienage discrimination,
there are additional questions of protection based on "intersec-
tionality," that is, whether the case of a black woman ought
to be analyzed differently than the case of an African-American
man or of a white woman, and relational questions, such as
the protection against employment discrimination because of
a person's relationship with a person of a different race.

Whether or not there is a sufficient basis to draw an inference
of discrimination depends in part on the group to which the
plaintiff belongs. In Taken v. Oklahoma Corp. Commn., 125
F.3d 1366 (9th Cir. 1997), the court held that members of
groups historically *favored* in employment are not entitled to the
McDonnell Douglas presumption unless they prove "background
circumstances that support an inference that the defendant is
one of those unusual employers who discriminates against the
majority."

In Fisher v. Vassar College, 114 F.3d 1332 (2d Cir. 1997) (en
banc), the opinion of Judges Jacobs and Leval for six members
of the court found that a prima facie showing under *McDonnell
Douglas* does *not* finally support an inference of discrimination.
"In our diverse workplace, virtually any decision in which one
employment applicant is chosen from a pool of qualified
candidates will support a slew of prima facie cases of discrimination. The rejected candidates are likely to be older, or to differ
in race, religion, sex and national origin from the chosen
candidate."

ii. **Qualified.** In *McDonnell Douglas,* the employer conceded that
the plaintiff was qualified since he had performed the job in
question before his layoff. In Patterson v. McLean Credit Union,
491 U.S. 164 (1989), the Court indicated that for a prima
facie case the plaintiff need only show she met the minimal
qualifications for the job in question. The employer can always
put in issue that she was not sufficiently qualified, or not as
qualified as the worker who got the job, at the rebuttal stage
and then it becomes an issue of fact to be decided at the third,
pretext stage of analysis.

       iii. Rejection. This is rarely at issue since plaintiffs typically do not bring suit unless something adverse to them happens.

       iv. Job remained open. The thrust of this is that the employer had the opportunity to treat the plaintiff favorably but did not do so. Thus, in a failure to promote case, this part is satisfied when the plaintiff shows that someone else was promoted. In a **downsizing** situation in which age discrimination is claimed, the plaintiff must show that a younger worker was retained. Beaird v. Seagate Technology, 145 F.3d 1159 (10th Cir. 1998).

EXAM TIP

Make sure you analyze each of the four parts to the establishment of a prima facie case. Most important is the issue of plaintif's qualifications, which plays a part in the prima facie case and, quite frequently, in the employer's rebuttal. Plaintiff must show she met the basic qualifications, while defendant may well assert that another person was more qualified. The issue is then decided at the final pretest stage.

 ## EXAMPLES AND ANALYSIS

1. Plaintiff, age 46, was a middle manager of a company that distributed and serviced vending machines. After 12 years on the job, he was discharged during a period in which the company was reorganizing and downsizing. His job, however, continued without change and his replacement was age 40. He claimed age discrimination by showing that (1) he was in the age group protected by the ADEA; (2) he was discharged; (3) at the time of his discharge, he was performing at a level that met his employer's legitimate expectations; and (4) his replacement was substantially younger than the plaintiff.

    The employer argued that plaintiff did not establish a prima facie case based on *McDonnell Douglas* because the plaintiff's replacement was himself within the age group protected by the ADEA. The Court rejected the employer's approach, saying, "the fact that a replacement is substantially younger than the plaintiff is a far more reliable indicator of age discrimination than is the fact that the plaintiff was replaced by someone outside the protected class." O'Connor v. Consolidated Coin Caterers Corp., 517 U.S. 308 (1996).

2. The lower court in *O'Connor* had modified the prima facie case showing in a reduction-in-force case claiming age discrimination: (1) the employee was pro-

tected by the ADEA; (2) he was selected for discharge from a larger group of candidates; (3) he was performing at a level substantially equivalent to the lowest level of those of the group retained; and (4) the process of selection produced a residual workforce of persons in the groups containing some unprotected persons who were performing at a level lower than that at which he was performing. Plaintiff, the court found, failed to satisfy this articulation of the prima facie case requirements because there was an identifiable person who replaced him. In a reduction in force the jobs are reorganized so that it is not clear who, if anyone, actually replaces any particular employee. O'Connor v. Consolidated Coin Caterers Corp., 56 F.3d 542 (4th Cir. 1995), *rev'd on other grounds,* 517 U.S. 308 (1996).

---

    b.   Limiting the scope of circumstantial evidence. In Hazen Paper v. Biggins, 507 U.S. 604, 611 (1993), the Court restricted the scope of circumstantial evidence upon which the inference of discrimination can be based. Plaintiff pleaded both age discrimination and pension interference in violation of ERISA, the Employee Retirement Income Security Act. The Court held that pension status was not even circumstantial evidence of age discrimination. Even though age and pension status frequently are correlated in the sense that as workers grow older they are more likely to be eligible for a pension, that correlation is not proof of age discrimination: "an employee's age is analytically distinct from his years of service. . . . Because age and years of service are analytically distinct, an employer can take account of one while ignoring the other, thus it is incorrect to say that a decision based on years of service is necessarily 'age-based.' "

 ## EXAMPLE AND ANALYSIS

Suppose a 38-year-old woman is discharged and she sues, claiming sex discrimination in violation of Title VII, and uses supplemental federal court jurisdiction to sue on a state antidiscrimination statute that protects employees from age discrimination generally, not limiting the protection to those over age 40. Plaintiff may be trapped by the part of *Biggins* that dilutes the strength of any particular claim as more claims are brought. Thus, the power of the evidence to support an inference of sex discrimination diminishes as the finder of fact is presented with claims that the discrimination could have been based on age and vice versa.

---

    c.   The consequences of establishing a prima facie case. In *Burdine,* the Court described the consequence of a plaintiff establishing a prima facie case. "Establishment of the prima facie case in effect creates a presumption that the employer unlawfully discriminated against the employee. If the trier of fact believes the plaintiff's evidence, and if the employer is silent in the face of the presumption, the court must enter judgment for the plaintiff because no issue of fact remains in the case." 450 U.S. at 254. In a footnote, the Court emphasized that a prima facie case creates "a legally mandatory, rebuttable presumption." 450 U.S. at 254 n.7.

In Fisher v. Vassar College, 114 F.3d 1332 (2d Cir. 1997) (en banc), Judges Jacob and Leval, writing for six members of the court, held that evidence sufficient to establish a prima facie case does not necessarily justify judgment for a plaintiff should the employer fail to rebut: "a plaintiff alleging discrimination can satisfy the prima facie case and avoid dismissal at the conclusion of the plaintiff's direct case without submitting evidence sufficient to support a finding in his favor on each element that the plaintiff must ultimately prove to win."

2.   Employer's Rebuttal

The second step in a *McDonnell Douglas/Burdine* case requires the employer to rebut the inference of discrimination based on the prima facie showing of intent to discriminate. **In *McDonnell Douglas*, the Court described this rebuttal burden to require the defendant to "articulate some legitimate, nondiscriminatory reason"** for its action. McDonnell Douglas had satisfied its rebuttal burden by showing that the plaintiff had been engaged in criminal activity aimed at the employer, a "stall-in" to block access to defendant's plant, to protest the employer's policies that discriminated.

In *Burdine,* the Court clarified the significance of this rebuttal burden: **"The defendant need not persuade the court that it was actually motivated by the proffered reasons. It is sufficient if the defendant's evidence raises a genuine issue of fact as to whether it discriminated against the plaintiff."** The *Burdine* Court also described the effect of the employer carrying this burden of production: "If the defendant carries this burden of production, the presumption raised by the prima facie case is rebutted." Such a showing "suffices to meet the prima facie case," but that does not end the dispute. 450 U.S. at 255.

In *Hazen Paper,* the Court indicated that a reason need not even be legal, much less legitimate, to suffice as a rebuttal. In the case, the finding that the employer acted because of illegal pension interference foreclosed a finding of age discrimination: Further, the existence of a finding of pension interference all but precludes finding age discrimination: "inferring age-motivation from the implausibility of the employer's explanation [that plaintiff was fired for doing business with competitors] may be problematic in cases where other unsavory motives, such as pension interference, were present." 450 U.S. at 613.

EXAM TIP

Remember that, since *Biggins,* the employer's rebuttal opportunity has expanded. While bizarre and even illegal reasons will work procedurally as rebuttals, a factfinder may not believe these reasons and might therefore be more inclined to find that the plaintiff was the victim of intentional discrimination.

 # EXAMPLE AND ANALYSIS

Suppose the same 38-year-old woman as in the above example cannot join a state law claim with her Title VII action. Because the ADEA's protection from age discrimination protects people over age 40, she has no basis for a federal claim of age discrimination. If the woman sues only on sex discrimination, the employer can rebut that claim by "admitting" that it acted because of her age. While neither legitimate nor nondiscriminatory, *Biggins* would find the explanation sufficient as a rebuttal. Thus, *Biggins* pushes plaintiffs to sue on every available ground lest they give the employer a way to "admit" its way out of liability.

---

3. **Plaintiff's Showing of Pretext**

The third step in the *McDonnell Douglas/Burdine* analysis gives the plaintiff a chance to show that the reasons advanced by the employer were a "pretext" hiding the employer's actual discriminatory motivation.

In *McDonnell Douglas,* the Court said "pretext" is where "the presumptively valid reasons for [plaintiff's] rejection were in fact a coverup for a racially discriminatory decision." This final stage of analysis required giving plaintiff a "fair opportunity to demonstrate that [the employer's] assigned reason for refusing to re-employ was a pretext or discriminatory in its application." 411 U.S. at 804.

In *Burdine,* the Court restated the pretext showing as demonstrating "that the proffered reason was not the true reason for the employment decision." The Court then joined the pretext issue with the ultimate issue requiring plaintiff to prove intentional discrimination. "The burden now merges with the ultimate burden of persuading the court that she has been the victim of intentional discrimination. She may succeed in this either directly by persuading the court that a discriminatory reason more likely motivated the employer or indirectly by showing that the employer's proffered explanation is unworthy of credence." 450 U.S. at 256.

In St. Mary's Honor Ctr. v. Hicks, 509 U.S. 502 (1993), the Court held that a finding of pretext, in the sense that the employer's proffered reason was not the true reason for its actions, did not justify finding as a matter of law that the employer had discriminated against the plaintiff. Although the "plaintiff has proven the existence of a crusade to terminate him, he has not proven that the crusade was racially rather than personally motivated." 509 U.S. at 508. **A finding of Title VII liability must be based on a finding of the ultimate question of "whether [the] plaintiff has proven 'that the defendant intentionally discriminated against [him] because of his race.' " 509 U.S. at 511.**

If the finder of fact finds that the employer's explanation was not true, it would be permitted, but not required, to draw the inference that the employer acted with an intent to discriminate. "Even though . . . rejection of the defendant's proffered reasons is enough at law to sustain a finding of discrimination, *there must be a finding of discrimination*." 509 U.S. at 511, n.4.

In Fisher v. Vassar College, 114 F.3d 1332, 1337 (1998) (en banc), the court, in a case involving a multi-decision-maker process for making tenure decisions, described why a finding that the reason the employer advances for its action is false does not necessarily lead to the conclusion that the actual reason for the action was discrimination.

> Individual decision-makers may intentionally dissemble in order to hide a reason that is non-discriminatory but unbecoming or small-minded, such as backscratching, log-rolling, horse-trading, institutional politics, envy, nepotism, spite, or personal hostility.

There is some other language in *Hicks* that "a reason cannot be proved to be a 'pretext' for discrimination unless it is shown both that the reason was false and that discrimination was the real reason." 509 U.S. at 515. The Court, however, disavowed that statement, saying "rejection of the defendant's reasons is enough at law to sustain a finding of discrimination." 509 U.S. at 511. Nevertheless, some courts are requiring plaintiff to prove pretext as well as discrimination. In McCullough v. Real Foods, 140 F.3d 1123, 1127 (8th Cir. 1998), the court found that at the pretext stage, the burden is on the plaintiff "to present evidence sufficient to support two findings. . . . First, the plaintiff must present evidence which creates a fact issue as to whether the employer's proffered reasons are mere pretext. . . . Second, she must present evidence which creates a reasonable inference that the adverse employment decision was an act of intentional racial discrimination."

 # EXAMPLE AND ANALYSIS

Plaintiff, an African-American male, was a shift commander at a correctional facility. With a new administration taking over the management of the facility, plaintiff, who had a satisfactory employment record, suddenly became the subject of repeated, and increasingly severe, disciplinary actions, ultimately leading to his demotion. In response to plaintiff's prima facie case of race discrimination, the employer introduced evidence that its action was motivated by plaintiff's rule violations. In a bench trial, the trial judge found that the reason the employer gave for its action was not the real reason for the demotion but he also found that the demotion was not because of his race: "although [plaintiff] has proven the existence of a crusade to terminate him, he has not proven that the crusade was racially rather than personally motivated." The Supreme Court agreed, holding that a finding of pretext is not sufficient by itself to establish liability because "there must be a finding of discrimination." But, the "factfinder's disbelief of the reasons put forward by the defendant . . . may, together with the elements of the prima facie case, suffice to show intentional discrimination." St. Mary's Honor Ctr. v. Hicks, 509 U.S. 502, 511 (1993).

Despite that language in *Hicks,* the Fifth Circuit requires plaintiff at the pretext stage to introduce evidence over and above the evidence sufficient to make out a prima facie case. In Reeves v. Sandford Plumbing Products, Inc., 197 F.3d 688 (5th Cir. 1999), *cert. granted,* _____ U.S. _____, 1999 U.S. LEXIS 7400 (Nov. 8, 1999), plaintiff proved that the reason defendant asserted for terminating him was not true, yet the court overtuned plaintiff's jury verdict because the evidence plaintiff introduced was insufficient under the court's pretext-plus rule.

a. **The types of evidence showing pretext.** In *McDonnell Douglas,* the Court described a broad array of types of evidence that could show pretext, including the employer's treatment of other workers, the employer's treatment of the plaintiff when he had previously worked for the employer, and the employer's general policy and practice, including statistical evidence, with respect to minority employment. In Patterson v. McLean Credit Union, 491 U.S. 164 (1989), the Court narrowed somewhat the scope of the types of evidence a plaintiff could rely on to prove pretext by not mentioning statistical evidence. While not including statistical evidence that had been mentioned in *McDonnell Douglas,* this holding still allows a broader array of evidence than is allowed under the general litigation rule that surrebuttal is limited to answering directly only what was raised in rebuttal.

4.   Level of Showing.

As the Court said in *Burdine,* "the ultimate burden of persuading the trier of fact that the defendant intentionally discriminated against the plaintiff remains at all times with the plaintiff." 450 U.S. at 256. Thus, plaintiff must prove, by a preponderance of evidence, that the action she challenges was motivated by an intent to discriminate that rises to a level of **but-for causation.** But for the employer's intent to discriminate, the adverse action would not have been taken against the plaintiff. In Hazen Paper Co. v. Biggins, the Court described this in slightly different language, as "a determinative influence" or **a determinative factor.** Thus, **"a disparate treatment claim cannot succeed unless the employee's protected trait actually played a role in that process and had a determinative influence on the outcome."** 507 U.S. at 610.

EXAM TIP

After *Hicks,* the key to establishing liability is the ultimate question of whether the defendant discriminated against the plaintiff.

 # EXAMPLE AND ANALYSIS

Assuming on remand in *Hicks* that the finder of fact decides that race did play a role in the demotion of the plaintiff, but that the accumulation of rule violations also played a part, plaintiff can win, even though he did not establish that the rule violation reason was a pretext for discrimination, as long as he can convince the factfinder that race, and not the rule violations, was the determinative influence on the outcome.

F.   THE BACKGROUND OF THE DIRECT EVIDENCE OR MIXED MOTIVE TEST OF INTENT

By the time Price Waterhouse v. Hopkins, 490 U.S. 228 (1989), was decided in 1989, the *McDonnell Douglas/Burdine* circumstantial evidence approach was well established, though it had yet to be cut back by the 1993 decisions in Hazen Paper Co. v. Biggins and *Hicks.* Unlike the circumstantial evidence cases, *Price Waterhouse* involved statements by the employer that revealed an intent by the employer to discriminate or at least its reliance upon stereotypical thinking about the plaintiff as a woman. Plaintiff was put on hold in her bid to become a partner in a large accounting firm. The plaintiff introduced circumstantial evidence showing her to be a comparatively strong candidate as well as evidence showing few incumbent partners to be women. Additionally, the plaintiff relied on written evaluations by partners that suggested gender had played a role in their decision: one partner "described her as 'macho'; another suggested that she 'overcompensated for being a woman'; and a third advised her to take 'a course at charm school.'" Further, the partner who informed her of the negative decision counselled her to "walk more femininely, wear make-up, have her hair styled, and wear jewelry." 490 U.S. at 235.

In deciding for Hopkins, the Supreme Court was quite splintered. Nevertheless, this case ultimately is the basis for the creation of a second method of proving individual disparate treatment discrimination. It involves plaintiff introducing "direct" evidence of discrimination sufficient to create a question of fact whether sex, or other protected characteristic, was "a motivating factor" in the employer's decision. If that is established, then the employer has an opportunity to prove an affirmative defense that it would have made the same decision even if it had not considered sex in its decision.

1. The Test for a Prima Facie Case

A plurality of four members of the Court found that the plaintiff had established a prima facie case of liability by using this evidence to show that gender was "a motivating factor" in the challenged decision. To make a majority, the approach of one of the two concurring Justices was required. Justices White and O'Connor differed with the plurality but agreed with each other that the plaintiff must show that race or gender was "a substantial factor" in the employer's decision-making. That test is more difficult for a plaintiff to prove than the "motivating factor" test picked by the plurality.

Calling *Price Waterhouse* a "mixed motive" approach to proving individual disparate treatment comes from the fact that a showing that intent to discriminate was either "a substantial factor" or the lesser "motivating factor." That means that at least one other factor also played a role in the employer's decision. Thus discriminatory motive was mixed with a nondiscriminatory motive to produce the decision. However, the *McDonnell Douglas/Burdine* circumstantial evidence approach also involves mixing discriminatory motivation with nondiscriminatory motivation: Showing that race, gender, or other characteristic protected against discrimination was "a determinative factor" admits to the possibility that another factor did play some role, though not a decisive one.

2. The Same Decision Defense to Liability

The plurality and the two concurring Justices did agree as to the effect of the prima facie case established in *Price Waterhouse:* such a showing created a presumption of liability that could be rebutted by the employer if it could prove, by a preponderance of the evidence, that it would have made the same decision even if gender had not been considered.

3.   The Direct Evidence Approach as an Independent Theory of Proving Intent

While characterizing the case as one involving mixed motives and rejecting the idea that all individual disparate cases need be analyzed according to *McDonnell Douglas/Burdine*, the plurality appeared to treat this burden-shifting as an affirmative defense to all individual disparate treatment cases, including *McDonnell Douglas/Burdine*-type cases based on circumstantial evidence. In contrast, Justice O'Connor envisioned *Price Waterhouse* as creating a new, and separate, track of individual disparate treatment theory. For her, there was a fundamental difference between cases that depended on direct versus circumstantial evidence to attempt to prove discrimination. In cases based only on circumstantial evidence of intent to discriminate, the plaintiff must carry the heavier burden of proving that, but for the gender or race of the plaintiff, the defendant would not have taken the action plaintiff challenges. However, in direct evidence cases, the plaintiff could establish a prima facie case by proving race or gender was "a substantial factor" in the employer's decision because direct, or "smoking gun," evidence is of higher quality than mere circumstantial evidence. That showing, then, would shift the burden of persuasion to the employer to prove that it would have made the same decision even if it had not considered race or gender.

Most of the lower courts initially followed Justice O'Connor's position and have treated *Price Waterhouse* as creating a separate method of proving intent to discriminate based on the threshold showing of "direct" evidence of discrimination.

4.   Congressional Modification of *Price Waterhouse*

In passing the Civil Rights Act of 1991, Congress modified *Price Waterhouse*. As a result, the level of showing necessary to make out a prima facie case was reduced from "a substantial factor" to "a motivating factor." Further, the same decision affirmative defense was changed from one that would free the employer of all liability to one that instead limited plaintiff's relief to an injunction prohibiting future discrimination and to attorney's fees.

Since the amendments in question were made only to Title VII, it is not clear whether the approach that now governs direct evidence cases under Title VII also applies to similar cases brought under the ADEA or 42 U.S.C. §1981.

G.   THE PRESENT APPROACH TO DIRECT EVIDENCE CASES

As a result of the amendments added to Title VII by the 1991 Civil Rights Act, direct evidence cases involve two steps, the plaintiff's prima facie case followed by the employer's affirmative defense.

1. The Prima Facie Showing of "A Motivating Factor"

New §703(m), which was added to Title VII by the 1991 Civil Rights Act, rejects the "substantial factor" test that Justices O'Connor and White had insisted upon in *Price Waterhouse*. Instead, Congress adopted the **"motivating factor"** threshold that the plurality had relied upon. Thus, new §703(m) provides that "an unlawful employment practice is established when the complaining party demonstrates that race, color, religion, sex, or national origin was a motivating factor for any employment practice, even though other factors also motivated the practice."

This level of showing is less difficult for a plaintiff to make out than the but-for or determinative factor test required in *McDonnell Douglas/Burdine* circumstantial evidence cases.

EXAMPLE AND ANALYSIS

Suppose plaintiff introduces evidence that triggers the use of the direct evidence method by showing that shortly before deciding to lay off plaintiff, his boss told him, "You are too damn old for this kind of work." In addition to claiming that this was said in jest, the employer introduces evidence that the plaintiff had failed to call back some of his customers who had complained about the company's service. If the factfinder believed that both the age of the plaintiff and his failure to call back customers motivated the employer, then plaintiff loses if he must prove age was the sole cause of his layoff. If the but-for or determinative factor test is used, plaintiff can win only if the factfinder believes that he would not have been laid off but for the employer's consideration of his age. Under the "substantial factor" test, the factfinder must determine that more of the motivation for the layoff was age discrimination than plaintiff's failure to respond to customer complaints. Using the "motivating factor" test, plaintiff can win by convincing the factfinder that his age motivated the employer to some extent even if the failure to return customer calls played a larger role in the employer's motivation for the layoff. See O'Connor Consolidated Coin Caterers Corp., 56 F.3d 542 (4th Cir. 1995), *rev'd on other grounds,* 116 U.S. 1307 (1996).

2. The Same Decision Defense to Full Remedies

Congress changed the consequences of the same decision defense from a defense to liability to a limitation on remedies. According to §706(g)(2)(B), where the employer proves that it "would have taken the same action in the absence of the impermissible motivating factor, the court—(i) may grant declaratory relief, injunctive relief . . . and attorney's fees and costs directly attributable only to the pursuit of a claim under section 703(m), and (ii) shall not award damages or issue an order requiring any admission, reinstatement, hiring, promotion or payment [of backpay]." The plaintiff would only receive declaratory relief that the employer had discriminated, injunctive relief prohibiting such discrimination in the future, and attorney's fees and costs. If, however, the employer fails to carry its burden, the plaintiff would be entitled to full legal and equitable relief.

EXAM TIP

To use *Price Waterhouse,* the Supreme Court's approach, as modified by the 1991 amendments, still requires plaintiff to (1) use direct evidence, and (2) prove that an impermissible reason was "a motivating factor" in the employer's decision. That establishes defendant's liability, but defendant can, nevertheless, restrict the remedies to which plaintiff is entitled by proving that it would have made the same decision even if it had not relied on the impermissible reason.

 # EXAMPLES AND ANALYSIS

1. In the above example, assume that a jury finds that age was "a motivating factor" for the plaintiff's layoff. With that finding, liability is established. But the employer can attempt to prove that it would have made the same decision to lay him off because of his failure to respond to customer complaints, even if it had not taken age into account in making the decision. If the jury finds that the employer carried its burden of persuasion on this affirmative defense, then plaintiff is only entitled to the limited relief of declaratory or injunctive relief against further discrimination plus attorney's fees and costs. While age is "a motivating factor" justifying limited relief, the but-for reason of his loss of job was the failure to respond to customer complaints.

   If the jury finds that the employer failed to carry its burden of persuasion on the same decision defense, then the plaintiff is entitled to full equitable and legal relief because age discrimination was the but-for motivation of the employer.

2. Plaintiff applied for but was not hired as principal of a high school. In challenging that decision, plaintiff introduced testimony that, during the selection process, the school superintendent told the school board that "we did not need to employ a black as principal at Thompson High School." Assuming this is direct evidence that the jury relies upon to find that race was a motivating factor in not hiring plaintiff, the school board won on its same decision defense by proving that the person it did appoint as principal was so much more qualified than plaintiff that

it would have made that appointment even if it had not considered plaintiff's race at all. See Harris v. Shelby County Bd. of Educ., 99 F.3d 1078 (11th Cir. 1996).

H. THE RELATIONSHIP BETWEEN THE CIRCUMSTANTIAL AND DIRECT EVIDENCE APPROACHES TO INDIVIDUAL DISPARATE TREATMENT DISCRMINATION

Given that there are two separate methods of proving individual disparate treatment discrimination, it is necessary to find the boundary that divides them.

1. Only One of the Two Approaches Applies to a Case

The plurality in *Price Waterhouse* appeared to assume that, while a plaintiff could claim both approaches in any case, at some point the trial judge must decide which of the two methods is applicable. In Fuller v. Phipps, 67 F.3d 1137, 1142 n.2 (4th Cir. 1995), the court described how this works: "A plaintiff need not decide at the outset whether to classify his case as a 'pretext' or a 'mixed-motive' case. Instead, the district court makes this determination after evaluating the evidence, and instructs the jury."

2. *McDonnell Douglas/Burdine* Is the Default Approach

In deciding which approach applies, first decide if the *Price Waterhouse* direct evidence approach applies, and, if not, then the *McDonnell Douglas/Burdine* approach applies as the default position.

EXAM TIP

In analyizing an individual disparate treatment case, always start with a discussion of whether *Price Waterhouse* applies by arguing that the facts include evidence that can be characterized as "direct."

3. The Existence of "Direct Evidence" Is the Boundary Between Circumstantial and Direct Evidence Cases

While long disfavored as a distinction in evidence law, "direct evidence" is evidence that proves a factual issue without the need to resort to drawing any inferences, while "circumstantial evidence" is evidence that only supports drawing an inference to resolve a factual issue. Some courts have defined "direct evidence" more broadly than the classic test.

EXAMPLES AND ANALYSIS

1. Suppose an employer does not hire an applicant and says, "I did not hire the plaintiff because this is no job for a woman." This admission is quite powerful, probative evidence of intent to discriminate. But what makes it powerful is that it is against the interest of the employer to make it, so there is little reason not to believe it. This is, however, not direct evidence of the employer's state of mind. Even if said in open court to the jury, this statement is still circumstantial evidence of the employer's state of mind. The factfinder, who perceives the statement through her senses by hearing and observing the speaker, is drawing an inference in deciding whether the statement is to be believed as expressing the employer's actual state of mind. The statement could be a lie, a joke, or a mistake. The decision, while easy, does require the factfinder to draw an inference in deciding the employer's state of mind.

2. Assume the plaintiff thinks she is the victim of age discrimination even though the employer told her, "I did not discriminate against you because of your age but because you are overqualified." While denying it was plaintiff's age that motivated him, the speaker may have admitted relying on age but just not have been aware of it. The statement that plaintiff was "overqualified" may signify an unconscious reliance on stereotypical thinking about older workers, and, thus, is a code word for "old." Alternatively, it might be a legitimate, nondiscriminatory description of plaintiff as someone who would not do a good job or would not stay long because she would find the job too boring. See Taggart v. Time, Inc., 924 F.2d 43 (2d Cir. 1991).

  a. **The two different definitions of what is direct evidence.** The lower courts have taken several different positions as to what evidence is sufficiently direct to trigger the use of the *Price Waterhouse* method of proving individual disparate treatment discrimination. In Harris v. Shelby County Bd. of Educ., 99 F.3d 1078 (11th Cir. 1996), the court adopted the classical definition of **direct evidence as "evidence, which if believed, proves the existence of the fact in issue without an inference or presumption."**

  In contrast, in Deneen v. Northwest Airlines, 132 F.3d 431 (8th Cir. 1998), the court defined direct evidence as evidence that supports an inference of discrimination. **Direct evidence "demonstrates a specific link between the alleged discriminatory animus and the challenged decision, sufficient to support a finding by a reasonable fact finder that an illegitimate criterion actually motivated the employer's decision."** This approach is sometimes called the **"circumstantial-plus"** approach to the threshold for the use of the *Price Waterhouse* approach because it requires that ''circumstantial evidence must be tied directly to the alleged discriminatory animus. For example, purely statistical evidence would not warrant such a charge; nor would evidence merely of the plaintiff's qualification for and the availability of a given position; nor would 'stray' remarks in the workplace by persons who are not involved in the pertinent decision-making process.'' Ostrowski v. Atlantic Mut. Ins. Cos., 968 F.2d 171 (2d Cir. 1992).

EXAM TIP

Because two methods of proof exist, it is important to analyze whether the fact situation includes anything that can be characterized as ''direct'' evidence, since that is the trigger to the application of the *Price Waterhouse* rather than the *McDonnell Douglas/Burdine* approach. As the definition of what is ''direct'' evidence expands, so does the scope of application of *Price Waterhouse*.

EXAMPLE AND ANALYSIS

A former employee provided plaintiff with an affidavit relaying a conversation he had with the manager of the employer, who decided not to promote plaintiff, in which the manager said ''she identified in herself a bias against blacks and she found that they were difficult for her to trust or get along with.'' This would be rejected as direct evidence under the strict test of the *Harris* court because it is subject to more than one interpretation: it could mean that she was trying to overcome her prior prejudice. Even under the broader circumstantial-plus approach of the *Ostrowski* court, this might not be admissible to trigger the *Price Waterhouse* approach because it was not directly connected to plaintiff's promotion decision. However, the fact that it was made by the manager who decided to deny plaintiff a promotion may suffice so that this satisfies *Ostrowski*. See Carter v. Three Springs Res. Treatment, 132 F.3d 635 (11th Cir. 1998).

I. THE COLLAPSE OF THE EXISTING ORDER AND THE EMERGENCE OF A NEW APPROACH

There is much criticism of the present state of the *McDonnell Douglas/Burdine* approach because it has been turned from a device to give plaintiffs every chance to prove discrimination into a means for dumping cases out of court without a trial. Professor Deborah C. Malamud, The Last Minuet: Disparate Treatment After *Hicks,* 93 Mich. L. Rev. 2229, 2237 (1995), argues:

A review of district court summary judgment cases demonstrates that to accord legal significance to the plaintiff's satisfaction of the "requirements" of the prima facie "stage" and the pretext "stage" of *McDonnell Douglas-Burdine* is to engage in an act of misplaced concreteness. The world of practice under *McDonnell Douglas-Burdine* remains a disorderly one, in which the assignment of categories of facts to "stages" is unstable. Furthermore, to the extent that *McDonnell Douglas-Burdine* does constrain fact finding, it tends to discourage the kind of holistic fact finding that is most likely to reveal the truth about discrimination in the workplace.

Maintaining two separate methods of approach may also allow deserving cases to fall between the cracks. And, even if each of the two separate approaches makes some sense, having two tracks makes the law too complicated for jurors, lawyers, and even judges to understand and to operate. There have been several alternative approaches suggested.

1. Applying the 1991 Civil Rights Act Provisions to All Individual Disparate Treatment Cases

Since §§703(m) and 707(g)(2)(B) already apply to *Price Waterhouse* direct evidence cases, these same provisions could easily be read to apply to *McDonnell Douglas/Burdine* circumstantial evidence cases as well. Circumstantial evidence cases involve the proof of intent to discriminate and it could be argued that §703(m) applies whenever plaintiff proves race, gender, or other protected characteristic is "a motivating factor" in the decision the plaintiff challenges.

The effect of this approach would be twofold. First, the burden on plaintiff in the first instance would be lowered from having to prove that the protected characteristic was the "determinative influence" to the lesser "motivating factor" level. Second, if plaintiff establishes a prima facie case, defendant would have a new affirmative defense under §706(g)(2)(B) not previously available under the *McDonnell Douglas/Burdine* approach to try to limit full remedies by proving it would have made the same decision even if it had not considered plaintiff's prohibited characteristic in making the decision.

The lower courts have not adopted this approach. In Fuller v. Phipps, 67 F.3d 1137 (4th Cir. 1995), the Fourth Circuit, faced with applying the new provisions added to Title VII by §107 of the Civil Rights Act of 1991, found that the new law did not apply to pretext cases: "Section 107 was intended to benefit plaintiffs in mixed-motive cases; it has nothing to say about the analysis in pretext cases such as this one."

Judge Tjoflat, in Wright v. Southland Corp., 187 F.3d 1287 (11th Cir. 1999), has articulated a new approach that ultimately treats all individual disparate treatment cases that get to the factfinder as *Price Waterhouse* cases. Under his approach, *McDonnell Douglas* is only used to "smoke out" of the defendant evidence of its reason for having taken the action that plaintiff challenges. Once evidence of the defendant's reason is in the record, *McDonnell Douglas* drops out of the case. Defining all the evidence in the record as "direct" evidence in the sense that it is aimed at finding whether discrimination is proven by a preponderance of the evidence, Judge Tjoflat then would apply *Price Waterhouse,* as modified by the 1991 Act amendments, to determine if an impermissible factor was "a motivating factor" and, if so, whether the defendant carried its same decision defense to limit remedies.

EXAMPLE AND ANALYSIS

Assume that a Latina worker claims she was discharged because of race and sex discrimination. She claims she was a member of two protected groups, was doing a satisfactory job, but was discharged and her job filled by a white male. The employer argues that she was discharged for excessive tardiness. The evidence includes testimony that the manager who made the decision to fire the plaintiff had been heard to say, "Women and good workers are oil and water." Further, plaintiff showed some evidence that several white workers had records of tardiness as bad as plaintiff, yet they had not been discharged. In contrast, the employer introduced the testimony of the manager denying he had made the statement claimed of him and evidence that the white workers with as many tardy days had accumulated them over a longer period of employment than had the plaintiff.

Using the separate *Price Waterhouse* and *McDonnell Douglas/Burdine* approaches, the first question is whether *Price Waterhouse* applies. The statement of the supervisor reveals prejudice against women but it is not directly linked to plaintiff's discharge. If this is sufficient to trigger a direct evidence case, then the jury must decide if, by that statement, plaintiff proved that race and/or sex was "a motivating factor" in the employer's decision, even if tardiness was also a factor in the decision. That establishes liability but, if the employer successfully proved that it would have made the same decision even if race and/or sex had not been considered, then plaintiff's remedies will be limited to declaratory and injunctive relief and attorney's fees.

If *McDonnell Douglas/Burdine* applies because *Price Waterhouse* is held not to apply, a prima facie case exists but the question is whether, at the pretext step of analysis, the factfinder believes, based on the preponderance of the evidence, that plaintiff has proven that either her race or her sex had a determinative influence in the employer's decision. Presumably, as among the three possibilities—her race, her sex, and her tardiness—only one can be the determinative influence.

Under an approach unified under §§703(m) and 706(g)(2)(B), the jury would look at the record as a whole, including all the evidence however categorized, to determine whether race and/or sex was "a motivating factor" in the employer's decision. If so, that would open up the possibility of the same decision affirmative defense to full remedies.

2. A Gravitational Move Toward a Unified Approach

The lower courts may be moving toward a unified approach to individual disparate treatment cases, even without saying so. For example, in Fields v. New York State Office of Mental Retardation and Developmental Disabilities, 115 F.3d 116 (2d Cir. 1997), the court rejected the argument that the 1991 Civil Rights Act abolished the distinction between *Price Waterhouse* and *McDonnell Douglas* cases. It indicated that the "motivating factor" level of showing applied in both *Price Waterhouse* and *McDonnell Douglas/Burdine* cases but held that the same decision limitation on full remedies is available only as a defense to cases where plaintiff has introduced direct or circumstantial-plus evidence necessary to the use of the *Price Waterhouse* approach. In contrast, in Deneen v. Northwest Airlines, 132 F.3d 431 (8th Cir. 1998), the court found that the employer's requirement that the pregnant plaintiff obtain a doctor's note before she could return to work was direct evidence of discrimination just because he knew she was pregnant. Such a broad definition of direct evidence, and with it the application of §703(m), encompasses most circumstantial evidence.

3. The Traditional Approach of General Litigation

Rhodes v. Guiberson Oil Tools, 75 F.3d 989, 993–94 (5th Cir. 1996) (en banc), may be a good example of a court applying the basic inference-drawing standard of general civil litigation to an individual disparate treatment case. While cast in terms of a *McDonnell Douglas/Burdine* case, the court emphasized that "traditional sufficiency-of-the-evidence analysis" applies. "To sustain a finding of discrimination, circumstantial evidence must be such as to allow a rational factfinder to make a reasonable inference that age was a determinative reason for the employment."

EXAM TIP

If your professor spends time on the emerging approaches that diverge from the Supreme Court's bifurcated *McDonnell Douglas* or *Price Waterhouse* structure, then add this as a third part to your discussion in individual disparate treatment cases.

REVIEW QUESTIONS AND ANSWERS

Question: How many approaches to individual disparate treatment has the Supreme Court adopted?

Answer: Two. The *McDonnell Douglas/Burdine* approach applies where circumstantial evidence is the basis for drawing the inference that the determinative influence in the employer's decision was race, gender, or other prohibited characteristic. The *Price Waterhouse* approach applies where direct evidence is the basis for finding that race, gender, etc., was a motivating factor in the employer's decision. The lower courts appear to be moving toward several different approaches.

Question: What are the steps used to analyze a *McDonnell Douglas/Burdine* case based on circumstantial evidence?

Answer: There are three steps in a *McDonnell Douglas/Burdine* case.

1. Plaintiff's prima facie case is established when plaintiff introduces evidence sufficient to reject the most typical legitimate reasons for the employer's action and to support the inference that it was plaintiff's race or gender that motivated the employer's action.

2. To rebut plaintiff's prima facie case, defendant must introduce evidence of a reason other than discrimination that it says explains the action taken.

3. In carrying its ultimate burden of persuasion, plaintiff must convince the fact-finder by a preponderance of the evidence that defendant's intent to discriminate was the determinative influence in defendant's decision. The evidence to support that finding may include the evidence that made out the prima facie case, evidence supporting a finding that the defendant's rebuttal reason was a pretext, as well as other evidence.

Question: What level of showing must a plaintiff prove to establish a *McDonnell Douglas/Burdine* case?

Answer: The Supreme Court has indicated in *Biggins,* 507 U.S. at 610, that plaintiff must prove that "the employee's protected trait actually played a role in [the employer's decision-making process] and had a determinative influence on the outcome." This appears to be a but-for showing.

Question: Is the same decision defense available in a *McDonnell Douglas/Burdine* case?

Answer: No, that defense is yet to be recognized outside of the *Price Waterhouse*-type case. It would, however, be available if a uniform approach to individual disparate treatment cases based on the 1991 Civil Rights Act would be adopted.

Question: What two steps are necessary in a *Price Waterhouse* case?

Answer: The two steps are:

1. Based upon direct or at least circumstantial-plus evidence, plaintiff will establish liability by proving that race, gender, age, etc., was "a motivating factor" in the decision the employer made.

2. The employer can limit plaintiff's remedies to declaratory and injunctive relief and attorney's fees if it can prove that it would have made the same decision, even if it had not considered the protected characteristic in making its decision.

Question: Can both *McDonnell Douglas/Burdine* and *Price Waterhouse* apply to the same case?

Answer: Although not finally decided by the Supreme Court, it appears that a plaintiff can initiate a case under either or both approaches, but that, before the case is submitted to the finder of fact, the trial judge must decide which of the two approaches applies.

Question: How do you analyze whether the *Price Waterhouse* or the *McDonnell Douglas/Burdine* approach applies?

Answer: The first step is to determine whether *Price Waterhouse* applies by determining if plaintiff has introduced direct or circumstantial-plus evidence of the employer's intent to discriminate. If *Price Waterhouse* does not apply, *McDonnell Douglas/Burdine* is the default approach that applies.

Question: What is the difference between the type of evidence that triggers the application of *Price Waterhouse* and of *McDonnell Douglas/Burdine?*

Answer: The classic definition of direct evidence that triggers the use of the *Price Waterhouse* approach is evidence that proves a fact at issue without the need to draw an inference. Some courts have used the term "direct" to mean evidence connected more or less directly with the decision the plaintiff challenges as discriminatory. Some courts characterize "circumstantial-plus" evidence as sufficient to trigger the use of *Price Waterhouse,* which is evidence other than statistical evidence, plaintiff's qualification for and the availability of an opening, or "stray" remarks in the workplace by persons not involved in the decision that plaintiff challenges.

Circumstantial evidence as used by *McDonnell Douglas/Burdine* is all the evidence in the record where the trial judge has ruled that *Price Waterhouse* does not apply.

3 SYSTEMIC DISPARATE TREATMENT DISCRIMINATION

CHAPTER OVERVIEW

Systemic disparate treatment discrimination addresses the broadest claims of intentional discrimination because of its focus on policies or general practices of discrimination. As in individual disparate treatment discrimination, the key is intent to discriminate, which can be proved in one of two ways. The first is to show a formal policy of discrimination and the second is to show, through the cumulation of employment decisions, that an employer has a general practice of discriminating. There are two established rebuttals potentially available to the employer. The first is to rebut plaintiff's prima facie case; the second is the bona fide occupational qualification.

- **Formal Policy of Discrimination:** One way to establish a prima facie case of systemic disparate treatment discrimination is to show the existence of a formal, usually written, policy of discrimination. At present, these most typically exist where the employer admits the policy but claims a justification because of the bona fide occupational qualification defense.

- **Voluntary Affirmative Action:** Employer use of voluntary affirmative action plans is a special case of a formal policy of discrimination. The burden of persuasion is on the ''reverse'' discrimination plaintiff using Title VII to challenge an affirmative action plan. He must not only prove that the employer had a plan but also that the plan violated the standards set for Title VII. The plan will be upheld as long as it breaks down old patterns of segregation or diminishes a manifest imbalance in the workforce, does not trammel unnecessarily the interests of majority workers and is a temporary measure. The constitutional equal protection standards for using race for affirmative action purposes by public employers are much stricter, including imposing the burden of persuasion on the employer to justify its use as narrowly tailored to a compelling governmental interest.

- **General Practice of Discrimination:** The second way to prove systemic disparate treatment discrimination is to prove, typically with statistical and anecdotal evidence, that it is the general practice of the employer to discriminate. If a **"gross and longlasting" disparity** exists between the number of women or minority group members working for the employer and the number of women or minority group members who are available to do the work involved, then a prima facie case of systemic disparate treatment discrimination is established.

- **The Two Rebuttals to a Systemic Disparate Treatment Case:** Theoretically, there are two defenses available to a prima facie case of systemic disparate treatment discrimination.

  - **Rebut Plaintiff's Showing:** The defendant can refute the inference of discriminatory intent in three ways: (1) by arguing that the formal policy plaintiff proved does not exist or is not discriminatory; (2) by undermining the statistical evidence plaintiff relied upon to establish a practice of discrimination; or (3) by showing that the employer took its actions "despite," rather than "because of" its racial or gender impact. Defendant does not bear the burden of persuasion on this rebuttal since these are not affirmative defenses.

  - **Bona Fide Occupational Qualification:** When the prima facie case is established with the showing of a formal policy of discrimination, the BFOQ defense is available if the employer can prove that the challenged qualification goes to the essence of the job and either no one of the excluded group can do the job or the difficulty of picking the few qualified members in the excluded group make that impractical. The BFOQ defense applies to formal discrimination because of religion, sex, national origin, or age but **not** because of race or color. This is an affirmative defense, so that the employer bears the burden of persuasion to prove the BFOQ defense.

A. POLICY OR PRACTICE OF INTENTIONAL DISCRIMINATION

The broadest definition or theory of discrimination is systemic disparate treatment discrimination. It is a system of discrimination, that is, a formal policy or a general practice of an employer to discriminate on a basis prohibited by an antidiscrimination statute. In International Brotherhood of Teamsters v. United States, 431 U.S. 324, 335 n.15 (1977), the Supreme Court described disparate treatment: "The employer simply treats some people less favorably than others because of their race, color, religion, sex or national origin." More recently, the Supreme Court in Hazen Paper Co. v. Biggins, 507 U.S. 604, 610 (1993), said

In a disparate treatment case, liability depends on whether the protected trait . . . actually motivated the employer's decision. The employer may have relied upon a formal, facially discriminatory policy requiring adverse treatment of employees with that trait. . . . Or, the employer may have been motivated by the protected trait on an ad hoc, informal basis.

B. ESTABLISHING A PRIMA FACIE CASE

The structure of systemic disparate treatment in part mirrors individual disparate treatment law in that it can be proven in two ways. First, the plaintiff may demonstrate that the employer has an announced, formal policy of discrimination. This approach is analogous to a *Price Waterhouse* case of individual disparate treatment based on direct evidence. Second, failing proof of a formal policy, a plaintiff may nevertheless establish that the employer's pattern of employment decisions, its general practice, reveals that a de facto policy of disparate treatment exists. This approach is somewhat analogous to a *McDonnell Douglas/Burdine* case of individual disparate treatment based on circumstantial evidence.

EXAM TIP

The key similarity of systemic and individual disparate treatment theories is the focus on the employer's intent to discriminate. The key difference is the focus on an individual's treatment versus a formal policy or general practice of discrimination by the employer. The key difference between systemic disparate treatment and systemic disparate impact is that there is no intent to discriminate element in disparate impact.

 # EXAMPLES AND ANALYSIS

1. If a town has a rule that it will only hire white applicants for public jobs, that rule will be a formal policy of discriminating on the basis of race. Proving that this formal policy exists will be proof of discriminatory intent since it would be hard to imagine a court accepting the argument that the rule was enacted "in spite of" its impact on African Americans. Further, the BFOQ defense is not available in race cases and an affirmative action plan to benefit whites would be highly unlikely.

2. Assume that another town has a substantially all-white population and it has a rule limiting hiring of public employees to town residents. While not a policy that on its face demonstrates race discrimination, a pattern or practice of discrimination case could be established by showing that there were none or very few minority group members working for the town while many would be available but for the town residency rule. While the employer would attempt to show that it enacted the rule "despite" rather than "because" of its racial impact, that defense is not

likely to be successful where the racial impact is so overwhelming and the rule is not connected to the performance of the work. See NAACP v. Town of Harrison, 940 F.2d 792 (3d Cir. 1991).

C. FORMAL POLICIES OF DISCRIMINATION

Historically, formal systems of discrimination were common. In nineteenth century Boston, the sign on the employer's door, "Irish Need Not Apply," or, more recently, sex-segregated advertisements in the classified section of the newspaper typify formal policies of discrimination. With the passage of Title VII in 1964, most formal policies of exclusion ended. When the ADEA was amended in 1978 to eliminate the use of age as a basis for mandatory retirement, employer policies requiring such retirement also generally ended. In the present era, formal policies of discrimination exist in two situations.

1. The Employer Admits the Policy

Since the BFOQ defense is tied to a formal policy of discrimination, an employer trying to defend a policy based on the BFOQ defense may admit the existence of a formal policy of discrimination. For example, in Dothard v. Rawlinson, 433 U.S. 321 (1977), the employer, a state prison system, required prison guards in "contact" positions with inmates to be of the same gender as the inmates. The existence of the formal policy of discrimination was admitted, with the whole focus of the case turning on whether that segregation of prison guards by gender was justified by the BFOQ defense. The Court ultimately found that it was. In International Union, UAW v. Johnson Controls, Inc., 499 U.S. 187 (1991), the company adopted a rule that "women who are pregnant or who are capable of bearing children will not be placed into jobs involving lead exposure." The employer did not deny that this was a gender explicit policy but instead argued, unsuccessfully, that it was legal because it was to protect the children of workers and was not implemented with an evil motive.

EXAM TIP

When the obvious thrust of the question is either the BFOQ defense or the affirmative action defense, make sure you point out the threshold issue that these typically involve formal policies that discriminate.

---

a. **Voluntary affirmative action.** "Reverse" discrimination challenges to employer use of affirmative action are analyzed using very different standards depending on whether the case is brought under an antidiscrimination statute, such as Title VII, or pursuant to equal protection under the Constitution.

i. **The Title VII standards for affirmative action.** The Supreme Court has upheld the use of race and gender by an employer under Title VII attack where the employer was acting pursuant to a voluntary affirmative action plan that meets certain standards.

   (a) **The burden of persuasion is on the plaintiff.** Not only must the use of affirmative action be shown by the "reverse" discrimination plaintiff but also the plaintiff must prove that its use violates Title VII's standards. In Johnson v. Transportation Agency of Santa Clara County, 480 U.S. 616 (1987), the Court held that a **plaintiff challenging an affirmative action plan under Title VII "bears the burden of establishing the invalidity of the employer's affirmative action plan."** Although an employer relying on an affirmative action plan may concede that it used race or gender in its decision-making, the "existence of an affirmative action plan provides [a nondiscriminatory] rationale." By analogy to the individual disparate treatment cases, *McDonnell Douglas* and *Burdine*, this nondiscriminatory reason does not shift the burden of persuasion to the employer. "The burden of proving invalidity remains on the plaintiff."

   (b) **The standards for using affirmative action.** The following standards apply under Title VII to voluntary affirmative action plans.

      (1) **The purpose is to break patterns of discrimination.** In United Steelworkers of America v. Weber, 443 U.S. 193 (1979), the Court, in laying out the basic standards to find that Title VII did not prohibit affirmative action, said as to the particular plan that operated to integrate skilled craft jobs in a manufacturing plant, **"The purposes of the plan mirror those of the statute. Both were designed to break down old patterns of racial segregation and hierarchy."** In another statement, the Court said the intent of the plan must be to **"eliminate a manifest racial imbalance."**

      Limiting the use of affirmative action to breaking down patterns of segregation and hierarchy means that the beneficiaries of affirmative action must be women and members of minority groups since it would be very rare for a pattern of segregation and hierarchy to operate to the disadvantage of white males.

In Johnson v. Transportation Agency of Santa Clara County, 480 U.S. 616 (1987), the Court, in upholding an affirmative action plan benefitting women, held that the validity of an affirmative action plan does not turn on the employer pointing to "its own prior discriminatory practices, nor even to evidence of an 'arguable violation' on its part. Rather, it need point only to a 'conspicuous . . . imbalance in traditionally segregated job categories.' "

(2) **The plan does not unnecessarily trammel the rights of majority workers.** The second element necessary to uphold an affirmative action plan from attack under Title VII was described by the Court in *Weber.* The **"plan does not unnecessarily trammel the interest of the white employees.** The plan does not require the discharge of white workers and their replacement with new black hires. . . . Nor does the plan create an absolute bar to the advancement of white employees." 443 U.S. at 208.

(3) **The plan must be temporary.** The Court in *Weber* added the requirement that **"the plan is a temporary measure; it is not intended to maintain racial balance, but simply to eliminate a manifest racial imbalance."** 443 U.S. at 208. In *Johnson,* the Court found this element satisfied by the plan in that case since it "was intended to *attain* a balanced work force, not to maintain one." 480 U.S. at 639. The absence of an explicit end date for the plan was not fatal, given the long, slow process that was expected in order to achieve the goal of a balanced workforce.

 # EXAMPLES AND ANALYSIS

1. Kaiser Aluminum bargained with its union to create a new program to allow incumbent workers into a training program to fill skilled jobs in the plant. Previously, the employer hired all its skilled workers from outside the company so no incumbent workers could transfer to skilled jobs in the plant. Because of discrimination by craft unions, all the skilled workers in the locale of the plant were white. Thus, Kaiser's skilled workers were also all white. The purpose of the new program was to integrate the skilled jobs at the plant. Seniority was used to select incumbent workers to participate. But since incumbent African-American workers had less seniority than the white incumbents, the plan provided one-for-one selection of black and white workers. The Court found that Title VII did not prohibit the plan

adopted by Kaiser and the union. "The purposes of the plan mirror those of the statute. Both were designed to break down old patterns of racial segregation and hierarchy. . . . At the same time, the plan does not unnecessarily trammel the interest of the white employees. The plan does not require the discharge of white workers and their replacement with new black hires. . . . Nor does the plan create an absolute bar to the advancement of white employees; half of those trained in the program will be white. Moreover, the plan is a temporary measure; it is not intended to maintain racial balance, but simply to eliminate a manifest racial imbalance." 433 U.S. at 208.

2. In Johnson v. Transportation Agency of Santa Clara County, 480 U.S. 616 (1987), the Supreme Court reaffirmed *Weber* and applied its tests in another Title VII case to uphold a voluntary affirmative action plan of a public employer that benefitted women. While plaintiff Johnson was rated by an interview panel at 75, Joyce, the woman who was given the job, was rated a 73. The director of the agency, who made the decision, said that both candidates were equally qualified, that the rating difference was not significant and that he had looked at the whole picture including "affirmative action matters." With over 36 percent of the area labor market made up of women and over 22 percent of the employer's employees being women but with none of its 238 skilled craft worker positions filled by a woman, the employer's affirmative action plan called for a long-range goal of 36 percent women in the skilled craft worker category. The plan did not set a short-term goal but "authorized the consideration of ethnicity or sex as a factor when evaluating qualified candidates for jobs in which members of such groups were poorly represented."

3. Recently, the Third Circuit, sitting en banc, rejected an affirmative action plan because its purpose was not to remedy prior discrimination by the employer. That appears to be inconsistent with *Weber* and *Johnson* and reads Title VII in a way that appears to evoke the strict scrutiny that is now applicable to the use of race by governmental actors under the equal protection clause of the Fourteenth Amendment to uphold affirmative action. In Taxman v. Board of Educ. of Township of Piscataway, 91 F.3d 1547 (3d Cir. 1996) (en banc), a case that was settled while on the docket of the Supreme Court, a school board relied on affirmative action to break a tie in a layoff situation where two teachers, one black and one white, had equal seniority to the day and had been found to be equally qualified. The school board decided to retain the African-American teacher in order to have at least one black teacher in the high school's business education department. The Third Circuit found that the affirmative action plan of the school district had been required by the state so there had been no prior discrimination by the school board. Claiming to only be applying Title VII, the court held that "unless an affirmative action plan has a remedial purpose, it cannot be said to mirror the purposes of [Title VII], and, therefore, cannot satisfy the first prong of the *Weber* test. Further, the affirmative action was not narrowly tailored since it trammeled the rights of the equally situated white teacher."

ii. **Affirmative action and the Constitution.** A much stricter test applies to affirmative action when the case is brought on equal protection grounds under the Constitution. In Adarand Constructors v. Pena, 515 U.S. 200, 229 (1995), the Court declared quite broadly: **"Accordingly, we hold today that all racial classifications, imposed by whatever federal, state, or local governmental actor, must be analyzed by a reviewing court under strict scrutiny. In other words, such classifications are constitutional only if they are narrowly tailored measures that further compelling governmental interests."**

In contrast, the Court has yet to decide what level of scrutiny applies to the use of affirmative action to aid women. In Craig v. Boren, 429 U.S. 190 (1976), the Court adopted intermediate scrutiny for reviewing gender classification generally: "classifications by gender must serve important governmental objectives and must be substantially related to the achievement of those objectives."

(a) **A compelling governmental interest.** So far, a limited list of interests have been found to be compelling enough to satisfy strict scrutiny.

(1) **Remedy defendant's discrimination.** In United States v. Paradise, 480 U.S. 149 (1987), the Court made it clear that providing a remedy for a governmental actor's discrimination is a compelling state interest, even if some beneficiaries of the remedy are not themselves the victims of the defendant's discrimination.

(2) **Remedy present effects of past discrimination.** There is authority that remedying the present effects of past discrimination is a compelling governmental interest. In Podberesky v. Kirwan, 38 F.3d 147 (4th Cir. 1994), the court upheld, as a compelling governmental interest, a governmental actor's interest in curing the present effects of its own past discrimination where the defendant had, at an earlier point, engaged in *de jure* segregation. But the court found that the defendant had failed to prove that there were any effects that continued to the present.

(3) **Diversity.** In Regents of University of California v. Bakke, 438 U.S. 265 (1978), Justice Powell, in an opinion that broke a 4-to-4 tie, upheld the use of affirmative action, using race as a plus in admissions, to serve the interest of diversity. In Hopwood v. Texas, 78 F.3d

932 (5th Cir. 1996), the court rejected diversity as a compelling governmental interest justifying the use of affirmative action by a law school, finding that *Bakke* had not survived *Croson* and *Adarand.*

(4) **Remedying societal discrimination is *not* a compelling governmental interest.** It is clear since Wygant v. Jackson Bd. of Educ., 476 U.S. 267 (1986), that a governmental actor's attempt to cure the effects of societal discrimination that is not attributable to its discrimination is not a compelling state interest.

(b) **Narrowly tailored remedy.** If the defendant is successful in arguing that its use of affirmative action serves a compelling governmental interest, it then must prove that its use is narrowly tailored to that interest. The narrowly tailored test has two aspects.

(1) **The remedy must serve only the compelling interest.** The use of a racial classification must serve only the compelling interest that justifies its use and it cannot serve interests other than the articulated compelling interest.

(2) **The plan does not unnecessarily trammel the rights of the majority.** It appears that this aspect of the narrowly tailored requirement is shared with Title VII's approach to affirmative action.

EXAM TIP

Where the employer is a government employer and the issues involves affirmative action, remember to analyze the question under both Title VII and equal protection under the Constitution.

2. The Policy Is Shown by Inference

Formal policies of discrimination may be found to exist even though the nature of the classification is not always immediately clear but must be based on the drawing of an inference. For example, early in the development of Title VII, the Supreme Court, in General Electric Co. v. Gilbert, 429 U.S. 125 (1976), refused to draw the inference that the exclusion of pregnancy from health insurance coverage was sex discrimination. It took the passage of an amendment to Title VII, the Pregnancy Discrimination in Employment Act, for Congress to make it clear that pregnancy discrimination is a formal policy of sex discrimination.

EXAMPLES AND ANALYSIS

1. In Los Angeles Dept. of Water & Power v. Manhart, 435 U.S. 702 (1978), the employer deducted for its pension fund a greater percentage of a woman's salary than of a man making the same salary. This was clearly a gender classification since all women were treated in one way and all men another, even though the employer argued that it was not discriminatory since women as a group lived longer than men and so the greater deduction was necessary to fund equal monthly pension benefits for life once they retired. The Court nevertheless found that difference in treatment to be a formal policy of discrimination. "An employment practice that requires 2,000 individuals to contribute more money into a fund than 10,000 other employees simply because each of them is a woman, rather than a man, is in direct conflict with both the language and the policy of the Act. Such a practice does not pass the simple test of whether the evidence shows 'treatment of a person in a manner which but for that person's sex would be different.' " 435 U.S. at 711.

2. In Trans World Airlines, Inc. v. Thurston, 469 U.S. 111 (1985), a contract with the union allowed pilots to "bump" down to flight engineer jobs if they became disqualified as pilots. An FAA rule required pilots and co-pilots, but not flight engineers, to retire at age 60. Pilots who bumped down to flight engineer before they reached age 60 could continue to fly, while they were forced to retire at age 60 if they had not bumped down by their birthday. The Court found this to be a formal policy of age discrimination. "Since it allows captains who become disqualified for any reason other than age to 'bump' less senior flight engineers, TWA's transfer policy is discriminatory on its face." 469 U.S. at 121.

EXAM TIP

When dealing with something that seems to be a general practice issues first try to argue that it is a policy of discrimination based on drawing inferences. In contrast, a general practice of discrimination is shown by the cumulation of employer decisions demonstrating a pattern of discrimination.

D. PATTERNS AND PRACTICES OF DISCRIMINATION

Even if no formal, announced policy of discrimination can be proved to exist, a systemic disparate treatment case can still be established if the plaintiff can prove that the practices of the employer reveal an intent on the part of the employer to discriminate. In Bazemore v. Friday, 478 U.S. 385, the Court found that an employer engaged in systemic disparate treatment in its practice of paying African American employees less than similarly situated white employees. In

International Brotherhood of Teamsters v. United States, 431 U.S. 324 (1977), the Court found that a trucking employer and the union had, despite their availability, excluded virtually all African Americans and Latinos from the favored line or over-the-road driving jobs.

1. The Comparison of the Workforce and the Labor Pool

Statistical evidence can be probative of systemic disparate treatment because statistics can show the result, by race, gender, or other protected class, of all the individual hiring and assignment decisions that the employer made over time and can then compare that pattern with the representation of minority group members in the labor pool from which the employer could be expected to pick its workers if it was not discriminating. The starkness of the comparison determines whether it is appropriate to draw the inference that the employer was acting with an intent to discriminate in its hiring practices. In other words, the employer's actions may speak louder than its words.

a. Comparing the workforce with the labor pool is central. Simply showing that an employer has hired few or no members of a group protected by antidiscrimination law does not by itself make out a case of systemic disparate treatment discrimination. "Title VII imposes no requirement that a workforce mirror the general population." *Teamsters,* 431 U.S. at 339 n.20. The simple workforce statistic does not reveal the state of mind of the employer because it does not show that the employer could have hired a more diverse workforce. The core of a statistical showing of a practice of systemic disparate treatment discrimination is a comparison of the employer's workforce and the labor pool available to the employer. It is only when it is shown that the employer had the opportunity to hire members of that group but failed to do so that it is safe to draw the inference that the employer had a practice of discriminating against that group.

 # EXAMPLES AND ANALYSIS

1. Suppose that Subaru Car Company opens an auto assembly plant in Fargo, North Dakota. After the initial hiring is done for the workers in the plant, less than 1 percent are African Americans. Without some showing that African Americans were available for the kind of jobs that Subaru was hiring for, this statistical showing fails to make out a prima facie case of systemic disparate treatment discrimination. Assuming that the African-American population in the Fargo area is quite small, it would not be a surprise that few African Americans were hired.

2. In contrast, now assume that there is a population of 25 percent Native Americans in the Fargo labor market and assume that Subaru hired less than 1 percent of

them. Showing such a comparison would likely support drawing an inference that the employer had a practice of systemic disparate treatment because it acted out of an intent to discriminate.

---

2. "Gross and Longlasting Disparity" or the "Inexorable Zero"

The level of showing necessary to draw the inference that the employer has a practice of discriminating is "gross and longlasting disparity." Showing that the impact rises to the level of a "gross and longlasting disparity is a telltale of purposeful discrimination." *Teamsters,* 431 U.S. at 335 n.20. Further, the Court rejected all of the employer's challenges to the use of statistics to prove that it followed a practice of systemic disparate treatment, saying that none of those arguments could explain away the "inexorable zero" of African-American and Hispanic over-the-road truck drivers.

a. "Eyeballing" the statistics. While more sophisticated statistical techniques can be used in systemic disparate treatment cases, the Supreme Court in *Teamsters* relied on a straightforward "eyeballing" of the statistical evidence to find that the employer had a practice of excluding African Americans and Hispanics from over-the-road truck driving jobs.

 # EXAMPLE AND ANALYSIS

Suppose a trucking company has almost no African-American or Latino over-the-road drivers. To determine if this is the result of an intent to discriminate, the first place to look is at the written policies of the employer. If a formal policy exists saying, "No African American or Latinos will be assigned to line driver jobs," we need look no further to find the intent to discriminate of the employer. Even if no written policy is found to exist, the result of all the hiring and assignment decisions the employer has made over time may still demonstrate that a general practice of discrimination exists.

The Court in *Teamsters* relied on the statistical evidence comparing the employer's workforce of over-the road drivers with its city drivers as well as with the population of the cities in which the employer had terminals to find that the employer engaged in a practice of systemic disparate treatment discrimination. "Of [6,472 company employees], 314 (5%) were Negroes and 257 (4%) were Spanish-surnamed Americans. Of the 1,828 line drivers, however, there were only 8 (0.4%) Negroes and 5 (0.3%) Spanish-surnamed persons, and all of the Negroes had been hired after the litigation had commenced. . . . [T]here were terminals in areas of substantial Negro population where all of the company's line drivers were white." Since the company did not have even one African-American line driver until 1969, this "inexorable zero" led the Court to conclude that intent to discriminate should be "inferred from the mere fact of differences in treatment." See International Brotherhood of Teamsters v. United States, 431 U.S. 324, 335 n.15, 342 n.23 (1977).

3. The Employer's Post-Act Workforce

In Hazelwood School District v. United States, 433 U.S. 299 (1977), the Court refined the *Teamsters* approach to the use of statistical evidence to prove systemic disparate treatment discrimination. The school district, located in a suburban area near St. Louis, was sued for race discrimination because only 1.8 percent of its teachers were black. In refining the use of statistical evidence to prove systemic disparate treatment, the Court found that hiring decisions made before the effective date of the employer's coverage under the antidiscrimination statute could not be used in the analysis. The reason to exclude **pre-Act hiring** from the comparison is that the employer was presumably not under an obligation not to discriminate before the statute applied to the employer. If the employer from the effective date of Title VII "forward made all of its employment decisions in a wholly nondiscriminatory way [that] would not violate Title VII even if it had formerly maintained an all-white work force by purposefully excluding Negroes." 433 U.S. at 309.

4. The Qualified Labor Pool

Hazelwood School District also refined the other side of the comparison by limiting the labor market pool concept to **qualified potential workers in the geographic area** where, absent discrimination, the employer would hire its employees. What constitutes the qualifications of workers in this qualified labor market for a job and what constitutes the appropriate geographic limits to the labor pool can have a significant effect on the comparison of the workforce with the qualified labor pool.

a. **The probability theory underpinning statistical evidence.** Probability theory explains why statistical evidence of an employer's hiring, assignment and transfer policies can support a finding of that the employer follows a practice of systemic disparate treatment discrimination. In *Teamsters,* the Court said, **"Absent explanation, it is ordinarily to be expected that nondiscriminatory hiring practices will in time result in a workforce more or less representative of the racial and ethnic composition of the population of the community from which employees are hired."** 431 U.S. at 339–40 n.20.

5. Anecdotal Evidence Supports the Inference of Discrimination

Evidence by fact witnesses can support the inference that the employer excluded minority group members from line driver jobs because of their race. In *Teamsters,* there was testimony of over 40 instances of individual disparate treatment. One company official told an employee that a minority line driver would cause "a lot of problems on the road . . . with different people, Caucasians." Another supervisor told an employee seeking a transfer to the over-the-road jobs that "there isn't a Chicano driver in the system." 431 U.S. at 338 n.19. Some lower court cases emphasize the importance of introducing anecdotal evidence in order to bring the cold numbers to life.

EXAM TIP

In analyzing an issue of a general pattern or practice of discrimination, look to statistical evidence comparing the cumulative result of what the employer did with what the employer's workforce would have looked like if it had not discriminated. Any evidence of how the employer treated individuals is important as anecdotal evidence of what the employer's general practice is.

E. USING STATISTICAL EVIDENCE TO PROVE SYSTEMIC DISPARATE TREATMENT DISRIMINATION

The comparison of the statistics of the employer's workforce versus the labor pool is the key to making out a practice of systemic disparate treatment discrimination. Both parties try to manipulate the statistics to their own advantage: Plaintiff wants to show few minority workers in the employer's workforce with many available in the labor pool. As the gap between the representation of the protected group among the employer's workers and their availability to work for the employer widens, it becomes ever more possible to find a gross and longlasting disparity that is the basis for drawing the inference that the employer practices systemic disparate treatment because of its intent to discriminate. Conversely, the employer wants to show as many minority group members in its workforce with few available in the appropriate labor pool. As the gap between the two narrows, it becomes ever more difficult to find a gross and longlasting disparity. Manipulation is possible on both sides of the equation but the nature of that manipulation is much more legal than statistical.

1. The Employer's Observed Post-Act Workforce

Both *Teamsters* and *Hazelwood* were based on a "snapshot" of the racial representation of the employer's workers in the target jobs on the day the lawsuit commenced. In other words, the incumbent workforce of the employer on one particular day was simply recorded by their race. Since the Court's decision in *Hazelwood,* that snapshot then must be refined by subtracting all pre-Act hiring. Since *Hazelwood* had been brought shortly after Title VII had been extended to public employers, the removal of pre-Act hires could have made a real difference in the representation of minority workers in the employer's workforce that counted for the comparison necessary to make out a prima facie case. Title VII coverage has not been expanded since 1972, so subtracting pre-Act hires will now rarely be significant in a Title VII case: the total number of workers with 40 years of seniority is only a tiny percentage of the total number of employees of most employers. The Americans with Disabilities Act, however, was enacted in 1991 and so removing pre-Act employment decisions may still have a substantial effect on the count of the employer's workforce under that statute.

EXAMPLE AND ANALYSIS

If the snapshot statistics taken of the racial representation of the teachers in a school district showed only 2 of 100, or 2 percent, of teachers to be African Americans, that is quite dramatic. By itself, however, that statistic would not make out a prima facie case of systemic disparate treatment discrimination. But such a showing would be significant for comparison with a labor market pool of teachers if that pool included 20 percent African Americans. Assume, however, that 90 of those 100 teachers had been hired before Title VII became applicable to the school district and were, therefore, subtracted from the employer's workforce for the purposes of making the comparison in a systemic disparate treatment case. Taking the 90 pre-Act hires out of the count leaves the relevant representation of African Americans in the workforce of 2 out of the total of 10, or 20 percent. The comparison of an employer's workforce with 20 percent African Americans to a labor market pool that also included only 20 percent African Americans would certainly not support finding any disparity, much less the gross and longlasting disparity necessary to support drawing the inference that the employer had a practice of systemic disparate treatment race discrimination.

2. The Qualified Labor Pool

To make out a systemic disparate treatment case, the plaintiff must also show that, given their availability in a qualified labor pool, so many fewer women or minority group members are working for the employer than would be expected that it is possible to conclude that a "gross and longlasting disparity" exists between the employer's workforce and the labor pool from which workers are selected. *Hazelwood School District* made clear that the appropriate statistical showing was the labor pool made up of people qualified to do the work performed by the employer's employees. There are two related dimensions to establishing the relevant labor pool. One is set by the qualifications for the job and the other is set by the geographic area from which workers would be expected to be recruited.

a. Qualifications. In *Teamsters* and *Hazelwood,* the Court differentiated between two different kinds of jobs and the labor pools that would be appropriate for each.

i.   **Unskilled or low skilled jobs.** Where the employer's workforce involves unskilled or low skilled workers, the general population may be used as the qualified labor pool for comparison with the makeup of the employer's workforce. Thus, in *Teamsters,* the Court approved the use as the qualified labor pool of the general population statistics in the cities in which the employer had its truck terminals. In *Hazelwood,* the Court explained why the use of general population statistics for truck driver jobs was appropriate in *Teamsters.* "In *Teamsters,* the comparison between . . . the employer's work force and the . . . general areawide population was highly probative, because the job skill there involved—the ability to drive a truck—is one that many persons possess or can fairly readily acquire." 433 U.S. at 308 n.13.

ii. **Skilled jobs.** In contrast to the truck driver jobs in *Teamsters,* in *Hazelwood* the Court limited the labor pool used for the comparison with the employer's workforce to "qualified public school teacher[s]" because of the special skills and education teachers have that are not shared by the general population. "When special qualifications are required to fill particular jobs, comparisons to the general population (rather than to the smaller group of individuals who possess the necessary qualifications) may have little probative value." 433 U.S. at 308 n.13.

EXAM TIP

The key to analyzing qualified labor market questions is the nature of the work: the general population is a good comparison for low-skill jobs; a more specialized pool of potential workers is needed for skilled jobs.

---

b.   **Geographic labor pool.** The second basis for manipulation of the labor market statistics is the geographic area used for the comparison. As to racial and national origin groups, rather extreme patterns of residential segregation makes the choice of geographic area outcome determinative in many cases. In contrast, the residential patterns of men and women appear to be geographically more or less evenly distributed. In *Teamsters,* the Court found that the general population in the cities in which the employer had terminals was appropriate because the employer hired most of its truck drivers from those areas. In *Hazelwood,* the residential pool of teachers to be used for the comparison was outcome determinative: with only 1.8 percent of the Hazelwood teachers being African American, it is much easier to draw an inference that the employer engaged in a practice of intentional discrimination if the comparison is made to the pool of licensed teachers in the St. Louis metropolitan area, with 15.4 percent of those teachers being African Americans, than if the pool is the metropolitan area but carving out from that area the City of St. Louis. In that doughnut-shaped area, only 5.7 pecent of the teachers were African Americans.

In EEOC v. Chicago Miniature Lamp Works, 947 F.2d 292 (7th Cir. 1991), the court rejected the use of the entire city of Chicago as the labor market because it was too large considering that the jobs in question were low-paying, entry-level jobs. "Low-paying, unskilled jobs are more likely to be filled by those living closer to the site of the job, simply because the cost (including the opportunity cost of time lost) of commuting cannot be justified." 947 F.2d at 302.

i. **The relation between job qualifications and geographic labor market.** It is expected that for some jobs there may be a national labor market that the employer might be expected to use to find particularly highly skilled workers. Thus, for highly skilled jobs, the geographic labor market can be quite broad. In contrast, few employers can be expected to search very broadly for entry-level jobs requiring few skills. Thus, for those jobs, a narrower geographic area may be appropriate.

EXAMPLE AND ANALYSIS

Suppose that Quality University advertises in the national edition of the *New York Times* and in the *Chronicle of Higher Education,* a journal that many professors and college administrators subscribe to, to fill academic positions, such as professors and high-level academic administrators. Given that these jobs involve very special skills, training and expertise not shared by the general population, the appropriate geographic area to use as the qualified labor pool may be the nation.

3. **Sources of Qualified Labor Pool Statistics**

There are a number of potential sources of statistical evidence to show the pool of qualified workers and the geographic area in which the employer would look for employees, absent discrimination.

a. **The employer's own workforce as a labor pool.** From a plaintiff's point of view, it is best if possible to use some portion of the employer's own workforce. In *Teamsters*, for example, the employer's blue-collar workforce included a substantially greater number of African-American and Latino employees, including some working as city drivers, than "the inexorable zero" among over-the-road drivers. Thus, the labor pool used for comparison with the workforce of line drivers was the employer's own workforce performing similar work. The Court in *Hazelwood* made it clear that it was appropriate to use these statistics in *Teamsters* because there was no substantial difference between the qualifications necessary for any of these jobs. Since these workers were already working for the employer, this eliminated any issue of the geographic labor pool.

b. **Applicants for employer's jobs.** The pool of applicants for work at the employer is the next best labor pool. Applicants showed they were interested in working for the employer and available and they are likely to meet the minimal qualifications the employer announced for its jobs. Justice White, in *Hazelwood*, argued that the relevant labor pool be limited to applicants. In Dothard v. Rawlinson, 433 U.S. 321, 330 (1977), the Court rejected that. "There is no requirement, however, that a statistical showing . . . must always be based on analysis of the characteristics of actual applicants. . . . The application process might itself not adequately reflect the actual potential applicant pool."

c. **Labor market statistics.** Statistical evidence of appropriate labor markets may also be used. The labor market must be defined as those potential workers who meet the employer's minimal qualifications. General population statistics may serve as a proxy for the pool of qualified workers where the jobs involved are unskilled or involve skills that can be quickly learned by most people.

4. Sophisticated Statistical Techniques

The probability assumption that the Court stated in *Teamsters*—that "absent explanation, it is ordinarily expected that nondiscriminatory hiring practices will in time result in a work force more or less representative of the racial and ethnic composition of the population in the community from which employees are hired"—is the basis for the use of sophisticated statistical techniques to prove systemic disparate treatment discrimination. While *Teamsters* did not involve the use of sophisticated statistical techniques to analyze the data, *Hazelwood* and Bazemore v. Friday, 478 U.S. 385 (1986), uphold the use of such sophisticated statistical techniques to prove systemic disparate treatment.

a. **A statistical expert report establishes a prima facie case.** In *Bazemore,* the Court found that a prima facie case of systemic disparate treatment is established if a witness, qualified as a statistical expert, presents a statistical report that concludes that race, gender, or other protected characteristic was a statistically significant factor explaining the difference between the employer's treatment of black and white workers. Such a statistical report will establish a prima facie case unless the trial court determines that it is "so incomplete as to be inadmissible as irrelevant." *Bazemore* involved salary discrimination between African-American and white employees. While the average salary of black employees was less than for whites, it was not obviously the result of discrimination since many factors other than race could explain this result. Thus, plaintiffs would have lost if they had to rely on the sort of "eyeballing" approach the Court used in *Teamsters*. Similarly, in *Hazelwood* the possible comparison of 1.8 percent representation of African Americans as teachers in the school district with a labor pool of 5.7 percent African Americans in the metropolitan St. Louis area, surrounding but not including the City of St. Louis, was not so obviously "gross and longlasting" that one would be confident in just eyeballing the figures to determine whether to draw the inference that the employer intended to discriminate.

Thus, more sophisticated statistical studies can help the finder of fact decide whether to draw an inference of intent to discriminate. While there could be many variations on the type of statistical technique used, all are based on the probability assumption that is the basis of the science of statistics.

i. **The null hypothesis.** All statistical studies start with the statement of the null hypothesis. **The null hypothesis** is a statement made at the outset of what the study will test to be true or false. The null hypothesis is stated as the opposite of what the study is expected to find. In a race discrimination case where plaintiff expects to prove that there was race discrimination, the null hypothesis is that race is not a factor in the employer's employment decisions. The null hypothesis will be rejected if, as a result of the study, the expert concludes that it cannot be said that the null hypothesis is true. Having rejected the null hypothesis that race was not a factor in the employer's decision, it is reasonable to conclude that race was a factor.

ii. **Expected probability, the "P."** Once the null hypothesis is stated, the expert then decides what probability to expect. In a study dealing with employment discrimination, the probability would be set by the representation of women or minority group members in the qualified labor pool. All of the manipulation to establish the qualified labor pool, discussed above, is done solely to establish the probability number, the "P." That number is the key to the comparison between the employer's workforce and the labor pool: if the labor pool has a large representation of women or minority group members, the "P" is high. As the "P" goes up, the likelihood of finding liability goes up because that tends to increase the gap between the employer's workforce and the labor pool. In contrast, a low probability makes it more difficult to show a gross and longlasting disparity between the employer's workforce and the qualified labor pool.

iii. **Level of confidence.** The fact that the probability is set does not mean that anyone would have much confidence that it is correct. Thus, if you are given a coin to flip to determine if it is fair, the probability before you flipped at all would be .5 or 50 percent. After 10 flips resulting in 4 heads and 6 tails, you would set the probability for the outcome in the next 10 flips to be .6 or 60 percent tails and .4 or 40 percent heads. But you would not be very confident in that prediction because you have so little experience with that particular coin. Your confidence would rise, however, as you flip the coin and discover that over 1,000 sets of 10 flips (10,000 flips), 4,000 are heads and 6,000 are tails. While it is not certain what the outcome will be in the next set of 10 flips, you should be reasonably confident that there will be more tails than heads.

Statisticians choose a **level of confidence** in deciding whether the null hypothesis should be accepted or rejected Since statistical testing involves a risk of making a mistake, the level of confidence determines the risk of mistake the study will tolerate. There are two types of mistakes.

(a) **Type I error.** A Type I error is where an innocent employer is found liable for discriminating (false inculpation).

(b) **Type II error.** Type II errors are where a guilty employer is found innocent (false exculpation).

(While Type II errors will go down as Type I errors go up, there is no direct relationship between the two types of errors.)

(c) **Risk of Type I error sets level of confidence.** Statisticians set the level of confidence by setting the risk of Type I errors. They typically set the risk at 5 percent. This means that there is a 5 percent chance that an innocent employer will be found liable. It also means that there is something like a 50 percent chance of a Type II error, that a guilty employer will be found not liable.

iv. **Accepting or rejecting the null hypothesis.** The key question is whether race, gender, or other protected characteristic is a factor in the employer's decision-making. If the outcome of the study could occur more than 5 percent of the time by chance, then the statistician will accept the null hypothesis because the risk of finding an innocent employer guilty is judged too high. Correspondingly, if the particular statistical technique shows that these outcomes would occur by chance less than 5 percent of the time, then the null hypothesis—that race is not a factor—would be rejected. When the chance that an innocent employer will be mistakenly found liable is less than 5 percent, the null hypothesis should be rejected to avoid the substantial risk of finding a guilty employer innocent. Based on the rejection of the null hypothesis, it is then reasonable and logical to conclude that race was a factor in the employer's decision-making. Such a showing establishes a prima facie case of systemic disparate treatment discrimination.

v.   **Choosing the type of statistical study.** Statisticians have available a number of techniques that can be useful to prove systemic discrimination. The Court approved the use of **binomial distribution** in *Hazelwood* and the use of **multiple regression** was accepted in *Bazemore*.

(a)   **Binomial distribution.** This technique is used to compare two groups of data, such as the employer's workforce and the labor pool from which the employees are selected, by one variable such as race or gender. It is the technique discussed in *Hazelwood*.

(b)   **Multiple regression.** This technique is used to compare the influence any number of factors or variables have on a "continuous variable" such as salary. A variable is continuous when it moves up or down in increments of equal value. Thus, salary is the perfect example because each dollar of salary is of equal value. A computer is needed to run the study but multiple regression is a way to hold constant all the factors that might go into determining something like salary, including education, seniority with the employer and on the particular job, experience in the industry, etc., and then decide if race or gender is also a variable that explains salary.

EXAM TIPS

Few professors expect you to know how to do the sophisticated statistics involved, but it is useful to understand the concept of probability, the names of the two approaches used—binomial distribution and multiple regression—and the fact that an expert's report supporting a finding that an impermissible factor was statistically significant is sufficient to establish a prima facie case of systemic disparate treatment discrimination.

F. DEFENSES TO DISPARATE TREATMENT CASES

There are two ways to defend a systemic disparate treatment case. The first is to undermine the basis for the plaintiff's case by rebuttal. The second way is for the defendant to assert the BFOQ defense. Finally, the employer may be able to limit full remedies that go to the individual employees and applicants affected by its systemic disparate treatment discrimination if it can prove that it did not discriminate against particular individuals.

1. Rebutting the Inference of Discriminatory Intent

A prima facie case can be undermined and overcome through rebuttal.

a. Rebutting a formal policy case. In a prima facie case based on a formal policy of discrimination, **the defendant can argue that in fact no such policy exists or that the policy that does exist is not discriminatory.** For example, in General Electric Co. v. Gilbert, 429 U.S. 125 (1976), the employer's health insurance policy excluded pregnancy from coverage. While only women get pregnant, the employer persuaded the Court not to draw the inference that the exclusion of pregnancy from health insurance coverage was sex discrimination because all men and some women never get pregnant. It took the amendment of Title VII in the Pregnancy Discrimination Act to make clear that a pregnancy classification is a formal policy of sex discrimination.

b. Rebutting a practice case. Where the prima facie case is based on a showing of practice of systemic disparate treatment, **the employer can rebut the evidence plaintiff relies upon by challenging the statistics plaintiff uses or by challenging the inference of discrimination that is based on those statistics.** For example, the employer was successful in earning a remand in *Hazelwood* by arguing successfully that the lower court may have relied on the wrong geographic labor pool to use for the comparison with the employer's workforce.

 # EXAMPLES AND ANALYSIS

1. A chain of nine Dairy Queen stores in Houston was charged with systemic disparate treatment because of race in hiring. Plaintiff relied on two statistical studies—one compared the employer's workforce with the percentage of African-American food preparation workers in the Houston Standard Metropolitan Area, and the other compared the employer's workforce with the percentage of African-American applicants for jobs at the Dairy Queen stores. Both studies rejected the null hypothesis that race was not involved in the employer's decision and, thus, would support a finding that the employer did have a practice of discriminating on the basis of race. The employer attempted to rebut plaintiff's showing with its own statistical study,

focused on one of the nine stores, that showed that the incumbent employees tended to be white high school students who lived relatively near the store. The court rejected this rebuttal since it did not explain the large number of African Americans who did not live near the store yet did apply for jobs with the employer. EEOC v. Olson's Dairy Queens, Inc., 989 F.2d 165 (5th Cir. 1993).

2. Women faculty members at a university relied on multiple regression studies to prove salary discrimination because of sex. The variables included in the study were years teaching before coming to the university, years teaching at the university, possession of a doctorate degree, number of years since receiving the doctorate, number of publications, other experience before coming to the university and years of full-time high school teaching. The study did not include academic rank— instructor, assistant professor, associate professor, and professor. Plaintiffs claimed that rank was not included because women were discriminated against in the ranks to which they were assigned. While the court was not persuaded by defendant's attempt to prove that rank was not discriminatorily assigned, plaintiffs lost because the court was not persuaded by plaintiff's statistical and anecdotal evidence that the university did engage in a practice of salary discrimination because of sex. Ottaviani v. University of New York at New Paltz, 875 F.2d 365 (1990).

---

i. **Rebut the inference of discrimination.** Even if plaintiff's statistics hold up, employers can try to rebut plaintiff's case by challenging the inference that the employer intended to discriminate.

 EXAMPLES AND ANALYSIS

---

1. In Personnel Administrator v. Feeney, 442 U.S. 256 (1979), plaintiff challenged an absolute preference for military veterans for Massachusetts' civil service jobs: if just one veteran applied for a job, non-veterans would not even be considered for a job. In the typical situation, preferred jobs were filled from a pool of applicants who were all military veterans. That rule had a drastic effect on women since at that time 98 percent of veterans were men. Nevertheless, the Court found that the veterans' preference was not the result of an intent on the part of Massachusetts to discriminate against women. The impact of the rule on women was the result of the actions of the national government in limiting the number of women who could serve in the military. If few women could serve in the military, few women would become veterans. The Court found that intent to discriminate "implies more than intent as volition or intent as awareness of consequences. . . . It implies that the decisionmaker, in this case a state legislature, selected or reaffirmed a particular course of action at least in part **'because of,' not merely 'in spite of,'** its adverse effects upon a particular group." 442 U.S. at 279.

Since *Feeney* was decided, the percentage of women in the military and, therefore among veterans, has increased substantially. So, the impact on women of Massachusetts' rule would be much less now than it was when *Feeney* was decided over 20 years ago. This shows that it may be wrong to draw an inference of intent to discriminate when over time the employer's policy does not change but the impact of that policy does change.

2. In EEOC v. Sears, Roebuck & Co., 839 F.2d 302 (7th Cir. 1988), the EEOC challenged the exclusion of women from the higher-paid commission sales jobs at Sears. While 61 percent of applicants for sales jobs were women, only 27 percent of commission salespeople were women. Of the lower-paid non-commission jobs, 75 percent went to women. Using the actual pool of applicants to Sears resolved any disputes about the appropriate geographic pool. But the employer argued successfully to the court that the shortfall of women in commission sales jobs was the result of their lack of interest in, and qualifications for, those jobs. Bolstering that argument was the fact that the EEOC failed to introduce any anecdotal evidence of individual women who requested but were denied commission sales jobs by Sears. That being so, the court found that plaintiff's statistics and statistical studies did not support drawing the inference that the employer intended to discriminate.

EXAM TIP

The focus of the rebuttal of a systemic disparate treatment case based on statistics is whether the employer did what it did because of, rather than in spite of, its impact in terms of race or other impermissible factors.

G. BONA FIDE OCCUPATIONAL QUALIFICATIONS

Title VII and the ADEA include bona fide occupational qualification defenses to systemic disparate treatment cases. Thus, §703(h) of Title VII provides that "it shall not be an unlawful employment practice for an employer to hire and employ employees . . . on the basis of religion, sex, or national origin in those certain instances where religion, sex, or national origin is a bona fide occupational qualification reasonably necessary to the normal operation of that particular business or enterprise." The BFOQ defense is available as to **religion, sex, national origin and, through the ADEA, age** but **not** to disparate treatment where the claim is discrimination **because of race or color.** While not explicit in the statutory language, the BFOQ is only available, as a practical matter, as a defense to formal policies of discrimination because the test for it is so narrow that it requires great focus by the employer. Further, the BFOQ is a classic example of an affirmative defense, with the burden of persuasion on the employer. The BFOQ defense involves two steps.

1. The Qualification Must Be Necessary to the Essence of the Business

In Western Air Lines v. Criswell, 472 U.S. 400 (1985), a challenge to an airline rule that flight engineers must retire at age 60, the Court adopted the prevailing lower court test for the BFOQ. The first step of that test, based on Diaz v. Pan American World Airways, 442 F.2d 385 (5th Cir.), *cert. denied,* 404 U.S. 950 (1971), requires that **the job qualification must be reasonably necessary to the** *essence* **of the business, not to something peripheral to the central mission of the employer's business.** In *Criswell,* the essence of the business was the safe transportation of the airline's passengers. So, the first step was satisfied because the employer claimed that its retirement policy was justified by its concern for safety in the air.

In contrast, in Los Angeles Dept. of Water & Power v. Manhart, 435 U.S. 702 (1978), the BFOQ defense was found unavailable as a defense to discrimination in take-home pay and pension contributions. The language in the statute makes it clear that the BFOQ applies only ''in those certain instances'' where sex, religion, national origin, or age is necessary to perform particular jobs. Thus, discrimination in employment benefits cannot be defended by the BFOQ.

2. Either No Person in Excluded Group Can Do the Job or It Is Impractical to Determine Who Can Do It

The second step of the BFOQ is for the employer to prove one of two different tests.

a. **No member of the protected group can perform the job.** The first alternative to the second step in proving the BFOQ defense is for **the employer** to prove that it **had reasonable cause to believe that no one in the excluded group can perform the functions of the job in question safely and efficiently.** This is a very difficult test that is probably limited to such jobs, if there are any, as sperm donors or host wombs, or, perhaps, jobs involving significant privacy concerns. In Dothard v. Rawlinson, 433 U.S. 321 (1977), however, the Court did uphold a rule requiring prison guards in ''contact'' positions with inmates to be the same sex as the inmates. Because the prisons in Alabama at that time were almost completely out of control, a woman guard of male prisoners could trigger an attack and a riot simply because she was a woman. Thus, the BFOQ was upheld because control within the prison would be ''directly reduced by her womanhood.''

b. **Highly impractical to determine qualifications on individualized basis.** The second alternative is for the **employer to show that sex, national origin, religion, or age was a legitimate proxy for the safety-**

related job qualifications because it is "impossible or highly impractical" to determine on an individualized basis whether workers in that excluded category could safely perform the job in question. In *Criswell*, the airline failed to justify its mandatory retirement rule for flight engineers even under this broader test. Because other airlines employ flight engineers over age 60, the FAA had not extended its mandatory retirement rule from pilots to flight engineers, and all flight officers, including flight engineers, over age 60, had to pass individualized and regular physical exams, it would be hard to find a BFOQ under either prong of the second step.

EXAM TIP

Since there are few instances when no member of the protected group can perform the job in question, the main focus of the BFOQ is on the employer's claim that it is impractical to determine who can do the job individual by individual.

 # EXAMPLE AND ANALYSIS

In International Union, UAW v. Johnson Controls, Inc., 499 U.S. 187 (1991), the employer manufactured lead batteries for automobiles. In 1977, the employer left it to women workers to decide whether to work in areas with lead exposure since there was some health risk from exposure of lead to them and from them to their fetuses. In 1982, the employer shifted to a policy of exclusion: "women who are pregnant or who are capable of bearing children will not be placed into jobs involving lead exposure or which could expose them to lead through the exercise of job bidding, bumping, transfer or promotion rights." Despite the gender explicit classification, the lower court applied business necessity, which is a defense to disparate impact discrimination, to uphold the rule on the ground that the employer did not intend to discriminate against women. The Supreme Court found that the gender explicit nature of the rule established the intent to discriminate sufficient to make out a prima facie case of systemic disparate treatment discrimination, even in the absence of an evil motive. "Respondent's fetal-protection policy . . . excludes women with childbearing capacity from lead-exposed jobs and so creates a facial classification based on gender. . . . Moreover, the absence of a malevolent motive does not convert a facially discriminatory policy into a neutral policy with a discriminatory effect." 499 U.S. at 197, 199. Congress reaffirmed *Johnson Controls* in its amendments to Title VII in the Civil Rights Act of 1991. Section 703(k)(2) of Title VII now provides: **"A demonstration that an employment practice is required by business necessity may not be used as a defense against a claim of intentional discrimination under this title."**

The Court went on to find that the BFOQ defense had not been established. "Fertile women, as far as appears in the record, participate in the manufacture of batteries as efficiently as anyone else." Concern over the safety of the fetuses cannot "be considered a part of the 'essence' of Johnson Control's business." While it is impossible to tell which fertile women will become pregnant while working with lead, "Johnson Controls has shown no 'factual basis for believing that all or substantially all women would be unable to perform safely and efficiently the duties of the job involved.' " 499 U.S. at 206–207.

H.   THE DEFENSE AGAINST INDIVIDUAL'S REMEDIES

Establishing a systemic disparate treatment case creates a presumption of relief to affected workers or applicants. Franks v. Bowman Transp. Co., 424 U.S. 747 (1976). That means that, to preclude relief to any affected individual on a case-by-case basis, the employer must carry the burden of proving that it did not discriminate against that individual.

REVIEW QUESTIONS AND ANSWERS

Question: What are the two kinds of systemic disparate treatment discrimination?

Answer: The first is a formal policy of discrimination of an employer and the second is a general practice, typically shown through statistical and anecdotal evidence, of disparate treatment by the employer because of race, gender, or other protected characteristic.

Question: What is a formal policy of discrimination?

Answer: A formal policy of discrimination is an announced, often written but sometimes orally stated, declaration by the employer that it discriminates.

Question: How is voluntary affirmative action treated?

Answer: To use Title VII to attack the employer's use of affirmative action, the "reverse" discrimination plaintiff must prove that the plan **fails** to satisfy the following test: that it was designed to eliminate manifest imbalances in employment; it does not unnecessarily trammel the rights of majority workers, and it is temporary in nature. A much more stringent standard applies when public employer's use of affirmative action is attacked using constitutional equal protection.

Question: What is a practice of discrimination?

Answer: A practice of discrimination involves an employer whose cumulative employment decisions support the inference that it in fact discriminates, even if it denies it.

Question: What are the two ways for an employer to defend a systemic disparate treatment discrimination?

Answer: The two are: (1) rebut plaintiff's statistical evidence or the inference based on that showing; or (2) prove the bona fide occupational qualification (BFOQ). The employer must show that the discriminatory classification goes to the essence of the business, involves the requirements for a particular job, and either no member of the protected class can do the job or so few can that it is impractical to make individual determinations.

4 SYSTEMIC DISPARATE IMPACT DISCRIMINATION

CHAPTER OVERVIEW

Systemic disparate impact discrimination involves the use of practices by an employer without the intent to discriminate, which practices nevertheless have a greater impact on women and minority group members than on the majority. An employer is liable for the use of such a practice unless it can prove that it is job related and necessary for business, or is justified by one of three other statutory exceptions.

The structure of the law of systemic disparate impact discrimination is now determined by §703(k), which was added to Title VII by the Civil Rights Act of 1991. There are three steps in a systemic disparate impact case.

- **The Prima Facie Showing of an Employment Practice Causing Impact:** To establish a prima facie case of disparate impact discrimination, plaintiff must prove that the employer "uses a particular employment practice that causes a disparate impact on the basis of race, color, religion, sex, or national origin." There are five subparts to proving this prima facie case.

  - **A Particular Employment Practice:** The plaintiff must show that the employer uses a particular employment practice and cannot generally rely on "bottom line" statistics showing few women or minority group members among the employer's workforce. Employment practice has been construed very broadly to include such practices as subjective evaluations of employees. There are, however, four exceptions to the general rule.

    - **The "Bottom Line" Exception:** If plaintiff can demonstrate to the court that the elements of an employer's decision-making process are not capable of separation for analysis, the decision-making process may be analyzed as one employment practice.

- **The Exception for Rules Prohibiting Drug Use:** Employer rules prohibiting the illegal use of drugs are by statute exempt from disparate impact attack.

- **The Passivity Exception:** There is lower court authority that passivity by the employer that results in disparate impact is not subject to disparate impact attack.

- **The Fringe Benefits Exception:** There is lower court authority that, at least in age discrimination cases, changes in fringe benefits are not subject to disparate impact attack.

- **The Employer's Use of the Practice:** The employer must use the practice plaintiff challenges but a prima facie case can be established with national data or data based on the use of the practice by other employers.

- **Amount of Impact:** The Supreme Court has "eyeballed" the statistics to determine whether the amount of impact suffices to establish a prima facie case. The EEOC has a "four-fifths" rule and various sophisticated statistical techniques are available to assist in determining the sufficiency of the amount of impact.

- **The Impact Is Adverse:** The impact must not only be real, it must be adverse to the plaintiffs.

- **The Impact Is to a Protected Group:** Only members of groups that have historically been the victims of employment discrimination may use the disparate impact theory of discrimination.

- **Defendant's Rebuttal:** There are five different rebuttal possibilities open to an employer to defend against a prima facie case of disparate impact discrimination.

  - **The Employer's Use Does Not Cause the Impact:** Where plaintiff relies on national data of impact to establish a prima facie case, the employer has an affirmative defense if it can carry the burden of persuasion to prove that the practice does not cause an impact in its use.

  - **Business Necessity and Job Relatedness:** The employer has an affirmative defense if it can carry its burden of persuasion to prove that the practice is both job related and justified by business necessity.

  - **Professionally Developed Tests:** An employer can escape liability for disparate impact discrimination if the employment practice challenged is a test and the employer can prove that the test has been properly validated according to professional testing standards.

- **Bona Fide Seniority System:** The employer has an affirmative defense if it can prove that the challenged practice is a traditional part of a bona fide seniority system in a collective bargaining agreement with a union.

- **Bona Fide Merit and Piecework System:** This affirmative defense for merit and piecework systems has been treated like the exception for professionally developed tests.

- **Alternative Employment Practice Surrebuttal:** The final step of the analysis allows the plaintiff to win by proving that an alternative employment practice existed that caused less impact but would serve the employer's legitimate business needs and that the employer refuses to adopt it.

A.   THE DISPARATE IMPACT CONCEPT

Systemic disparate impact discrimination is the unjustified use by an employer of practices that, while neutral on their face as to race or gender, nevertheless heavily burden groups that have historically been the victims of discrimination. The fundamental difference between systemic disparate *impact* and either systemic or individual disparate *treatment* is that disparate impact does not include the intent to discriminate element that is the key to both of the disparate treatment theories. Thus, disparate impact discrimination "involve[s] **employment practices that are facially neutral in their treatment of different groups but that in fact fall more harshly on one group than another and cannot be justified by business necessity. Proof of discriminatory motive . . . is not required under a disparate impact theory.**" International Brotherhood of Teamsters v. United States, 324 U.S. 324, 336 n.15 (1977).

EXAM TIP

It is important to distinguish disparate impact, which does not involve the employer's intent to discriminate, from systemic disparate treatment, which focuses on intent to discriminate.

B.   A BRIEF BACKGROUND

Systemic disparate impact discrimination was first established in Griggs v. Duke Power Co., 401 U.S. 424 (1971), and was finally incorporated explicitly into the terms of Title VII by the Civil Rights Act of 1991. While the new statutory structure governs cases presently being decided, it is important to understand the background of that statute in order to understand how it works.

1. Griggs v. Duke Power Co.

In *Griggs,* the Court created the disparate impact theory of discrimination.

> The Act proscribes not only overt discrimination but also practices that are fair in form, but discriminatory in operation. The touchstone is business necessity. If an employment practice which operates to exclude Negroes cannot be shown to be related to job performance, the practice is prohibited. 401 U.S. at 431.

EXAMPLE AND ANALYSIS

As Title VII became effective, the employer ended the formal racial segregation of its work departments. However, it required employees to have a high school diploma or a passing score on standardized tests of general intelligence for eligibility to transfer or be promoted between departments. These requirements tended to keep African-American workers in their former all-black departments, therefore causing a disparate impact on blacks: while 34 percent of whites in North Carolina had completed high school, only 12 percent of blacks had graduated. As to the standardized tests, an EEOC decision in another case found that 58 percent of whites passed the test in comparison with 6 percent of African Americans. Without overturning the lower court finding that the test and educational requirements had been adopted with no intent to discriminate, the Court found the employer liable for disparate impact discrimination.

2. Albemarle Paper Co. v. Moody

In Albemarle Paper Co. v. Moody, 422 U.S. 405, 424 (1975), the Court created a three-step litigation structure out of the holding in *Griggs.*

   a. Plaintiff's prima facie showing of impact. The *Albemarle* Court described the plaintiff's prima facie case as showing a practice of an employer is "discriminatory in effect" and "that the tests in question select applicants for hire or promotion in a racial pattern significantly different from that of the pool of applicants."

   b. Defendant's job related and business necessity rebuttal. Once a prima facie case is established, the employer has, quoting *Griggs,* "the burden of showing that any given requirement [has] . . . a manifest relationship to the employment in question." 422 U.S. at 425. The Court also described this as a showing that the requirement was "job related."

   c. Plaintiff's pretext surrebuttal. The *Albemarle* Court created a new, third step, which allows the plaintiff to succeed even if the employer carries its rebuttal burden.

If an employer does then meet the burden of proving that its tests are "job related," it remains open to the complaining party to show that other tests or selection devices, without a similarly undesirable racial effect, would also serve the employer's legitimate interest in "efficient and trustworthy workmanship." Such a showing would be evidence that the employer was using its tests merely as a "pretext" for discrimination. 422 U.S. at 425.

3. Wards Cove v. Atonio

In Wards Cove Packing Co. v. Atonio, 490 U.S. 642 (1989), the Court cut back the *Griggs/Albemarle* approach by making four changes in how disparate impact cases were structured.

a. **Plaintiff must prove a particular practice caused the impact.** The Court made it clear that the focus of disparate impact theory was on employer's practices. "Our disparate-impact cases have always focused on the impact of *particular* hiring practices on employment opportunities for minorities. . . . As a general matter, **a plaintiff must demonstrate that it is the application of a specific or particular employment practice that has created the disparate impact under attack.** Such a showing is an integral part of the plaintiff's prima facie case in a disparate-impact suit under Title VII." 490 U.S. at 656–657. That means that it is inappropriate to use "bottom line" statistics—the representation of minority group members in the employer's workforce—to establish disparate impact.

b. **Job related and business necessity become business justification.** The Court expanded the scope of the employer's rebuttal defense from job related and business necessity to **"business justification."** "[A]t the justification stage of such a disparate-impact case, the dispositive issue is whether a challenged practice serves, in a significant way, the legitimate employment goals of the employer. . . . The touchstone of this inquiry is a reasoned review of the employer's justification for his use of the challenged practice." 490 U.S. at 659.

c. **The employer does not carry the burden on business justification.** The most significant change wrought by *Wards Cove* was lowering the employer's business justification burden to the need to produce evidence rather than requiring the employer actually to prove its practice justified. "[T]he employer carries the burden of producing evidence of a business justification for his employment practice. **The burden of persuasion, however, remains with the disparate-impact plaintiff.**" 490 U.S. at 659.

d. **Pretext becomes "alternative practices."** The Court changed *Albemarle*'s pretext concept of plaintiff's surrebuttal to **"alternative practices."**

> If [plaintiffs], having established a prima facie case, come forward with alternatives to [the employers'] hiring practices that reduce the racially disparate impact of practices currently being used, and [the employers] refuse to adopt these alternatives, such a refusal would belie a claim . . . that their incumbent practices are being [used by the employers] for nondiscriminatory reasons. 490 U.S. at 660–661.

4.   The Civil Rights Act of 1991

Wards Cove was the most notorious of a number of civil rights decisions made by the Supreme Court in 1989 that provoked concern that civil rights were being unjustifiably cut back. In response, Congress enacted the Civil Rights Act of 1991, which incorporated a specific statutory structure for systemic disparate impact cases, which structure governs cases presently being brought. The following sections will analyze how this statutory structure works.

C.   THE PRESENT STATUTORY STRUCTURE OF DISPARATE IMPACT DISCRIMINATION

The 1991 Act amended Title VII to add a new §703(k), which for the first time in the statute uses the term "disparate impact." A principal feature of the 1991 Act was to attempt to restore a useful disparate impact theory. The Act did this by modifying *Wards Cove,* but did not go entirely back to *Griggs/Albemarle Paper.* The Act basically maintains the structure of three steps of the judicially created disparate impact analysis that preceded it while changing the articulation of some of those elements.

EXAM TIP

While the background leading up to the Civil Rights Act of 1991 is helpful in understanding disparate impact discrimination, the focus of your analysis of a disparate impact problem should be on the 1991 amendments.

D.   THE PRIMA FACIE SHOWING OF AN EMPLOYMENT PRACTICE CAUSING IMPACT

The 1991 Act does not change the general rule articulated in *Wards Cove* that the plaintiff bears the burden of proving that a particular employment practice causes a disparate impact. New §703(k)(1)(A)(i) provides that a prima facie case based on disparate impact is established if **"a complaining party [plaintiff] demonstrates [by carrying the burden of persuasion] that a respondent [employer] uses a particular employment practice that causes a disparate impact on the basis of race, color, religion, sex, or national origin."**

EXAMPLE AND ANALYSIS

An employer requires all its employees have a college degree. Since the diploma requirement is a particular employment practice and since a smaller percentage of African Americans and Latinos than whites have earned college degrees, this showing makes out a prima facie case of disparate impact discrimination.

1. A Particular Employment Practice

A broad array of employer policies and practices have been found to be employer practices subject to disparate impact analysis. *Griggs* involved short-form IQ tests and educational prerequisites, Dothard v. Rawlinson, 433 U.S. 321 (1977), involved height and weight prerequisites, and New York City Trans. Auth. v. Beazer, 440 U.S. 568 (1979), a rule excluding people who were in methadone maintenance programs. In Watson v. Fort Worth Bank & Trust, 487 U.S. 977 (1988), the Court concluded that the use of subjective criteria could be attacked using disparate impact theory. "[D]isparate impact analysis is in principle no less applicable to subjective employment criteria than to objective or standardized tests."

There are four exceptions to the requirement that plaintiff point to a particular employment practice in order to make out a prima facie case of systemic disparate impact discrimination. The "bottom line" exception expands the application of disparate impact discrimination while the exception for anti-drug rules, the passivity, and the fringe benefits exceptions limit the scope of application of disparate impact discrimination.

a. **The "bottom line" exception.** In *Wards Cove*, the Court rejected the use of "bottom line" statistics for disparate impact cases. Thus, plaintiffs could not use the representation of minority workers in one category of jobs, heavily minority cannery workers at a summer fish factory in Alaska, as a basis of comparison with their representation in another category of jobs, the mostly white non-cannery workers at the same factory. It is out of the concern that "bottom line" disparities in group representation among an employer's workforce could easily trigger disparate impact liability that the Court limited disparate impact cases to those that focus on particular employment practices.

The Civil Rights Act of 1991 amendments modify this aspect of *Wards Cove*. While maintaining the general rule that disparate impact must focus on particular employment practices, §703(k)(1)(B)(i) adds an exception that allows the plaintiff to use "bottom line" statistics to establish a prima facie case of disparate impact discrimination:

With respect to demonstrating that a particular employment practice causes a disparate impact . . . the [plaintiff] shall demonstrate that each particular challenged employment practice causes a disparate impact, **except that if the [plaintiff] can demonstrate to the court that the elements of [an employer's] decisionmaking process are not capable of separation for analysis, the decisionmaking process may be analyzed as one employment practice.**

EXAM TIP

Remember that even if you conclude that the plaintiff cannot show that a "particular" employment practice is at issue, then analyze the exception to that requirement. The "bottom line" exception applies where the elements of the employer's decision-making process can't be separated into particular employment practices.

---

    b. No impact defense. The following subsection, §701(k)(1)(B)(ii), provides that the employer can then escape having to justify any practice that makes up part of the decision-making process if it can prove that its use does not cause an impact: **"If the [employer] demonstrates that a specific employment practice does not cause the disparate impact, the [employer] shall not be required to demonstrate that such practice is required by business necessity."**

 # EXAMPLES AND ANALSYIS

1. If an employer uses a series of pass-fail steps in its selection process, a plaintiff can attack each and every step that results in a disparate impact. Suppose an employer requires all applicants to have a high school diploma in order to be considered for a job. Applicants with a high school diploma must then pass a pen-and-pencil test in order to be interviewed for the job. Finally, only those who pass the interview are hired. Each step in this process would be susceptible to attack as a particular employment practice if separate data existed as to the performance on each criteria. Thus, a plaintiff challenging the selection system could not rely on the "bottom line" statistics of the representation of women or minority group members in the employer's workforce as a basis of a disparate impact attack.

2. Assume the same multi-step process for hiring, but the data reveals that only the pen-and-pencil test has a disparate impact and there is no impact at the "bottom line" when the hiring is complete. The use of the pen-and-pencil test is subject to disparate impact discrimination, even in the absence of impact at the "bottom

line" when the hiring process is completed. Connecticut v. Teal, 457 U.S. 440 (1982).

3. If, instead of the multi-step process described above, the employer requires all applicants to fill out a form that asks about educational level, prior work experience, their SAT scores, etc., but then the employer subjectively weighs all this information in making decisions to hire, the only data that is likely to be available are the "bottom line" statistics of the racial or gender representation of those people the employer hired. *Wards Cove* would not allow plaintiff to use that as a basis of comparison with the representation of the protected group who applied. Section 703(k)(1)(B)(i), however, allows the plaintiff to use that evidence if she can convince the court that it is not possible to separate these different elements of the process. If the court agrees, the plaintiff should be allowed to treat "bottom line" statistics of the result of the whole process as one employment practice for purposes of establishing a prima facie case of disparate impact discrimination.

The employer can escape having to justify any particular element of its overall decision-making process by proving its use of that element does not cause a disparate impact.

---

c. The exception for rules prohibiting drug use. The 1991 Act added an exception excluding the use of disparate impact discrimination to attack employer rules barring the illegal use of drugs. Section 703(k)(3) provides that "a rule barring the employment of an individual who currently and knowingly uses or possesses a controlled substance . . . other than the use or possession of a drug taken under the supervision of a licensed health care professional, . . . shall be considered an unlawful employment practice under this title only if such rule is adopted or applied with an intent to discriminate because of race, color, sex, or national origin."

This complete exception of employer drug rules from disparate impact attack appears to resolve the tension created with the Court's decision in New York City Trans. Auth. v. Beazer, 440 U.S. 568 (1979), involving a drug use rule, in which the Court applied disparate impact law more favorably to employers than it had in other disparate impact cases.

 # EXAMPLE AND ANALYSIS

The plaintiffs challenged the employer's rule prohibiting the employment of people on methadone maintenance. The statistics showed that 81 percent of all Transit Authority employees suspected of drug use were African American or Hispanic and that between 62 and 65 percent of all methadone-maintained people in the city were African American or Hispanic. The Supreme Court found this showing inadequate and imposed a quite severe test of what is necessary to show impact: "[Plaintiffs] have only challenged the rule to the extent that is construed to apply to methadone users, and [the statistics about overall drug use] tell us nothing about the racial composition of the employees suspected of using methadone. Nor does the record give us any information about the number of black, Hispanic, or white persons who were dismissed for using methadone. . . . We do not know . . . how many of these persons [in methadone maintenance programs] ever worked or sought to work for the TA." 440 U.S. at 584–585 The Court then also used a relaxed notion of business necessity and job relatedness in overturning the challenge to the employer's drug rule.

The suspicion has always been that *Beazer* was treated specially because it involved a rule about drug use. But since the Court did not say so, the decision has influenced how disparate impact law has developed generally. Section 703(k)(3)'s more direct approach, creating an exception for employer rules concerning drug use, may be preferable because it is straightforward and clear.

Ironically, the same rule attacked in *Beazer* would not be within the §703(b)(3) exception since "the use or possession of a drug [was] taken under the supervision of a licensed health care professional." Therefore, the general disparate impact rules created in §703(k) would apply.

---

    d. **The passivity exception.** In EEOC v. Chicago Miniature Lamp Works, 947 F.2d 292 (7th Cir. 1991), the employer, to fill job openings, relied on "word-of-mouth" recruitment by incumbent workers telling people they knew to apply for jobs as they opened up. The court, in a opinion by Judge Posner, held that no employer practice existed. "The [lower] court erred in considering passive reliance on employee word-of-mouth recruiting as a particular employment practice for the purposes of disparate impact. Their practices here are undertaken solely by employees." While clearly not a policy, it is harder to conclude that the employer's conduct did not amount to a "practice" of hiring people through word-of-mouth recruitment by incumbent employees.

    e. **The fringe benefits exception.** In Finnigan v. Trans World Airlines, Inc., 967 F.2d 1161 (7th Cir. 1992), the employer, facing a severe economic downturn, capped vacations at 4 weeks per year. This had a disparate impact on older workers who as a group were more likely than younger workers to have enough seniority to qualify for more than 4 weeks vacation. Saying that "*this* case makes no sense in disparate impact terms," Judge Posner held that disparate impact analysis did not apply to changes in fringe benefits, at least in age discrimination cases: "A company that for legitimate business reasons decides to cut wages across the board, or to cut out dental insurance, or to curtail the use of company cars is not required to conduct a study to determine the impact of the measure on employees grouped by age and if it is nonrandom to prove that the same amount of money could not have been saved in some different fashion." 967 F.2d at 1163. It may be that *Finnegan* is really a foreshadowing of a broader question that is as yet unanswered by the Supreme Court. That question is whether disparate impact applies in Age Discrimination in Employment Act cases.

2. The Employer's Use of the Practice

Section 703(k)(1)(A)(i) requires plaintiff to prove that the employer "uses a particular employment practice that causes a disparate impact." That can be done with data of the employer's own use of the practice or with data from other sources, such as national data or data developed from its use by other employers, but that does not say that the employer's use of the practice must cause the impact. If the plaintiff proves the impact necessary to establish a prima facie case by relying on sources other than the employer's own use of the challenged practice, the employer then has an affirmative defense by proving that its use does not have a disparate impact. Section 701(k)(1)(B)(ii) of Title VII provides that, "If the [employer] demonstrates that a specific employment practice does not cause the disparate impact, the [employer] shall not be required to demonstrate that such practice is required by business necessity."

The 1991 Act's provisions clear up a confusion caused by earlier Supreme Court cases. In *Griggs,* the Court upheld the use of data to show impact that was not based on the employer's use of the challenged practices. Nationwide statistics of height and weight differences between women and men were sufficient to make a case in Dothard v. Rawlinson, with the Court commenting that "reliance on general population data was not misplaced where there was no reason to suppose that physical height and weight characteristics of Alabama [the site of the employer] men and women differ markedly from those of the national population." 433 U.S. at 330. In contrast, in Espinoza v. Farah Mfg. Co., 414 U.S. 86 (1973), the Court conceded that disparate impact applied to a national origin challenge to a no-alien rule but held that the employer could escape liability because it had shown that no impact existed at its place of business. "[P]ersons of Mexican ancestry make up more than 96% of the employees at the company's San Antonio division, and 97% of those doing the work for which Mrs. Espinoza applied. . . . Farah does not discriminate against persons of Mexican national origin with respect to employment in the job Mrs. Espinoza sought." 414 U.S. at 93.

The 1991 Act appears to resolve the dilemma by allowing plaintiff's use of national data or data derived from the use of the challenged practice by other employers to prove a prima facie case of impact. The employer can then use data from its own use of the practice to escape liability under §701(k)(1)(B)(ii).

EXAM TIP

Analyzing the data in the question as involving the impact of the challenged practice when used nationally or by employers other than the defendant sets up a discussion of plaintiff's burden to prove impact versus the affirmative defense of the employer proving that its use of the practice did not cause an impact.

 # EXAMPLES AND ANALYSIS

1. A police department requires that all officers use a Smith & Wesson Model 59 service revolver. That revolver is quite large and powerful and has a correspondingly large hand grip. National data shows that over 50 percent of all women and 10 percent of all men would be unable to handle the gun because the hand grip is too big. A prima facie case of disparate impact was found because of the national data on impact. At the particular police department, however, 75 out of 80 women officers in fact qualified using the revolver. Presumably, the employer can use the data from its own experience with the revolver to carry its burden of rebutting plaintiff's showing of impact pursuant to §701(k)(1)(B)(ii). Cf., Burne v. City of Naperville, 1991 U.S. Dist. LEXIS 15873 (ND. Ill. 1991).

2. Suppose another police department adopts the same police revolver but the department cannot carry its burden of proving no local impact and cannot escape liability pursuant to §701(k)(1)(B)(ii). The employer may still attempt to escape liability by proving the use of this revolver was job related and a business necessity. Pumpfrey v. City of Coeur d' Alene, 1994 U.S. App. LEXIS 3892 (9th Cir. 1994).

---

3. Amount of Impact

In its disparate impact decisions, the Supreme Court has used an "eyeballing the numbers" approach to determine whether the impact was "disparate," that is, sufficient to support a disparate impact case. The EEOC's Uniform Guidelines on Employee Selection Procedures, 29 C.F.R. §1607.4D (1993), adopt a "four-fifths rule" for purposes of the administrative enforcement of Title VII. A sufficient amount of impact will be shown where the "selection rate for any race, sex, or ethnic group which is less than four-fifths (4/5) (or eighty percent) of the rate for the group with the highest rate." The EEOC Guidelines, however, fail to take into account the size of the sample being tested: If an employer uses a practice involving a handful of workers, 5 men and 5 women, the four-fifths rule is violated if 3 women and 4 men pass the test since the passing rate for women is only 75 percent of the passing rate for men. That may not be a very convincing showing of impact.

a. **Statistically significant showings of impact.** The Supreme Court decisions finding disparate impact have not involved the use of sophisticated statistical techniques. Nevertheless, such techniques may prove useful and some lower courts have required their use. In Fudge v. City of Providence Fire Dept., 766 F.2d 650, 659 (1st Cir. 1985), the court concluded, "[w]idely accepted statistical techniques have been developed to determine the likelihood an observed disparity resulted from mere chance. . . . [T]he better approach is for the courts to require a showing that the disparity is statistically significant, or unlikely to have occurred by chance, applying basic statistical tests as the method of proof."

b. **Real but low-level impact.** Statistical techniques can be used as a basis to conclude that race or gender had a real impact but, nevertheless, the quantum of difference might be so small that a prima facie case is not established. In Thomas v. Metroflight, Inc., 814 F.2d 1506, 1511 n.4 (10th Cir. 1987), the court found disparate impact not established simply because a statistically significant difference was shown: "*Hazelwood* [School District v. United States, 433 U.S. 299 (1977)] does not say that 'statistically significant' is 'significantly discriminatory' as used in *Dothard*. Beyond a requirement of statistical significance, the Court may require in disparate impact cases that the disparity be 'substantial' as well."

4. The Impact Is Adverse

Plaintiffs rarely challenge employer practices unless the practices operate adversely to them. Nevertheless, the issue of adversity has arisen in several cases involving claims of national origin discrimination involving bilingual employees. Although there was impact, it was not adverse. In Garcia v. Spun Steak Co., 998 F.2d 1480 (9th Cir. 1993), the challenged employer policy required bilingual workers to speak only English while working. "When the privilege [of self-expression] is defined at its narrowest (as merely the ability to speak on the job), we cannot conclude that those employees fluent in both English and Spanish are adversely impacted by the policy. Because they are able to speak English, bilingual employees can engage in conversation on the job." 998 F.2d at 1487.

5. The Impact Is to a Protected Group

Title VII protects all persons against employment discrimination because of race, color, sex, religion, and national origin. McDonald v. Santa Fe Trail Trans. Co., 427 U.S. 273 (1976). That protection extends to disparate treatment discrimination but it is not clear that disparate impact theory is available to whites or males. All of the disparate impact cases decided by the Supreme Court involved claims by women or minority men. *Griggs* emphasized that Title VII was "to achieve equality of employment opportunities and remove barriers that have operated in the past to favor an identifiable group of white employees over other employees." 401 U.S. at 429–30 (1971). Los Angeles Dept. of Water & Power v. Manhart, 435 U.S. 702, 710 n.20 (1978), dealt with the argument that equalizing both pension benefits and contributions for men and women to eliminate the use of an illegal gender classification would produce a disparate impact on men, who as a group do not live as long as women. The Court suggested that men would not be able to use the disparate impact theory. "Even a completely neutral practice will inevitably have some disproportionate impact on one group or another. *Griggs* does not imply, and this Court has never held, that discrimination must always be inferred from such consequences."

The most powerful reason to limit disparate impact theory to groups that have been historically the victims of discrimination is that otherwise, to the extent that neutral practices will impact some group, all employer practices would have to be justified as job related and necessary for business. That might make antidiscrimination law too intrusive into the operation of business.

EXAM TIP

Remember that the law is not clear on whether men or whites can use disparate impact law in a question that impacts on these groups.

E. DEFENDANT'S REBUTTAL

There are five different responses potentially open to an employer to rebut a prima facie case of disparate impact discrimination. Two have their source in the Civil Rights Act of 1991 and the other three are found in Title VII as originally enacted.

1. The Employer's Use Does Not Cause the Impact

Even before the 1991 Act amendments, it was always clear that the employer could try to undermine the plaintiff's showing of a prima facie case by introducing evidence that the data plaintiff relied on was flawed. That rebuttal possibility does not change the basic rule that the plaintiff has the burden of persuasion to prove a prima facie case. Section 703(k)(1)(A)(i) states the general rule that "a complaining party demonstrates that a respondent uses a particular employment practice that causes a disparate impact," with "demonstrate" being separately defined in §701(l) as "meets the burdens of production and persuasion." **Section 703(k)(1)(B)(ii), however, appears to create an affirmative defense which imposes on the employer the burden of persuasion to prove that "a specific employment practice does not cause the disparate impact."**

Since the burden of persuasion cannot be on both the plaintiff and the defendant on the same issue, the way to resolve this apparent conflict is by differentiating the types of proof used by plaintiff to establish the prima facie case. If the plaintiff makes out a prima facie case based on data showing the experience of the employer's use of the challenged practice, the employer may rebut such a showing by challenging the accuracy of the evidence that plaintiff relied upon. The defendant, presumably, does not carry the burden of persuasion when it undermines the evidence the plaintiff relies on to establish a prima facie case. However, if the plaintiff makes out a prima facie case of disparate impact relying on national data or with the experience of other employers and the employer is unable to rebut that showing, then §701(k)(1)(B)(ii) shifts the burden to the employer to prove that its own use of the practice does not have a disparate impact.

 # EXAMPLE AND ANALYSIS

In Dothard v. Rawlinson, 433 U.S. 321 (1977), the plaintiff established a prima facie case using national statistics to show that, among the population generally, the height and weight prerequisites the employer used for its prison guard jobs had a disparate impact on women. Defendant did not attempt to rebut that showing of impact at a national level. Because the plaintiff relied on national statistics, §701(k)(1)(B)(ii) would shift the burden of persuasion to the employer to prove that its own use of these prerequisites did not have an impact.

2. Business Necessity and Job Relatedness

If the plaintiff is successful in establishing a prima facie case and the efforts of the employer to rebut it fail, the next affirmative defense available to the employer is **§701(k)(1)(A)(i), which requires the employer to prove "that the challenged practice is job related for the position in question and consistent with business necessity."**

This language is significant in three ways. First, it replaces the *Wards Cove* language about reasoned review of the employer's justification for the challenged practice. Congress rejected the Court's view that the practice need not be "essential" or "indispensable" and returned to the notion of business *necessity.*

Second, the plain meaning of the section makes it clear that the burden on the employer on these issues is one of persuasion and not, as the Court would have had it in *Wards Cove,* just of production.

Third, the plain meaning of the section requires the *employer* to demonstrate *both* that the challenged practice is (1) job related for the position involved and (2) justified by business necessity. Both terms originally come from Griggs v. Duke Power Co., and the Court's usage in that case suggests that job relatedness is a narrower, more difficult, justification than business necessity. To prove something is job related the employer must prove that the practice affects the performance of the employee on the particular job that she performs. Business necessity is broader in that it may take into account factors not directly related to employee performance on a particular job. Requiring both should make this a difficult defense to prove.

 # EXAMPLE AND ANALYSIS

Suppose a stock brokerage requires all of its brokers to have MBAs because it wants to tout to potential customers the high quality of its brokers, and suppose that requirement has a disparate impact on women and members of minority groups. Since many successful brokers working for other firms do not have MBA degrees, the employer would be hard pressed to prove the requirement was "job related for the position in question." An MBA is not required to become a licensed broker nor is an MBA necessary to place securities trades for customers. If the job related standard was somehow satisfied, it would also be quite difficult, despite the employer's desire to publicize its expertise, to find that the requirement is "consistent with business necessity."

　　　　a.   **Legislative history limited to pre-*Wards Cove* Supreme Court decisions.** In adding new §703(k), Congress took the unusual step of defining the relevant legislative history that may be relied on in interpreting the terms "business necessity" and "job related." Section 105(b) of the Civil Rights Act of 1991 limits the legislative history on the terms "business necessity" and "job related" to a single Interpretive Memorandum, which says that those terms "are intended to reflect the concepts enunciated by the Supreme Court in *Griggs* and other decisions prior to *Wards Cove.*" Obviously, *Wards Cove* should not be a source used to interpret these terms and it also seems clear that *only* Supreme Court cases can be so used.

b. **The pre-*Wards Cove* Supreme Court decisions.** The Supreme Court has used various formulations of the terms "business necessity" and "job related" in its disparate impact decisions. *Griggs* uses both terms at various times, but the only use close to a definition is the statement, "What Congress has forbidden is giving these [testing or measuring] devices and mechanisms controlling force unless they are demonstrably a reasonable measure of job performance." 401 U.S. at 436.

Both Albemarle Paper Co. v. Moody, 422 U.S. 404, 425 (1975), and New York City Trans. Auth. v. Beazer, 440 U.S. 568, 587 (1979), spoke in terms of "manifest relation to the employment in question," and Connecticut v. Teal, 457 U.S. 440, 451 (1982), required the employer to show that a test "measure[s] skills related to effective performance of [the job]." All these descriptions make the defenses quite narrow.

Beazer, however, also involved a rather permissive application of business necessity. After saying that the Transit Authority's goals of safety and efficiency required that drug users be excluded from employment, the Court went on to say that those goals "are significantly served by—even if they do not require—TA's rule as it applies to all methadone users including those who are seeking employment in safety-sensitive positions." 440 U.S. at 587 n.31.

i. **Empirical evidence required.** Dothard v. Rawlinson, 433 U.S. 321 (1977), requires that the employer must base its defense on empirical evidence and not merely on an argument.

c. **Lower court reading of the 1991 Act.** With one exception, the lower courts are beginning to interpret the terms "business necessity" and "job related" in a reasonably strict manner. In Lanning v. Southeastern Pa. Transp. Auth., 181 F.3d 478, 489 (3rd Cir. 1999), the court, in a case dealing with the appropriate cutoff score on a physical fitness test, held that "the employer must demonstrate that its cutoff measures the minimum qualifications necessary for successful performance of the job in question." Thus, it rejected the idea that the employer could use a "more is better" approach by setting the performance cutoff in a way that was unconnected to the minimum performance requirements for the job.

EXAMPLES AND ANALYSIS

1. In Lanning v. Southeastern Pa. Transp. Auth., 181 F.3d 478, (3rd Cir. 1999), the defendant's police force established a physical fitness test for applicants requiring

them to run 1.5 miles within 12 minutes, which test had a disparate impact on women. The court reversed a finding of the trial court that this test was justified by business necessity by holding that the defendant had failed to carry its burden of proving that the test measured the "minimum qualifications necessary for the successful performance of the job in question."

2. The Hispanic male plaintiff in Melendez v. Illinois Bell Telephone Co., 79 F.3d 661, 669 (7th Cir. 1996), proved that a test used by the employer, the Basic Skills Abilities Test (BSAT), had a disparate impact on African Americans and Hispanics. Defendants had conducted a validation study but the court found that the test was not justified as job related just because "the BSAT can predict a person's job performance 3 percent better than chance alone." In other words, improving job performance by 3 percent over chance was not sufficient to justify the use of the test.

3. In Fitzpatrick v. City of Atlanta, 2 F.3d 1112 (11th Cir. 1993), African-American firefighters challenged a new employer rule that required all firefighters to be clean-shaven. The plaintiffs all suffered from pseudofolliculitis barbae (PFB), a bacterial disorder that disproportionately afflicts African-American men and causes their faces to become infected if they are shaved. The employer claimed that the rule was justified because facial hair could interfere with the operation of the respirators firefighters must sometimes wear. The firefighters responded that a prior rule had allowed firefighters with PFB to wear very short "shadow" beards and that no one had a problem using the respirators under that rule. In upholding summary judgment for the fire department, the court first described business necessity as a demonstration "that the practice or action is necessary to meeting a goal that, as a matter of law, has been found to qualify as an important business goal for Title VII purposes." 2 F.3d at 1119. The court then accepted worker safety as such a goal and found no question of material fact to exist because of an unrebutted expert witness report.

Some factors considered in earlier cases may continue to be important in the future development of business necessity and job relatedness.

   i. **Sliding scale.** In Fitzpatrick v. City of Atlanta, 2 F.3d 1112 (11th Cir. 1993), may be an example of a view developed in pre-1991 Act cases that greater deference be given an employer when human safety was at issue rather than some other goal. *See* Spurlock v. United Airlines, Inc., 475 F.2d 216 (10th Cir. 1972) (sliding scale business necessity test applied to uphold 500-hour flight time and college degree prerequisites for commercial pilot training program).

   ii. **Subjective practices.** In Watson v. Fort Worth Bank & Trust, 487 U.S. 977 (1988), the Court was reluctant to find subjective practices applicable to disparate impact analysis even while acknowledging the difficulty in proving them justified. While the American Psychological Association argued in its amicus brief in *Watson* that subjective practices could be validated pursuant to the test validation standards, the *Watson* plurality thought courts should to some extent defer to employers who use such practices. 487 U.S. at 999.

 iii. **Cost justification.** Judge Posner in Finnegan v. Trans World Airlines, Inc., 967 F.2d 1161 (7th Cir. 1992), indicated that he would accept cost justification as a defense to the employer's imposition of a 4-week cap on employee vacations. However, the court in Geller v. Markham, 635 F.2d 1027 (2d Cir. 1980), *cert. denied,* 451 U.S. 945 (1981), found that a policy against hiring teachers in higher pay scales was not justified as a cost-cutting measure required by tight budgetary constraints.

EXAM TIP

The scope of the business necessity/job related defense is the key to the application of disparate impact law.

---

3. Professionally Developed Tests

Title VII as originally enacted included **§703(h), which provides an exception to liability for "an employer to give and to act upon the results of any professionally developed ability test provided that such test, its administration or action upon the results is not designed, intended, or used to discriminate** because of race, color, religion, sex, or national origin." This is an affirmative defense, with the employer carrying the burden of persuasion to prove the test is valid.

Griggs looked to the EEOC test guidelines, which looked to the professional test validation standards of the American Psychological Association for the proper approach to the test exception. In other words, only tests that satisfy these professional standards would satisfy §703(h).

 a. **Defining a "test."** Since the professional test validation standards emphasize job relatedness, the test exception is in essence a subset of the job related defense. Those employment practices that are deemed to be "tests" must be validated pursuant to professional test validation standards. Presumably all paper-and-pencil tests must be validated, whether used for purposes like general intelligence or mechanical ability like the tests attacked in *Griggs* and *Albemarle* or to judge "honesty."

Use of a "performance assessment center," which is a simulation of important elements of a job, is a test. See Talbert v. City of Richmond, 648 F.2d 925 (4th Cir. 1981).

b. The professional test validation standards. The professional test standards set forth a complex system for validating tests.

    i. Job analysis. The first step in any validation is a job analysis: to determine the nature of the skills, knowledge, etc., entailed in doing it. The job analysis forms the basis for the threshold decision determining whether any test would be appropriate, and, if so, what the test should be composed of and how it can be validated.

    ii. Two methods of validation. The standards recognize two basic methods of validating employment tests: **criterion-related** and **content validation.** The court in Guardians Assn. v. Civil Service Commn., 630 F.2d 79, 92 (2d Cir. 1980), *cert. denied,* 452 U.S. 940 (1981), said the choice between them is usually outcome determinative. **"Content validation is generally feasible while [criterion-related] validation is frequently impossible."** Thus, employers attempt to rely on the content approach, even if it is a stretch to do so.

        (a) Criterion-related validation. This method of validation is a controlled experiment. The employer administers the tests and records the scores to a sample of applicants, hires all of them and then, after the workers have been on the job for a while, evaluates their work performance using trained evaluators and standard scoring measures. A statistical technique, called the correlation coefficient, is then used to compare the test scores with the job performance scores to determine whether the test is valid. If there is a high correlation between the scores workers get on the test and on the job, then the test is considered valid because a high test score predicts good job performance.

 # EXAMPLES AND ANALYSIS

1. In Albemarle Paper Co. v. Moody, 422 U.S. 405 (1975), the employer attempted an eve-of-litigation criterion-related validation of the Wonderlic and Bennett Mechanical tests it had been using. The Supreme Court reviewed this validation technique very closely and struck down the test as not having been properly validated. The fundamental failure was that no job analysis had been done, either when the tests were first adopted or by the expert hired to attempt the validation. It was no surprise that test performance did not correlate well with job performance where the employer adopted the tests not knowing what skills and abilities were

involved in the job.

Instead of being able to do a classic predictive study, where the employer gives a test to a sample of applicants and then hires all of them to determine how well the test predicts their job performance, here the expert had no choice but to do a "concurrent" study in which he gave the tests to incumbent workers and then compared their scores on the tests with their job performance. Concurrent validation raises many problems. First, there is the question of causation, that is, whether incumbent workers who earned high scores on the test did so because they learned how to do well on the test because of their experience on the job. Second, using incumbent workers meant that the test-taking group was different from the group of applicants. "Albemarle's validation study dealt only with job-experienced, white workers; but the tests themselves are given to new job applicants, who are younger, largely inexperienced, and in many instances nonwhite." 422 U.S. at 435. Third, using incumbent workers means that the study only looks at people who were hired. There is no data about the job performance of applicants who would get low test scores.

2. In contrast to the close scrutiny given to the validation study in *Albemarle Paper*, the Court was much more relaxed in its review of the test in Washington v. Davis, 426 U.S. 229 (1976). The test attacked there was used to select recruits for a police training program. It was designed to test verbal ability, reading, and comprehension. The criterion against which the test scores were correlated was performance in the training school and not the performance of police work. While there was a correlation between test scores and performance tests in the recruit program, the test was not shown to predict any aspect of the job of being a police officer. Nevertheless, the Court accepted the use of training program performance as the sole criterion on which test validity was judged.

(b)   **Content validation.** This technique of test validation involves the construction of a test that is actually a sample of the job the employee will hold. If the test is a good sample of what workers who get the job will do, then it is valid. Rather than the analysis of data and the use of the statistical technique involved in criterion-related validation, proof of content validation basically turns on the testimony of the test maker that the test in fact is a sample of the job for which the test is used.

EXAMPLE AND ANALYSIS

Gillespie v. Wisconsin, 771 F.2d 1035 (7th Cir. 1985), *cert. denied*, 474 U.S. 1083 (1986), is typical of the approach courts have recently taken to content validation.

The employer did undertake a job analysis and then constructed an essay test in which each test taker was asked to write a job description, prepare a memo for a hypothetical meeting, and plan an itinerary for a business trip. Since the job involved writing these sorts of documents, these elements of the test were close to elements of the actual job. Thus, the court found the test to be a valid sample of the job and, therefore, content valid.

(c) Differential validation and race test scores. One way an employer might consider continuing to use a test that had a disparate impact because of race or gender would be to raise the scores of the disadvantaged group. The Civil Rights Act of 1991 added §703(l) to prohibit that. "It shall be an unlawful employment practice for a respondent, in connection with the selection or referral of applicants or candidates for employment or promotion, to adjust the scores of, use of different cutoff scores for, or otherwise alter the results of, sex, or national origin."

EXAM TIP

If "content validation" applies because you can argue that the test is really a sample of the job for which it will be used, then the test will likely be upheld. If the validation attempted is "criterion-related" then the test will likely be struck down unless there is data favorably comparing test scores with job evaluations of the workers.

4. Bona Fide Seniority System

Section 703(h), as originally adopted in Title VII, also **provides an exception "for an employer to apply different standards of compensation, or different terms, conditions, or privileges of employment to a bona fide seniority . . . system** . . . provided that such differences are not the result of an intention to discriminate because of race, color, religion, sex, or national origin." This is an affirmative defense to a disparate impact case so the employer carries the burden of persuasion that the seniority system exception applies.

In International Brotherhood of Teamsters v. United States, 431 U.S. 324 (1977), the Supreme Court held that seniority systems are sheltered by §703(h) from disparate impact attack: "an otherwise neutral, legitimate seniority system does not become unlawful under Title VII simply because it may perpetuate pre-Act discrimination. **Congress did not intend to make it illegal for employees with vested seniority rights to continue to exercise those rights,** even at the expense of pre-Act discriminatees."

a. **Collective bargaining agreement seniority systems.** Only seniority systems that are collective bargaining agreements between an employer and a union representing the employees are sheltered by §703(h). All the seniority system cases decided by the Supreme Court have involved union-negotiated collective bargaining agreements. In Nashville Gas Co. v. Satty, 434 U.S. 136 (1977), the Court did not discuss the seniority system exception where the employer unilaterally promulgated a pregnancy leave policy based on seniority.

b. **The traditional component of seniority systems test.** In addition to proving that the seniority system involves a collective bargaining agreement, §703(h) requires the employer to prove that the challenged policy is in fact a traditional component of a system of seniority.

 # EXAMPLES AND ANALYSIS

1. In California Brewers Assn. v. Bryant, 444 U.S. 598 (1980), the plaintiffs challenged a clause in a collective bargaining agreement that required a temporary employee to work at least 45 weeks in a single calendar year to become a permanent employee in the brewing industry. Because brewing beer is so seasonal, it was difficult to become a permanent employee; the employer had discretion to choose which workers would be retained long enough to become permanent and no African American had ever become a permanent employee. While the court of appeals had found the rule not part of a seniority system because it did not measure length of total time worked by an employee, the Supreme Court reversed. " '[S]eniority' is a term that connotes length of employment. A 'seniority system' is a scheme that, alone or in tandem with non-'seniority' criteria, allots to employees ever improving employment rights and benefits as their relative lengths of pertinent employment increase. . . . **Every seniority system must, moreover, contain rules that particularize the types of employment conditions that will be governed or influenced by seniority, and those that will not.** Rules that serve these necessary purposes do not fall outside §703(h) simply because they do not, in and of themselves, operate on the basis of some factor involving the passage of time." 444 U.S. at 605–08.

    However, §703(h) does not shelter: "[E]mployment rules that depart fundamentally from commonly accepted notions concerning the acceptable contours of a seniority system, simply because those rules are dubbed 'seniority' provisions or have some nexus to an arrangement that concededly operates on the basis of seniority." 444 U.S. at 608.

2. Assume that a collective bargaining agreement puts hiring rules, such as education or test prerequisites, under the heading "seniority system." Since an employee cannot earn seniority without being hired, the argument would be that these rules are protected by §703(h). However, the placement of such hiring prerequisites is not within the "commonly accepted notions concerning the acceptable contours of a seniority system." Thus, these hiring rules would not be exempted from disparate impact attack because of the bona fide seniority system exception.

---

    c. **Seniority systems with their "genesis in discrimination."** In *Teamsters*, the Court recognized that **§703(h) would not shelter seniority systems that were the product of an intention to discriminate.** "The seniority system in this litigation is entirely bona fide. . . . [I]t is conceded that the seniority system did not have its genesis in racial discrimination, and that it was negotiated and has been maintained free from any illegal purpose." 431 U.S. at 355–56.

In James v. Stockman Valves & Fittings Co., 559 F.2d 310, 352 (5th Cir. 1977), *cert. denied,* 434 U.S. 1034 (1978), the court created a four-factor test to determine whether a seniority system fell outside the protection of §703(h) because it did have its genesis in discrimination: (1) whether the seniority system operates to discourage all employees equally from transferring between seniority units; (2) whether the seniority units are in the same or separate bargaining units (if the latter, whether that structure is rational and in conformance with industry practice); (3) whether the seniority system has its genesis in racial discrimination; and (4) whether the system was negotiated and has been maintained free from any illegal purpose.

5. Bona Fide Merit and Piecework System

Finally, **§703(h) provides an exception to disparate impact liability for bona fide merit systems or systems "which measures earnings by quantity or quality of production** . . . provided that such differences are not the result of an intention to discriminate because of race, color, religion, sex, or national origin."

In Maxwell v. City of Tucson, 803 F.2d 444, 447 (9th Cir. 1986), the court emphasized that, to be within the exception, there must be a merit "system," which must be "an organized and structured procedure whereby employees are evaluated systematically according to predetermined criteria."

In Guardians Assn. v. Civil Service Commn., 633 F.2d 232 (2d Cir. 1980), the defendant failed to prove its test was strongly enough validated under the test exception to support the use of rank order scoring to hire police officers. The employer then tried to argue that the rank order use of test scores to hire was a merit system. The court rejected the argument, holding that "a hiring system that ranks applicants according to their performance on discriminatory examinations cannot claim the status of a 'bona fide merit system' within the meaning of the statute. . . . Section 703(h) makes sense only if the term 'bona fide merit system' is understood to refer to merit in areas related to the necessities of the business, not 'merit' in the abstract." 633 F.2d at 252–53.

F. ALTERNATIVE EMPLOYMENT PRACTICE SURREBUTTAL

Section 703(k)(1)(A)(ii) defines the third, surrebuttal stage of a disparate impact case as involving the plaintiff proving the existence of an alternative employment practice that the employer refuses to adopt: **"the complaining party makes the demonstration described in subparagraph (C) with respect to an alternative employment practice and the respondent refuses to adopt such alternative employment practice."**

1. Defining "Alternative Employment Practice"

Instead of defining what "an alternative employment practice" is, §703(k)(1)(C), which is referred to above, indicates that the demonstration of the alternative employment practice "shall be in accordance with the law as it existed on June 4, 1989." That is the day before *Wards Cove* was decided. The problem is that prior to *Wards Cove* the Supreme Court did not use the exact language, "an alternative employment practice."

Section 703(k)(1)(A)(ii) replaces the idea of "pretext" with "alternative employment practice." That would appear to remove the connotation that the state of mind of the employer is at issue. That leaves the content of the concept in Court's pre-*Wards Cove* decisions as the showing of a less discriminatory alternative. In Fitzpatrick v. City of Atlanta, 2 F.3d 1112 (11th Cir. 1993), the first case applying the provisions of the new Act, the court described **an alternative employment practice as "alternative policies with lesser discriminatory effects that would be comparably as effective at serving the employer's identified business needs."**

2. The Employer's Refusal to Adopt the Alternative

The statutory language requires the plaintiff to show that the employer "refuses to adopt" the alternative practice. **"Refuses" seems to mean more than the mere failure to use the alternative practice. At a minimum, it connotes that the employer was somehow aware of the existence of the alternative practice and made the conscious decision not to adopt it. "Refuses" also suggests that the refusal is a continuing one.** So all of this raises a difficult question of the timing of this refusal. It may be that an employer can escape liability by adopting the alternative even while a disparate impact trial is going on.

EXAMPLE AND ANALYSIS

Suppose that a fire department uses a physical fitness test to pick recruits for the department, the test emphasizes physical strength, and it causes a disparate impact on women. Further, assume that the court finds that the fire department has justified the test as a business necessity and as job related. That leaves the issue of the alternative employment practice. The plaintiffs present the fire department with an alternative test that emphasizes endurance rather than strength and that does not have as dramatic an impact on women as the strength test. If the court finds that firefighting requires both strength and endurance and that the proposed endurance test is comparable to the strength test in picking qualified recruits for the fire department, then the refusal of the fire department to adopt the alternative establishes liability. Cf. Zamlen v. City of Cleveland, 906 F.2d 209 (6th Cir. 1990).

EXAM TIP

The 1991 Act does not make it clear whether the third step of the case—the alternative employment practice—applies to tests, seniority and merit systems, or only to other employment practices that the employer must justify with the business necessity/job related defense.

3. The Alternative Employment Practice as an Independent Cause of Action

The plain meaning of §703(k)(1)(A) provides two ways to establish disparate impact liability. The first is in (i), which provides for liability if the plaintiff proves the employer uses a practice that has a disparate impact which the employer then fails to justify by business necessity and job relatedness. The alternative employment practice surrebuttal step is not included. The second, and completely independent, method in (ii) involves proving an alternative employment practice that the employer refuses to adopt. It can be argued that (ii) creates an independent cause of action, free from having to prove disparate impact on a protected class and not dependent on the defendant proving business necessity and job relatedness.

G. THE SAME DECISION DEFENSE TO LIMIT INDIVIDUAL'S REMEDIES

As with systemic disparate treatment cases, the employer can escape providing remedies to individuals adversely affected by its systemic disparate impact discrimination by proving that, as to each individual, it had not discriminated against them.

H. PROCEDURES AND REMEDIES

While Congress codified disparate impact law in the Civil Rights Act of 1991, disparate impact law did not benefit from several expansions of rights and remedies provided for disparate treatment claims. While the 1991 Act added a right to jury trial and compensatory and punitive damages in intentional discrimination cases, those rights were not provided for disparate impact cases. 42 U.S.C. §1981 a(c) creates a right to jury trials but that is limited to cases in which the plaintiff seeks compensatory or punitive damages. Compensatory and punitive damages are provided in 42 U.S.C. §1981a(a)(1) but they are limited to actions brought against an employer "who engaged in unlawful intentional discrimination (not an employment practice that is unlawful because of its disparate impact)."

I. DISPARATE IMPACT IN OTHER ANTIDISCRMINATION STATUTES

Since the enactment of the Civil Rights Act of 1991, disparate impact discrimination has been codified in Title VII, which is in part modeled on the disparate impact provisions in §102(b)(3) of the Americans with Disabilities Act. 42 U.S.C. §1981, however, has been construed as not including the disparate impact theory of discrimination. General Building Contractors Assn. v. Pennsylvania, 458 U.S. 375 (1982). Whether disparate impact discrimination is incorporated within the Age Discrimination in Employment Act is yet to be definitively determined. See Chapter 10.

EXAM TIP

A question to look for is whether disparate impact applies in age discrimination cases.

REVIEW QUESTIONS AND ANSWERS

Question: What is the essence of systemic disparate impact discrimination?

Answer: The use by an employer of a practice that causes a disparate impact because of race, color, religion, sex, or national origin.

Question: Is the employer's intent to discriminate an element in a systemic disparate impact case?

Answer: Proof of discriminatory intent or motive is not an element in a systemic disparate impact case.

Question: What are the three steps used to structure systemic disparate impact cases?

Answer: The three steps that structure a systemic disparate impact case are:

1. Plaintiff's prima facie case showing the employer uses a particular employment practice that causes disparate impact.

2. The defendant's rebuttal based on one of five statutory defenses.

3. The plaintiff's proof that an alternative employment practice exists that the employer refuses to use.

Question: What must a plaintiff show to establish a prima facie case of systemic disparate impact discrimination?

Answer: The plaintiff must prove that the employer "uses a particular employment practice that causes a disparate impact on the basis of race, color, religion, sex, or national origin."

Question: What are the five subparts that make up the showing of a prima facie case of systemic disparate impact discrimination?

Answer: The five subparts making up a prima facie case are:

1. The employer uses a particular employment practice.

2. That practice causes an impact.

3. That impact is sufficient to support a finding that the impact is disparate.

4. The impact is adverse to members of the protected group.

5. A protected group suffers the impact.

Question: What are the five possible rebuttals the employer has to a prima facie case of disparate impact discrimination?

Answer: The five possible rebuttals are:

1. The employer's use of the practice does not cause impact.

2. The practice is both job related and justified by business necessity.

3. The practice is a test that has been validated using professional test validation standards.

4. The practice is a traditional component of a bona fide seniority system.

5. The practice is a bona fide merit or piecework system.

Question: What are the two parts to the alternative employment practice issue at the surrebuttal stage of a systemic disparate impact case?

Answer: The plaintiff must prove that:

1. An alternative employment practice exists that serves the employer's interest, and;

2. The employer refuses to adopt it.

THE INTERRELATION OF THE THEORIES OF DISCRIMINATION

CHAPTER OVERVIEW

Figuring out the relationship among the three theories derived from different definitions of the term "discrimination" is very important. Many fact patterns give rise to the possible application of more than one of the theories. Thus, it is important not only to understand how each of the three theories applies to a fact pattern but also to understand how the application of the three theories is interrelated.

- **The Key to Disparate Treatment Is Intentional Discrimination.** The key to both individual and systemic disparate treatment is intent to discriminate.

- **No Intent Issue in Disparate Impact Actions.** Systemic disparate impact does not include an intent-to-discriminate element.

- **General Practices Exist in Both Systemic Theories.** The basic similarity between systemic disparate treatment and systemic disparate impact is that both apply to the general practices of the employer.

- **Individual Disparate Treatment Applies to Ad Hoc Discrimination.** Individual disparate treatment theory is not relevant to claims of systemic discrimination by the employee but it does apply to her individual treatment by the employer pursuant to those practices or on an ad hoc basis.

- **Individual Class Members Presumed Entitled to Relief.** When a case of systemic disparate treatment or impact is established, the class of individuals affected are presumed to be entitled to relief unless the employer can prove that it had not engaged in discrimination against them.

- **Defending Against Disparate Treatment May Concede a Disparate Impact Case.** In defending against a systemic disparate treatment case, the employer may point to employment practices it uses that cause the impact to undermine the inference that it acted "because of" rather than "in spite of" the impact. In doing so, the employer may concede that these practices cause a disparate impact. Thus, to avoid a finding of disparate impact discrimination, the employer must also justify these practices pursuant to one of the defenses and may still be liable if the plaintiff can prove an alternative employment practice exists that the employer refuses to use.

EXAM TIP

When you first finish reading your exam questions, figure out which of these general theories of discrmination apply in which questions.

A.   THE DIFFERENCES BETWEEN THE THREE THEORIES OF DISCRIMINATION

The three main theories that apply in antidiscrimination statutes all derive from different definitions of the term "discrimination." In order to understand the interaction among them, it is first necessary to show how they differ.

1.   Systemic Disparate Treatment Discrimination

The broadest definition of discrimination is systemic disparate treatment discrimination since any policy or practice that is discriminatory is systemic disparate treatment discrimination. Because of its breadth and because Title VII now provides a right to a jury trial and compensatory and punitive damages in systemic disparate treatment cases, it is the approach plaintiffs prefer. The key element in a systemic disparate treatment case is the intent of the employer to discriminate because of a characteristic prohibited by an antidiscrimination statute. Congress, in the Civil Rights Act of 1991, provided a right to trial by jury in all intentional discrimination cases. **Intent to discriminate to support a systemic disparate treatment case can be proven in two different ways.**

  a.   **Formal policies of discrimination.** Intent to discriminate is established by showing a formal policy, in writing or admitted by the employer to exist, of discrimination.

    i.   **Voluntary affirmative action.** A "reverse" discrimination Title VII plaintiff must not only prove that the employer used affirmative action but also that the use fails to satisfy standards.

    ii.   **The defenses to a formal policy case.** If the employer cannot rebut the existence of the policy or the inference that it is a policy of discrimination, only one defense is available:

(a) **Bona fide occupational qualification.** The BFOQ defense applies to religion, sex, and national origin, but not to race or color discrimination.

(b) **Defenses that do not apply.** The following defenses do **not** apply to a systemic disparate treatment case based on a formal policy of discrimination:

(1) **Business Necessity.** The business necessity defense, which applies in systemic disparate impact cases, does not apply in systemic disparate treatment cases. International Union, UAW v. Johnson Controls, Inc., 499 U.S. 187 (1991) and §703(k)(2) of Title VII.

(2) **Lack of Disparate Impact.** The fact that a formal policy of discrimination does not result in disparate impact upon the group discriminated against is not a defense. Los Angeles Dept. of Water & Power v. Manhart, 435 U.S. 702 (1978).

EXAM TIP

A voluntary affirmative action plan and the BFOQ defense apply to systemic disparate treatment cases but the business necessity/job related defenses do not apply.

---

b. **Practice of discrimination.** As an alternative to showing a formal policy of discrimination, systemic disparate treatment can be shown by evidence, both statistical and anecdotal, that the employer as a general practice treats employees or applicants differently because of their race, gender, or other characteristic protected against discrimination.

i. **No affirmative defense to a practice case.** If the employer cannot rebut the evidence supporting plaintiff's prima facie case or the inference that it acted "because of" rather than "in spite of" the discriminatory impact, no defense is available since the employer will not win if it first denies discriminating and then, when found to have discriminated, turns around and tries to argue that the discrimination was justified as a BFOQ.

2. Systemic Disparate Impact

In contrast to systemic disparate treatment with its key being the employer's intent to discriminate, **systemic disparate impact does not require proof of intent to discriminate. Instead, its focus is on employer practices that weigh more heavily on a protected group than on the majority.** Because the provision for a right to a jury trial and for compensatory and punitive damages requires the action be for intentional discrimination, these rights are not available in systemic disparate impact cases.

a. Plaintiff's prima facie case. The key to systemic disparate impact discrimination is plaintiff's proof that the employer uses an employment practice that causes a disparate impact because of race, color, religion, sex, or national origin.

b. Defendant's rebuttal. There are five possible defenses to a prima facie case of systemic disparate treatment.

  i. Employer's use does not cause impact. The employer bears the burden of proving its use of the practice did not cause an impact at least where plaintiff establishes impact using data not connected with the employer.

  ii. Business necessity and job relatedness. The employer bears the burden of proving its practice is job related for the position in question and consistent with business necessity.

  iii. Professionally developed test. The employer bears the burden of proving that the test it used was validated by professional test standards.

  iv. Bona fide seniority system. The employer bears the burden of proving that the challenged practice is a traditional component of a bona fide seniority system.

  v. Bona fide merit or piecework system. The employer bears the burden of proving the challenged practice is a bona fide merit or piecework system.

c. Plaintiff's alternative practice surrebuttal. Even if the defendant carries its burden of proving one of the defenses, plaintiff can still prevail by proving that an alternative employment practice exists and that the employer refuses to adopt it.

3. Individual Disparate Treatment Discrimination

While both systemic disparate treatment and systemic disparate impact apply broadly to employer policies and practices, **individual disparate treatment discrimination focuses on the treatment by the employer of individuals.** As in systemic disparate treatment cases, the key in individual disparate treatment cases is the intent to discriminate. As in systemic disparate treatment cases, there is a right to a trial by jury and to compensatory and punitive damages. Intent to discriminate to support an individual disparate treatment case can be proven in two different ways.

a.   Direct evidence of intent. While a formal policy of discrimination establishes a prima facie case of systemic disparate treatment discrimination, **direct evidence of intent, such as an admission by the employer that it discriminated, establishes a prima facie case of individual disparate treatment discrimination.** Liability is established when the finder of fact finds that race, gender, etc., was "a motivating factor" in the decision of the employer that plaintiff challenges.

   i.   Defense to a direct evidence case. In addition to attempting to rebut the evidence establishing plaintiff's case, defendant can limit full remedies to the plaintiff by proving an affirmative defense upon which it carries the burden of persuasion that it would have made the same decision even if it had not relied on an impermissible factor such as race, gender, etc.

b.   Circumstantial evidence of intent. If there is no direct evidence establishing intent to discriminate, **a case of individual disparate treatment can still be established through circumstantial evidence sufficient to support drawing an inference that the employer acted with an intent to discriminate.** There is sufficient evidence when plaintiff has shown that the most likely nondiscriminatory reasons for the employer's action did not apply to the plaintiff.

   i.   Defendant's rebuttal. The employer can rebut the plaintiff's prima facie case by introducing **evidence sufficient to raise an issue of fact that a reason other than a discriminatory one was what motivated the employer.** Defendant bears the burden of production but does not bear the burden of persuasion to prove that the nondiscriminatory reason actually motivated its action.

   ii.   Plaintiff's surrebuttal. Since an employer always can introduce evidence for its action other than discrimination, **the final step requires the plaintiff to carry its burden of persuasion to prove that the employer's intent to discriminate was the determinative factor in its decision.** The evidence supporting the prima facie case as well as evidence that defendant's rebuttal explanation was a pretext can support that finding of discrimination.

   iii.   No same decision defense. Unlike a case based on direct evidence, there is no same decision affirmative defense available to the employer in an individual disparate treatment case based on circumstantial evidence because that possibility is foreclosed once the factfinder finds that race was "a determinative factor" in the employer's decision.

B.   THE RELATIONSHIP BETWEEN THE TWO SYSTEMIC THEORIES

Both systemic disparate treatment and systemic disparate impact theories focus on the general policies and practices of an employer that affect many employees and applicants.

EXAM TIP

Where an exam question deals with the general policies and practices of an employer, analyze the problem under both systemic disparate treatment and impact theories.

---

1.   Plaintiffs Prefer Systemic Disparate Treatment

The systemic disparate treatment theory is the broadest theory of discrimination since it applies to employment policies and practices of intentional discrimination of employers no matter where they occur. Plaintiffs prefer the systemic disparate treatment approach because it provides a right to trial by jury and the potential for compensatory and punitive damages, which are not available in systemic disparate impact cases. Further, in systemic disparate treatment cases, the defenses available to the employer are limited to the BFOQ, while in systemic disparate impact cases, there are defenses for showing the employer's use of the practice did not cause an impact, for business necessity and job relatedness, for professionally developed tests, and for bona fide seniority systems and bona fide merit or piecework systems.

2.   Both Systemic Theories Do Not Always Apply

While the Court in *Teamsters* said that, "Either theory may, of course, be applied to a particular set of facts," 431 U.S. at 336 n.15, it is not always true that both systemic disparate treatment and systemic disparate impact cases apply to any particular case.

a.   The disparate impact theory is not used in formal policy cases.
Plaintiffs have little incentive to use systemic disparate impact when both systemic theories apply but the plaintiff can win on the disparate treatment claim. The advantages in a limited defense, broader remedies, and the right to jury trial available in systemic disparate treatment cases make that theory more attractive.

Further, it is clear that the absence of impact is not a defense to a systemic disparate treatment case based on a formal policy of discrimination. In Los Angeles Dept. of Water & Power v. Manhart, 435 U.S. 702 (1978), a systemic disparate treatment case involving a formal policy of salary discrimination in which the employer deducted more for pension contributions from women, the employer argued that the lack of impact on women, because they would get monthly pension benefits equal to men but would get them over their longer lifetimes, was a defense to the disparate treatment case. The Court rejected the argument, saying that the lack of discriminatory effect "does not defeat the claim that the practice, on its face, discriminated against every individual employed by the Department."

b. The scope of disparate impact theory is more limited than for disparate treatment. *Wards Cove* made it clear that the focus of systemic disparate impact actions was on particular practices used by an employer rather than the "bottom line" representation of women and minority group members in the employer's workforce.

While the Civil Rights Act of 1991 modifies *Wards Cove,* the plaintiff is still required to try to prove the impact of each specific employment practice that she is challenging. Section 703(k)(1)(B), however, creates an exception allowing the use of "bottom line" statistics of the employer's workforce "if the complaining party can demonstrate to the court that the elements of a respondent's decisionmaking process are not capable of separation for analysis."

3. Where Both Disparate Treatment and Disparate Impact Theories Apply

Both systemic disparate treatment cases based on proof of an employer practice of discriminating and systemic disparate impact actions require proof of disparate impact. When both apply to the same case, two issues of the relationship between the theories are raised.

a. Less impact establishes disparate impact than disparate treatment. A less drastic level of impact is necessary to make out a disparate impact case than is required to prove that the employer's use of the practice was the product of discriminatory intent. The kind of "gross and longlasting" disparity showing necessary to draw the inference of intent to discriminate in a systemic disparate treatment case requires a showing of a more substantial amount of impact than the "disparate" impact necessary to support a disparate impact case. **The difference in language between the "gross and longlasting" disparity for systemic disparate treatment and the "disparate" impact showing for systemic disparate impact highlights that less impact will satisfy the impact rather than the treatment case.**

Some lower courts, however, require a plaintiff to show that the impact is statistically significant to make out a disparate impact case. While it is clear that showing a statistically significant reliance on race or gender would suffice to make out a disparate impact case, it does not follow, however, that a lesser amount of impact will not establish the necessary level of impact for an impact case.

Thus, a plaintiff claiming that a practice is both systemic disparate treatment and impact discrimination may fail to convince the finder of fact that the employer used the practice out of an intent to discriminate. Nevertheless, even though the amount of impact is insufficient to establish disparate treatment, the showing of impact may still suffice to make out a prima facie case of disparate impact discrimination.

b. Defending disparate treatment claims can concede disparate impact claims. The employer's defense strategy to a systemic disparate treatment claim may concede a prima facie case of disparate impact discrimination. Employers, facing potential liability for systemic disparate treatment discrimination, have a strong incentive to try to undermine plaintiff's case because they face the risk of full legal remedies that are not available in disparate impact actions. The employer can try to explain away the inference of intent to discriminate, particularly of "bottom line" statistics showing a drastic shortfall of women or minority men from what would be expected, by pointing out one or more employment practices that it uses that together produce the impact. Because those practices caused the impact, the employer lacked the intent to discriminate because it made its decisions "in spite of" rather than "because of" the impact. If accepted as a defense to the disparate treatment claim, that showing would operate as an admission that the practices the employer used caused a disparate impact.

The question following the codification of disparate impact in §703(k) by the Civil Rights Act of 1991 is whether only a "complaining party"—a plaintiff—can be the one who "demonstrates that a respondent"—the employer—uses a practice that causes the impact. It would seem that an employer should be liable if it admits a practice it uses has a disparate impact, thereby conceding a prima facie case of disparate impact discrimination.

Once a prima facie case of disparate impact discrimination is established, the employer can escape disparate impact liability only by proving that "the challenged practice is job related for the position in question and consistent with business necessity" or is justified by one of the §703(h) defenses for professionally developed tests and bona fide seniority and merit systems. Even with such a showing, liability for disparate impact discrimination might still attach if plaintiff can establish the existence of an alternative employment practice that the employer refuses to adopt.

EXAM TIP

When a systemic disparate treatment case is based on statistics showing a gross and long-lasting disparity between the employer's workforce and the labor pool from which the employer picks employees, a possible defense is that the employer used a particular practice that caused that impact. The use of that defense triggers a prima facie case of disparate impact discrimination, however, so the employer must try to prove the practice was within one of the defenses to disparate impact cases, such as business necessity/job relatedness, professionally developed test, or seniority or merit system.

 # EXAMPLE AND ANALYSIS

The employer runs a fishing factory every summer season in Alaska. While many of its cannery workers are members of minority groups, almost all of the non-cannery jobs are filled with whites. Systemic disparate treatment theory can be used to attack the exclusion of minority group members from the non-cannery jobs if the comparison of the workforce with the representation of minority group members in the qualified labor pool reveals that there is a "gross and longlasting disparity." The incumbent cannery workers might be the basis for the comparison if those workers in fact have the basic qualifications for the non-cannery jobs, or there may be another way to construct a comparison pool sufficient to be used for the systemic disparate treatment comparison.

If the factfinder makes a finding of gross and longlasting disparity that supports finding intentional systemic disparate treatment discrimination, liability is established if nothing else is involved. If, however, the finder of fact concludes that the amount of impact shown is not sufficient to establish the employer's intent to discriminate, then plaintiff loses on her systemic disparate treatment claim.

No disparate impact case exists unless the plaintiff has, in addition to the disparate treatment claim, claimed disparate impact discrimination by focusing on a particular employment practice or has convinced the court that the elements of the employer's decision-making process are not capable of separation for analysis. If, however, plaintiff has identified an employment practice of the employer that causes the impact, or, if the court finds plaintiff can, pursuant to §703(k)(1)(B)(i), treat the "decisionmaking process as one employment practice" for disparate impact purposes, then the court must determine if the amount of impact shown is substantial enough to support a prima facie case of disparate impact discrimination.

If, instead, the amount of impact is sufficient to support a finding of "gross and longlasting" impact that makes out a prima facie case of systemic disparate treatment and if the employer responds by introducing evidence of one or more employment practices that it uses that produce the impact, then the first question is whether the proof that these employment practices caused the impact is sufficient to support the conclusion that the employer did not act "because of" the discriminatory impact but "in spite of" it. If believed, that would support a finding that the employer did not act with the intent to discriminate necessary to make out a systemic disparate treatment case.

The showing that would allow the defendant to escape systemic disparate treatment liability would, however, appear to make out a prima facie case of disparate impact discrimination. The employer, however, would be liable for disparate impact discrimination unless the employer also proved the practices were justified by business necessity and were job related, were professionally developed tests, or were parts of a bona fide seniority system or of a bona fide merit or piecework system and the plaintiff failed to prove an alternative employment practice that the employer refuses to use. Cf., Wards Cove v. Atonio, 490 U.S. 642 (1989).

C. THE REALTIONSHIP BETWEEN THE TWO SYSTEMIC THEORIES AND INDIVIDUAL DISPARATE TREATMENT DISCRIMINATION

The relationship between systemic disparate treatment and systemic disparate impact on one hand and individual disparate treatment on the other has two aspects, depending on whether the systemic case is successful or not.

1. A Successful Systemic Case

Where a systemic disparate treatment or a systemic disparate impact case is successful and the action has been certified as a class action, all members of the class affected by the employer's discrimination are presumed to be entitled to relief. In Franks v. Bowman Transp. Co., 424 U.S. 747 (1976), the Court held that the employer could overcome that presumption by carrying the burden of persuasion by proving that it had not discriminated against particular individuals. Just because an employer generally discriminated does not mean necessarily that it discriminated in each individual's case. But, since the employer has been proven to be a discriminator, it is fair to require that the employer prove that it did not discriminate against the individual members of the class.

2. An Unsuccessful Systemic Case

Where a class action claiming a systemic theory of discrimination fails, that failure does not cut off the right of individuals within the class from pursuing their own claims of individual disparate treatment discrimination. Just because an employer has been shown not to discriminate generally does not mean that it did not discriminate in treating an individual on an ad hoc basis. The individual may proceed with her own action but she has the burden of proving that she was discriminated against. In Cooper v. Federal Reserve Bank of Richmond, 467 U.S. 867 (1984), the Supreme Court described what it called the manifest difference between individual and general practice claims of discrimination. "The inquiry regarding an individual's claim is the reason for a particular employment decision, while 'at the liability stage of a pattern-or-practice trial the focus often will not be on individual hiring decisions, but on a pattern of discriminatory decisionmaking.'"

EXAM TIP

A successful systemic case for plaintiff creates a presumption of relief for affected employees or applicants, but an unsuccessful systemic case does not cut off the claims of individuals.

EXAMPLE AND ANALYSIS

The employer operates a warehouse to supply its supermarkets. It installed a very rigorous computer-operated system of reviewing the performance of the employees who were order selectors. The computer calculated the amount of time each order should take to be filled and then compared that with the actual time the selector took to fill the order. The bottom 20 percent of the selectors who did not perform at the 100 percent level were subject to progressive discipline leading up to discharge. Eleven of the 52 selectors were discharged, with 10 of those discharged being age 40 or older. Because of "mistakes" in applying the system, eight younger workers who should have been fired were not and six older workers were fired when they should have been retained. After a number of older workers were discharged, the number of instances of discipline went down and, finally, the company stopped using its system.

At the broadest level, the question is whether this computer program was used with the intent to discriminate and was thus systemic disparate treatment discrimination. Not only were all but one of the discharged workers over age 40 with the result that 10 of the 27 older workers were discharged, but also the so-called errors in the system mostly worked to wrongly discharge older workers while wrongly saving the jobs of younger employees. This statistical and anecdotal evidence could support a finding of "gross and longlasting" disparity sufficient to draw an inference of intentional systemic discrimination by the employer.

Assume, instead, that the finder of fact does find not enough evidence, statistical and anecdotal, to support a finding of "gross and longlasting disparity" necessary to draw an inference that the employer acted with an intent to discriminate. Even with that finding, the use of the computer system is surely an employment practice that has a disparate impact on older workers. While there is a split of authority as to whether the disparate impact theory is available to plaintiffs under the ADEA, if it is, the question is whether the computer program with such impact is nevertheless justified because the employer can demonstrate that it is job related for the position in question and consistent with business necessity or is within one of the other defenses for professionally developed tests or a seniority or merit system. Defendants have a strong claim that the system is job related because it does measure job performance, even though it does so against an absolute and almost impossibly stringent standard. While filling orders from a warehouse is essential to the business of a supermarket chain, an absolute standard of performance may not be necessary for business. The system is not a test to determine whether someone will be able to perform a job and so it is not within the test exception. However, the argument may suffice that it is a merit system because it does determine actual performance levels of the employees. Since most other warehouses probably review selector performance in some less strenuous way, plaintiff may be able to show an alternative employment practice that the employer refuses to use.

Finally, the older workers who lost their jobs through the "errors" of the employer in running its system are likely to be successful in their individual age discrimination claims. While there was no "smoking gun" direct evidence, the suspicious circumstances that so many older workers were "erroneously" evaluated and then discharged based on those errors and that the program ended once many older workers were discharged makes it likely the finder of fact would conclude that it was age discrimination and not the operation of a fair system of job evaluation that caused the employees to be discharged. While making a mistake in evaluating workers is a reason other than age discrimination, most factfinders would, nevertheless, be likely to find that explanation a pretext for discrimination and that the employer in fact intended to discriminate because of age. See Fisher v. Transco Services-Milwaukee, Inc., 979 F.2d 1239 (7th Cir. 1992).

REVIEW QUESTIONS AND ANSWERS

Question: What is systemic disparate treatment discrimination?

Answer: Systemic disparate treatment discrimination is a formal policy of discrimination or a general practice of discriminating because of an intent to discriminate.

Question: What affirmative defense is available in a systemic disparate treatment case based on a formal policy of discrimination?

Answer: If the employer fails to rebut the existence of a policy of discrimination, only the BFOQ defense is available.

Question: What defenses are available to a systemic disparate treatment case based on proof of an employer practice of discriminating?

Answer: The only rebuttal is for the employer to undermine the evidence supporting plaintiff's case or the inference that the employer acted "because of" rather than "in spite of" the discriminatory impact.

Question: Is business necessity a defense to systemic disparate treatment discrimination?

Answer: No.

Question: What is systemic disparate impact discrimination?

Answer: Systemic disparate impact discrimination is the use of an employment practice that causes disparate impact to a group protected by an antidiscrimination statute which use is not justified by business necessity and job relatedness or one of the other statutory defenses.

Question: Is intent to discriminate an element of systemic disparate impact discrimination?

Answer: No.

Question: Does the employer necessarily win if it proves the challenged practice in a disparate impact case is job related and justified by business necessity?

Answer: Not necessarily, because the plaintiff still has the opportunity to prove the existence of an alternative employment practice that the employer refuses to adopt.

Question: What is individual disparate treatment discrimination?

Answer: Individual disparate treatment is adverse treatment of an employee or applicant because of the employer's intent to discriminate. Intent to discriminate can be proved by direct or circumstantial evidence.

Question: Is the same decision affirmative defense to full remedies available to all individual disparate treatment discrimination?

Answer: No, the same decision defense has so far only been available for cases based on direct evidence of discrimination.

Question: Do both systemic theories always apply to the same case?

Answer: Systemic disparate treatment is broader than systemic disparate impact. Systemic disparate impact does not apply to cases of systemic disparate treatment based on formal policies of discrimination. Further, systemic disparate impact does not apply unless plaintiff can prove that a particular employment practice causes the impact unless the elements of the employer's decision-making process are not capable of separation, in which case the whole process can be analyzed as one employment practice.

Question: Why do plaintiffs prefer bringing systemic disparate treatment to systemic disparate impact cases?

Answer: Intentional discrimination cases include the right to trial by jury and the possibility of compensatory and punitive damages in addition to the equitable remedies available in disparate impact cases.

Question: If both systemic theories apply, will the same amount of impact make out both?

Answer: The amount of impact to prove the impact is "substantial" to establish a disparate impact case is less than the amount necessary to conclude there is a "gross and longlasting disparity" for a disparate treatment case.

Question: Where both systemic theories apply, what happens if the employer rebuts the disparate treatment case by showing that practices it uses caused the impact, so that it did not act with an intent to discriminate since it acted "in spite of" the impact, not "because of" it?

Answer: Conceding that its employment practices cause such impact concedes a prima facie case of disparate impact which the employer must defend successfully to avoid liability for systemic disparate impact discrimination.

Question: Are the members of a class of employees entitled to relief if their employer is found liable for systemic discrimination?

Answer: Members of the class of employees affected by their employer's systemic discrimination are presumptively entitled to relief. The employer, however, can avoid liability to each individual in the class by proving that it had not discriminated against the individual.

Question: If the plaintiffs lose their systemic case against the employer, does that cut off the individual disparate treatment actions of the members of the class in the systemic action?

Answer: No, just because the employer does not engage in systemic discrimination does not mean it has not discriminated against individuals in an ad hoc way.

6 SPECIAL PROBLEMS OF GENDER DISCRIMINATION

CHAPTER OVERVIEW

This chapter covers four problems of gender discrimination not covered by the general theories of discrimination.

- **Pregnancy Discrimination.** The Pregnancy Discrimination Act amended Title VII to make pregnancy discrimination sex discrimination. The law, however, does not treat pregnancy exactly the same way as race, color, religion, sex, or national origin. **While the first clause of the PDA makes pregnancy discrimination discrimination because of sex, the second clause imposes an equal treatment requirement that pregnant women be ''treated the same . . . as other persons not so affected but similar in their ability or inability to work.''** The second clause affects how the three general theories of discrimination apply to claims of pregnancy discrimination.

  - **Individual Disparate Treatment.** Some courts have relied on this equal treatment test to require plaintiff to prove that another employee is similarly situated but for not being pregnant in order to establish discrimination because of pregnancy.

  - **Systemic Disparate Treatment.** The use of formal pregnancy classifications that treat pregnancy less favorably than other similar situations is systemic disparate treatment discrimination. Formal polices that treat pregnancy more favorably than other similar situations are not systemic disparate treatment.

- **Systemic Disparate Impact.** The equal treatment test of pregnancy discrimination means that disparate impact analysis is not directly applicable to a practice that has a disparate impact because of pregnancy.

- **Sexual Harassment.** There are three elements in a sexual harassment claim.

  - **The Harassment Is Either Quid Pro Quo or Hostile Environment Harassment.** Plaintiff must prove one of two kinds of harassment to make out a case of sexual harassment.

    - **Quid Pro Quo Harassment.** The essence of quid pro quo harassment is that the employee is threatened by a supervisor, "sex or your job." **Quid pro quo harassment is established if the employee enters a sexual relation in order to save her job or if the employee is punished with a tangible employment act for refusing to have sex.**

    - **Hostile Environment Harassment.** Claims of harassment other than quid pro quo claims are treated as hostile environment harassment. The essence of hostile environment harassment is when the workplace is "permeated with 'discriminatory intimidation, ridicule, and insult.'"

      - **Severe or Pervasive to Alter Employment Conditions.** To make out hostile environment harassment, **the harassment must be "sufficiently severe or pervasive to alter the conditions of the victim's employment and create an abusive working environment."**

      - **All the Circumstances Test.** All circumstances must be evaluated to determine if the harassment rose to the level of being severe or pervasive.

      - **Objective and Subjective.** The harassment must be both subjectively abusive and objectively abusive to a reasonable person in her position.

  - **The Harassment Must Be Because of Sex.** Whether the harassment is between male and female or between members of the same sex, harassment must be shown to be because of sex in order to violate Title VII.

  - **Employer Responsibility for Harassment.** To impose liability on the employer in either a quid pro quo or hostile environment case, the basis of employer liability depends on whether a supervisor or only co-workers were involved in the harassment.

    - **Supervisor Harassment. If a supervisor was the harasser,** then the employer is presumed liable because the supervisor's authority as an agent of the employer aids him in his harassment.

- **Tangible Employment Action.** If a supervisor was the harasser and the employee suffered a tangible employment action taken against her, the employer is liable to the employee.

- **No Tangible Employment Action.** If no tangible action was taken against the employee, the employer overcomes the presumption that the supervisor was aided in his harassment by his authority by proving an affirmative defense, which has two elements:

  - **Reasonable Employer Care to Prevent Harassment.** The employer must prove that it exercised reasonable care to prevent and correct promptly any sexually harassing behavior by having an effective anti-harassment policy that worked.

  - **Employee Failed to Take Advantage.** The employer must also prove that the plaintiff employee unreasonably failed to take advantage of any preventive or corrective opportunities provided by the employer or to avoid harm otherwise.

  - **Employer Negligence for Co-Worker Harassment.** Employer liability for co-worker harassment is limited to situations where the "employer is negligent with respect to sexual harassment if it knew or should have known about the conduct and failed to stop it."

- **Grooming and Dress Codes.** There is an exception to the rule that formal policies of sex discrimination are systemic disparate treatment violations for gender explicit dress and grooming codes unless those codes portray women as in less authority than similarly situated men.

- **Sexual Preference and Orientation.** Title VII does not protect against discrimination because of sexual preference or orientation, although same sex harassment does violate Title VII if proven to be because of sex.

A. THE FOUR SPECIAL GENDER DISCRIMINATION PROBLEMS

The general theories of discrimination studied in earlier chapters apply to sex discrimination cases. There are, however, four special problems that need be addressed that arise in gender discrimination. This chapter will look at the law concerning **pregnancy, sexual harassment, grooming and dress codes,** and **sexual orientation.**

B. PREGNANCY

Originally, Title VII was construed such that discrimination because of pregnancy was not sex discrimination. The Supreme Court, in General Electric Co. v. Gilbert, 429 U.S. 125 (1976), held that discrimination based the exclusion of pregnancy from health insurance coverage was not sex discrimination prohibited by Title VII. The pregnancy exclusion was not sex discrimination because the employer's insurance plan divided "potential recipients into two groups—

pregnant women and nonpregnant persons. While the first group is exclusively female, the second includes members of both sexes.''

1.   The Pregnancy Discrimination Act

Congress amended Title VII in the Pregnancy Discrimination Act of 1978 to overturn *Gilbert* by defining ''sex'' to include ''pregnancy.'' **Section 701(k),** which was added to Title VII, **has two separate clauses dealing with the employer's treatment of pregnancy:**

- **The terms ''because of sex''** or ''on the basis of sex'' **include,** but are not limited to, because of or **on the basis of pregnancy,** childbirth, or related medical conditions; and

- **women affected by pregnancy,** childbirth, or related medical conditions **shall be treated the same** for all employment-related purposes, including receipt of benefits under fringe benefit programs, **as other persons not so affected but similar in their ability or inability to work,** and nothing in section 703(h) of this title shall be interpreted to permit otherwise.

a.   The first clause. Had Congress merely added the first clause, making pregnancy sex discrimination, then cases involving pregnancy could proceed under the three general antidiscrimination theories—individual disparate treatment, systemic disparate treatment, and systemic disparate impact. The application might not be completely straightforward since women workers do get pregnant and at some point in the pregnancy and childbirth the employer would have to take account of the pregnancy.

b.   The second clause. The addition of the second clause—''women affected by pregnancy . . . shall be treated the same for all employment-related purposes, including receipt of benefits under fringe benefit programs, as other persons not so affected but similar in their ability or inability to work''—supposedly deals with the fact that pregnancy at some point does affect employment but the clause adds great complexity to pregnancy issues.

EXAM TIP

The second clause of the PDA clouds the application of the general concepts of individual disparate treatment to pregnancy and may foreclose directly the application of disparate impact law to pregnancy.

EXAMPLE AND ANALYSIS

Depending on the particular woman and on the nature of the job, most pregnant women need to stop working at some point near the end of the pregnancy and need some time to recover from childbirth. Susan Lee is near the end of her pregnancy and asks her employer, Mississippi.com, for three weeks off before her due date, plus leave for three weeks after she gives birth. If the employer grants or denies the pregnancy leave, it is acting "because of or on the basis of pregnancy, childbirth, or related medical conditions." Either taking account of or failing to take account of the effect of the pregnancy on the worker's ability to work violates the first clause. The second clause, "women affected by pregnancy . . . shall be treated the same for all employment-related purposes, including receipt of benefits under fringe benefit programs, as other persons not so affected but similar in their ability or inability to work," sets an equal treatment standard for determining what the employer should do and whether it violates Title VII. Under the equal treatment standard, Mississippi.com should grant her the pregnancy leave if it grants leaves to workers who are similarly situated in their inability to work. Thus, if Mississippi.com grants leaves to workers having knee replacement surgery, or triple bypass surgery, then it would violate Title VII to deny it to Lee. If, however, it does not give any leaves for any reason, then if does not violate Title VII by denying the leave to Lee.

2. The Effect of the PDA on the Main Theories of Discrimination

The following section shows how the Pregnancy Discrimination Act amendments to Title VII affect the three main theories of discrimination—individual disparate treatment discrimination, systemic disparate treatment discrimination, and systemic disparate impact discrimination.

a. Individual disparate treatment. The second, equal treatment clause of the PDA has proved to cause major problems in the application of individual disparate treatment law to pregnancy because it is not entirely clear what equal treatment means. While there is a split of authority, equal treatment should mean that the employer treats the pregnant employee in the same way it would have treated another employee similarly situated in terms of the ability to work but who was not pregnant.

 ## EXAMPLES AND ANALYSIS

1. Willa Sparrow is an employee of a major department store in a mall. During her pregnancy she was repeatedly tardy, which she ascribed to severe morning sickness.

The employer put her on probation because of the tardiness and discharged her, allegedly for continued tardiness, the day before she would have been eligible to take paid maternity leave under a fringe benefit plan of the employer. In Troupe v. May Department Stores Co., 20 F.3d 734 (7th Cir. 1994), the court relied on the second clause of the PDA as a basis for finding that plaintiff failed to prove a violation of the PDA because she could not prove that another employee was similarly situated with her in terms of tardiness but who was not discharged. "We must imagine a hypothetical Mr. Troupe, who is as tardy as Ms. Troupe was, also because of health problems, and who is about to take a protracted sick leave growing out of those problems at the expense of Lord & Taylor equal to that of Ms. Troupe's maternity leave. If Lord & Taylor would have fired our hypothetical Mr. Troupe, this implies that it fired Ms. Troupe not because she was pregnant but because she caused the company more trouble than she was worth to it." 20 F.3d at 738.

2. In Byrd v. Lakeshore Hospital, 30 F.3d 1380 (11th Cir. 1994), the Court took a different approach, holding that an employee alleging pregnancy discrimination need not show that the employer provided better treatment to nonpregnant employees but can win by showing that she was discharged for trying to use the fringe benefits generally available to workers: "it is a violation of the PDA for an employer to deny a pregnant employee the benefits commonly afforded temporarily disabled workers in similar positions, or to discharge a pregnant employee for using those benefits."

b. **Formal pregnancy policies are systemic disparate treatment.** Whether a formal classification of pregnancy violates the PDA depends on whether the classification serves to treat pregnancy less favorably or more favorably than other similar situations. The Family and Medical Leave Act ameliorates the need for the PDA in regard to employer policies regarding leaves of absences because it mandates family leaves.

i. **Formal policies treating pregnancy less favorably.** The use of formal pregnancy classifications that treat pregnancy less favorably than other similar situations is systemic disparate treatment discrimination. In Newport News Shipbuilding and Dry Dock Co. v. EEOC, 462 U.S. 669 (1983), a formal pregnancy classification put a cap on the pregnancy-related hospital benefits for spouses of employees but not for employees themselves. "The 1978 Act makes clear that it is discriminatory to treat pregnancy-related conditions less favorably than other medical conditions. Thus petitioner's plan unlawfully gives married male employees a benefit package for their dependents that is less inclusive than the dependency coverage provided to married female employees."

ii. **Formal policies treating pregnancy more favorably.** In California Federal Savings & Loan Assn. v. Guerra, 479 U.S. 272 (1987), the Court, echoing its treatment of affirmative action in *Weber* and *Johnson*, found that the second clause of §701(k) does not forbid employers from giving special preference for pregnancy benefits. The Court said that "Congress intended the PDA to be 'a floor beneath which pregnancy disability benefits may not drop—not a ceiling above which they may not rise.'" Thus, Title VII did not preempt a state law that required employers to provide an unpaid leave of absence to pregnant workers.

EXAMPLE AND ANALYSIS

In the above example concerning Susan Lee's request for six weeks pregnancy and childbirth leave from Mississippi.com, the employer may provide pregnancy and childbirth leave without violating Title VII, even if it does not provide leaves of absence for reasons other than pregnancy.

iii. **The family and medical leave act.** The Family and Medical Leave Act of 1993, 29 U.S.C.A. §2601 (1993), resolves some of the problems faced by pregnant women and parents of small children that are not fully resolved by the PDA. **FMLA requires that covered employers provide up to 12 weeks of unpaid leave "because of the birth of a son or daughter of the employee and in order to care for such son or daughter,** because of the placement of a son or daughter with the employee for adoption or foster care, in order to care for the spouse, or a son, daughter, or parent, of the employee, if such spouse, son, daughter, or parent has a serious health condition and because of a serious health condition that makes the employee unable to perform the functions of the position of such employee."

c. **Systemic disparate impact.** Since the second clause of the PDA appears to set an equal treatment test of discrimination, that may mean that disparate impact analysis is not available concerning pregnancy.

i. **Impact on pregnant women may be impact on women.** Since only women can get pregnant, but not all women do get pregnant, an employer rule that causes a disparate impact on pregnant women may not necessarily cause an impact on women generally. Nevertheless, where the impact of a rule on pregnant workers by that fact causes impact on women, the general disparate impact doctrine applies. EEOC v. Warshawsky & Co., 768 F. Supp. 647 (N.D. Ill. 1991).

 ## EXAMPLE AND ANALYSIS

United Airlines requires all customer service personnel to be able to lift 75 lb. bags and packages, even though not all the customer service personnel actually lift bags as a part of their job. At some point during pregnancy, it becomes increasingly difficult to lift heavy weights. Since disparate impact theory does not appear to apply to pregnancy discrimination claims under the PDA, the way to use the disparate impact approach would be to prove that this rule would have a disparate impact on women generally. If that could be shown, the employer would have to prove it was job related and necessary for business. Since lifting relatively heavy bags is at least part of the work some customer service workers must perform, the rule may be justified. Even so, the plaintiff might still be able to show that an alternative employment practice existed—such as allowing employees to work togther on heavy packages or assigning pregnant workers the jobs that did not entail heavy lifting—and that United Airlines refuses to adopt it. Cf., Deneen v. Northwest Airlines, 138 F.3d 204 (5th Cir. 1998).

C. SEXUAL HARASSMENT

There are three elements to a sexual harassment case.

EXAM TIP

Sexual harassment law is a very hot topic.

1. Harassment Is Either Quid Pro Quo or Hostile Environment Harassment

The first step in establishing a case of sexual harassment is to show that the case is either a quid pro quo or a hostile environment case. If sexual relations between a boss and a subordinate is involved, it is a quid pro quo case. Where sexual relations are not involved, the case is a hostile environment case. Thus, the **hostile environment rules apply if the case is not a quid pro quo case.** The range of fact patterns in which hostile environment can occur is quite broad, while quid pro quo harassment is focused on sexual relations between an employee and a supervisor.

EXAM TIP

When a question involves harassment, your answer should start with quid pro quo—"sex or your job"—and then analyze under the hostile environment approach as well.

a. **Quid pro quo sexual harassment.** The essence of quid pro quo harassment is that the employee is threatened by a supervisor, "sex or your job." The case is quid pro quo harassment if the employee relents and has sex or if she refuses and suffers a tangible employment action being taken against her.

   i. **Unwelcomeness focus on the victim.** In Meritor Savings Bank v. Vinson, 477 U.S. 57 (1986), the Court said, the **"gravamen of any sexual harassment claim is that the alleged sexual advances were 'unwelcome.'"** This element of unwelcomeness focuses on the victim's behavior. "The correct inquiry is whether [plaintiff] by her conduct indicated that the alleged sexual advances were unwelcome, not whether her actual participation in sexual intercourse was voluntary." 477 U.S. at 68. Turning the focus on the victim has a danger that the litigation will turn on her lifestyle rather than the conduct of the alleged perpetrator. Thus, in *Meritor,* the Court found that plaintiff's "sexually provocative speech or dress is [not] irrelevant as a matter of law in determining whether he or she found particular sexual advances unwelcome." 477 U.S. at 69. Nevertheless, the court in Burns v. McGregor Electronic Indus., 989 F.2d 959 (8th Cir. 1993), reversed a lower court that had found the conduct unwelcome but not offensive to the plaintiff based on her conduct off the job of posing nude for photos in motorcycle magazines. Plaintiff's private life "did not provide lawful acquiescence to unwanted sexual advances at her work place by her employer."

 EXAMPLE AND ANALYSIS

In Meritor Savings Bank v. Vinson, 477 U.S. 57 (1986), a worker claimed that she had been harassed by her manager who made repeated demands for sexual favors over a four-year period. In addition to having intercourse 40 to 50 times, plaintiff testified that the manager "fondled her in front of other employees, followed her into the women's restroom when she went there alone, exposed himself to her, and even forcibly raped her on several occasions." This was treated as a quid pro quo case because it involved sexual relations with a supervisor where plaintiff testified that, though unwelcome, she had sex with her supervisor out of a fear for loss of her job.

---

b. **Hostile environment harassment.** Where sexual relations between a supervisor and a subordinate is not involved, the Court in Harris v. Forklift Sys., Inc., 510 U.S. 17 (1993), said that a hostile environment case still can be made out when the workplace is "permeated with 'discriminatory intimidation, ridicule, and insult.'"

   i. **Severe or pervasive to alter employment conditions.** In *Harris,* the Court said that to make out hostile environment harassment, **the harassment must be 'sufficiently severe or pervasive to alter the conditions of the victim's employment** and create an abusive working environment.'" 510 U.S. at 21.

   ii. **All relevant circumstances test.** In deciding whether there is a hostile environment, it is necessary to look at all the circumstances, which include "the frequency of the discriminatory conduct; its severity; whether it is physically threatening or humiliating, or a mere offensive utterance; and whether it unreasonably interferes with an employee's work performance." 510 U.S. at 23.

   iii. **Objective and subjective harassment. The harassment must be both subjectively abusive to the plaintiff and objectively abusive** to a reasonable person in the position of the plaintiff. In *Harris,* the Court said, "Conduct that is not severe or pervasive enough to create an objectively hostile or abusive work environment—an environment that a reasonable person would find hostile or abusive—is beyond Title VII's purview. Likewise, if the victim does not subjectively perceive the environment to be abusive, the conduct has not actually altered the conditions of the victim's employment, and there is no Title VII violation." 510 U.S. at 21.

 # EXAMPLE AND ANALYSIS

In Harris v. Forklift Sys., Inc., 510 U.S. 20 (1993), the company president insulted the plaintiff because of her gender and often made her the target of unwanted sexual innuendo. For example, in the presence of others, he said such things as, "You're a woman, what do you know?," "We need a man as the rental manager," and he told her she was "a dumb-ass woman." Further, he suggested they go to the Holiday Inn to negotiate her raise and he occasionally asked plaintiff and other female employees to retrieve coins from his front pants pocket. Finally, while plaintiff was arranging a deal with a customer, he asked her, "What did you do, promise the guy some [sex] Saturday night?" Plaintiff eventually quit.

While the boss was the harasser, this was a hostile environment case since no sexual relations were threatened between the boss and the employee. The Court found these facts sufficient to prove hostile environment harassment.

---

c. **The boundary between quid pro quo and hostile environment harassment.** Quid pro quo harassment occurs when a supervisor threatens an employee's job if she does not have sex with him. If she gives in to his demands or if she refuses and the supervisor acts on the threat, it is a quid pro quo case. If, however, she refuses and the supervisor does not take the action he threatened, it is a hostile environment case. In Burlington Indus., Inc. v. Ellerth, 524 U.S. 742 (1998), the Court said, "Because Ellerth's claim involves only unfulfilled threats, it should be categorized as a hostile environment claim which requires a showing of severe or pervasive conduct."

EXAM TIP

Even if a supervisor threatens an employee's job if she does not have sex with him, the case may be a hostile environment case and not a quid pro quo case if she says no but the supervisor does not take action against the employee.

2. **The Harassment Must Be Because of Sex**

In Oncale v. Sundowner Offshore Servs., Inc., 523 U.S. 75 (1998), the Court found that harassment violates Title VII only when the plaintiff proves that the harassment was because of sex. Plaintiff **"must always prove that the conduct at issue was not merely tinged with offensive sexual connotations, but actually constituted 'discrimination . . . because of . . . sex.'"** That element of a sexual harassment case involves the following scenarios:

a. **Male-female quid pro quo harassment.** The *Oncale* Court said that, in quid pro quo cases, the inference that the harassment is because of sex is "easy to draw **in most male-female harassment situations, because the challenged conduct typically involves explicit or implicit proposals of sexual activity;** it is reasonable to assume those proposals would not have been made to someone of the same sex." 523 at 80.

b. Homosexual quid pro quo harassment. The Court in *Oncale* further elaborated that same sex harassment also establishes that the harassment was because of sex. "The same chain of inference would be available to a plaintiff alleging same-sex harassment, if there were credible evidence that the harasser was homosexual." 523 at 80.

c. Hostile environment harassment not motivated by sexual desire. Harassment not motivated by sexual desire can still violate Title VII where the harassment is shown to be because of sex. "A trier of fact might reasonably find [harassment because of sex], for example, if a female victim is harassed in such sex-specific and derogatory terms by another woman as to make it clear that the harasser is motivated by general hostility to the presence of women in the workplace. A same-sex harassment plaintiff may also, of course, offer direct comparative evidence about how the alleged harasser treated members of both sexes in a mixed-sex workplace." 523 at 80–81. Presumably, the "sex-specific and derogatory terms" of the harasser would establish that the hostile environment harassment was because of sex where the harasser was a man and the victim a woman, or vice versa, or where they were the same sex.

EXAM TIP

As long as the harassment is because of sex—whatever that means—it may violate Title VII even if the harassment does not involve sexual desire. This is important in some same sex harassment situations, as well as in jobs where women are pioneers, such as firefighting, where the harassment is used to drive them from the job.

 # EXAMPLE AND ANALYSIS

Joseph Oncale worked as a roustabout on an eight-man crew on an oil platform in the Gulf of Mexico. Apparently because his fellow crew members, including the two with supervisory power, thought he was a homosexual, they subjected him to sex-related, humiliating actions, physical assaults in a sexual manner, and threats of rape. Since there were no threats made to his job, this was not a quid pro quo case. It was, however, a hostile environment harassment case because his treatment was because of his sex. Oncale v. Sundowner Offshore Servs., Inc., 523 U.S. 75 (1998).

d. Harassment because of race, color, religion, and national origin also violates Title VII. Title VII's protection against harassment is not limited to harassment because of sex. The Court in *Harris* made it clear that hostile environment claims could be based on all the types of discrimination prohibited by Title VII: "a work environment abusive to employees because of their race, gender, religion, or national origin offends Title VII's broad rule of workplace equality." 510 U.S. at 22.

3. Employer Responsibility for Harassment

In *Meritor*, the Court held that plaintiff need not show that she suffered economic or tangible harm from the harassment to make out a case of harassment and, in *Harris,* the Court made clear that to establish harassment, plaintiff need not show that she suffered psychological injury. But the failure of plaintiff to prove that she suffered a tangible employment action raises an affirmative defense to employer liability where a supervisor is the harasser.

In *Meritor,* the Court found that the law of agency was the source for determining the liability of the employer for workplace harassment. The main focus of the agency question is whether a harassing supervisor is aided in his harassment by his authority as a supervisor and whether, as to co-worker harassment, the employer was negligent in that it knew or should have known of the harassing conduct and failed to stop it. In Burlington Industries, Inc. v. Ellerth, 524 U.S. 742, 757 (1998), the Court stated the general rule of employer liability for workplace harassment: "The general rule is that sexual harassment by a supervisor is not conduct within the scope of employment." There are, however, three major exceptions that can be the basis of employer liability for harassment in the workplace, depending on whether a supervisor or co-workers harass the victim and, where a supervisor is involved, whether the supervisor takes a tangible employment action against the victim.

a. A broad general rule of employer vicarious liability. In *Ellerth,* and in Faragher v. City of Boca Raton, 524 U.S. 775 (1998), decided with *Ellerth* and sharing the identical holding, the Court stated a broad rule of vicarious employer liability, with an affirmative defense if the supervisor did not take a tangible employment action against the victim. **"An employer is subject to vicarious liability to a victimized employee for an actionable hostile environment created by a supervisor with immediate (or successively higher) authority over the employee."** 524 U.S. at 765.

b. The supervisor takes a tangible employment action against the victim. Where it is shown that a supervisor has taken a tangible employment action against a victim of sex harassment, the employer is liable to the victim. **"No affirmative defense is available . . . when the supervisor's harassment culminates in a tangible employment action."** 524 U.S. at 765.

      i.   **Tangible employment action.** The Court in *Ellerth* broadly defined tangible employment action: **"A tangible employment action constitutes a significant change in employment status,** such as hiring, firing, failing to promote, reassignment with significantly different responsibilities, or a decision causing a significant change in benefits." 524 U.S. at 761.

EXAM TIP

Employers are liable to the victims of tangible employment actions by supervisors who harass, whether they are quid pro quo or hostile environment cases, even if the employer has an antiharassment policy in place.

---

    c.   **The supervisor does not take a tangible employment action.** The *Ellerth* Court created an affirmative defense to the general rule of employer vicarious liability for supervisor harassment if no tangible action was taken against the employee: **"When no tangible employment action is taken, a defending employer may raise an affirmative defense to liability or damages,** subject to proof by a preponderance of evidence. **The defense comprises two necessary elements: (a) that the employer exercised reasonable care to prevent and correct promptly any sexually harassing behavior, and (b) that the plaintiff employee unreasonably failed to take advantage of any preventive or corrective opportunities** provided by the employer or to avoid harm otherwise." 524 U.S. at 765.

        i.   **Employer acts to prevent harassment.** Presumably, there are two aspects to this element.

          (a)   **Anti-harassment policy.** At a global level, **employers now have a very strong incentive to adopt a sexual harassment policy.** As the Court said, "While proof that an employee had promulgated an anti-harassment policy with complaint procedure is not necessary in every instance as a matter of law, the need for a stated policy suitable to the employment circumstances may appropriately be addressed in any case when litigating the first element of the defense." 524 U.S. at 765.

If an employee did make use of an available complaint procedure, then the issue is whether the employer investigated promptly, corrected any harassing behavior, and protected the employee, even if the employer ultimately found that no harassment took place.

(b) **Employee failure to mitigate.** The second element looks to the behavior of the employee to determine if she took steps to avoid the harm, including the use of a complaint procedure made available in an anti-harassment policy. The Court said as to this element, "And while proof that an employee failed to fulfill the corresponding obligation of reasonable care to avoid harm is not limited to showing any unreasonable failure to use any complaint procedure provided by the employer, a demonstration of such failure will normally suffice to satisfy the employer's burden under the second element of the defense." 524 U.S. at 765.

When an employer claims it has an available anti-harassment policy that the employee failed to use, the main focus will be whether the policy was a safe way for an employee to complain of harassment that would lead the employer promptly to investigate the complaint and to correct any harassing behavior. The way in which the complaint procedure is structured as well as the way in which the employer administered it will be relevant to deciding whether the employee was unreasonable in failing to take advantage of the procedure.

EXAMPLES AND ANALYSIS

1. Kim Ellerth was a salesperson for Burlington Industries. Ted Slowik was a middle manager, one level above Ellerth's supervisor. On a business trip, Slowik invited Ellerth to a hotel lounge. When Ellerth gave no encouragement to remarks Slowik made about her breasts, he told her to "loosen up" and warned, "you know, Kim, I could make your life very hard or very easy at Burlington." Subsequently in a review for a promotion which Ellerth received, Slowik again told her to "loosen up" and he reached over and rubbed her knee. When Slowik called to announce her promotion, he told her that the men in the factories where she would be going as part of her new job "like women with pretty butts/legs." Finally, when Ellerth called to ask permission to help a customer, Slowik first told her that he did not have time to talk "unless you want to tell me what you're wearing." In a second call, Slowik asked whether she "was wearing shorter skirts yet, Kim, because it

would make your job a whole heck of a lot easier.'' Ellerth quit several days later after her immediate supervisor cautioned her to return promptly customer phone calls. She faxed the employer a letter with her reasons for quitting but she did not mention Slowik's harassment until she sent another letter three weeks later.

The Supreme Court found a summary judgment for Burlington was error and reversed for a trial. At trial, Ellerth will have to convince the finder of fact that Slowik's remarks amounted to threats to retaliate if she refused his sexual advances. Unless Ellerth can show at trial that she had suffered a tangible employment action, her claim will be subject to the employer's affirmative defense of proving that it had a reasonable anti-harassment policy with a complaint procedure and that Ellerth was unreasonable in not using it.

2. Beth Ann Faragher worked summers as a lifeguard for the city of Boca Raton, with her immediate supervisors being Bill Terry and David Silverman. In bringing a hostile environment harassment claim, Faragher claimed that both Terry and Silverman repeatedly subjected female lifeguards to offensive touching and lewd and offensive remarks. Faragher quit without making any complaint to the city concerning their behavior. Since Faragher did not claim that any tangible employment action had been taken against her, the employer theoretically had available the newly articulated affirmative defense. But, the Court upheld the judgment for Faragher because the city failed to exercise reasonable care, failed to disseminate its anti-harassment policy to its employees, did not track the conduct of supervisors, and did not include in the policy any assurance that employees could safely bypass their supervisors to file complaints of harassment against them. Since Faragher sought only nominal damages, there was no reason to remand for consideration of Faragher's duty to mitigate.

---

d. **Co-worker hostile environment harassment.** Where the harasser or harassers are not in a supervisory position over the victim of the harassment, the case is treated as a hostile environment case, even if demands are made for sexual relations. That is because co-workers typically lack the power to threaten the job of the victim. In *Ellerth*, the Court described this lack of power: "one co-worker (absent some elaborate scheme) cannot dock another's pay, nor can one co-worker demote another." 524 U.S. at 762.

Employer liability for co-worker harassment is limited to situations where the "employer is negligent with respect to sexual harassment if it knew or should have known about the conduct and failed to stop it."

EXAM TIP
Employers are liable for harassment by co-workers (versus supervisors) only if the employer was negligent in allowing known harassment to continue.

D. GROOMING AND DRESS CODES

There is an exception from Title VII's proscription of formal policies of sex discrimination for gender explicit dress and grooming codes. Willingham v. Macon Telegraphy Publ. Co., 507 F.2d 1084 (5th Cir. 1975).

There is, however, some authority that while separate dress codes for men and women are not per se disparate treatment, those codes must be applied so that they do not create an erroneous impression as to the authority or rank of men and women. In Carroll v. Talman Federal Savings & Loan Ass'n, 604 F.2d 1028 (7th Cir. 1979), *cert. denied,* 445 U.S. 929 (1980), the court struck down a bank's rule that required women but not men in the same job category to wear uniforms. "While there is nothing offensive about uniforms per se, when some employees are uniformed and others not, there is a natural tendency to assume that the uniformed women have a lesser professional status than their male colleagues attired in normal business clothes."

E. SEXUAL ORIENTATION

Title VII does not protect employees against discrimination because of homosexuality, transexuality, or bisexuality. In DeSantis v. Pacific Telephone & Telegraph Co., 608 F.2d 327 (9th Cir. 1979), the court concluded that, "Title VII's prohibition of 'sex' discrimination applies only to discrimination on the basis of gender and should not be judicially extended to include sexual preference such as homosexuality." The basis for that conclusion was a finding that Congress did not intend the term "sex" to include sexual orientation or preference. Since Congress did not intend to protect workers against sexual orientation discrimination, the *DeSantis* court also found that the disparate impact theory of discrimination was also not available even in the face of the claim "that discrimination against homosexuals disproportionately affects men because of the greater incidence of homosexuality in the male population and because of the greater likelihood of an employer's discovering male homosexuals compared to female homosexuals." Characterizing the claim as a "bootstrap," the court concluded "that the *Griggs* disproportionate impact theory may not be applied to extend Title VII protection to homosexuals."

Sexual harassment is the one area in which Title VII has provided some protection. Thus, same-sex harassment was found to violate Title VII where the plaintiff can prove that the harassment was because of sex. In Oncale v. Sundowner Offshore Servs., Inc., 523 U.S. 75 (1998), the Court overturned a lower court ruling that same-sex harassment was not prohibited by Title VII. Plaintiff claimed the harassment was because he was perceived to be a homosexual and that the sexual nature of the harassment showed it to be because of sex. Conversely, the Court acknowledged that, in the same-sex situation, if the harasser is a homosexual, it is reasonable to draw the inference that the harassment was because of sex.

REVIEW QUESTIONS AND ANSWERS

Question: Do the PDA amendments to Title VII mean that pregnancy is treated the same as sex discrimination?

Answer: While the first clause of the PDA says discrimination because of pregnancy is discrimination because of sex, the second clause adds an equal treatment test that means pregnancy cases are not treated exactly like other sex discrimination cases.

Question: What does the second clause of the PDA mean in individual disparate treatment cases?

Answer: While there is a split among courts, plaintiff must at least show that she was not treated the same as others similarly situated who are not pregnant.

Question: Does the PDA prohibit all formal employer classifications dealing with pregnancy?

Answer: No. While formal policies treating pregnancy unfavorably violate the PDA, this law sets a floor, not a ceiling, so that employers can enact formal policies treating pregnancy more favorably than similar situations not involving pregnancy.

Question: Does an employer practice, neutral on its face as to pregnancy, violate Title VII if it causes an impact on pregnant workers?

Answer: The equal treatment test of the second clause of the PDA probably means that disparate impact discrimination theory does not apply to pregnancy itself. But an employer practice concerning pregnancy may be subject to disparate impact analysis if the practice can be shown to have an impact on women generally.

Question: How many different types of sexual harassment violate Title VII?

Answer: Two types of sexual harassment—quid pro quo and hostile environment—violate Title VII.

Question: What are the three elements in a sexual harassment action?

Answer: The first is to prove either quid pro quo or hostile environment harassment. The second is that the harassment is because of sex. And, to establish employer liability, the third is that a supervisor was a harasser or, if co-workers were the harassers, that the employer knew or should have known of the harassment and failed to do anything about it.

Question: What is quid pro quo harassment?

Answer: The essence of quid pro quo harassment is that the employee is presented by a supervisor with an unwelcome threat, "sex or your job."

Question: What is hostile environment harassment?

Answer: The essence of hostile environment harassment is when the workplace is permeated with discriminatory intimidation, ridicule, and insult, that is so severe or pervasive that it alters a condition of employment when judged objectively by a reasonable person in the position of the plaintiff as well as subjectively by the plaintiff herself.

Question: If a supervisor is a harasser, is the employer always liable to the employee?

Answer: The employer is vicariously liable if a supervisor is a harasser and if a tangible employment action is taken against the employee. If a supervisor is the harasser and no tangible employment action is taken, the employer can escape liability to the employee if it can prove that it had acted reasonably to prevent and correct harassment and that the employee unreasonably failed to mitigate her injury.

Question: Do formal policies of gender explicit dress and grooming codes violate Title VII?

Answer: Not unless the policy operates to wrongly suggest women have less authority than similarly situated men.

Question: Does Title VII prohibit discrimination because of sexual preference or orientation?

Answer: Although homosexuals are protected against harassment because of their sex, Title VII does not prohibit discrimination because of sexual preference or orientation.

SPECIAL PROBLEMS OF RELIGIOUS DISCRIMINATION

 CHAPTER OVERVIEW

The three general theories of discrimination apply to religious discrimination claims. In addition, Title VII provides a cause of action to employees if their employers fail to reasonably accommodate their religious beliefs and practices, two special exemptions allowing discrimination by certain religious employers in favor of members of particular religions, as well as the general BFOQ defense to disparate treatment discrimination. Since Congress enacted these provisions, these statutes raise questions as to their constitutionality under the Establishment Clause of the First Amendment. Finally, the Free Exercise Clause may give religious employers the right to discriminate because of race, color, sex, and national origin in employment decisions involving employees key to their religious mission.

- **Section 701(j) Reasonable Accommodation Action.** Title VII requires employers to accommodate the religious beliefs of its employees, but the Supreme Court has read this duty to accommodate quite narrowly.

- **Plaintiff's Prima Facie Case.** There are four elements a plaintiff must prove to establish a prima facie case of failure to accommodate.

  - **A Sincere Religious Belief.** Plaintiff must prove that his religious belief is sincere.

  - **The Belief Conflicts with Employer's Rule.** The accommodation duty only arises when the religious needs of the employee conflict with an employment rule.

- **The Employer Knew of Conflict.** The employer cannot accommodate the religious beliefs of an employee if it does not know that those beliefs conflict with an employment rule.

- **The Employer Did Not Satisfy Plaintiff's Belief.** Whether or not the employer took any action to attempt to accommodate the plaintiff, the conflict between the employee's belief and the employer's rule must not be fully resolved.

- **The Employer's Rebuttal Burden.** Proof of a prima facie case shifts the burden of persuasion to the employer to demonstrate either:

  - **A Reasonable Accommodation Was Provided.** If the court finds that the employer did provide an accommodation that it finds to be reasonable, that ends plaintiff's case under §703(j), even if that accommodation did not satisfy the plaintiff.

  - **Any Cost Over a De Minimis Cost Is An Undue Hardship.** The issue of undue hardship of the accommodation plaintiff proposes becomes relevant only if the employer fails to offer the employee any accommodation or the accommodation offered is not reasonable. The standard of what is undue hardship is any cost above a de minimis level.

- **Title VII's Exemptions for Employers to Discriminate Because of Religion.** There are three statutory grounds that allow an employer to discriminate because of religion: (1) religious discrimination by religious institutions; (2) religious discrimination by educational institutions that propagate a particular religion in their curriculum; and (3) specific instances of religious discrimination by the employer, whether or not it is a religious organization, that can prove that religion is a bona fide occupational qualification reasonably necessary to the normal operation of that particular business or enterprise.

- **The Constitutionality of Title VII's Treatment of Religion.** The Free Exercise and Establishment Clauses of the First Amendment raise questions concerning the constitutionality of Title VII's treatment of religion.

  - **Section 703's Duty Not to Discriminate and the Free Exercise Clause.** The Free Exercise Clause makes the application of the basic proscriptions against discrimination unconstitutional when applied to key positions of religious institutions.

  - **Section 702's Religious Institutions Exemption and the Establishment Clause.** Section 702(a), which gives to religious organizations, and §703(e)(2), which gives to schools that use their curricula to propagate religion, the authority to discriminate in favor of members of their own religion do not violate the Establishment Clause of the First Amendment.

- **Section 701(j)'s Accommodation Duty and the Establishment Clause.** The duty of an employer to reasonably accommodate the religious practices and beliefs of employees required by §701(j) probably does not violate the Establishment Clause.

A. THE FOUR SPECIAL PROBLEMS OF RELIGIOUS DISCRIMINATION

The three general theories of discrimination apply to claims of religious discrimination. One wrinkle is that, in an individual disparate treatment case claiming religious discrimination, plaintiff must prove that defendant knew plaintiff's religion. Van Koten v. Family Health Management, Inc. 1998 U.S. App. LEXIS 1837 (7th Cir. 1998).

While it is individual disparate treatment discrimination to refuse to hire or to fire someone because of her religion, it is also religious discrimination to discriminate against an employee for not belonging to a particular religion. For example, in Shapolia v. Los Alamos Natl. Laboratory, 992 F.2d 1033 (10th Cir. 1993), plaintiff claimed he was discriminated against because of religion because he was *not* a Mormon.

Title VII also treats religions specially in three ways and that special treatment raises the fourth special problem, the constitutionality of that treatment under the Free Exercise and Establishment Clauses of the First Amendment.

B. THE DUTY TO ACCOMMODATE EMPLOYEES' RELIGIOUS PRACTICES

In 1972, **Congress amended Title VII to create a special cause of action for the failure of an employer to reasonably accommodate the religious beliefs and practices of employees or applicants.** Section 701(j) imposes this reasonable accommodation duty on employers through its definition of "religion."

The term "religion" includes all aspects of religious observance and practice, as well as belief, unless an employer demonstrates that he is unable to reasonably accommodate to an employee's or prospective employee's religious observance or practice without undue hardship on the conduct of the employer's business.

1. The Contrast with Disparate Treatment and Disparate Impact

Unlike disparate treatment, which is premised on the requirement that the employer not take religion into account in making employment decisions, the reasonable accommodation concept requires the employer to focus on at least the consequences for its workplace of the religious practices of the employee. Reasonable accommodation is like an individualized disparate impact theory because it requires the employer to review and modify its general policies and practices for each worker to be able to work and to practice her religion.

EXAMPLES AND ANALYSIS

1. In Wilson v. U.S. West Communications, 58 F.3d 1337 (8th Cir. 1995), plaintiff made a religious vow that she would wear an anti-abortion button until abortion ended. The face of the button included a color photograph of an 18- to 22-week old fetus and included the phrases "Stop Abortion" and "They're Forgetting Someone." When other employees, including some who shared her religious views about abortion, objected to the button, the employer offered the accommodation that she cover the button at work. Therefore, the case was analyzed as a reasonable accommodation case and the employer's preferred accommodation was found reasonable, even though it did not satisfy the plaintiff. Note, however, that if the objections of plaintiff's employer or her co-workers had been shown to be religious-based, then this would appear to be an individual disparate treatment case and not one of failure to reasonably accommodate.

2. In Brown v. Polk County, Iowa, 61 F.3d 650 (8th Cir. 1995) (en banc), plaintiff, a born-again Christian who served as director of the data processing department of Polk County, was terminated in part because of his religious activities such as having a secretary type his notes from a Bible study class as well as his spontaneous prayer and references to Bible passages during meetings of his department. In response to plaintiff's claim that he was the victim of individual disparate treatment because of his religion, the court, instead, analyzed the case as a reasonable accommodation case. Had it been treated as a disparate treatment case, it is clear that the employer took its actions against Brown because of his religion. The issue would be whether that action was nevertheless justified based on the bona fide occupational qualification that employees of public employers cannot be allowed to act in ways that cause the employer to violate the Establishment Clause of the First Amendment.

---

2. **The Structure of a §703(j) Case**

Plaintiff must prove four elements to establish a prima facie case that the employer failed to reasonably accommodate his religious beliefs and practices. The employer's rebuttal may be made on either of two possible grounds.

a. **The prima facie accommodations case.** There are four elements a plaintiff must prove to establish a prima facie case of failure to accommodate. The prima facie case is relatively easy to establish.

i.   **A sincere religious belief. Plaintiff must prove that his religious belief is sincere. Religious belief is broadly defined and is hard to rebut.** Based on the jurisprudence developed in conscientious objector cases dealing with military service, a sincere religious belief is one that assumes the function of religion in the person's life. The fact that plaintiff's belief evolved over time or even changed after the need to accommodate issue passed does not necessarily undermine the finding of sincerity. See EEOC v. IBP, Inc., 824 F. Supp. 147 (C.D. Ill. 1993) (employee's belief sincere even though, both before Sabbath work became an issue and after he left the company, plaintiff worked on his Sabbath).

ii. **The belief conflicts with employer's rule.** It is usually easy for the plaintiff to prove that his religious belief, or the practice or observance required by his belief conflicts with the employer's rule since it is that conflict that generated the problem in the first place.

iii. **The employer knew of conflict.** An employer need have "only enough information about an employee's religious needs to permit the employer to understand the existence of a conflict between the employee's religious practices and the employer's job requirements." Heller v. EBB Auto Co., 8 F.3d 1433, 1439 (9th Cir. 1993).

iv. **The employer did not satisfy plaintiff's belief.** The plaintiff must prove that, whether or not the employer took any action to attempt to accommodate the plaintiff, the employer did not satisfy plaintiff so that the conflict between the employee's belief and the employer's rule is not fully resolved.

b. **The employer's rebuttal burden.** Proof of a prima facie case shifts the burden of persuasion to the employer to demonstrate either that it made an accommodation that was reasonable or that any accommodation that would meet the employee's needs would be an undue burden on the employer's business. Despite the broad formulation of the accommodation duty in the statute, the Supreme Court has read §701(j) quite narrowly.

i.   **An accommodation that is reasonable need not fully accommodate the employee's belief.** In Ansonia Bd. of Educ. v. Philbrook, 479 U.S. 60 (1986), the Court ruled that, "By its very terms the statute directs that **any reasonable accommodation by the employer is sufficient to meet its accommodation obligation.**" Thus, the fact that the accommodation provided plaintiff did not completely satisfy his religious practice needs was irrelevant once the employer provided some accommodation that a court found "reasonable." Once the employer has "reasonably accommodated the employee's religious needs, the statutory inquiry is at an end. The employer need not further show that each of the employee's alternative accommodations would result in undue hardship."

Unlinking the needs of the employee from the determination that the employer's accommodation was reasonable makes it very difficult to figure out what is reasonable in the abstract.

EXAM TIP

In a religious accommodations case, the plaintiff can lose as long as the employer does something to meet the religious needs of the plaintiff, even if that accommodation does not actually solve the conflict between the employer's rules and the employee's needs. This can happen without getting to the undue hardship issue—but you should always argue that in the alternative.

 # EXAMPLES AND ANALYSIS

---

1. Philbrook was a member of a religion that required its members to attend religious meetings that would take him from his work on six days a year. In its collective bargaining agreement with a union, the employer had provided for three paid days for religious observances. The Court found that the three-day leave was a reasonable accommodation, even though it did not fully meet the needs of Philbrook. Because of that, the employer did not need to consider whether plaintiff's proposed accommodation, which would allow him to use three paid personal days of leave that were provided by the employer for reasons other than the leaves specified in the union contract, was an undue hardship on the employer's business. Ansonia Bd. of Educ. v. Philbrook, 479 U.S. 60 (1986).

2. In Wilson v. U.S. West Communications, 58 F.3d 1337 (8th Cir. 1995), the employer offered an accommodation to the plaintiff, whose religious beliefs required her to wear a graphic anti-abortion button, that she could wear the pin but had to keep it covered while at work. The court found this accommodation reasonable by narrowly defining her belief as requiring her only to wear the pin and not to be a "living witness" to that belief. Finding the employer's accommodation reasonable, the court found it did not have to address whether the accommodation plaintiff sought would be an undue hardship.

Both *Philbrook* and *Wilson* involved an accommodation that at least partially met the needs of the plaintiff but it is not clear how the "reasonableness" of the accommodation is to be determined if it does not meet the needs of the employee.

         ii.   Any cost over a de minimis cost is an undue hardship. Only if the employer fails to offer the employee any accommodation or the accommodation offered fails to meet the reasonable test of *Philbrook*, does the issue of the undue hardship become relevant. In Trans World Airlines, Inc. v. Hardison, 432 U.S. 63 (1977), the employer failed to offer any accommodation to the scheduling needs of a Saturday Sabbatarian but the Court held that any accommodation that would satisfy the employee would involve undue hardship when judged against a de minimis cost standard. "To require TWA to bear more than a de minimis cost in order to give Hardison Saturdays off is an undue hardship."

 ## EXAMPLE AND ANALYSIS

In Brown v. Polk County, Iowa, 61 F.3d 650 (8th Cir. 1995) (en banc), the court analyzed plaintiff's case that he was terminated because of his religious practices on the job as a reasonable accommodation case like *Hardison* where the employer made no attempt to accommodate plaintiff's religious activities. The court found that the employer did not violate Title VII by disciplining the plaintiff for directing a secretary to type his Bible study notes since it would be an undue hardship to allow such activity. But, as to allowing spontaneous prayers, occasional affirmations of Christianity, and isolated references to the Bible during meetings of the department, the employer failed to prove any undue hardship. Simply arguing that Brown's actions might foster favoritism for born-again Christians or create religious divisions in plaintiff's department did not rise to the level of proof. Thus, the burden defendants' "would have to bear by tolerating trifling instances such as those complained of are insufficiently 'real,' and too 'hypothetical,' to satisfy the standard required to show undue hardship."

C.   TITLE VII'S EXEMPTIONS FOR EMPLOYERS TO DISCRIMINATE BECAUSE OF RELIGION

There are three statutory grounds that allow an employer to discriminate because of religion.

1. The Religious Employer Exemption

Section 702(a) provides that Title VII shall **not** apply "to a **religious corporation, association, educational institution, or society** with respect to the employment of **individuals of a particular religion** to perform work connected with the carrying on by such corporation, association, educational institution, or society of its activities."

In EEOC v. Kamehameha Schools/Bishop Estate, 990 F.2d 458 (9th Cir. 1993), the schools, which had been set up by a will and trust, required, pursuant to the grantor's will, that "the teachers of said school shall forever be persons of the Protestant religion." In deciding that the schools were not religious institutions for purposes of §702(a), the court applied a case-by-case factual approach and found that the "ownership and affiliation, purpose, faculty, student body, student activities, and curriculum of the Schools are either essentially secular, or neutral as far as religion is concerned." 990 F.2d at 461. The religious characteristics consisted of "minimal, largely comparative religious studies, scheduled prayers and services, [and] quotation of Bible verses in a school publication. . . . [T]he addition of nominally Protestant teachers does not alter [the conclusion that the school was not a religious institution]." 990 F.2d at 463.

2. The Religious Curriculum Exemption

Section 703(e)(2) provides that, "It shall not be an unlawful employment practice for a school . . . to hire and employ employees of a particular religion . . . if the curriculum of such school . . . is directed toward the propagation of a particular religion." The court in *Kamehameha Schools* found that since the schools did not propagate a particular religion, the curriculum was not within the §703(e)(2) exemption. "Courses *about* religion and a general effort to teach good values do not constitute a curriculum that propagates religion, especially in view of the Schools' express disclaimer of any effort to convert their non-Protestant students." 990 F.2d at 465.

3. The Bona Fide Occupational Qualification

Section 703(e)(1) provides that it shall not be unlawful for an employer "to employ any individual in any certain instances where religion . . . is a bona fide occupational qualification reasonably necessary to the normal operation of that particular business or enterprise." See Chapter 3.G, supra, for a general discussion of the BFOQ defense. In *Kamehameha Schools*, the court found the BFOQ defense did not apply to the teachers' positions because there is "nothing to suggest that adherence to the Protestant faith is essential to the performance of this job." Employers that are not religious need not be religious organizations to assert the BFOQ if the nature of their business requires that religion be taken into account.

EXAMPLES AND ANALYSIS

1. In Pime v. Loyola University of Chicago, 803 F.2d 351 (7th Cir. 1986), the court upheld a quota that reserved three positions in the philosophy department for members of the Jesuit religious order on the ground that a Jesuit "presence" was important to the successful operation of the university, even though Loyola was not a religious institution entitled to the §702(a) exemption. That decision, however, predated and may not survive the Supreme Court's narrowing of the BFOQ defense to the essence of the business in International Union, UAW v. Johnson Controls, Inc., 499 U.S. 187 (1991).

2. An employer is not a religious organization but is in the business of flying helicopter tours over Mecca in Saudi Arabia. Saudi Arabia law forbids non-Moslems from entering or even flying above holy sites. The employer's rule that all helicopter pilots be Moslems was upheld as a BFOQ since flying over Mecca is the essence of the business and no one who is not a Moslem can legally do it. Kern v. Dynalection Corp., 577 F. Supp. 1196 (N.D. Tex. 1983).

D. THE CONSTIUTIONALITY OF TITLE VII'S TREATMENT OF RELIGION

The First Amendment of the Constitution provides: "Congress shall make no law respecting an establishment of religion, or prohibiting the free exercise thereof." Because Title VII is a statute enacted by Congress that concerns religion, there are two First Amendment issues involving Title VII's treatment of religion based on the religion clauses of the First Amendment. The first is whether, even with the availability of the BFOQ defense for religion, §703's basic prohibition against discrimination because of race, color, sex, and national origin violates the Free Exercise Clause as applied to a church, temple, or mosque. The second question is whether Title VII's special exemptions in §702(a) for religious institutions, §703(e)(2) for educational institutions with a religious curriculum, and §701(j)'s requirement that employers accommodate the religious beliefs of employees violate the Establishment Clause.

EXAM TIP

If an employer in a fact pattern is in some sense religiously affiliated, make sure to deal with both the question of statutory exclusion and the question of the constitutionality of such an exclusion.

1. **Section 703's Duty Not to Discriminate and the Free Exercise Clause**

While §702 exempts religious institutions from the proscription of religious discrimination in employment, the basic antidiscrimination provision, §703, applies to discrimination by religious employers because of race, color, national origin, and sex. The argument for the unconstitutionality of §703 is that it violates the Free Exercise Clause by interfering with the ability of a religious organization to fill core positions necessary to carry out the mission of the organization and that it violates the Establishment Clause because the enforcement of §703 entangles the government in the operations of religions.

In EEOC v. The Catholic University of America, 83 F.3d 455, 461 (D.C. Cir. 1996), the court held that **§703 violated the Free Exercise Clause. "[T]he Free Exercise Clause exempts the selection of clergy from Title VII** and similar statutes and, as a consequence, precludes civil courts from adjudicating employment discrimination suits by ministers against the church or religious institutions employing them." This so-called ministerial exception is not limited to members of the clergy, but applies to lay employees whose "primary duties consist of teaching, spreading the faith, church governance, supervision of a religious order, or participation in religious ritual and worship." 83 F.3d at 461.

 ## Examples and Analysis

In EEOC v. The Catholic University of America, plaintiff claimed that the university had discriminated against her because of her sex in denying her tenure as a professor in the canon law department. The university defended, claiming that the application of §703's proscription of sex discrimination to such a position violated the Free Exercise Clause of the First Amendment. The court agreed, finding that plaintiff's responsibilities as a member of the canon law faculty would be essentially religious because the job was to teach "sacred doctrine."

While in the *Catholic University* case a decision on the merits would have required the court to evaluate plaintiff's scholarship on canon law, which would have raised issues of religious doctrine, the court in Combs v. Central Texas Annual Conference of the United Methodist Church, 173 F.3d 343 (5th Cir. 1999), applied the ministerial exception to the discharge of a minister where no doctrinal disputes were involved.

2.   Section 702's Religious Institutions Exemption and the Establishment Clause

The special treatment §702(a) gives to religious organizations and §703(e)(2) gives to schools that use their curricula to propagate religion to discriminate in favor of members of their own religion does not violate the Establishment Clause of the First Amendment. In Corporation of the Presiding Bishop v. Amos, 483 U.S. 327 (1987), where the religious employer required employees of a gym it owned to be Mormon, the Supreme Court, applying the three-part test from Lemon v. Kurtzman, 403 U.S. 602 (1971), upheld the constitutionality of §702(a)

a.   **The law serves a secular purpose.** The first element of the *Lemon* test is that the law at issue must serve a **"secular legislative purpose."** Section 702 was found to have a secular purpose because it alleviated significant governmental interference with the ability of religious organizations to define and carry out their religious missions. 483 U.S. at 335.

b.   **The primary effect must not advance religion.** The second part of the *Lemon* test is that the law in question must have a principal or **primary effect** that neither advances nor inhibits religion. While acknowledging that §702 better allows religious organizations to advance their purposes, the Court found that its primary effect was not to advance religion. For a law to have the forbidden effect the government itself must be advancing religion through its own activities and influence. Here, none of the advancement of religion by the gymnasium could "be fairly attributed to the Government, as opposed to the Church." 483 U.S. at 337. The employee's "freedom of choice in religious matters was impinged upon but it was the Church, . . . and not the Government, who put him to the choice of changing his religious practices or losing his job." 483 U.S. at 337 n.15. The fact that only religious organizations, and not a larger category of charitable organizations, are subject to the §702 exemption and that there is no historical tradition for such an exemption was not determinative.

c.   **No impermissible entanglement of church and state.** The third prong in the *Lemon* test is that the law in question does not impermissibly entangle the state in the operations of a church. Rather than entangle the church and state, the Court found that §702 "effectuates a more complete separation of the two and avoids the kind of intrusion into religious belief" that occurs when there is impermissible entanglement. 483 U.S. at 339.

The concurring opinions of Justices Brennan and O'Connor emphasized that the gymnasium involved in the case was a nonprofit operation. They thought that an Establishment Clause claim would be made out if a religious organization attempted to rely on the §702 exemption to discriminate because of religion in profit-making activities. That would give the religions an unfair advantage in business competition with nonreligious employers.

 EXAMPLE AND ANALYSIS

Plaintiff, who had been an employee for 16 years of a gymnasium owned and operated by the Mormon church, was discharged because he did not qualify as a member of the Mormon church. While Corporation of the Presiding Bishop v. Amos, 483 U.S. 387 (1987), will defeat plaintiff's suit if the gym is not profit-making, a suit might be successful if the gym was a money-making venture that just happened to be owned by a church.

3.   Section 701(j)'s Accommodation Duty and the Establishment Clause.

It seems likely that §701(j) would be found constitutional, though it may be a close case based on Estate of Thornton v. Caldor, Inc., 472 U.S. 503 (1986). The state law attacked in *Thornton* prohibited an employer from requiring an employee to work on a day designated as her Sabbath and thus required absolute accommodation and not just the reasonable accommodation without undue influence required by §701(j). In upholding §701(j) in Protos v. Volkswagen of America, Inc., 797 F.2d 129 (3d Cir.), *cert. denied*, 479 U.S. 972 (1986), the court distinguished *Thornton*. "Unlike the Connecticut statute, Title VII does not require absolute deference to the religious practices of the employee, allows for consideration of the hardship to other employees and to the company, and permits an evaluation of whether the employer has attempted to accommodate the employee. . . . Any effect the statute had of advancing religion, therefore, would appear to be incidental to its primary effect of promoting freedom of conscience and prohibition discrimination in the workplace."

REVIEW QUESTIONS AND ANSWERS

Question: Do employers have the duty to accommodate the religious beliefs and practices of employees?

Answer: Section 701(j) requires employers to reasonably accommodate the religious beliefs and practices of employees and applicants unless the accommodation causes undue hardship on the business of the employer.

Question: What must plaintiff prove to establish that the employer failed in its duty to accommodate?

Answer: Plaintiff must prove four elements:

1. that she held a sincere religious belief;

2. that her belief was in conflict with a rule of an employer;

3. that her employer knew of the conflict; and

4. that the employer did not fully accommodate the needs of the plaintiff.

Question: What are the rebuttal possibilities for the employer in a reasonable accommodation case?

Answer: The employer can prove either:

1. that the employer did provide an accommodation that was reasonable; or

2. that the accommodation that would satisfy plaintiff's needs causes an undue hardship on the employer.

Question: What are the three statutory exemptions that Title VII provides for religion?

Answer: The three exemptions are:

1. Section 702(a) exempts religious institutions from Title VII's prohibition of religious discrimination if they hire employees of their own religion.

2. Section 703(e)(2) exempts schools that use their curricula to propagate their religion if they hire employees of their own religion.

3. Section 703(e)(1), the general BFOQ defense, applies to religion.

Question: Does the basic proscription in §703 against discrimination because of race, color, sex, or national origin violate the Free Exercise Clause of the First Amendment?

Answer: Yes, if the proscription is applied to key positions of a religious institution.

Question: Do the special exemptions from religious discrimination claims for religious institutions and for schools that use their curricula to promulgate their religions violate the Establishment Clause of the First Amendment?

Answer: As long as the institution is not profit-making, these exemptions do not violate the Establishment Clause.

Question: Does the duty to accommodate required in §701(j) violate the Establishment Clause?

Answer: Probably not, since the accommodation duty is not absolute.

SPECIAL PROBLEMS OF NATIONAL ORIGIN AND ALIENAGE DISCRMINATION

8

CHAPTER OVERVIEW

Most of the problems of national origin and alienage discrimination result from the difficulty of defining those terms, as well as "race" and "ancestry," for purposes of different antidiscrimination statutes that have different scopes of application. Beyond that, the most significant problem of national origin discrimination involves English language issues.

- Alienage discrimination is not national origin discrimination under Title VII.

- National origin discrimination is discrimination because of the country you or your forbears came from.

- 42 U.S.C. §1981 prohibits race and ancestry but not national origin discrimination and it may prohibit alienage discrimination.

- The Immigration Reform and Control Act of 1986 (IRCA) requires employer to discriminate against "unauthorized aliens" but prohibits discrimination because of national origin or authorized alien status.

- It is not clear whether discrimination because of a foreign accent is national origin discrimination.

- Requiring employees to be able to speak English is not national origin discrimination where workers need to be able to communicate in a common language.

- Requiring bilingual employees to speak English on the job is not national origin discrimination.

A. THE SPECIAL PROBLEMS OF NATIONAL ORIGIN AND ALIENAGE DISCRMINATION

Difficult definitional problems result from the interaction of the concepts of national origin, alienage, ancestry, and race. First, Title VII prohibits national origin discrimination but not alienage discrimination. Second, 42 U.S.C. §1981 prohibits discrimination because of "ancestry or ethnic characteristics," race and alienage, but not because of national origin. Third, in addition to prohibiting discrimination because of national origin, the Immigration Reform and Control Act of 1986 (IRCA) prohibits discrimination by employers against aliens who are "lawfully admitted for permanent residence."

Beyond the problems of definition and different statutory coverage, the most significant special problem in the application of the basic theories of discrimination to national origin involves discrimination because of language or accent.

EXAM TIP

If a fact pattern deals with citizenship (or alienage), national origin, and ethnic origin, distinguish them because they play out differently in Title VII and Section 1981.

B. ALIENAGE DISCRMINATION IS NOT PROHIBITED BY TITLE VII

In Espinoza v. Farah Mfg. Co., 414 U.S. 86 (1973), the employer refused to hire a lawfully admitted alien from Mexico because an employer rule limited employment to citizens of the United States. The Court made two points in finding for the employer.

1. Title VII's Prohibition of National Origin Discrimination Does Not Prohibit Discrimination Based on Alienage

The Court held that **discrimination based on alienage, that is, one's citizenship, is not treated as national origin discrimination** under Title VII. Looking to Title VII's legislative history, the Court quoted Congressman Roosevelt: National origin "means the country from which you or your forebears came. . . . You may come from Poland, Czechoslavkia, England, France, or any other country." 414 U.S. at 89.

Since everyone in the United States, including Native Americans, ultimately came, either directly or through their forebears, from some other nation, everyone is protected by Title VII against national origin discrimination.

EXAMPLES AND ANALYSIS

1. Holly Higgins was born in the United States, so the United States is the country she comes from. If Globalized, Inc., refuses to hire Holly because it has decided it has too many employees who come from the United States, that is national origin discrimination.

2. While she comes from the United States, Holly Higgins' forebears come from Ireland. If an employer refuses to hire her because her forebears were Irish, that, too, is national origin discrimination.

2. Disparate Treatment and Disparate Impact Theories Do Apply to National Origin Discrimination

In *Espinoza*, the Court found that both disparate treatment and disparate impact discrimination theories apply to national origin discrimination. Since the alienage rule was not a formal policy of disparate treatment because of national origin, the Court analyzed it as a case of disparate impact because of national origin but found for the employer. Because over 95 percent of all of the defendant's employees were of Mexican national origin, the Court found that the citizens-only rule did not have a disparate impact on persons of Mexican ancestry.

 EXAMPLE AND ANALYSIS

Olga Petroff, a Russian citizen, is not hired by Faberge, Inc. While Title VII will not protect her if Faberge refused to hire her because of her Russian citizenship or because she was not a United States citizen, she can bring claims of national origin discrimination if Faberge did not hire her because she came from Russia.

C. 42 U.S.C. §1981 PROHIBITS RACE, ANCESTRY, AND ETHNIC BUT NOT NATIONAL ORIGIN DISCRMINATION

Section 1981 provides: "All persons within the jurisdiction of the United States shall have the same right . . . to make and enforce contracts . . . as is enjoyed by white citizens."

In Saint Francis College v. Al-Khazraji, 481 U.S. 604 (1987), plaintiff, a United States citizen who had been born in Iraq, claimed in a §1981 action that he was denied tenure because of his Arab ancestry. The Court found that he had stated a claim upon which relief could be granted: "Congress intended to protect from discrimination identifiable classes of persons who are subjected to intentional discrimination solely because of their ancestry or ethnic characteristics. Such discrimination is racial discrimination that Congress intended §1981 to forbid, whether or not it would be classified as racial in terms of modern scientific theory. . . . **If respondent can prove that he was subjected to intentional discrimination based on the fact that he was born an Arab, rather than solely on the place of nation of his origin, or his religion, he will have made out a case under §1981."** 481 U.S. at 613.

1.   Section 1981 Prohibits Private Alienage Discrimination

The Fifth Circuit, in Bhandari v. First Natl. Bank of Commerce, 887 F.2d 609 (5th Cir. 1989) (en banc), found that alienage discrimination was prohibited by §1981 for public actors but not for private actors. Recently, the Second Circuit found that alienage discrimination is proscribed by §1981 whether the employer is public or private. "The statute's juxtaposition of 'all' and 'white' suggests that it prohibits race discrimination, while the juxtaposition of 'persons' and 'citizens' suggest that it prohibits alienage discrimination. A 'person' who is denied employment because he or she is not a citizen cannot be said to enjoy the 'same right . . . to make and enforce contracts . . . as is enjoyed by white citizens.'" Further, the 1991 Act amendments added new §1981(c), which provides that the "rights protected by this section are protected against impairment by nongovernmental discrimination and impairment under color of State law." The court then found that the Civil Rights Act of 1991 amendments extended the protection against alienage discrimination to private conduct. Anderson v. Conboy, 156 F.3d 167 (2d Cir. 1998). The Supreme Court had granted certiorari in *Anderson,* but the case was then settled.

D.   THE IMMIGRATION REFORM AND CONTROL ACT PROHIBITS ALIENAGE AND NATIONAL ORIGIN DISCRIMINATION

Section 101 of the Immigration Reform and Control Act of 1986 requires employers to discriminate against "unauthorized aliens." An unauthorized alien is any person who is not a citizen of the United States and who is not lawfully admitted for permanent residence or authorized by IRCA or the Attorney General to be employed.

Section 102 of IRCA makes it an "unfair immigration-related employment practice" to discriminate because of a person's "national origin" or protected status. An individual is protected if she is a citizen or national of the United States or an authorized alien.

IRCA requires claimants to elect remedies by choosing between pursuing claims under it or other remedies such as §1981 or Title VII.

EXAM TIP

When the fact pattern involves a noncitizen lawfully in the U.S. or someone whose national origin is identified, remember to apply the Immigration Reform and Control Act.

 ## EXAMPLE AND ANALYSIS

Sam Dawavendewa, who is a member of the Hopi tribe, applied for and was not hired by the Big Casino, Inc. Native Americans have been treated as a racial minority, Morton v. Mancari, 417 U.S. 535 (1974), and have also been protected from discrimination on the basis of national origin. If Dawavendewa challenges his failure to be hired, he may use Title VII to claim it was because of race and national origin discrimination, although the claim of national origin discrimination has the BFOQ affirmative defense that is not available as to race. He can also use 42 U.S.C. §1981 to claim race and ancestry discrimination. While he could join together his Title VII and §1981 claims, he could decide to forego those by making a claim under IRCA for national origin discrimination. Cf., Dawavendewa v. Salt River Project Agricultural Improvement & Power Dist., 154 F.3d 1117 (9th Cir. 1998).

E.   ACCENT AND LANGUAGE AS NATIONAL ORIGIN DISCRMINATION

Speaking English with an accent, not being able to speak English, or speaking languages in addition to English are all potentially related to a person's national origin.

EXAM TIP

Where a fact pattern involves speaking English with an accent or speaking languages other then English, look at national origin and ethnic discrmination.

---

1.   Speaking English with an Accent

In both Jiminez v. Mary Washington College, 57 F.3d 369 (4th Cir. 1995), and Bina v. Providence College, 39 F.3d 21 (1st Cir. 1994), the courts did not regard as national origin discrimination the fact that defendant colleges considered plaintiff's foreign accents when speaking English where the teaching positions involved required the ability to communicate in English. In Fragante v. City and County of Honolulu, 888 F.2d 591 (9th Cir. 1989), plaintiff was not hired for a civil service clerk's position, allegedly because of his heavy Filipino accent. Distinguishing several decisions in which plaintiffs won national origin cases where their noticeable Filipino or Polish accents did not interfere with job performance, the court concluded that, "Fragante was not selected because of the deleterious *effect* his Filipino accent had upon his ability to communicate orally, not merely because he had such an accent." 888 F.2d at 599.

2.   Requiring the Ability to Speak English

Employer rules requiring the ability to speak English have generally withstood attack under Title VII. In Garcia v. Rush-Presbyterian-St. Luke's Med. Ctr., 660 F.2d 1217 (7th Cir. 1981), the court upheld such a rule as a BFOQ to any claim of disparate treatment, as not having an impact on Spanish speakers versus other foreign language speakers, and as a business necessity to a claim of disparate impact. Characterizing the hospital as "somewhat of a Tower of Babel," the Court found that "English is most likely to be the common language of a majority of patients and staff alike, and, therefore, a deficiency in English is the language deficiency most likely to be troublesome with an employer."

3.   English-Only Rules

Employer rules requiring bilingual employees to speak English on the job have been upheld. In Garcia v. Gloor, 618 F.2d 264, 270 (5th Cir. 1980), the court held that Title VII "does not support an interpretation that equates language an employee prefers to use with his national origin [since] the language a person who is multi-lingual elects to speak at a particular time is by definition a matter of choice." In Garcia v. Spun Steak Co., 998 F.2d 1480 (9th Cir. 1993), the court rejected an attack of an English-only rule under disparate impact since the impact was found not to be adverse as to bilingual employees.

REVIEW QUESTIONS AND ANSWERS

Question: Does Title VII prohibit alienage discrimination?

Answer: No, national origin, which is prohibited by Title VII, does not directly include alienage discrimination, although it may be disparate impact discrimination if an alienage rule causes disparate impact because of national origin.

Question: What does 42 U.S.C. §1981 prohibit?

Answer: While not prohibiting national origin discrimination as such, §1981 does prohibit race, ancestry, and alienage discrimination.

Question: Does IRCA prohibit alienage discrimination?

Answer: While IRCA *requires* an employer to discriminate against "unauthorized aliens," it does prohibit discrimination because of national origin or because of the protected status as a U.S. citizen or national or an "authorized alien."

Question: Is discrimination because a person speaks English with an accent national origin discrimination?

Answer: While some courts find that it is, others easily find against the plaintiff on the ground that it is not national origin discrimination, that it is a legitimate nondiscriminatory reason, or that it is justified by the BFOQ defense.

Question: Will employer rules requiring English to be spoken be struck down as national origin discrimination?

Answer: Such a rule will be struck down only where the job is shown not to require much speaking in any language.

Question: Will employer rules that bilingual employees speak English on the job be struck down as national origin discrimination?

Answer: These rules have been upheld on the ground that they do not cause an impact that is adverse on workers who are bilingual.

9 SPECIAL PROBLEMS OF AGE DISCRIMINATION

 CHAPTER OVERVIEW

This chapter addresses five major issues that concern age discrimination.

- **The Protected Class.** Section 4(a) of the ADEA generally prohibits discrimination "because of such individual's age" rather than discrimination "because of such individual's race, color, religion, sex or national origin." Section 12, however, provides that the protection against discrimination because of age "shall be limited to individuals who are at least 40 years of age."

  - **Exceptions.** While employers may not require workers to retire because of age, the ADEA provides exceptions for bona fide executives and police and firefighters.

- **Individual Disparate Treatment Discrimination.** The Civil Rights Act of 1991 amended Title VII to modify the Price Waterhouse v. Hopkins "direct evidence" approach to proving individual disparate treatment discrimination. The failure to similarly amend the ADEA may lead to diverging approaches to individual disparate treatment cases under the two statutes.

- **The ADEA and Disparate Impact Discrimination.** The Supreme Court has never decided whether or not disparate impact discrimination is available in ADEA actions and there is a split within the circuit courts. There are differences in statutory terms between Title VII and the ADEA that bear on this question.

  - **Title VII Specifically Includes Disparate Impact Discrimination.** The 1991 Act explicitly included disparate impact discrimination by amending Title VII, but not the ADEA.

153

- **ADEA Provisions Not in Title VII.** The ADEA has two provisions, "good cause" and the "reasonable factor other than age," which have no correlative Title VII provisions and which emphasize that only intentional discrimination because of age is prohibited.

- **Fringe Benefit Plans.** Congress has made several amendments to the ADEA dealing with employee fringe benefit plans.

  - **Equal Cost or Equal Benefit Rule.** Congress has adopted the equal cost or equal benefit test for legality of fringe benefit plans.

  - **Pension Plans May Use Age to Establish Eligibility.** The ADEA allows pension plans to define a normal retirement age for purposes of the plan.

- **Downsizing, Reductions in Force, and Early Retirement Incentive Plans.** This era of downsizing and corporate reorganization raises two age discrimination issues:

  - **Reductions in Force and Individual Disparate Treatment Cases.** Some courts have created a modified form of the prima facie case as established in *McDonnell Douglas/Burdine* to be applied in reduction-in-force cases.

  - **Early Retirement Plans.** Congress, in the Older Workers Benefit Protection Act of 1990, added new §7(f), which deals with waiver of ADEA rights generally as well as adding some additional procedural requirements for early retirement programs.

A.   THE FIVE SPECIAL PROBLEMS OF AGE DISCRMINATION

This chapter addresses five major issues. The first describes the special definition of the group of workers protected against age discrimination, with several exceptions from the rule that the employer cannot retire workers involuntarily because of age. The second deals with the potential splitting of the present uniform structure for dealing with individual disparate treatment discrimination claims under the ADEA and Title VII. The third addresses the still unresolved question whether the disparate impact theory of discrimination is available to claimants in ADEA actions. The fourth looks at special provisions of the ADEA dealing with employee fringe benefit plans. The fifth deals with the special ADEA provisions that address employee downsizing, which is a significant problem for workers over age 40.

EXAM TIP

The most significant issues involving age discrmination that might appear on an exam are the question of whether the disparate impact theory applies, and the question of how downsizing or reductions in force are analyzed, including questions of the validity of agreements to voluntarily retire.

B.   THE PROTECTED CLASS

Section 4(a) of the ADEA generally tracks the language of §703(a) of Title VII but prohibits discrimination "because of such individual's age" rather than discrimination "because of such individual's race, color, religion, sex or national origin." Section 12, however, provides that the protection against discrimination because of age "shall be limited to individuals who are at least 40 years of age." In O'Connor v. Consolidated Coin Caterers Corp., 517 U.S. 308 (1996), the Court described the interaction of those two sections. "This [statutory] language does not ban discrimination against employees because they are aged 40 or older; it bans discrimination against employees because of their age, but limits the protected class to those who are 40 or older." Thus, a substantial difference in age between plaintiff and his replacement supports an inference that plaintiff was replaced because of his age, while the fact that the replacement was over age 40 is irrelevant.

1.   No Involuntary Retirement Because of Age

When the ADEA was initially passed, it protected workers from age discrimination only up to age 65, which cap was first raised to age 70 and then generally eliminated. A benefit plan exception initially allowed the employer to retire employees involuntarily pursuant to a mandatory retirement age established in the plan even at an age below 65. After several amendments, **the ADEA now protects workers without an age cap and, with two exceptions, prohibits employers from involuntarily retiring employees because of age.** Section 4(f)(2)(B)(ii) provides that no "employee benefit plan or voluntary early retirement incentive plan shall excuse the failure to hire any individual, and no such employee benefit shall require or permit the involuntary retirement of any individual . . . because of the age of such individual."

a.   Bona fide executive exception. Section 12(d)(1) allows employers to impose a mandatory retirement age of 65 for employees, who for the two-year period immediately before retirement, are employed in a "bona fide executive or high policymaking position," and who are entitled to an immediate, non-forfeitable retirement benefit of at least $44,000, with that amount indexed for inflation.

The biggest issue is who is a "bona fide executive." The head of a division of an employer with 25 employees and a $4 million budget is one, Passer v. American Chem. Socy., 935 F.2d 322 (D.C. Cir. 1991), while a corporation's in-house chief labor counsel is not, Whittlesey v. Union Carbide Corp., 742 F.2d 724 (2d Cir. 1984).

b.   Police and firefighter exception. Congress, in the Age Discrimination in Employment Amendments of 1996, 104 Pub. L. No. 208 (1996), made permanent the earlier temporary exception allowing an age cap on hiring and the mandatory retirement of police and firefighters if done pursuant to a "bona fide hiring or retirement plan that is not a subterfuge to evade the purposes of the Act." Generally the exception sets a minimum age of not younger than age 55, with no minimum for state laws that were passed before March 3, 1983 (the date the application of the ADEA to state and local governmental employers was upheld in *EEOC v. Wyoming*, 460 U.S. 226 (1983)).

A firefighter is an employee whose duties entail work directly connected with the control and extinguishment of fires or the maintenance and use of firefighting apparatus and equipment. Law enforcement officers includes employees whose duties include investigation, apprehension, or detention of individuals suspected or convicted of offenses against the criminal laws of a state. Police and firefighters who are transferred to desk jobs, such as supervisory or administrative positions, stay covered by the exception.

C.   INDIVIDUAL DISPARATE TREATMENT DISCRIMINATION

The Civil Rights Act of 1991 amended Title VII by adding §§703(m) and 706(g)(2)(B) that modify the Price Waterhouse v. Hopkins "direct evidence" approach to proving individual disparate treatment discrimination. The "a motivating factor" level of proof of employer state of mind set in §703(m) and the same decision affirmative defense to full remedies in §706(g)(2)(B) may also come to have effect in *McDonnell Douglas/Burdine* cases of circumstantial evidence of intent to discriminate in Title VII cases.

Since these amendments were made only to Title VII, it is clear that Congress did not amend the ADEA to include them. Congress, by amending only Title VII, did not in any way suggest, however, that these new provisions could not be referred to in the ongoing judicial enforcement of ADEA law. Thus, the courts can, where relevant, look to the amendments to Title VII to help determine the meaning of the ADEA. It may be, however, that the approaches of individual disparate treatment cases brought under Title VII and the ADEA will begin to diverge.

EXAM TIP

The key issue is whether the 1991 amendments to Title VII dealing with individual disparate treatment discrimination will be applied to the ADEA or whether the prior uniformity in analysis will begin to diverge.

D.   THE ADEA AND DISPARATE IMPACT DISCRIMINATION

The Supreme Court has never decided whether or not disparate impact discrimination is available in ADEA actions. There are differences in statutory terms between Title VII and the ADEA and a split within the circuits.

1. Differences in the ADEA and Title VII Statutes

While the ADEA and Title VII largely parallel each other, there are now substantial differences in each that may bear on whether the disparate impact theory is available in ADEA actions.

a. **Title VII specifically includes disparate impact discrimination.** Until passage of the Civil Rights Act of 1991, neither Title VII nor the ADEA specifically included provision for disparate impact discrimination claims. The 1991 Act, however, amended Title VII to include new §703(k), which does establish a specific statutory scheme addressing disparate impact discrimination. The 1991 Act did not amend the ADEA in that regard, so the ADEA still does not include specific provision for disparate impact discrimination.

b. **ADEA provisions not in Title VII.** The ADEA has two provisions, with no correlative Title VII provisions, that emphasize that the ADEA only prohibits intentional discrimination because of age.

   i. **"Good cause."** Section 4(f)(3) of the ADEA provides that it "shall not be unlawful . . . to discharge or otherwise discipline an individual for good cause."

   ii. **"Reasonable factors other than age."** Section 4(f)(1) makes it not unlawful "to take any action otherwise prohibited . . . where the differentiation is based on reasonable factors other than age."

2. The Split in the Circuits

There is a split in the circuits and the Supreme Court has yet to resolve the issue of whether disparate impact actions can be brought under the ADEA.

a. **Disparate impact applies to the ADEA.** The EEOC, 29 C.F.R. §1625.7(d), and the Second Circuit are of the view that the disparate impact theory applies under the ADEA. In Geller v. Markham, 635 F.2d 1027 (2d Cir. 1980), *cert. denied,* 451 U.S. 945 (1981), the Second Circuit found and applied disparate impact where a school district policy limited the hiring of teachers to those eligible for the lower pay grades. The policy had an impact on older teachers who, because their greater experience slotted them in at higher pay grades, would be precluded from being hired. Justice Rehnquist dissented to the denial of certiorari, arguing that the Court should hear the case to decide that disparate impact did not apply to ADEA claims.

b. **Disparate impact does not apply.** In Hazen Paper Co. v. Biggins, 507 U.S. 604 (1993), Justices Kennedy and Thomas indicated they would join Justice Rehnquist in questioning the reasoning of *Geller.* Since

Biggins, two appellate courts have found disparate impact theory not applicable to ADEA cases.

 EXAMPLES AND ANALYSIS

1. In EEOC v. Francis W. Parker School, 41 F.3d 1073 (7th Cir. 1994), the Seventh Circuit held that disparate impact did not apply to facts similar to *Geller.* Here a school refused to hire a teacher because his qualifications required that he be paid a higher salary than the school was willing to pay. That salary cap imposed a disparate impact upon older teachers because their greater experience slotted them in at a higher level. The court, quoting from *Biggins,* found that since "age and years of service are analytically distinct, an employer can take account of one while ignoring the other." 41 F.3d at 1076–77.

   The court also read the ADEA's "reasonable factor other than age" provision to "suggest that decisions which are made for reasons independent of age *but which happen to correlate with age* are not actionable under the ADEA." 41 F.3d 1077 (emphasis added).

2. In Ellis v. United Airlines, Inc., 73 F.3d 999 (10th Cir. 1996), plaintiffs were applicants for employment who were denied employment on the basis of not meeting the weight prerequisites of the employer. Plaintiffs claimed that the denial, while based on the age-neutral weight requirements, caused disparate impact to older applicants, who as a group weigh more than younger workers.

   In rejecting the plaintiff's disparate impact claim, the court relied on the fact that amendments made in the Civil Rights Act of 1991 specifically incorporate disparate impact theory in Title VII but not in the ADEA.

E. FRINGE BENEFIT PLANS

Congress has made several amendments to the ADEA dealing with employee fringe benefit plans.

1. Benefits Paid or Cost Incurred Must Be Equal

Congress has adopted the equal cost or equal benefit test for legality of fringe benefit plans. Section 4(f)(2)(B) now provides that it shall not be an unlawful employment action for an employer "to observe the terms of a bona fide employee benefit plan—(i) where, for each benefit or benefit package, the actual amount of payment made or cost incurred on behalf of an older worker is no less than that made or incurred on behalf of a younger worker."

Examples and Analysis

1. Employer *X* has created an employee benefit plan to provide term life insurance for its employees with a policy for $100,000 for each employee. This does not violate §4(f)(2)(B) since it provides equal benefits to all workers, even though the cost per older employee exceeds the cost for younger employees.

2. Alternatively, Employer *Y* decides to provide term life insurance for each employee by paying a premium of $1,000 for each employee. This does not violate §4(f)(2)(B) since the employer can pay an equal sum of money as a life insurance premium for all workers, even though that will provide more life insurance for younger than for older workers.

2. Pension Plans May Use Age to Establish Eligibility

After a long period of uncertainty about the scope of the ADEA benefit plan exception, Congress, in the Older Workers Benefit Protection Act of 1990, resolved certain questions. Section 4(l)(1)(A) now provides that **pension plans will not violate the ADEA solely because the plan "provides for the attainment of a minimum age as a condition of eligibility for normal or early retirement benefits."**

Exam Tip

One area where the use of age is explicitly authorized is in setting retirement plan eligibility.

F. DOWNSIZING, REDUCTIONS IN FORCE, AND EARLY RETIREMENT INCENTIVE PLANS

In this era of downsizing and corporate reorganization, employers have devised various means to reduce the number of their employees, which raises two issues:

1. Reductions in Force and Individual Disparate Treatment Cases

Reductions in force involve the discharge of a group of workers while at the same time the jobs of the remaining employees are reorganized so it is not possible to point to a specific person who has replaced each discharged worker. Some lower courts, in dealing with reduction-in-force situations in individual disparate treatment cases, have created a modified form of the *McDonnell Douglas/Burdine* showing required for plaintiff to establish a prima facie case. In O'Connor v. Consolidated Coin Caterers Corp., 56 F.3d 542 (4th Cir. 1995), the Fourth Circuit described it as follows:

a. The employee was protected by the ADEA.

b. He was selected for discharge from a larger group of candidates.

c. He was performing at a level substantially equivalent to the lowest level of those of the group retained.

d. The process of selection produced a residual workforce of persons in the groups containing some unprotected persons who were performing at a lower level than that at which he was performing.

2. Early Retirement Plans

Early retirement incentive plans are used by employers who are involved in a downsizing or a reorganization as a way to minimize the need to discharge any workers if a sufficient number accept the early retirement offer. The way these plans work is that the employer defines a group of employees by some formula of age and seniority who are offered incentives to retire early. If, at the end of the period during which the incentive plan is offered, not enough employees have opted to retire, then the employer lays off workers involuntarily. Given the threat of layoff if not enough employees in the target group accept the incentive package, there is some question whether the decisions of employees to retire early are ever truly voluntary. Other employees may complain because they would like to retire early but are ineligible under the formula for the early retirement plan.

Congress, in the Older Workers Benefit Protection Act of 1990, addressed these problems in two steps. The Act added new §7(f), which deals with waiver of ADEA rights generally as well as adding some additional requirements only for early retirement programs.

EXAM TIP

Whenever a fact pattern involves the settlement of a discrimination claim, even if it doesn't involve claims of age discrimination, look to the potential application of the ADEA standards for waiver of rights.

---

a. **Conditions for waiver of ADEA rights.** The seven minimum conditions for the waiver of any and all rights under the ADEA, including but not limited to early retirement programs, are:

(1) the waiver must be part of an agreement between the individual and the employer that is written in a manner calculated to be understood by that individual, or by the average individual eligible to participate;

(2) the waiver must specifically refer to rights or claims arising under the ADEA;

(3) the agreement cannot waive rights or claims that may arise after the date the waiver is executed;

(4) the individual must receive in exchange for her waiver consideration in addition to anything of value to which the individual already is entitled;

(5) the individual must be advised in writing to consult with an attorney prior to executing the agreement;

(6) the individual must be given a period of at least 21 days within which to consider the agreement; and

(7) the agreement must provide that for a period of at least 7 days following the execution of such agreement, the individual may revoke the agreement, and the agreement shall not become effective or enforceable until the revocation period has expired.

b. **Additional conditions for early retirement program waivers.** If the waiver of ADEA rights is part of an early retirement program, §7(f) adds the following requirements in addition to those required for all other ADEA waivers:

(1) Section 7(f)(F)(ii) extends the time period for the employee to consider the offer from the 21 days provided in §7(f)(F)(i) to at least 45 days.

(2) Section 7(f)(H) requires that the employer inform "the individual in writing in a manner calculated to be understood by the average individual eligible to participate, as to—
    (a) any class, unit, or group of individuals covered by such program, any eligibility factors for such program, and any time limits applicable to such program; and
    (b) the job titles and ages of all individuals eligible or selected for the program, and the ages of all individuals in the same job classification or organizational unit who are not eligible or selected for the program.

EXAMPLE AND ANALYSIS

Employer offers an early retirement incentive program to its employees. The formula for eligibility is a "rule of 75." The "rule of 75" allows workers to retire whose age plus years of service with the employer total at least 75 years. They receive a $600 a month early retirement plan until they reach age 62 when they begin to receive regular pension benefits.

Employee *A*, who is 60, will never be eligible for early retirement before the normal retirement age of 62 because she began working for the company only ten years ago—her total of age and seniority is 70.

Employee *B* can take early retirement. He satisfies the "rule of 75" because he is 48 years old and has 30 years seniority since he began working for the company at age 18. His total age plus seniority is 78 and he will receive $600 per month for 14 years.

Employee *C* is also contemplating early retirement. He is 60 years old with 15 years of seniority, so his age and years of service do equal 75. If he accepts the program, he will receive the $600 per month for the two years until he reaches age 62.

Employee *D* joined the company 20 years ago. But because she is only 45 now, her total of age and service is only 65, so she is not eligible for early retirement under the plan.

Assuming employees *B* and *C* chose to accept early retirement, their potential ADEA claims will be waived if the employer can prove the plan satisfied the formal requirements of both parts of §7(f). If the agreement was "written in a manner calculated to be understood" by *B* and *C* and by the "average individual eligible to participate," if the waiver specifically refers to ADEA claims, if the agreement does not purport to waive ADEA claims arising after the waiver is signed, if the waiver advises the employee to consult an attorney, if the agreement gave the employee a "window" of at least 45 days in which to decide to accept, if the employer provided the information about eligibility factors and demographic characteristics of which workers are eligible and which are not, then *B* and *C* will be found to have waived their ADEA claims because the $600 a month benefit is adequate additional consideration. See Raczak v. Ameritech Corp., 72 F.3d 1337 (8th Cir. 1997).

As to employees *A* and *D*, who do not qualify for early retirement, the fact that the employer establishes age 62 as the normal retirement age does not violate the ADEA as long as the employer does not force employees to retire at that age. Also, the employer is permitted to use age in a formula for incentive plans, even though that excludes younger workers because of their age. See Hamilton v. Caterpillar, Inc., 966 F.2d 1226 (7th Cir. 1992).

c. **No "tender back" of benefits necessary to challenge waiver of ADEA rights.** In Oubre v. Entergy Operations, Inc., 522 U.S. 422 (1998), the Court held that an individual is not required to "tender back" consideration given for a waiver agreement in order to bring a claim under the ADEA. Retention of the consideration does not constitute a ratification of the release.

 # EXAMPLE AND ANALYSIS

Dolores Oubre received a poor performance rating and was given the option of improving her performance in the coming year or accepting voluntary severance. She was given a packet of information about the severance agreement and had 14 days to consider her options. After consulting an attorney, she accepted. She signed a release agreeing to "waive, settle, release, and discharge any and all claims . . . against Entergy." In exchange, she received six payments over four months, totaling $6,258.

The release was deficient in three ways. It did not give her the full statutory time period to decide; it did not give her the required seven days after signing to change her mind; and the release made no specific reference to claims under the ADEA. Oubre then brought an ADEA case, despite not tendering back to the employer the money she received in the settlement.

The Court held that the statute did not require a claimant to tender back the benefits and that it could not read such a requirement into this statute since Congress had required strict compliance with the ADEA waiver rules. "Congress imposed specific duties on employers who seek releases of certain claims created by statute. Congress delineated these duties with precision and without qualification: An employee 'may not waive' an ADEA claim unless the employer complies with the statute. Courts cannot with ease presume ratification of that which Congress forbids." 522 U.S. at 427.

REVIEW QUESTIONS AND ANSWERS

Question: Does the ADEA prohibit discrimination because of age for all workers?

Answer: While the ADEA prohibits age discrimination in employment, it limits the protected class to those who are age 40 or older.

Question: May an employer force an employee to retire because she reaches a certain age?

Answer: In general, the ADEA prohibits mandatory retirement because of age, but there are exceptions for bona fide executives and police and firefighters.

Question: Are individual disparate treatment cases treated the same in ADEA as well as Title VII actions?

Answer: So far the structure of individual disparate treatment cases has been uniform as between ADEA and Title VII actions. However, the 1991 amendments as to individual disparate treatment law were only made to Title VII, so the approaches may begin to diverge.

Question: Can a plaintiff bring a disparate impact claim under the ADEA by showing that an employer practice causes a disparate impact on older workers?

Answer: There is a split in the circuit courts and there are differences in statutory language between the ADEA and Title VII that might support finding that the disparate impact theory is not available in ADEA actions.

Question: How strictly do the courts read the standards for waiving ADEA claims?

Answer: The Court refused to read into those waiver standards a requirement that a claimant must tender back benefits in order to challenge the waiver and claim age discrimination because the waiver standards were intended to be read strictly.

10 RETALIATION

CHAPTER OVERVIEW

Retaliation is adverse action taken by an employer in response to an employee who has opposed the employer's discrimination. An action for retaliation is independent of any action claiming discrimination, though the two claims may be joined.

- **The Structure of a Retaliation Case.** There are three elements to a retaliation case.

  - **Section 704 Protects Applicants, Present and Former Employees.** Section 704 has been held to bar retaliation not only against applicants and present employees, but also against former employees.

  - **The Plaintiff Must Show She Engaged in Either Free Access or Opposition Conduct.** Two types of employee conduct are protected by §704(a) against employer retaliation—**"free access"** and **"opposition."** The courts have interpreted the clauses protecting each differently.

    - **Free Access Retaliation.** Where the plaintiff can show that she filed a charge of discrimination or otherwise participated in a proceeding claiming discrimination, a free access claim is established and she is absolutely protected.

    - **Opposition Clause Retaliation.** Where the plaintiff cannot make out a free access clause case, she can rely on the opposition clause, which

165

bars employer retaliation if an employee "has opposed any practice made an unlawful employment practice by this title." There are two parts to proving that the employee engaged in protected opposition conduct.

- **Plaintiff Reasonably Believes Employer Has Discriminated.** While the opposition clause of §704 literally only protects opposition to a "practice made an unlawful employment practice," an employee engaging in opposition conduct will be protected if she, in subjective good faith, believes the employer has discriminated and, in objective fact, has a reasonable basis for that belief.

- **Plaintiff's Opposition Conduct Was Reasonable.** This is the crux of most opposition clause cases. Not all opposition conduct will be protected; only opposition conduct that the court finds reasonable.

- **The Plaintiff Must Show That the Employer Took Adverse Action Against Her Because of Her Protected Conduct.** Where the adverse action occurred in a reasonably close proximity to the time the employer learned of the employee's protected conduct, then it is easy to conclude that the adverse action was because of that conduct and was, therefore, retaliation.

- **Plaintiff Suffers an "Ultimate Employment Decision.** Several lower courts have restricted the scope of §704 by reading into it a requirement that plaintiff must suffer an "ultimate employment decision" in order to be protected from retaliation. Ultimate employment decisions include acts such as hiring, firing, promoting, and granting leaves of absence.

A.   THE ESSENCE OF RETALIATION

Retaliation is the adverse response of an employer to the actions of its employee who participates in proceedings to remedy employer discrimination or who opposes employer discrimination. An action for retaliation is independent of an action for discrimination, although a plaintiff claiming discrimination may join it with an action also claiming retaliation.

B.   STATUTORY AUTHORITY

Title VII in §704(a), the ADEA in §4(d) and 42 U.S.C. §1981 all prohibit employer retaliation.

1. **Section 704(a) of Title VII provides that "it shall be an unlawful employment practice for an employer to discriminate against any of his employees or applicants for employment because . . . he has opposed** any practice made an unlawful employment practice by this title or because he has made a charge, testified, assisted, or **participated** in any manner in an investigation, proceeding, or hearing under this title."

2. Section 4(d) of the ADEA prohibits retaliation using language similar to Title VII's

3. The basic language of §1981 has been interpreted to protect people against retaliation: "All persons . . . shall have the same right . . . to make and enforce contracts . . . and to the full and equal benefit of all laws . . . as is enjoyed by white citizens."

C. THE STRUCTURE OF A RETALIATION CASE

There are three basic elements to a retaliation case. First, the plaintiff must show she is a person protected from retaliation. Second, she must prove that she engaged in either "free access" conduct or "opposition" conduct. Third, plaintiff must show that she was the victim of adverse action by the employer.

1. Section 704 Protects Applicants, Present and Former Employees

Section 704 has been held to bar retaliation not only against applicants and present employees, but also against former employees. In Robinson v. Shell Oil Co., 519 U.S. 337 (1997), the Court held that the term "employee," as used in §704, included former employees within its protections. Applying principles of statutory interpretation, the Court reasoned that §704 expressly protects employees who were fired for retaliation for filing a charge and, such a charge, in conjunction with §703, would necessarily have to be brought by a former employee. The "exclusion of former employees from the protection of §704(a) would undermine the effectiveness of Title VII by allowing the threat of post-employment retaliation to deter victims of discrimination from complaining to [the] EEOC, and would provide a perverse incentive for employers to fire employees who might bring Title VII claims." 519 U.S. at 346.

EXAMPLES AND ANALYSIS

1. In *Robinson*, the employer gave a former employee, who had filed a charge with the EEOC that claimed that he was discharged on the basis of his race, a negative reference to a prospective employer. The former employee claimed that the negative reference was in retaliation for his filing the charge. He is protected by §704(a).

2. In *Womack*, the present employer of the plaintiff was found to have retaliated against him based on the employee's behavior while working at a prior employer.

---

2. The Plaintiff Must Show She Engaged in Either Free Access or Opposition Conduct

Two types of employee conduct are protected by §704(a) against employer retaliation—**"free access"** and **"opposition."** The courts have interpreted the clauses protecting each differently.

a. **Free access retaliation. Where the plaintiff can show that she filed a charge of discrimination or otherwise participated in a legal proceeding claiming discrimination,** even as a witness in a case not directly involving her, **a free access claim is established.** On claims based on the free access clause, **the protection of** employees, who have been the **victims of retaliation for having participated in proceedings claiming discrimination, is virtually absolute.**

   i. **Plaintiffs prefer free access cases.** From a plaintiff's point of view, the free access basis for a retaliation claim is better than relying on the opposition clause because the case is a simple factual one answering three questions—is plaintiff a protected person, did she participate in a proceeding involving discrimination, and did the employer take adverse action against her because of that participation?

 ## EXAMPLES AND ANALYSIS

1. In Pettway v. American Cast Iron Pipe Co., 411 F.2d 998 (5th Cir. 1969), the employer fired a worker who filed a discrimination charge with the EEOC, claiming the charge was false. Rather than let the employer take any action based on an employee's charge of discrimination, the court stated that the free access clause would be frustrated if employers were permitted to determine the veracity of the charges. The employee is protected from retaliation for filing a charge, even if the charge is ultimately found baseless.

2. In Womack v. Munson, 619 F.2d 1292 (8th Cir. 1980), an African-American employee, who had been hired by the county prosecutor, brought a discrimination suit against his former employer, the sheriff of the same county. The prosecutor questioned the employee regarding the suit, which related to physical abuse of black suspects, and then discharged him. The *Womack* court held that the prosecutor violated the free access clause by firing the plaintiff, even though the plaintiff may

have lied or participated in physically abusing suspects while working in the sheriff's department.

b.   **Opposition clause retaliation.** Where the plaintiff cannot make out a free access clause case, she can rely on the opposition clause, which bars employer retaliation if an employee "has opposed any practice made an unlawful employment practice by this title." Unlike the almost absolute protection afforded under the free access clause, opposition clause cases, because they may involve a very wide array of different kinds of employee behavior, involve a balancing of interests so that some conduct that does oppose an employer's discrimination is nevertheless found not to be protected because it is seen as unreasonable.

There are two parts to proving that the employee engaged in protected opposition conduct.

   i.   **Plaintiff reasonably believes employer has discriminated.** While the opposition clause of §704 by its literal terms only protects opposition to a "practice made an unlawful employment practice," **an employee** engaging in opposition conduct **will be protected if she, in subjective good faith, believes the employer has discriminated and, in objective fact, has a reasonable basis for that belief.**

   ii. **Plaintiff's opposition conduct was reasonable. The crux of most opposition clause cases is the necessity of finding plaintiff's conduct reasonable.** While the Supreme Court has not directly decided any retaliation cases, it has indicated that not all conduct opposing discrimination will be protected. In McDonnell Douglas Corp. v. Green, 411 U.S. 792 (1973), a case in which the §704(a) issue was not appealed to the Supreme Court, the Court commented generally that, "Nothing in Title VII compels an employer to absolve and rehire one who has engaged in such deliberate, unlawful activity against it [such as the illegal lock-in and blockade of plant entrances]."

 EXAMPLE AND ANALYSIS

In Jennings v. Tinley Park Community Sch. Dist., 864 F.2d 1368 (7th Cir. 1988), the personal secretary of the superintendent of schools was a member of a group of secretaries protesting salary discrimination. She intentionally delayed delivery to the superintendent of the group's proposed salary schedule. Because of the delay, the superintendent was "blindsided" at a school board meeting and was unable to answer questions posed by school board members. He then dismissed the secretary, claiming her acts undermined the loyalty, trust, and support essential for a close working relationship. The court found against the plaintiff, by applying a test of reasonableness to judge whether or not plaintiff's opposition conduct was protected. Applying this reasonableness test, the court determined that the substance of plaintiff's protest, unlawful gender discrimination, was protected, but that the employee's conduct here exceeded the protection the statute afforded. Her delay in delivering the salary schedule to her supervisor, which subsequently affected his ability to respond to the board members, was unreasonable. In other words, the opposition clause protects conduct that furthers the protest but it does not extend to deliberate attempts to undermine a supervisor's ability to perform his job.

3. **The Plaintiff Must Show that the Employer Took Adverse Action Against Her Because of Her Protected Conduct**

Typically, people do not sue if they do not think something bad has happened to them, so this usually is easy to prove. **Where the adverse action occurred in a reasonably close proximity to the time the employer learned of the employee's protected conduct, then it is easy to conclude that the adverse action was because of that conduct and was, therefore, retaliation.**

REVIEW QUESTIONS AND ANSWERS

Question: What is retaliation?

Answer: Retaliation is the adverse response of an employer to the actions of its employee who participates in proceedings to remedy employer discrimination or who opposes employer discrimination.

Question: Is a retaliation action tied to an action for discrimination?

Answer: An action for retaliation is independent of an action for discrimination, though a plaintiff complaining of discrimination may join with it an action also claiming retaliation.

Question: What are the three elements of a retaliation case?

Answer: First, the plaintiff must show she is a person protected from retaliation. Second, she must prove that she engaged in either "free access" conduct or "opposition" conduct. Third, plaintiff must show that she was the victim of adverse action by the employer.

Question: Who is protected from retaliation?

Answer: Section 704(a) has been held to bar retaliation not only against applicants and present employees, but also against former employees.

Question: What is conduct that falls within the "free access" clause?

Answer: Plaintiff filed a charge of discrimination or otherwise participated in a proceeding claiming discrimination, even as a witness in a case not directly involving her.

Question: What is conduct that falls with the "opposition" clause?

Answer: The opposition clause bars employer retaliation where an employee "has opposed any practice made an unlawful employment practice by this title."

Question: Is all conduct that opposes practices made unlawful protected?

Answer: Only opposition conduct that is reasonable is protected.

Question: Is the opposition conduct of an employee protected if the employer is not found to have discriminated?

Answer: An employee engaging in opposition conduct will be protected if she, in subjective good faith, believes the employer has discriminated and, in objective fact, has a reasonable basis for that belief.

Question: How does a plaintiff show that the adverse action taken by the employer was retaliation?

Answer: Where the adverse action occurred in a reasonably close proximity to the time the employer learned of the employee's protected conduct, then it is easy to conclude that the adverse action was because of that conduct and was, therefore, retaliation.

11 RECONSTRUCTION CIVIL RIGHTS ACTS

CHAPTER OVERVIEW

Congress passed significant Reconstruction civil rights acts after the Civil War to bring about equality among the races, 42 U.S.C. §§1981, 1983 and 1985(c). All still have important application in the employment sector.

- **The Reconstruction Era Statutes.** Section 1981 prohibits race discrimination in all contracts; §1983 creates a remedy for the violation of rights created by the Constitution or other federal laws; and §1985(c) protects people from conspiracies to deprive them of their civil rights.

- **The Relationship of the Reconstruction Statutes and Title VII.** There are four reasons why the Reconstruction era statutes can sometimes still be quite useful.

  - **Reconstruction Era Statutes May Reach Conduct Exempted from Title VII.** Since Title VII includes some exemptions, the matters within those exemptions may be attacked using the Reconstruction statutes.

  - **No Administrative Agency Filing Is Required.** Unlike Title VII, the Reconstruction era statutes do not require the claimant to first file a claim with an administrative agency before filing a federal court action.

  - **Statutes of Limitation.** Not having the short filing period for filing claims with an administrative agency, the Reconstruction era statutes have longer statutes of limitations for filing claims in court, with the exact statute of limitation set by the analogous state law.

- • **Remedies.** The Reconstruction era statutes provide for compensatory and punitive remedies, not subject to the caps on damages in Title VII actions.

- • **The Scope of §1981 Protection.** There are four facets to §1981 that define its scope.

  - • **"Race" for §1981 Means "Ancestry" or "Ethnic" Background.** While the main thrust of §1981 is to prohibit race discrimination in contracts, race was defined at the time of its enactment to mean "ancestry" or "ethnic" background. That means that discrimination because of the ethnic group you or your predecessors are members of, not the country of your birth, is prohibited. Alienage discrimination is prohibited by §1981, but national origin and sex discrimination are not within the scope of §1981's protections.

  - • **Section 1981 Reaches Private Contracts.** Both private and public employers are prohibited by §1981 from discriminating in making and enforcing contracts.

  - • **Section 1981 Prohibits Race Discrimination for the Duration of the Contract Relationship.** The Civil Rights Act of 1991 made clear that §1981 is not limited in its protection to the formation of contracts, but extends to the duration of the contract.

  - • **Only Intentional Discrimination Is Prohibited by §1981.** The disparate treatment law from Title VII applies in §1981 actions but the disparate impact theory is not available to §1981 plaintiffs.

- • **42 U.S.C. §1983.** Unlike §1981, which creates a right against race discrimination in contracts, §1983 creates a remedy against state actors for their violation of rights created by the Constitution or other federal laws.

  - • **Scope of §1983 Actions.** Most §1983 actions involve the claim that a state actor interfered with the plaintiff's constitutional rights, such as equal protection under the Fourteenth Amendment. The violation of Title VII rights does not, however, trigger a §1983 remedy.

  - • **The State Actor as Defendant.** Private actors are not covered by §1983. The application to state actors is quite complex.

- • **42 U.S.C. §1985(c).** Like §1983, §1985(c) protects people against conspiracies to interfere with their federal rights. The violation of Title VII rights does not trigger a §1985(c) remedy.

A. THE RECONSTRUCTION ERA CIVIL RIGHTS STATUTES

After the Civil War, Congress passed a series of Reconstruction civil rights statutes to protect former slaves from renewed oppression in the states that had made up the Confederacy. Several survive and have continuing relevance as antidiscrimination statutes today. 42 U.S.C. §1981 is the most significant for employment discrimination of those that survive, but 42 U.S.C. §§1983 and 1985(c) will be treated briefly as well.

1. 42 U.S.C. §1981

Section 1981 provides: "All persons within the jurisdiction of the United States shall have the same right in every State and Territory to make and enforce contracts . . . as is enjoyed by white citizens. . . ." This act broadly prohibits race discrimination in all contracts, public and private. Since the employment relationship is generally characterized as based in contract law, §1981 prohibits race discrimination in employment.

EXAM TIP

In fact patterns involving race or ethnic discrmination, apply §1981 as well as Title VII. This is especially important if there are procedural issues concerning the timely filing of Title VII charges with the EEOC.

---

2. 42 U.S.C. §1983

Unlike §1981, which creates a cause of action against discrimination in contracts, §1983 does not create substantive rights but instead creates a remedy for the violation of rights created by the Constitution or other federal laws by a state actor.

EXAM TIP

Where a fact pattern involves a governmental employer, §1983 may be applicable.

---

3. 42 U.S.C. §1985(c)

Like §1983, this section does not create substantive rights but instead creates a remedy to protect people from conspiracies to deprive them of their civil rights.

B. THE RELATIONSHIP OF THE RECONSTRUCTION STATUTES AND TITLE VII

Title VII does provide a reasonably comprehensive scheme for the protection against race discrimination. But there are four reasons why the Reconstruction era statutes can be quite useful.

1. Reconstruction Era Statutes May Reach Conduct Exempted from Title VII

Title VII is a more fully developed statute than any of the Civil War era statutes, including a number of exceptions. The Reconstruction era statutes may be used to attack conduct sheltered by those exceptions. In Personnel Administrator v. Feeney, 442 U.S. 256 (1979), plaintiff challenged as sex discrimination a veterans' preference that was sheltered from attack in a Title VII action by §712's exemption. Plaintiff, therefore, relied on §1983 in her challenge, claiming the preference violated the Fourteenth Amendment's guarantee of equal protection.

2. No Administrative Agency Filing Required

Claimants relying on the Reconstruction statutes can go immediately to court without having to first file their claim with any administrative agency, as is necessary in Title VII action.

3. Statutes of Limitation

Title VII and the other recent antidiscrimination statutes have relatively short statutes of limitation within which plaintiff must file with the EEOC or a state agency. One reason to bring an action under one of the Reconstruction era civil rights statutes is if the Title VII limitations period for filing with the administrative agency has run. The Reconstruction era statutes do not themselves include any statutes of limitations but they all look to the appropriate state statutes of limitation.

In Wilson v. Garcia, 471 U.S. 261 (1986), the Court treated §1983 claims as claims for violations of personal rights so the appropriate state statute of limitations was the statute governing tort actions for recovery of damages for personal injuries. That general personal injury statute applied to §1983 actions even in states with a shorter limitations period for "intentional" torts. Owens v. Okure, 488 U.S. 235 (1989). State law rules concerning the accrual of causes of action, continuing violations, and tolling also apply in §1983 actions, but "considerations of state law may be displaced where their application would be inconsistent with the federal policy underlying the cause of action under consideration." Johnson v. Railway Express Agency, Inc., 421 U.S. 454, 463–65 (1975) (filing EEOC charge did not toll statute of limitations in §1981 action). The approach used in §1983 actions also applies to §1981 actions. Goodman v. Lukens Steel Co., 482 U.S. 656 (1987).

Filing a claim with an administrative agency such as the EEOC does not toll the running of the limitations period of a claim based on a Reconstruction era statute.

4. Remedies

Before the passage of the Civil Rights Act of 1991, the differences in remedies and in right to jury trial between Reconstruction era civil rights causes of action and Title VII were an incentive to bring Reconstruction era actions. While Title VII originally provided equitable remedies, including backpay and attorney's fees, the Reconstruction era statutes provided full compensatory and punitive damages and the Civil Rights Attorney's Fees Awards Act, 42 U.S.C. §1988, provided attorney's fees.

The Civil Rights Act of 1991 reduced but did not eliminate the incentive to bring Reconstruction era civil rights actions because it provided greater relief under Title VII. The Act added 42 U.S.C. §1981(a), which provided compensatory and punitive damages and the right to trial by jury to claims of intentional discrimination brought under Title VII. These new damages, however, are subject to caps which do not apply to actions brought under the civil rights statutes from the earlier era. Thus, some incentive still exists for bringing §§1981 and 1983 actions.

C.   THE SCOPE OF §1981 PROTECTION

There are four facets to §1981 that define its scope.

1.   "Race" for §1981 Means "Ancestry" or "Ethnic" Background

The main thrust of §1981 is to prohibit all race discrimination in contracts. Since, however, the statute was enacted in the nineteenth century, the definition of "race" at that time differs from more contemporary understandings and it is what race meant when §1981 was passed that Congress intended to apply. In Saint Francis College v. Al-Khazraji, 481 U.S. 604, 613 (1987), the Court, looking at what race meant when §1981 was passed, found that, "Congress intended to protect from discrimination identifiable classes of persons who are subjected to intentional discrimination solely because of their ancestry or ethnic characteristics." The Court remanded, saying, "If respondent on remand can prove that he was subjected to intentional discrimination based on the fact that he was born an Arab, rather than solely on the place or nation of his origin, or his religion, he will have made out a case under §1981." 481 U.S. at 613.

a.   **National origin versus ethnic or ancestral origin.** While national origin is the country where a person was born, or the country from which his or her ancestors came, ancestry is the ethnic group from which an individual and his or her forbears are descended. The two overlap substantially and are hard to differentiate. Justice Brennan, in his concurring opinion in *Al-Khazraji*, articulated when §1981 would not apply: "discrimination based on *birthplace alone* is insufficient to state a claim under §1981." 481 U.S. at 614 (emphasis in original).

EXAM TIP

To find "ethnic" discrimination, which is prohibited by §1983, rather than "national origin" discrimination, which is not, it is necessary to find something more than the fact that the individual was born in a particular country.

EXAMPLE AND ANALYSIS

1. In Saint Francis College v. Al-Khazraji, 481 U.S. 604 (1987), plaintiff claimed he had been denied tenure by the college because of his Arab ancestry. The trial court rejected his claim because Arabs are generally now considered to be Caucasians. Therefore any discrimination plaintiff suffered was not on the basis of race. The Supreme Court reviewed the background of the passage of §1981 and concluded that, at that time, race had not yet been divided into Caucasians, Mongolians, and Negro races. Instead, race meant different ethnic and ancestral groups and not any distinctive physiognomy. Thus, plaintiff would win if he could prove that the defendant discriminated against him because he was born an Arab, rather than because he was born in Iraq, an Arab country.

2. Plaintiff claimed to be the victim of derogatory remarks in the workplace about his having been born in Israel. If he were discriminated against because of his national origin, being born in Israel, that would not violate §1981. Discrimination because he is Jewish, however, would violate §1981. The court found that those comments, which focused on Israel and not Jewishness, nevertheless could be the basis for drawing an inference of race discrimination. "That Israel is a Jewish state, albeit not composed exclusively of Jews, is well established. Furthermore, it is undisputed that appellee is of Hebrew/Jewish descent, the stock primarily associated with Israel. The jury thus could have determined that [defendant] discriminated against appellee on the basis of his Hebrew/Jewish race by disparaging Israel." Sinai v. New England Telephone & Telegraph Co., 3 F.3d 471, 474 (1st Cir. 1993).

---

    b. Section 1981 protects whites against race discrimination. Despite the language that every person is entitled to the same protection "as is enjoyed by white citizens," the Court in McDonald v. Santa Fe Trail Transp. Co., 427 U.S. 273 (1976), found "that §1981 is applicable to racial discrimination in private employment against white persons."

2. Section 1981 Prohibits Alienage Discrimination

The Fifth Circuit, in Bhandari v. First Natl. Bank of Commerce, 887 F.2d 609 (5th Cir. 1989) (en banc), found that alienage discrimination was prohibited by §1981 for public actors but not for private actors. More recently, the Second Circuit found that alienage discrimination is proscribed by §1981 whether the employer is public or private. The court found that the Civil Rights Act of 1991 amendments extended the protection against alienage discrimination to private conduct by adding a new subsection (e): "The rights protected by this section are protected against impairment by nongovernmental discrimination and impairment under color of State law."

Anderson v. Conboy, 156 F.3d 167 (2d Cir. 1998). The Supreme Court granted certiorari in *Anderson* but the case then settled.

3.   Sex Discrimination Does Not Violate §1981

The courts have found sex discrimination not to be prohibited by §1981. See Bobo v. ITT, Continental Baking Co., 662 F.2d 340 (5th Cir. 1981), *cert. denied,* 456 U.S. 933 (1982).

4.   Section 1981 Reaches Private and Public Employers

Shortly after the Civil War, the Supreme Court raised doubts whether Congress had the power under the Fourteenth Amendment to reach private actors.

> *Civil rights cases, 109 U.S. 3 (1883).* That doubt was finally resolved in favor of Congress having the power to reach private action when the Supreme Court decided that 42 U.S.C. §1982, a companion statute to §1981 that prohibits race discrimination in property transactions, was constitutional when applied to private actors. Jones v. Alfred H. Mayer, 392 U.S. 409 (1968). In 1975, the Supreme Court said it joined with the lower courts in finding that "§1981 affords a federal remedy against discrimination in private employment on the basis of race." Johnson v. Railway Express Agency, Inc., 421 U.S. 454, 459–60 (1975). Congress, in the 1991 Act, ratified that interpretation by adding new subsection (c).

5.   Section 1981 Prohibits Race Discrimination for the Duration of the Contract Relationship

Patterson v. McLean Credit Union, 491 U.S. 164, 176 (1989), was among the 1989 cases in which the Supreme Court cut back the application of a number of antidiscrimination statutes. The Court held that §1981 applied "only to the formation of a contract, but not to problems that may arise later from the conditions of continuing employment." That meant that Patterson's claims of race harassment on the job, and of the failure to promote her because she was black, were not within the reach of §1981. In the Civil Rights Act of 1991, Congress overturned *Patterson,* by amending §1981 to add a new subsection (b): "For purposes of this section, 'make and enforce contracts' includes the making, performance, modification, and termination of contracts, and the enjoyment of all benefits, privileges, terms, and conditions of the contractual relationship."

6.   Only Intentional Discrimination Is Prohibited by §1981

a.   **The *McDonnell Douglas/Burdine* structure applies.** Even in absence of direct evidence of discrimination, the *McDonnell Douglas/Burdine* structure applies in §1981 cases. "We have developed, in analogous areas of civil rights law, a carefully designed framework of proof to determine, in the context of disparate treatment, the ultimate issue whether the defendant intentionally discriminated against the plaintiff. . . . [T]his scheme of proof should apply to claims of racial discrimination under §1981." 491 U.S. at 186.

b. **Disparate impact discrimination does not apply.** In General Bldg. Contractors Assn. v. Pennsylvania, 458 U.S. 375 (1982), the Court rejected a claim of disparate impact discrimination that was brought under §1981 since that theory does not include an intent-to-discriminate element. Only intentional discrimination is prohibited since, "§1981, like the equal protection clause, can be violated only by purposeful discrimination." Id. at 386.

D.   42 U.S.C. §1983

Unlike §1981, which creates a right against race discrimination in contracts, §1983 creates a remedy against state actors for their violation of rights created by the Constitution or other federal laws:

Every person, who, under color of any statute . . . of any State . . . subjects . . . any . . . other person . . . to the deprivation of any rights, privileges or immunities secured by the Constitution and laws, shall be liable to the party injured in an action, suit in equity, or other proper proceeding for redress.

1.   Scope of §1983 Actions

Since employment discrimination sometimes violates the equal protection requirements in the Constitution, §1983 is available as a cause of action to remedy that violation. While Title VII accords "rights . . . secured by [federal] laws" that theoretically could be protected in a §1983 action, Title VII has been held not to be a federal law that is protected by §1983 since it has it own enforcement and remedial scheme. Day v. Wayne County Bd. of Auditors, 749 F.2d 1199 (6th Cir. 1984). The existence of a Title VII action that applies to the same facts does not, however, bar a §1983 action based on the violation of some federal right other than Title VII. Thus, cases of intentional race and sex discrimination, which violate the Equal Protection Clause of the Fourteenth Amendment as well as Title VII, may be joined in the same action.

 # EXAMPLE AND ANALYSIS

In Personnel Administrator v. Feeney, 442 U.S. 256 (1979), Massachusetts had a rule that absolutely favored veterans in civil service jobs so that whenever at least one veteran applied for a job, no non-veteran would even be considered. Given that at that time very few women were veterans, the effect of this rule was to resrict good

civil service jobs to almost only men. Since Title VII's §712 exempts veteran preferences, plaintiff relied on §1983 in her challenge based on the Fourteenth Amendment's
guarantee of equal protection. The Court found, however, that §1983 was not violated
because the civil service rule was neutral on its face as to gender, served the legitimate
purpose of aiding veterans, and was not the result of purposeful discrimination against
women. Since the impact on women of this rule was the result of the exclusion of
women from the military by the federal government, Massachusetts would not be
liable for its rule unless it used the rule "because of, not in spite of, its impact on
women."

2.   The State Actor as Defendant

Since §1983 applies only to actions taken by a person under color of state
(not federal) law, the section does not apply to private employers. The state
itself is not a person for the purposes of a §1983 action. In an action for
damages but not injunctive relief, a state official acting in her official capacity
is barred because it is deemed an action against the state. Local governments
and their officials are persons acting under color of state law, so they can
be sued for damages and injunctive relief. Local governments, however, are
liable only when the action taken was pursuant to a local policy or custom.
When state or local governmental employees are sued for damages in their
individual capacity, there are immunities that apply. Legislators, judges,
and prosecutors are absolutely immune for their acts in their official capacity.
Other officials are sheltered by qualified immunity that applies when their
conduct does not violate "clearly established statutory or constitutional
rights of which a reasonable person would have known." Harlow v. Fitzger-
ald, 457 U.S. 800 (1982).

E.   42 U.S.C. §1985(c)

This section is designed to provide a remedy to protect people from conspiracies
to deprive them of their civil rights:

> If two or more persons . . . conspire . . . for the purpose of depriving . . . any
> person . . . of the equal protection of the laws . . . [and] if one or more persons
> engaged therein do . . . any act in furtherance of the object of such conspiracy,
> whereby another is injured . . . or deprived of having . . . any right or privilege
> of the United States, the party so injured . . . may have an action for the recovery
> of damages . . . against one or more of the conspirators.

Conspiracies based on race or other class-based animus interfering with employment opportunities protected by Title VII would seem to fit within §1985(c). The
Supreme Court in Great American Federal Savings & Loan Assn. v. Novotny,
422 U.S. 366, 378 (1979), however, concluded that "§1985 may not be invoked
to redress violations of Title VII." The rationale was that to allow §1985 to be

used to remedy conspiracies that interfered with Title VII rights would undermine the use of Title VII itself. Plaintiffs would tend to use §1985 to avoid the elaborate administrative process required by Title VII and go right to court to seek a §1985(c) recovery including compensatory and punitive damages, not subject to the caps set in Title VII.

REVIEW QUESTIONS AND ANSWERS

Question: What are the three Reconstruction era statutes that still have some application to employment discrimination?

Answer: Section 1981 prohibits race discrimination in all contracts, including employment contracts; §1983 gives a remedy to those whose constitutional and other federal law rights have been interfered with by a state court; and §1985(c) protects against conspiracies to interfere with constitutional and federal rights.

Question: What four reasons are there to bring a Reconstruction era action when Title VII is a comprehensive employment statute?

Answer: The four reasons are:

1.   Some conduct exempted from Title VII may violate a Reconstruction era statute.

2.   Plaintiffs can take their Reconstruction era claims directly to court, without having to first file with any administrative agency.

3.   Since the period for filing a Title VII charge with an administrative agency is quite short, the longer statute of limitations for claims based on Reconstruction era statutes may be available even when a Title VII claim is time barred.

4.   There are no caps to compensatory and punitive damages under Reconstruction era actions as there are in Title VII actions.

Question: What is the scope of the protection provided by §1981?

Answer: There are four facets to §1981 that define its scope.

1.   "Race" for §1981 means "ancestry" or "ethnic" background. The main thrust of §1981 is to prohibit all race discrimination in contracts, with the scope of protection provided to "identifiable classes of persons who are subjected to intentional discrimination solely because of their ancestry or ethnic characteristics." Section 1981 also prohibits discrimination because of alienage.

2. Section 1981 prohibits discrimination by both public and private employers.

3. Section 1981 protects against all discrimination in employment, including "the making, performance, modification, and termination of contracts, and the enjoyment of all benefits, privileges, terms, and conditions of the contractual relationship."

4. Section 1981 does apply the disparate treatment concepts of intentional discrimination developed in Title VII but it does not include the disparate impact theory of discrimination.

Question: Do §§1983 and 1985(c) create substantive rights?

Answer: Neither of these laws creates substantive rights but both provide remedies for the interference with constitutional and other federal rights.

Question: Are the federal rights created by Title VII protected by §§1983 and 1985(c)?

Answer: No, but other federal rights of employees, such as equal protection rights under the Fourteenth Amendment, are protected by those sections.

12 DISABILITY DISCRIMINATION

 CHAPTER OVERVIEW

The Americans with Disability Act, which prohibits disability discrimination, is a complicated statute. The basic thrust is to protect individuals against disparate treatment because of their disability. The structure of individual disparate treatment discrimination because of disability involves a series of statutory issues. In addition, the ADA includes a number of other theories of discrimination, including systemic disparate treatment, systemic disparate impact, and a reasonable accommodation duty, as well as special provisions dealing with the use of tests and protection for people because of their relationship with someone who is an individual with a disability.

- **Individual Disparate Treatment Case of Disability Discrimination.** The general rule prohibiting discrimination because of disability set forth in §102(a) is cast in terms of individual disparate treatment discrimination.

- **Plaintiff's Prima Facie Case.** There are three elements necessary for a plaintiff to prove a prima facie individual disparate treatment case.

  - **An Individual with a Disability.** The first step in establishing a disability case is for plaintiff to prove she is an individual with a disability under any one of three definitions of disability.

    - **Physical or Mental Impairment.** The basic definition of disability is a physical or mental impairment that substantially limits one or more major life activities. That showing has three facets.

- **Physical or Mental Impairment.** The Court has taken a broad view of what constitutes an impairment, even beyond regulations promulgated by the EEOC.

- **Major Life Activities.** Major life activities should be viewed broadly, including "caring for oneself, performing manual tasks, walking, seeing, hearing, speaking, breathing, learning, and working."

- **Substantially Limits.** The factors in determining whether an individual is "substantially limited" include the nature and severity of the impairment, its duration, and its permanent or long-term impact.

- **Mitigation of an Impairment.** If a person is taking measures to mitigate an impairment, the effect of those measures must be taken into account when judging whether that person is substantially limited.

- **Record of Impairment.** Someone who does not now have a disability is nevertheless protected by the ADA if she has been discriminated against because she has a record of having had a disability, even if she never was disabled.

- **Regarded as Having an Impairment.** A person is an individual with a disability if he is regarded by an employer as having a disability, because the employer either mistakenly believes (1) that a person has an impairment substantially limiting a major life activity, or (2) that a nonlimiting impairment substantially limits a major life activity.

- **Qualified Individual.** A person who is an individual with a disability within one of the definitions of disability described above must establish the second step of liability by showing that she is "qualified." According to the ADA, "The term 'qualified individual with a disability' means an **individual with a disability who, with or without reasonable accommodation, can perform the essential functions of the employment position** that such individual holds or desires."

  - **Essential Functions. To be qualified, the individual must be able to perform all the essential functions of the job.** While the ADA says that "consideration shall be given to the employer's judgment as to what functions of a job are essential," this language does not require that a court defer to the employer's judgment. Instead, the court must look to evidence of the actual functions of the employees doing the work of the job in question.

  - Am employee who fails to meet an applicable federal safety regulation is not qualified.

  - **Reasonable Accommodation.** An individual needs to be able to perform the essential functions of the job but that **performance is determined** "**with or without reasonable accommodation.**" While the ADA includes an extensive list of possible accommodations, the question of whether the cost versus the benefit of an accommodation enters into the determination of whether any accommodation is reasonable is not finally decided.

- **Proving the Employer Acted Because of Plaintiff's Disability.** If plaintiff proves she is "a qualified individual with a disability," then she must still prove that the employer took its action against her because of her disability. She may use *Price Waterhouse* direct evidence that the employer admitted or conceded it took her disability into account or, where the employer denies that it took disability into account, she may rely on the *McDonnell Douglas/Burdine* circumstantial evidence test to support the factfinder in drawing an inference that the employer acted because of plaintiff's disability.

- **Defenses to Individual Disparate Treatment Claims.** In addition to rebutting the facts of plaintiff's prima facie case of individual disparate treatment discrimination, the ADA provides two defenses—that any accommodation needed to make plaintiff qualified for the job would be an undue hardship or that employing the plaintiff would be a direct threat to others.

  - **Undue Hardship to the Employer.** Where plaintiff claims that she is qualified if the employer makes a reasonable accommodation, **§102(b)(5)(A) establishes an undue hardship defense if the employer "can demonstrate that the accommodation would impose an undue hardship on the operation of the business of such covered entity."**

  - **Direct Threat to Others.** A second defense is if the employer can prove that the plaintiff poses a direct threat to the health or safety of other individuals in the workplace. **"Direct threat" is "a significant risk to the health or safety of others that cannot be eliminated by reasonable accommodation."**

- **The Other Theories of Discrimination.** In addition to the central focus on individual disparate treatment discrimination, the ADA includes systemic disparate treatment, systemic disparate impact, a theory of liability based on the failure to provide a reasonable accommodation, which theory is independent of the duty not to discriminate against qualified individuals with disabilities, and special provisions dealing with testing and protection for a person who has a relationship with a person with a disability.

  - **Systemic Disparate Treatment Discrimination.** Formal policies or patterns and practices of discriminating because of disability amount to systemic disparate treatment discrimination.

    - **Benefit Plan Exception.** While the ADA prohibits employers from discriminating on the basis of disability in the provision of health care to its employees, the statute does provide an exception from systemic disparate treatment liability for bona fide benefit plans so that disparate treatment is permitted within these plans as long as the plan is not a subterfuge to evade the purposes of the ADA.

- **Systemic Disparate Impact Discrimination.** The ADA specifically includes disparate impact as a theory of discrimination so that it is discrimination for an employer to use "qualification standards, employment tests or other selection criteria that screen out . . . an individual with a disability or a class of individuals with disabilities unless the standard, test or other selection criteria . . . is shown to be job-related for the position in question and is consistent with business necessity."

- An employer need not justify an applicable federal safety regulation.

- **Failure to Reasonably Accommodate a Known Disability.** While reasonable accommodation is part of a basic disability discrimination case, §102(b)(5) creates a separate theory of liability if the employer fails to reasonably accommodate a known disability.

- **Testing That Causes Impact.** Section 102(b)(7) adds a special variant of disparate impact analysis for employment tests, requiring employers to show that "test results accurately reflect the skills, aptitude, or whatever other factor of such applicant or employee that such test purports to measure, rather than reflecting the impaired sensory, manual, or speaking skills of such employee or applicant."

- **Protected Relationship.** Section 102(b)(4) protects against discrimination because of a relationship with a person with a disability. Thus, the term "discriminate" includes: "excluding or otherwise denying equal jobs or benefits to a qualified individual because of the known disability of an individual with whom the qualified individual is known to have a relationship or association."

- **Special Disability Discrimination Problems.** There are a number of provisions that exclude alcohol and drug use rules, various sexuality-related conditions, kleptomania, etc., from the ADA. The ADA also establishes special rules concerning health examinations and questioning of employees about disabilities.

A. THE BROAD SCOPE OF THE AMERICANS WITH DISABILITIES ACT

The Americans with Disabilities Act of 1990, 42 U.S.C. §§12111 et seq., broadly prohibits discrimination against individuals with disabilities, including but not limited to employment discrimination. **While the general rule focuses on individual disparate treatment discrimination, the statutory scheme includes seven concepts within the meaning of the term "discrimination."** In addition to individual disparate treatment, the other concepts include systemic disparate treatment and systemic disparate impact, plus a reasonable accommodation duty, a special section dealing with testing, and protection against discrimination because one person has a relationship with another person who has a disability.

Because the central focus of the statute is on individual disparate treatment, the following sections will analyze an individual disparate treatment case before addressing the broader concepts of discrimination included within the scope of the ADA.

EXAM TIP

Disability issues are hot, so you should not be surprised to see an ADA question on an exam. These questions most always deal with individual disparate treatment because of disability. Unlike the other antidiscrimination statutes that are more open-ended definitions of the term "discrimination," the ADA involves a series of statutory definitions nested within each other.

B. INDIVIDUAL DISPARATE TREATMENT CASE OF DISABILITY DISCRIMINATION

The general rule prohibiting discrimination because of disability set forth in §102(a) is cast in terms of individual disparate treatment discrimination.

> No covered entity shall discriminate against a qualified individual with a disability because of the disability of such individual in regard to job application procedures, the hiring, advancement, or discharge of employees, employee compensation, job training, and other terms, conditions, and privileges of employment.

1. Exceptions to the definitions of disability.

There are several exceptions to the definition of "disability." Section 511(b) provides that the term "disability" shall not include—

    (i) transvestism, transsexualism, pedophilia, exhibitionism, voyeurism, gender identity disorders not resulting from physical impairments, or other sexual behavior disorders;

    (ii) compulsive gambling, kleptomania, or pyromania; or

    (iii) psychoactive substance use disorders resulting from current illegal use of drugs.

    The following sections will first discuss the requirements necessary to establish a prima facie case and will then describe the defenses available to the employer.

2. Plaintiff's Prima Facie Case

There are three elements necessary for a plaintiff to prove a prima facie individual disparate treatment case.

a. **An individual with a disability.** The first step for plaintiff to prove is that she is an individual with a disability. Subject to several exceptions, §3(2) sets forth three different definitions of "disability," with plaintiff having to prove she satisfies at least one of the three. Thus, "disability" means, with respect to an individual—

(A) a physical or mental impairment that substantially limits one or more of the major life activities of such individual;

(B) a record of such impairment; or

(C) being regarded as having such an impairment.

The following subsections will explore each of the three definitions.

i. **A physical or mental impairment that substantially limits a major life activity.** In Bragdon v. Abbott, 524 U.S. 624, 631 (1998), the Court, in deciding that a person who had HIV but was asymptomatic was an individual with a disability, set forth the three steps necessary to conclude that plaintiff had a physical or mental impairment that substantially limits a major life activity. "First, we consider whether respondent's HIV infection was a physical impairment. Second, we identify the life activity upon which respondent relies . . . and determine whether it constitutes a major life activity under the ADA. Third, tying the two statutory phrases together, we ask whether the impairment substantially limited the major life activity."

EXAM TIP

The first step of a prima facie case is to show that the plaintiff is an individual with a disability, which entails showing each of three parts: (1) a physical or mental impairment, (2) that implicates a major life activity, (3) because the impairment substantially limits the activity.

(a) **Physical or mental impairment.** The Court has taken a view of what constitutes an impairment that is broader than the regulations promulgated by the EEOC. The EEOC defines "physical or mental impairment" as follows:

(1) Any physiological disorder or condition, cosmetic disfigurement, or anatomical loss affecting one or more of the following body systems: neurological, musculo-

skeletal, special sense organs, respiratory (including speech organs), cardiovascular, reproductive, digestive, genito-urinary, hemic and lymphatic, skin, and endocrine; or

(2) Any mental or psychological disorder, such as mental retardation, organic brain syndrome, emotional or mental illness, and specific learning disabilities.

The Court in *Bragdon,* while acknowledging that HIV was not included in the list of specific disorders listed in regulations defining physical impairments, found that HIV did "fall well within the general definition set forth by the regulations." Thus, "HIV infection satisfies the statutory and regulatory definition of a physical impairment during every stage of the disease." 524 U.S. at 637.

(1) **Exceptions.** There are, however, two statutory limitations on what constitutes an impairment. Section 511(a) limits the scope of impairments by providing that "homosexuality and bisexuality are not impairments and as such are not disabilities under this Act."

(b) **Major life activities.** The Court, in *Bragdon,* indicated that major life activities should be viewed broadly and practically. Major life activities as stated in the ADA regulations include "caring for oneself, performing manual tasks, walking, seeing, hearing, speaking, breathing, learning, and working." 29 C.F.R. §1630.2(I). Even though the issue presented in *Bragdon* was limited to whether reproduction was a major life activity, the Court acknowledged that HIV raised broader issues so that it could be argued that "an HIV infection imposes substantial limitations on other major life activities." 524 U.S. at 637.

The Court rejected the attempt to limit major life activities to "those aspects of a person's life which have a public, economic or daily character." 524 U.S. at 638. As to reproduction as a major life activity, the Court concluded, "Reproduction falls well within the phrase 'major life activity.' 524 U.S. at 638.

Reproduction and the sexual dynamics surrounding it are central to the life process itself." 524 U.S. at 638.

(c) **Substantially limits.** The factors in determining whether an individual is "substantially limited" include the nature and severity of the impairment and the duration and the permanent or long-term impact resulting from the impairment. 29 C.F.R. §1630.2(j).

In *Bragdon,* the Court found that plaintiff's reproductive activity was substantially limited because of her HIV infection, even though having sex and getting pregnant were not impossible and were to some extent a question of personal choice. "The Act addresses substantial limitations on major life activities, not utter inabilities. Conception and childbirth are not impossible for an HIV victim but, without doubt, are dangerous to the public health." 524 U.S. at 641.

(1) **With or without mitigating measures.** In Sutton v. United Air Lines, Inc., 119 S. Ct. 2139 (1999), the Supreme Court held that whether an impairment substantially limits a major life activity is decided with whatever corrective measures the individual is taking. "Looking at the Act as a whole, it is apparent that if a person is taking measures to correct for, or mitigate, a physical or mental impairment, the effects of those measures—both positive and negative—must be taken into account when judging whether that person is 'substantially limited' in a major life activity and thus 'disabled' under the Act." 119 S. Ct. at 2146. Mitigating measures include wearing glasses, taking medicine and even a measure undertaken by the individual's own body systems to compensate for an impairment such as monocular vision. Albertson's Inc. v. Kirkenburg, 119 S. Ct. 2162 (1999).

EXAMPLES AND ANALYSIS

1. In Sutton v. United Air Lines, Inc., 119 S. Ct. 2139 (1999), plaintiffs were twin sisters who were commercial airline pilots for a regional commuter airline. They sued United after it refused to hire them to be major carrier pilots because their uncorrected vision was less than the 20/100 it required, even though their corrected vision was 20/20. While finding plaintiffs' vision to be a physical impairment within the meaning of the ADA, the Court found that plaintiff's vision as corrected did not substantially limit their major life activity of seeing.

2. In Murphy v. United Parcel Service, Inc. 119 S. Ct. 2133 (1999), plaintiff was found not "substantially limited" in a major life activity because his high blood pressure was mitigated with prescription medicine. Thus, he could be fired for his high blood pressure when unmedicated.

3. In Albertson's, Inc. v. Kirkenburg, 119 S. Ct. 2162 (1999), plaintiff was not "substantially limited" in a major life activity where his brain had itself mitigated his monocular vision so he could safely drive a truck. Thus, his termination because of his monocular vision did not violate the ADA.

---

(2) **Substantially limiting work.** With respect to the major life activity of working, the EEOC has further defined "substantially limited" as "significantly restricted in the ability to perform either a class of jobs or a broad range of jobs in various classes as compared to the average persons having comparable training, skills, and abilities. The inability to perform a single, particular job does not constitute a substantial limitation on the major life activity of working." 29 C.F.R. §1630.2(j)(3)(i). In Sutton v. United Air Lines, Inc., 119 S. Ct. 2139 (1999), plaintiffs were not hired to be "global airline" pilots by the defendant because of their poor uncorrected vision. Plaintiffs did not show that they were substantially limited in the major life activity of working because that was a single job and there were a number of other jobs available to plaintiffs utilizing their skills, such as regional airline pilot and pilot instructor.

 EXAMPLE AND ANALYSIS

In Forrisi v. Bowen, 794 F.2d 931 (4th Cir. 1986), plaintiff suffered from acrophobia (fear of heights) and he was discharged because his acrophobia prevented him from doing his engineering job, which involved climbing on high ladders. The Fourth Circuit concluded that, while acrophobia may be an impairment, it is not substantial enough to constitute a substantial limitation of the major life activity of working. Very few engineering jobs entail the exposure to heights that would trigger his acrophobia, so he could perform most engineering jobs.

---

ii. **A record of impairment.** People who may not now have a disability are nevertheless protected by the ADA if they are discriminated against because they have a record of having a disability. Thus, in School Bd. of Nassau County v. Arline, 480 U.S. 273 (1987), plaintiff had a long record of tuberculosis. If the employer had discriminated against her because of that record, she would still be within the statutory definition of an individual with a disability, even if, at the time the discrimination occurred, she had no present symptoms of the disease. Presumably, even a mistaken record that a person is an individual with a disability is a record of impairment.

iii. **Regarded as having an impairment.** If the employer regards someone as having a disability, the person is an individual with a disability even if the actual nature of their condition does not satisfy the requirement of "a physical or mental impairment that substantially limits one or more of the major life activities."

In Sutton v. United Air Lines, 119 S. Ct. 2139, plaintiffs were not regarded by defendant as having a disaiblity, even though the defendant refused to hire them because of their poor vision when uncorrected. "There are two apparent ways in which individuals may fall within [the 'regarded as'] statutory definition: (1) a covered entity mistakenly believes that a person has a physical impairment that substantially limits one or more major life activities, or (2) a covered entity mistakenly believes that an actual nonlimiting impairment substantially limits one or more major life activities." 119 S. Ct. at 2149–50. Here, defendant was not under either misperception since it did not perceive plaintiffs as being substantially limited in a major life activity. "[A]n employer is free to decide that physical characteristics or medical conditions that do not rise to the level of an impairment—such as one's height, build, or singing voice—are prefereable to others, just as it is free to decide that some limiting, but not *substantially* limiting, impairments make individuals less that ideally suited for a job." 119 S. Ct. at 2150 (emphasis in original).

b. **Qualified individual.** A person who is an individual with a disability within one of the definitions of disability described above must establish the second step of liability by showing that she is "qualified." Section 101(8) describes: "The term 'qualified individual with a disability' means an individual with a disability who, with or without **reasonable accommodation,** can perform the **essential functions** of the employment position that such individual holds or desires."

Section 104(a) limits qualified individuals by providing that "the term 'qualified individual with a disability' shall not include any employee or applicant who is currently engaging in the illegal use of drugs, when the covered entity acts on the basis of such."

EXAM TIP

The second issue of a prima facie case requires plaintiff to show that she is "qualified," which means being able to perform the "essential functions" of the job "with or without reasonable accommodation."

In Southeastern Community College v. Davis, 442 U.S. 397 (1979), the Court held that, in order to be a "qualified individual with a disability," the person must be able to meet the standards of a program considered as she is, with the disability, rather than looking at her other qualifications and deciding if she would be qualified if she did not have the disability.

In Albertson's, Inc. v. Kirkenburg, 119 S. Ct. 2162 (1999), the Court held that an individual who could not pass a vision test required by a federal regulation was not a "qualified individual" even though the government had undertaken an experimental program waiving the requirement.

Two factors are involved in determining if the plaintiff is qualified.

i.   **Essential functions.** To be qualified, the individual must be able to perform all the essential functions of the job. The ADA does not define "essential functions" but §101(8) does say that "consideration shall be given to the employer's judgment as to what functions of a job are essential, and if an employer has prepared a written description before advertising or interviewing applicants for the job, this description shall be considered evidence of the essential functions of the job." In Stone v. City of Mount Vernon, 118 F.3d 92 (2d Cir. 1997), the court indicated that this language does not require that it defer to the employer's judgment but it must look to evidence of the actual functions of the employees doing the job in question.

EXAMPLES AND ANALYSIS

1. In Simon v. St. Louis County, 656 F.2d 316 (8th Cir. 1981), a police officer, who became a paraplegic after he was shot while in the line of duty, could not perform many of the functions required of police officers as established in department regulations but he could perform desk jobs. The court found that requiring all officers to be able to undertake a forceful arrest was an essential function of a

police officer. The failure of the plaintiff to be able to do that meant he was not "qualified" and was not protected by the statute.

2. In contrast, in Kuntz v. City of New Haven, 2 A.D. Cas. (BNA) 905 (D. Conn. 1993), *aff'd without opinion*, 29 F.3d 622 (2d Cir. 1994), a police officer was denied a promotion to lieutenant on the ground that his heart condition prevented him from performing some of the duties of a lieutenant. The court looked at the essential functions of lieutenant and concluded that they were all supervisory in nature. Since Kuntz could perform all the supervisory functions, he was found to be a qualified individual with a disability and was protected against discrimination because of that disability.

---

    ii. **Reasonable accommodation as a component of the essential function element.** To be qualified, an individual needs to be able to perform the essential functions of the job but that performance is determined **"with or without reasonable accommodation."** Plaintiff can claim that she is qualified for the job in question without any accommodation. If that is plaintiff's claim, then reasonable accommodation is not at issue in an individual disparate treatment case. If, however, the plaintiff claims that she is qualified for the job if the employer makes some changes to accommodate her, then reasonable accommodation is at issue.

EXAM TIP

Unlike the reasonable accommodation issue in religion cases, the ADA defines what "reasonable accommodation" means.

    Section 101(9) says that the term "reasonable accommodation" may include: "(A) making existing facilities used by employees readily accessible to and usable by individuals with disabilities; and (B) job restructuring, part-time or modified work schedules, reassignment to a vacant position, acquisition or modification of equipment or devices, appropriate adjustments or modifications of examinations, training materials or policies, the provision of qualified readers or interpreters, and other similar accommodations for individuals with disabilities."

    (a) **Accommodation.** In Vande Zande v. State of Wisconsin Dept. of Administration, 44 F.3d 538, 542 (7th Cir. 1995), plaintiff, a paraplegic, argued that she should be allowed to work at home where she could better alleviate pressure ulcers. Judge Posner defined "accommodation" as follows: "It is plain enough what 'accommodation' means. The employer must be willing to consider making changes in its ordinary work rules, facilities, terms, and conditions in order to enable a disabled individual to work."

(b) **Reasonable accommodation.** In *Vande Zande,* the issue was whether cost versus benefit analysis played any role in determining whether an accommodation was reasonable or whether cost only came to bear as part of the undue hardship defense to a claim that the employer failed to reasonably accommodate the plaintiff.

> The difficult term is "reasonable." The plaintiff in our case, a paraplegic, argues in effect that the term just means apt or efficacious. An accommodation is reasonable, she believes, when it is tailored to the particular individual's disability. . . . Considerations of cost do not enter into the terms as the plaintiff would have us construe it. . . .
>
> [Rejecting that "questionable" interpretation, Posner said] at the very least, the cost [of an accommodation to be found reasonable] could not be disproportionate to the benefit. . . . The employee must show that the accommodation is reasonable in the sense both of efficacious and of proportional to costs. 44 F.3d at 542.

 # EXAMPLE AND ANALYSIS

In Borkowski v. Valley Central Sch. Dist., 63 F.3d 131 (2d Cir. 1995), a school teacher with neurological damage who had difficulty managing a classroom was denied tenure. The Second Circuit concluded that providing a teacher's assistant to help manage the class would be a reasonable accommodation because it would make the teacher a qualified individual with a disability. The failure to provide this accommodation was discrimination.

iii. **The relationship between the ADA and social security disability.** In Cleveland v. Policy Mgt. Sys. Corp., 526 U.S. 795, 119 S. Ct. 1597 (1999), the Court rejected the employer's argument that plaintiff's ADA claim was estopped by her prior claim for total disability benefits provided by Social Security. While disability for Social Security benefits means "inability to engage in any substantial gainful activity by reasons of any . . . physical or mental impairment," there are circumstances in which someone who has received Social Security benefits may nevertheless be a "qualified individual with a disability" under the ADA. First, the claimant may become qualified if the employer undertakes a reasonable accommodation of her needs. Second, the condition of a person in terms of disability may change over time. The Court did indicate that, to avoid summary judgment in her ADA case, the plaintiff must explain the inconsistency between her Social Security claim, that she is unable to work, and her ADA claim that she is a qualified individual with a disability.

c. **Proving the employer acted because of plaintiff's disability.** If plaintiff proves she is "a qualified individual with a disability," then she must still prove that the employer took its action against her because of her disability. She may use *Price Waterhouse* direct evidence that the employer admitted or conceded it took her disability into account or, where the employer denies that it took disability into account, she may rely on the *McDonnell Douglas/Burdine* circumstantial evidence test to support the factfinder in drawing an inference that the employer acted because of plaintiff's disability.

EXAM TIP

The ADA uses the *McDonnell Douglas* and *Price Waterhouse* approaches to link plaintiff's disability with the employment decision she challenges.

---

i. **Circumstantial evidence case.** In Norcross v. Sneed, 755 F.2d 113 (8th Cir. 1985), plaintiff claimed that she was not hired as a librarian because she was visually handicapped. In the absence of direct evidence of disability discrimination, *McDonnell Douglas/ Burdine* analysis applied. Since plaintiff was a qualified individual with a disability, who had applied for and been denied a job, which job was given to another, she made out a prima facie case of disability discrimination. Having established a prima facie case, the burden of production shifted to the employer to explain why it had acted. The employer denied that it had taken her disability into account at all in making its hiring decision and had considered her fully qualified for the job in question. The reason for not hiring plaintiff was that the person the employer selected instead was more qualified. The court agreed that the employer hired the most qualified individual and so plaintiff failed to prove that the employer had discriminated because of her disability.

    ii. **Direct evidence.** In Burns v. City of Columbus, Dept. of Public Safety, 90 F.3d 1173 (6th Cir. 1996), the court recognized that in some cases the employer acknowledges that it has taken plaintiff's disability into consideration in making its decision but argues that "the disability causes the plaintiff to be unqualified for the position . . . whether with or without reasonable accommodation of the disability. . . . Because direct evidence of the employer's discrimination exists, application of the *McDonnell Douglas* burden-shifting mechanism is inappropriate."

    The *Burns* court, however, found that the same decision defense of *Price Waterhouse* was not available in an ADA case because an employer is permitted to rely on the person's disability in determining whether she is "otherwise qualified" for the job.

3. Defenses to Disability Discrimination Claims

In addition to rebutting the facts of plaintiff's prima facie case of individual disparate treatment discrimination, the ADA provides two defenses—that any accommodation that is needed to make plaintiff qualified for the job would be an undue hardship to the employer or employing the plaintiff would be a direct threat to others.

EXAM TIP

There are two affirmative defenses in ADA cases: (1) where the plaintiff needs an accommodation, that accommodation is an undue hardship, which is defined as an action requiring a significant difficulty or expense, or (2) the plaintiff would be a direct threat to others.

---

    a. **Undue hardship to the employer.** Where plaintiff claims that she is qualified if the employer makes a reasonable accommodation, §102(b)(5)(A) establishes an undue hardship defense. Undue hardship is an exception to what would otherwise be discrimination where the employer "*can demonstrate that the accommodation would impose an undue hardship on the operation of the business of such covered entity.*"

    Section 101(10) further defines "undue hardship." "**In general.**—The term **'undue hardship' means an action requiring a significant difficulty or expense,** when considered in light of the factors set forth in subparagraph (b)." Subparagraph (b) lists factors including the nature and cost of the accommodation, the type of operation, and the overall financial resources of the facility involved and of the employer.

 # EXAMPLE AND ANALYSIS

In Dexler v. Tisch, 660 F. Supp. 1418 (D. Conn. 1987), plaintiff suffered a growth disorder which left him very short compared to the average adult. Having applied for a job in the post office, he requested as a reasonable accommodation that he be provided with a step stool or platform to help him load and unload trucks and mail containers he otherwise could not reach. The court concluded that the accommodation would be an undue hardship because of the safety and efficiency costs to the employer. Furthermore, assigning the tasks he could not do to someone else or providing another employee as an aide would amount to "doubling up" and would therefore be an undue hardship.

---

b.   **Direct threat to others.** Section 103(b) states that: "The term 'qualification standards' may include a requirement that an individual shall not pose a direct threat to the health or safety of other individuals in the workplace." **"Direct threat" is then defined in §101(3) as "a significant risk to the health or safety of others that cannot be eliminated by reasonable accommodation."**

In School Bd. of Nassau County v. Arline, 480 U.S. 273 (1987), the Court remanded the issue of whether Arline, who suffered from tuberculosis, was nevertheless qualified for a school teaching job or whether she was not qualified because she was a direct threat to the health or safety of others. In doing so, the Court said that the trial court must "conduct an individualized inquiry and make appropriate findings of fact." In saying that the basic factors were "well established," the Court approved the approach suggested by the American Medical Association, which defined the inquiry as including:

> [findings of] facts, based on reasonable medical judgments given the state of medical knowledge, about (a) the nature of the risk (how the disease is transmitted), (b) the duration of the risk (how long is the carrier infectious), (c) the severity of the risk (what is the potential harm to third parties) and (d) the probabilities the disease will be transmitted and will cause varying degrees of harm. 480 U.S. at 288.

In *Bragdon*, the Court rejected the idea that the good faith belief of the defendant, who was a dentist, that treating plaintiff was a direct threat to others was controlling. Instead, "courts should assess the objective reasonableness of the views of health care professionals without deferring to their individual judgments." The views of public health authorities are to be given special weight. But, a "health care professional [who is a defendant] who disagrees with the prevailing medical consensus may refute it by citing a credible scientific basis for deviating from the accepted norm." 524 U.S. at 650.

C. THE OTHER THEORIES OF DISCRIMINATION

In addition to the central focus on individual disparate treatment discrimination, the ADA includes systemic disparate treatment; systemic disparate impact; a theory of liability based on the failure to provide a reasonable accommodation, which theory is independent of the duty not to discriminate against qualified individuals with disabilities; a special provision dealing with testing; and protection for one person who has a relationship with another person who is an individual with a disability.

EXAM TIP

Even in an individual disparate impact case, it would be good if you find that one of the other theories of discrimination included within the ADA was also implicated in the question.

---

1. Systemic Disparate Treatment Discrimination

Formal policies or patterns and practices of discriminating because of disability amount to systemic disparate treatment discrimination.

 ## EXAMPLE AND ANALYSIS

In Galloway v. Superior Court, 816 F. Supp. 12 (D.D.C. 1993), plaintiff challenged an official policy in the local courts in the District of Columbia excluding blind individuals from jury duty as a violation of the Rehabilitation Act and Title II of the ADA. Blindness is a disability because it is a physical impairment which affects major life activities. The defense claimed that the blind could not perform the essential functions of jurors. Since blind judges and blind jurors were allowed in the federal courts, the court rejected the defense's argument that blind jurors were not qualified for the essential functions of a juror. Thus, systemic disparate treatment discrimination was established and the formal policy was struck down.

a. **Benefit plan exception.** While the ADA prohibits employers from discriminating on the basis of disability in the provision of health care to its employees, the statute does provide an exception from systemic disparate treatment liability for bona fide benefit plans. Section 501(c)(1) and (2) of the ADA allows disability-based distinctions in bona fide employee benefit plans based on different risks that are "based on or not inconsistent with State law." Section 501(c)(3) provides that the ADA does not prohibit or restrict "a person or organization covered by this Act from establishing, sponsoring, observing or administering the terms of a bona fide benefit plan that is not subject to State laws that regulate commerce." The final paragraph of §501(c) provides, "Paragraphs (1), (2), and (3) shall not be used as a subterfuge to evade the purposes of title I and III."

So far courts have upheld disability-based distinctions in insurance plans. In Ford v. Schering-Plough, 145 F.3d 601 (3d Cir. 1998), plaintiff attacked her employer's disability benefit plan because it differentiated between physical disabilities and mental disabilities. Benefits for physical disability continued until the disabled employee reached age 65, while mental disability benefits were capped at two years. The court rejected the challenge. "So long as every employee is offered the same plan regardless of that employee's contemporary or future disability status, then no discrimination has occurred even if the plan offers different coverage for various disabilities."

The only way to attack such formal policies of disability discrimination that are sheltered by the benefit plan exceptions is by showing the plan is a "subterfuge to evade the purposes" of the ADA. The court defined "subterfuge" as "a scheme, plan, stratagem, or artifice of evasion." 145 F.3d at 611. Where the disability benefit plan existed before the ADA was enacted, proving subterfuge may be impossible.

2. Systemic Disparate Impact Discrimination

The ADA specifically includes disparate impact as a theory of discrimination. Section 102(b) of the ADA defines the term "discriminate" to include two separate disparate impact concepts:

(3)   utilizing standards, criteria, or methods of administration . . . that have the effect of discrimination on the basis of disability; . . .

(6)   using qualification standards, employment tests or other selection criteria that screen out or tend to screen out an individual with a disability or a class of individuals with disabilities unless the standard, test or other selection criteria, as used by the covered entity, is shown to be job-related for the position in question and is consistent with business necessity.

The Interpretive Guidance issued by the EEOC, 29 C.F.R. pt. 1630, app. §1630.10, says that disparate impact analysis is "applicable to all types of selection criteria, including safety requirements, vision or hearing requirements, walking requirements, and employment tests." The EEOC further explains that selection criteria with a disparate impact that "do not concern an essential function of the job would not be consistent with business necessity."

In Albertson's, Inc. v. Kirkenburg, 119 S. Ct. 2162 (1999), the Court held that a vision requirement imposed by a federal regulation was not subject to disparate impact attack.

While showing job-relatedness and business necessity is an affirmitive defense, the exceptions included in Title VII for seniority, merit, and incentive systems are not available in ADA cases.

3. Failure to Reasonably Accommodate a Known Disability

As shown above, reasonable accommodation is an element in a basic disability discrimination case where the issue is whether an individual is qualified "with or without reasonable accommodation." Section 102(b)(5) creates a separate theory of liability by defining discrimination to include:

> (A) **not making reasonable accommodations to the known physical or mental limitations of an otherwise qualified individual with a disability who is an applicant or employee,** unless such covered entity can demonstrate that the accommodation would impose an undue hardship on the operation of the business of such covered entity; or

> (B) **denying employment opportunities** to a job applicant or employee who is an otherwise qualified individual with a disability, **if such denial is based on the need of such covered entity to make reasonable accommodation to the physical or mental impairments of the employee or applicant.**

EXAM TIP

The reasonable accommodation issue appears twice in the ADA, first as an issue imbedded in the question of whether an individual with a disability is "qualified," and, second, as a separate theory of liability. When the facts in a question raise issues of possible accommodation, deal with it in both contexts.

4. Testing that Causes Impact

Section 102(7) adds a requirement that employment tests test for the requirements of the job and not for the disabilities of the test takers. "Discriminate" includes:

failing to select and administer tests concerning employment in the most effective manner to ensure that, when such test is administered to a job applicant or employee who has a disability that impairs sensory, manual, or speaking skills, such test results accurately reflect the skills, aptitude, or whatever other factor of such applicant or employee that such test purports to measure, rather than reflecting the impaired sensory, manual, or speaking skills of such employee or applicant (except where such skills are the factors that the test purports to measure).

The job related or business necessity defense and the professional test exception that is applicable in Title VII test cases is not available in cases brought under §102(7).

5.   Protected Relationship

Section 102(b) protects against discrimination because of a relationship with a person with a disability. Thus, the term "discriminate" includes: "excluding or otherwise denying equal jobs or benefits to a qualified individual because of the known disability of an individual with whom the qualified individual is known to have a relationship or association."

D.   SPECIAL DISABILITY DISCRIMINATION PROBLEMS

There are a number of provisions of the ADA that deal with particular situations.

1.   Alcoholism and Illegal Drug Use

Section 511(b)(3) provides that the term "disability" shall not include "psychoactive substance use disorders resulting from current illegal use of drugs." Section 104(a) limits who is a qualified individual by providing that "the term 'qualified individual with a disability' shall not include any employee or applicant who is currently engaging in the illegal use of drugs, when the covered entity acts on the basis of such."

The ADA also specifies certain things employers may and may not do regarding drug and alcohol use. Section 104(c) provides that an employer

(1)   may prohibit the illegal use of drugs and the use of alcohol at the workplace by all employees;

(2)   may require that employees shall not be under the influence of alcohol or be engaging in the illegal use of drugs at the workplace; . . .

(4)   may hold an employee who engages in the illegal use of drugs or who is an alcoholic to the same qualification standards for employment or job performance and behavior that such entity holds other employees,

even if any unsatisfactory performance or behavior is related to the drug use or alcoholism of such employee.

Section 104(b) limits what an employer may do by providing that the provision that current users of illegal drugs are not qualified individuals with a disability shall not be construed to "exclude as a qualified individual with a disability an individual who . . . has successfully completed a supervised drug rehabilitation program and is no longer engaging in the illegal use of drugs, or has otherwise been rehabilitated successfully, . . . is participating in a supervised rehabilitation program and is no longer engaging in such use."

Section 104(d)(2) states that the ADA is neutral as to drug testing by employers: "Nothing in this title shall be constructed to encourage, prohibit, or authorize the conduct of drug testing for the illegal use of drugs by job applicants or employees or making employment decisions on such test results."

In Despears v. Milwaukee County, 63 F.3d 635 (7th Cir. 1995), plaintiff had his driver's license revoked for driving under the influence of alcohol. His employer then demoted him to a position that did not involve driving. The demotion was not disability discrimination because it was plaintiff's misuse of alcohol while driving that caused his loss of his license and demotion, not his alcoholism. The court differentiated discrimination because of status as an alcoholic, which is protected by the ADA, from discrimination because of the abuse of alcohol, which is not protected.

In Collings v. Longview Fibre, 63 F.3d 828 (9th Cir. 1995), the court held that the term "currently engaging in drug use" is not limited to the very moment at which the employer takes action against the employee but extends back even to weeks previous to the termination.

2. Sexuality Issues

The ADA has several provisions excluding persons from protection based on sexuality-related issues. Section 508 provides that "the term 'disabled' or 'disability' shall not apply to an individual solely because that individual is a transvestite." Further, §511(a) provides that, "For the purpose of the definition of 'disability' in section 3(2), homosexuality and bisexuality are not impairments and as such are not disabilities under this Act." Finally, §511(b)(1) provides that the term "disability" shall not include "transvestism, transsexualism, pedophilia, exhibitionism, voyeurism, gender identity disorders not resulting from physical impairments, or other sexual behavior disorders."

3. Gambling, Kleptomania, and Pyromania

Section 511(b)(2) provides that the term "disability" does not include compulsive gambling, kleptomania, and pyromania.

EXAM TIP

Alcoholism, illegal drug use, various sexuality issues, gambling, kleptomania, and pyromania have been popularly characterized as "morality" exceptions to the ADA.

---

4. Medical Examinations

While §102(d)(2)(B) allows an employer to "make preemployment inquiries into the ability of the applicant to perform job-related functions," §102(d)(2)(A) prohibits employers, before an offer of employment has been extended, from "conduct[ing] a medical examination or mak[ing] inquiries of a job applicant as to whether such applicant is an individual with a disability or as to the nature or severity of such disability." Once "an offer of employment has been made to a job applicant and prior to the commencement of the employment duties of such applicant," the employer may, according to §102(d)(3), condition the offer on the results of a medical examination if "all entering employees are subjected to such an examination regardless of disability" and the information collected is maintained in a separate, confidential medical record.

As to incumbent employees, §102(d)(4)(A) provides that employers may not require medical exams nor "make inquiries of an employee as to whether such employee is an individual with a disability or as to the nature or severity of the disability, unless such examination or inquiry is shown to be job-related and consistent with business necessity." Section 104(d)(1), however, provides that "a test to determine the illegal use of drugs shall not be considered a medical examination."

Employers may, according to §102(d)(4)(B), offer voluntary medical examinations that "are part of an employee health program available to employees at the work site" and "may make inquires into the ability of an employee to perform job-related functions."

REVIEW QUESTIONS AND ANSWERS

Question: What are the three elements of a plaintiff's prima facie case of individual disparate treatment disability discrimination?

Answer: The three elements plaintiff must prove to establish a prima facie case of individual disparate treatment discrimination because of the disability are:

1. The plaintiff is an individual with a disability.

2. The plaintiff is qualified.

3. The employer acted against plaintiff because of disability.

Question: What are the three ways of proving plaintiff is an individual with a disability?

Answer: Plaintiff must prove one of the three different statutory definitions of disability:

1. Plaintiff has a physical or mental impairment that substantially limits one or more major life activities.

2. Plaintiff has a record of a disability.

3. The employer regards plaintiff as an individual with a disability.

Question: What must plaintiff show to establish that she is qualified?

Answer: Plaintiff must prove that she can perform the essential functions of the job in question "with or without reasonable accommodation."

Question: If the plaintiff claims she is qualified for a job if the employer makes an accommodation, is cost a factor in whether that accommodation will be found reasonable?

Answer: There is not a final answer.

Question: What defenses are available to the employer in an individual disparate treatment case?

Answer: In addition to rebutting the basis of plaintiff's prima facie case, the employer can defend an individual disparate treatment case by proving that plaintiff poses a direct threat to others. Further, if plaintiff claims that she needs an accommodation to be qualified, the employer can defend by proving that the accommodation would cause it an undue hardship.

Question: Does the ADA prohibit other kinds of disability discrimination in addition to individual disparate treatment discrimination?

Answer: The ADA includes systemic disparate treatment; systemic disparate impact; a theory of liability based on the failure to provide a reasonable accommodation, which theory is independent of the duty not to discriminate against qualified individuals with disabilities; a special provision dealing with testing; and protection for a person who has a relationship with a person with a disability.

Question: May an employer ask a job applicant about a disability?

Answer: While the ADA allows an employer to "make preemployment inquiries into the ability of the applicant to perform job-related functions," it prohibits employers, before an offer of employment has been extended, from "conduct[ing] a medical examination or mak[ing] inquiries of a job applicant as to whether such applicant is an individual with a disability or as to the nature or severity of such disability."

13 EQUAL PAY FOR EQUAL WORK

CHAPTER OVERVIEW

Discrimination in compensation because of sex is governed by Title VII as well as by the Equal Pay Act of 1963.

- **Equal Work Focus of the EPA.** The Equal Pay Act limits its focus to guaranteeing "equal pay for equal work," where the jobs involve substantially the same content.

  - **Plaintiff's Prima Facie Case.** To make out an Equal Pay Act case, the plaintiff has the burden of proving that two workers of the opposite sex: (1) work in the same establishment (2) receive unequal pay (3) on the basis of sex (4) for work that is substantially identical.

    - **Equal Work Is Key Focus.** Since the jobs need not be identical in content, **the key element is proving that the job content is substantially equal.** Individual and classwide approaches have been used to determine whether the work is substantially equal.

  - **Defendant's Defenses.** Once plaintiff establishes a prima face case, the burden of persuasion shifts to the employer to prove the wages are paid pursuant to one of four affirmative defenses: (1) a seniority system; (2) a merit system; (3) a system that measures earnings by quality or quantity of production; or (4) a differential based on any other factor other than sex.

- **Factor Other than Sex Focus.** The defense that is most litigated is "any other factor other than sex." While there is a long list of factors, the key is that **a factor is not "other than sex" for EPA purposes if it would violate the disparate treatment definition of discrimination under Title VII.** Nevertheless, courts have found it hard to determine whether gender has played a part when compensation is based on the labor market or on economic benefit to the employer.

- **Title VII and Gender Compensation Claims.** Title VII prohibits discrimination in compensation because of sex. The Bennett Amendment to Title VII attempts to harmonize Title VII with the EPA by providing that, "It shall not be an unlawful employment practice under [Title VII] for any employer to differentiate upon the basis of sex in determining the amount of wages or compensation paid or to be paid to employees of such employer if such differentiation is authorized by [the Equal Pay Act]."

  - **EPA Defenses Apply in Title VII Cases.** In County of Washington v. Gunther, the Supreme Court decided that the Bennett Amendment means that the four affirmative defenses of the EPA are incorporated into Title VII claims of compensation discrimination since those differences described in the defenses are the only sex discrimination the EPA authorizes.

  - **Title VII Theories of Discrimination in Gender Compensation Cases.** Engrafting those four EPA affirmative defenses onto Title VII has lead to a constricted application of Title VII to claims of compensation discrimination because of sex.

    - **Individual Disparate Treatment.** Some courts have refused to apply *McDonnell Douglas/Burdine* and others have applied a modified form of it.

    - **Systemic Disparate Treatment Discrimination and Comparable Worth.** Evidence that would suffice to establish a general pattern of systemic disparate treatment discrimination in other areas of antidiscrimination law have been found not sufficient in claims of gender discrimination in compensation.

    - **Systemic Disparate Impact Discrimination.** Because the "any other factor other than sex" defense from the EPA applies to Title VII claims of sex discrimination in compensation, the systemic disparate impact theory is not applicable.

A. GENDER DISCRIMINATION IN COMPENSATION

Title VII prohibits sex discrimination and discrimination in compensation, so it does bear on the problem. The year before Title VII was enacted, Congress enacted the Equal Pay Act, 29 U.S.C. §206(d), which deals with one form of gender discrimination in wages by requiring employers to pay equal pay for equal work. This chapter will first look at the EPA and then look at how compensation discrimination because of sex is treated by Title VII.

EXAM TIP

Whenever a fact pattern involves discrimination against women in how much they are paid, it is necessary to look at both the Equal Pay Act and Title VII.

B. THE EQUAL PAY ACT

The Equal Pay Act (EPA) states: "No employer having employees subject to any provisions of this section **shall discriminate . . . on the basis of sex by paying wages to employees in such establishment at a rate less than the rate at which he pays wages to employees of the opposite sex . . . for equal work** on jobs the performance of which requires equal skill, effort, and responsibility, and which are performed under similar work conditions, except where such payment is made pursuant to i) a seniority system; ii) a merit system; iii) a system which measures earnings by quantity or quality of production; or iv) a differential based on any other factor other than sex." In Corning Glass Works v. Brennan, 417 U.S. 188 (1974), the Court outlined the basic structure of a case under the EPA:

1. **Plaintiff's Prima Facie Case**
   Plaintiff must show that an employer pays different wages to employees of the opposite sex "for equal work on jobs the performance of which require equal skill, effort, and responsibility, and which are performed under similar working conditions";

2. **Employer's Defenses**
   Once established, the burden of persuasion shifts to the employer to show that the differential is justified under one of the four exceptions to the act for payments made pursuant to i) a seniority system; ii) a merit system; iii) a system which measures earnings by quantity or quality of production; or iv) a differential based on any other factor other than sex.

 ## EXAMPLE AND ANALYSIS

In *Corning Glass,* the employer, a producer of glassware, began a night shift. Prior to that, Corning had only operated one shift per day and all the inspection work was performed by women. At the time the company introduced two shifts, state law prohibited women from working at night. Consequently, men were hired to perform the inspection function during the night shift but were paid at a substantially higher wage than the women who worked the day shift. Corning argued that the plaintiff had not established a prima facie case because the day shift work was not "performed under similar working conditions" as working the night shift. Relying on the legislative history of the EPA, the Court defined the term "working conditions" narrowly, limiting it to factors considered in formal job evaluation plans, and found that "working conditions" encompassed "surroundings" and "hazards" and not shift differentials. Consequently, the Court held that the work at issue was "equal work" regardless of whether performed at day or night.

The burden of persuasion then shifted to Corning to prove that the shift differential was "any other factor other than sex." While the wage differential appeared to be based on a shift differential, rather than a gender differential, the Court found it to be "on the basis of sex" because of the history of job segregation of day and night shift workers.

---

1. Plaintiff's Prima Facie Case

To establish a prima facie case, a plaintiff must prove that two workers of the opposite sex worked: (1) in the same "establishment"; (2) received unequal pay; (3) "on the basis of sex"; (4) for work that is "equal."

a. The establishment requirement. The EPA does not define the term "establishment." In the context of the Fair Labor Standards Act, the statute to which the EPA was attached, the Supreme Court defined establishment as a "distinct physical place of business." Phillips, Inc. v. Walling, 324 U.S. 490, 496 (1945). In EPA cases, however, "establishment" may be more expansively defined because the EPA's construction differs somewhat from that of the FLSA. Several EPA cases have suggested that the mere existence of physically separate operations is not necessarily fatal to an EPA claim. Relevant considerations include: (1) the degree to which one central authority administers all employment relations; (2) the movement of employees among locations; and (3) whether the duties and working conditions at the separate facilities are similar.

b. Unequal pay. Comparing the base pay of two jobs is not always as straightforward as it seems. Problems arise with regard to inflation, fringe benefits, and rates of pay. For example, in Bence v. Detroit Health Corp., 712 F.2d 1024 (6th Cir. 1983), cert. denied, 465 U.S. 1025 (1984), a spa chain, with segregated gyms for its male and female members, paid male employees a higher commission rate than female employees. The pay scale differed because the membership was predominately female and the company justified the pay differential on the need to pay men at a higher rate to achieve equal salaries for men and women.

While the employer argued that the males and females received "equal total remuneration," the court held that the employees established a prima facie case because the EPA commands an equal rate of pay for equal work.

c.   **Equal work.** This issue is central to an EPA case. The EPA only requires equal pay for "equal work on jobs the performance of which requires equal skill, effort, and responsibility, and which are performed under similar working conditions." The plaintiff bears the burden of establishing that the jobs are equal. **Equal work, however, has been construed to mean "substantially equal" and not identical. To constitute equal work, there must be a substantial, perhaps predominate, core set of tasks common to both jobs.** The more common the tasks, the greater the likelihood the court will find "equal work." Where the differences in the tasks performed are de minimis, the courts will often find "equal work," unless the positions require greatly different skill, effort, or responsibility.

EXAM TIP

The EPA is narrowly focused on people doing work that, while not identical, must be substantially the same. The issue of equal work requires intense factual analysis.

---

i.   **Job analysis.** The first step is a factual analysis, in which the court identifies the elements of the jobs to be compared and determines what, if any, common elements exist. The second step is to decide whether the differences are more or less equal with regard to skill, effort, responsibility, and working conditions.

ii. **Two approaches to comparing jobs.** Courts have developed two approaches to comparing jobs:

(a) **Comparing two individuals.** The easiest case involves the individual plaintiff comparing herself with a comparable male worker.

 EXAMPLE AND ANALYSIS

The Ninth Circuit in Hein v. Oregon College of Educ., 718 F.2d 910 (9th Cir. 1983) addressed the equal pay issue for professors. The plaintiffs sought to bring an EPA action by comparing their pay to that of various employees of the opposite sex. The question whether jobs are "substantially equal" is a question of fact that must be decided on a case-by-case basis. The court addressed each plaintiff separately. Consequently, the court examined the "skill, effort, responsibility, and working conditions" of each plaintiff as compared to a single male employee. In performing this task, the court noted that the EPA applies to *jobs* that require equal skills, and not to *employees* that possess equal skills. In this case, one of the plaintiffs chose the highest paid male employee for comparison. The court, however, found that the proper test was to compare the plaintiff's wages to the average wages paid to all employees of the opposite sex performing "substantially equal" work.

(b) **The Class Approach.** In broader scale actions, the court compares a predominately female classification with a predominately male classification. Shultz v. Wheaton Glass, 421 F.2d 259 (3d Cir. 1970), *cert. denied*, 398 U.S. 905 (1970) establishes the "least different" and "most alike" principles of job comparison. Both are based on the principle that where the job differences are insignificant, it is hard to believe that pay disparities are linked to those differences, rather than to gender. *Wheaton Glass* can also be read more broadly to mean that two jobs constitute equal work when they share a predominate common core set of tasks, in conjunction with extrinsic evidence that the difference in tasks does not explain the difference in pay.

(1) **The "least different" principle.** The least different principle compares the lower paid female job with the job held by a male whose tasks are the least different from those of the female, rather than with the typical male job.

(2) **The "most alike" principle.** The "most alike" principle looks to the male job that is most like the female job to determine if there is equal work for unequal pay.

EXAMPLE AND ANALYSIS

In *Wheaton Glass,* the government brought an action claiming that the employer violated the EPA by paying "female selector-packers" less than "male selector-packers." In this case, the male selector-packers performed additional duties during downtime in production that the women workers did not perform. Addressing the issue of equal work, the court stated that Congress did not require that the jobs be identical; they need only be substantially equal. As a result, the court found that the additional duties performed by the male selector-packers did not justify the wage differential because these tasks did not add enough real value to the employer to justify the pay differential favoring male employees.

---

d.   **On the basis of sex.** Plaintiff must prove that the wage differential is "on the basis of sex." Demonstrating that there exists a single person of the opposite sex who receives unequal wages for equal work in the same establishment appears to create a prima facie case, subject to the employer's rebuttal. But this element is not an intent-to-discriminate element. The sex basis need not be obvious. For example, in *Corning Glass*, the wage differential appeared to be based on a shift differential, rather than a gender differential, but the Court found it to be on the basis of sex because of the history of job segregation of day and night shift workers so that only men received the higher pay.

2.   **Defenses to the Prima Facie Case**

The defendant in an EPA case may avoid liability by proving one of the four statutory exceptions. **The requirement of equal pay for equal work does not apply where the wages are paid pursuant to: "i) a seniority system; ii) a merit system; iii) a system that measures earnings by quality or quantity of production; or iv) a differential based on any other factor other than sex."** Unlike a *McDonnell Douglas/Burdine* case under Title VII, where the defendant merely has the burden to produce a "legitimate nondiscriminatory reason" for its action, in an EPA case, the defendant bears the burden of persuasion in proving a statutory exception.

a.   **"Any other factor other than sex."** The bulk of the litigation relating to the exceptions has focused on the catch-all "any other factor other than sex" defense. For example, in Los Angeles Dept. of Water & Power v. Manhart, 435 U.S. 702 (1978), a group of female employees challenged their employer's pension plan, which required female employees to contribute more each pay period than men in order to fund an equal monthly retirement benefit. In *Manhart*, the employer claimed that the plan was based on differences in life expectancy, not gender, and therefore was within the EPA defense of "any other factor other than sex." The Supreme Court, however, rejected the defendant's argument and held that the plan was "on the basis of sex" because the employer used a gender classification. *Manhart* makes clear that a **factor cannot be "other than sex" for EPA purposes if it would violate the disparate treatment definition of discrimination under Title VII.**

Some examples of "other factors":

   i. Economic Benefit. In Hodgson v. Robert Hall Clothes, Inc., 473 F.2d 589 (3d Cir. 1973), *cert. denied*, 414 U.S. 866 (1973), the Third Circuit held that the employer was justified in paying higher commissions to salesmen selling men's clothes because those sales generated more profits for the company.

   ii. Market rate. Employers typically seek to explain the higher wage of a male employee by claiming that the higher salary was required in order to obtain the employee's services. Additionally, employers claim that the male employee bargained more effectively or had a stronger negotiating position. For example, in Horner v. Mary Institute, 613 F.2d 706 (8th Cir. 1980), the Eighth Circuit accepted the employer's argument that the male employees' experience and ability justified a higher salary. The market argument is difficult. On one hand, the EPA was not designed to relieve individuals of the consequences of their lack of value in the marketplace. On the other hand, the collective result of gender discrimination in employment gives men greater market value as workers than women.

   iii. Remedying past discrimination. In Board of Regents, University of Nebraska v. Dawes, 522 F.2d 380 (8th Cir. 1975), *cert. denied*, 424 U.S. 914 (1976), the university devised a plan to equalize the salaries of female employees and to remedy potential discrimination claims. Under the plan, the average male salary became the minimum female salary. Because the scheme left several male employees receiving less than the average, the Eighth Circuit found a violation of the EPA. The decision in *Dawes* creates a problem for employers deciding whether and how to correct possible equal pay violations against women. Several circuits have rejected similar claims by male employees that employer compensation plans favoring women violated the EPA. See, e.g., Winkes v. Brown University, 747 F.2d 792 (1st Cir. 1984) (court denied a claim that a salary increase given to a female professor to retain her services in the face of a competing offer was discriminatory); Grann v. City of Madison, 738 F.2d 786 (7th Cir.), *cert. denied*, 469 U.S. 918 (1984) (court held that remedying discrimination was "an absolute bar to a suit by fellow employees claiming that the action required by the remedial order constitutes a violation of Title VII"); Ende v. Board of Regents of Regency University, 757 F.2d 176 (7th Cir. 1985) (court held that a formula utilized to remedy perceived discrimination against women need not be applied to lower paid males).

   iv. Shift differentials as in *Corning Glass.*

   v. Temporary reassignments. The EEOC recognizes that employees may be temporarily assigned and paid the rate of their previous position instead of the wages applicable to the job currently being performed.

vi. **Temporary/part-time employees.** Employers traditionally have different pay rates for temporary and permanent employees. Though the interpretative bulletins allow such differentials, they may conceal sex discrimination if the temporary employees are women and the higher paid male employees are the permanent workers.

vii. **Education and experience.** Experience can be a valid basis for wage differentials, even if the work is found to be equal. Similarly, education-based differentials should be upheld provided that they are applied evenly to both genders.

viii. **Head of household.** Because head-of-household–based differentials bear no relationship to the requirements of the job, wage differentials based on this criteria will be closely scrutinized. Again, the employer must apply this criteria in a gender neutral manner to be successful with this defense.

b. **Seniority system.** In Mitchell v. Jefferson City Bd. of Educ., 936 F.2d 539, 545 (11th Cir. 1991), the court found that the alleged "seniority system" was not a seniority system within the meaning of either Title VII or the EPA since an increase in the employee's relative length of employment did not necessarily improve employment rights and benefits.

c. **Merit systems.** Unlike seniority systems, which are quantifiable and objective, merit systems range from objective to almost totally subjective. Some courts have required merit systems to involve an organized and structured procedure that enables employers to evaluate according to predetermined criteria.

d. **Incentive systems.** Most incentive pay systems can be characterized as objective and job related. Because the exception overlaps with the "equal work" determination, there are fewer interpretation problems. In Bence v. Detroit Health Corp., 712 F.2d 1024, 1029 (6th Cir. 1983), the court rejected an employer's argument that the different commission rates for men and women were an incentive system because the system differentiated between men and women.

C. USING TITLE VII TO ATTACK GENDER-BASED WAGE DISCRIMINATION

The EPA only applies where the content of the work is basically the same. Therefore, where the jobs at issue are not substantially equal, the only means to redress wage discrimination because of sex is Title VII. Clearly, Title VII's language prohibits sex discrimination in "compensation."

1. The Bennett Amendment Harmonizes the EPA and Title VII

Congress did attempt to harmonize Title VII with the EPA, via the Bennett Amendment to Title VII, which provides: "It shall not be an unlawful employment practice . . . for any employer to differentiate upon the basis of sex in determining the amount of the wages or compensation paid to employees . . . if such differentiation is authorized by the [EPA]." In County of Washington v. Gunther, 452 U.S. 161 (1981), the Supreme Court interpreted the Bennet Amendment. Based on the structure of the Bennett Amendment and the EPA, the Court found that the language of the Bennett Amendment intends only to incorporate the four affirmative defenses of the EPA into Title VII gender compensation cases, and nothing more.

EXAM TIP

A Title VII sex discrimination case involving compensation discrimination is different from all other Title VII cases because it is necessary to deal with the Bennett Amendment, which supposedly harmonizes Title VII with the narrower, more focused EPA. Beyond the Bennett Amendment, Title VII sex discrimination cases involving compensation have appeared to apply Title VII quite narrowly.

---

2. Title VII Theories of Discrimination in Gender Compensation Cases

Engrafting those four EPA affirmative defenses onto Title VII has lead to a constricted application of Title VII to claims of compensation discrimination because of sex.

a. **Individual disparate treatment.** The lower courts have taken a variety of approaches to individual disparate treatment cases claiming sex discrimination in compensation.

    i. *McDonnell Douglas/Burdine* **circumstantial evidence cases.** Some lower courts have found that the *McDonnell Douglas/Burdine* approach is unavailable while others allow it.

        (a) **Circumstantial evidence approach not available.** The Seventh Circuit views gender compensation claims narrowly, requiring evidence of discrimination that is "clear and straightforward" to make out a Title VII wage discrimination claim. See EEOC v. Sears, Roebuck & Co., 839 F.2d 302 (7th Cir. 1988). The Fifth Circuit holds that, in gender compensation discrimination claims, the plaintiff must show (1) a "transparently sex-based system for wage determination or; (2) offer direct evidence that the employer paid a female less than it would have paid a male." *See* Plemer v. Parsons-Gilbane, 713 F.2d 1127 (5th Cir. 1983).

(b) **Circumstantial evidence approach applies.** In Miranda v. B & B Cash Grocery Store, Inc., 975 F.2d 1518 (11th Cir. 1992), a buyer for a grocery store claimed that she was paid less than male employees who did similar but not equal work. The Eleventh Circuit concluded that the *McDonnell Douglas/Burdine* approach is the appropriate framework for evaluating gender-based wage discrimination claims under Title VII.

In Kouba v. Allstate Ins. Co., 691 F.2d 873 (9th Cir. 1982), the court held that *McDonnell Douglas/Burdine* applied, but in a modified form. Once a plaintiff makes out a prima facie case, then rather than shifting only the burden of production, the Bennett Amendment has the effect of shifting the burden of persuasion to the employer to prove one of the four EPA statutory defenses.

 # EXAMPLE AND ANALYSIS

In *Kouba,* several employees challenged Allstate's policy, which computed the minimum salary for new agent on the basis of ability, education, experience, and prior salary, claiming that it violated Title VII. As a result of the policy, female agents on average earned less than their male counterparts mostly because their prior salaries were lower. Because the court found that plaintiffs had established a prima facie case of discrimination and that shifted the burden of persuasion to the employer, the court remanded for a determination whether the employer could prove that the criteria it relied upon were factors other than sex.

b. **Systemic disparate treatment discrimination and comparable worth.**
While many women suffer discrimination by employers failing to pay men and women equally for doing equal work, continuing job segregation between men's and women's jobs that are not equal is a more significant problem of compensation discrimination. Attacking that discrimination has been given the name "comparable worth," with plaintiffs arguing that women should be paid equally for the value their efforts contribute to the employer with men making comparable contributions. Those efforts have not been fruitful.

In American Fedn. of State, County and Mun. Employees v. State of Washington, 770 F.2d 1401 (9th Cir. 1985), the Ninth Circuit held that the plaintiffs failed to establish the requisite elements of intent to discriminate by either circumstantial or direct evidence. In so holding, the court reasoned that intent to discriminate cannot be based on an employer's setting wages according to prevailing market rates. The free market system is based on a variety of factors including the value of a particular job, the availability of workers, and the effectiveness of collective bargaining. Nothing in Title VII or its legislative history indicates an intent to abrogate fundamental economic principles such as the laws of supply and demand or to prevent employers from competing in labor markets. At odds with the general systemic disparate treatment cases of *Teamsters, Hazelwood,* and *Bazemore,* the court held that job evaluation studies and comparable worth statistics alone are insufficient to establish the intent to discriminate required under disparate treatment theory. *American Federation* stands for the proposition that an employer's reliance on labor markets to set wages for jobs that are predominately segregated by gender is insufficient to establish an intent to discriminate.

 # EXAMPLE AND ANALYSIS

In *American Federation,* the state of Washington commissioned a study to determine whether a wage disparity existed between jobs held predominately by females and jobs held predominately by males. The study found a disparity of 20 percent for jobs of comparable worth. Comparable worth was calculated by evaluating jobs under four criteria: knowledge and skill, mental demands, accountability, and working conditions. Under *Bazemore,* the study would be sufficient to establish a prima facie case of systemic disparate treatment. But, in the area of gender compensation claims, the court found such a showing not sufficient.

---

    c. **Systemic disparate impact.** In the *American Federation* case, the Ninth Circuit held that for sex discrimination claims based on comparable jobs, the disparate impact theory of discrimination does not apply. The court held that relying on competitive market rates does not qualify as a facially neutral policy or practice within the disparate impact analysis because market prices are inherently job related; thus, they cannot be pretexts to shield intentional discrimination.

        A more persuasive reason that disparate impact may be unavailable in comparable worth cases is that the EPA's affirmative defenses—

including the "any other factor other than sex" defense—limits all Title VII compensation cases to disparate treatment theory. While reliance on the labor market has a disparate impact on women's salaries, the labor market is a factor other than sex.

REVIEW QUESTIONS AND ANSWERS

Question: Do the EPA and Title VII both apply to sex discrimination compensation claims?

Answer: Yes, though the EPA is sharply focused on situations where the jobs are substantially equal.

Question: What are the elements of a prima facie EPA case?

Answer: To make out an Equal Pay Act case, the plaintiff has the burden of proving that two workers of the opposite sex: (1) work in the same establishment (2) receive unequal pay (3) on the basis of sex (4) for work that is substantially equal.

Question: How can jobs be shown to be substantially equal?

Answer: Jobs can be shown to be substantially equal in content by comparing the work performed by two individual workers or by showing that two groups of workers do basically the same work, even if they have different job titles. Within groups, that comparison may be made by focusing on the workers who are least different and most alike.

Question: What are the defenses available to the employer to an EPA case?

Answer: In addition to rebutting the evidence plaintiff used to establish the prima facie case, the EPA provides four affirmative defenses, with the burden of persuasion on the defendant. Those are where the wages are paid pursuant to: "i) a seniority system; ii) a merit system; iii) a system that measures earnings by quality or quantity of production; or iv) a differential based on any other factor other than sex."

Question: What is included in the "any other factor other than sex" defense?

Answer: While there is a long list of factors, the key is that a factor cannot be "other than sex" for EPA purposes if it would violate the disparate treatment definition of discrimination under Title VII.

Question: Did Congress harmonize the EPA and Title VII in their respective approaches to compensation discrimination based on sex?

Answer: Congress added the Bennett Amendment to Title VII, which the Supreme Court has interpreted to mean that the four affirmative defenses of the EPA are incorporated into Title VII claims of compensation discrimination since the EPA "authorizes" only those differences described in these defenses.

Question: Do the courts apply the three general theories of discrimination to gender compensation cases in the same way these theories are applied in other cases?

Answer: The courts have not applied the traditional theories of discrimination to sex discrimination claims involving compensation in the same way these theories are generally applied.

1. While all courts find that the *Price Waterhouse* direct evidence approach applies, some courts refuse to apply the *McDonnell Douglas/Burdine* approach and others modify the application of this circumstantial evidence approach.

2. Statistical evidence that would establish a prima facie case of systemic disparate treatment discrimination has been held not to suffice in gender compensation cases.

3. Because of the EPA defense that applies in Title VII if wages are paid pursuant to "any other factor other than sex," disparate impact theory does not apply to gender compensation cases.

14 COVERAGE OF THE ANTIDISCRIMINATION STATUTES

CHAPTER OVERVIEW

Coverage issues are important because the coverage determination sets a floor below which an antidiscrimination statute does not apply.

- **Title VII Coverage.** The antidiscrimination statutes enacted since 1964 have their coverage provisions modeled on Title VII's provisions.

  - **An Employer Under Title VII.** Section 701(b) further defines an "employer" as a "*person* engaged in an *industry affecting commerce* who has fifteen or more *employees* for each working day in each of twenty or more calendar weeks in the current or preceding calendar year, and any agent of such a person." A person is an employee if she is on the employer's payroll.

    - **A "Person" as "Employer."** A "person" pursuant to §701(a) comports with our everyday notions of what a person should be: natural persons as well as legal entities acting as individuals.

    - **An "Industry Affecting Commerce."** Congress exercised its power under the Commerce Clause to reach the private sector to the extent an employer is engaged in "an industry affecting commerce."

  - **State and Local Government Employers.** In the 1972 amendments to Title VII, Congress expanded the coverage of Title VII to include state and local governmental employers. In doing so, Congress relied on its powers enumerated in both the Commerce Clause in Article I of the Constitution as well as §5 of the Fourteenth Amendment.

- **Federal Employment.** In the 1972 amendments to Title VII, Congress added a new §717, which extended Title VII to most federal employment but established specialized procedures for federal employees to advance their claims of discrimination.

- **Individual Liability of Agents.** Section 701(b) defines "employer" to include "any agent" of the employer. It is clear that "agents" were included in the definition of employer so that the employer was clearly liable for the acts of its agents. There is a split within the circuits whether the agents themselves are liable as employers for the discrimination that they cause.

- **Extraterritorial Employment.** Section 701(f) defines "employee" to apply Title VII extraterritorially: "With respect to employment in a foreign country, such term includes an individual who is a citizen of the United States."

- **An "Employee" Under Title VII.** Section 701(f) defines an "employee" as simply an individual employed by an employer. "Employee" does not, however, include any person elected to public office in any state or political subdivision of any state.

- **Coverage of the ADEA.** The ADEA coverage provisions mirror Title VII but coverage requires 20 employees, not the 15 that satisfies Title VII.

- **Reconstruction Civil Rights Statutes.** Three civil rights statutes survive from the Reconstruction period following the Civil War and have potential impact on employment discrimination.

  - **42 U.S.C. §1981.** 42 U.S.C. §1981 prohibits race discrimination in all contracts. Since so many relationships in our society are legally characterized as contractual, §1981 applies very broadly to all contracting parties in all contracts. It does not, however, reach the federal government as employer.

  - **42 U.S.C. §1983.** Liability under §1983 applies to "every person" acting "under color of law who interferes with constitutional rights." "Under color of law" includes actions by defendants "who carry a badge of authority of a state and represent it in some capacity whether they act in accordance with their authority or misuse it."

  - **42 U.S.C. §1985.** Section 1985 provides a remedy when two or more individuals conspire to deprive another of equal protection or equal privileges and immunities under the law, but the deprivation of Title VII rights are not included within the protection of §1985.

- **Americans with Disabilities Act.** Section 102(a) of the ADA creates the general rule prohibiting discrimination because of disability by any *covered entity.*

- **Covered Entities.** Section 101(2) defines "covered entity" as "any employer, employment agency, labor organization, or joint labor-management committee." The definition of an "employer" under this Act mirrors Title VII, so that a person who employs at least 15 people for each working day for 20 or more weeks is covered. Title II of the ADA provides for coverage for public entities.

- **An "Employer" Under the EPA.** The Equal Pay Act looks to the Fair Labor Standards Act to determine who is an employer within its coverage. There are two separate ways to establish coverage.

  - **The Individual Test.** If the individual plaintiff was "engaged in commerce" or "in the production of goods for commerce," then that person's employer is covered by the Fair Labor Standards Act and the Equal Pay Act.

  - **The Enterprise Test.** In 1961, FLSA was amended to create a new basis for coverage that looks to whether the enterprise is engaged in commerce by doing a particular dollar volume of business or was among a list of specified industries where the enterprise had individual employees who were engaged in commerce or in the production of goods for commerce.

A.   COVERAGE ISSUES ARE IMPORTANT TO SCOPE OF APPLICATION

Congress has passed a number of different antidiscrimination statutes, which vary somewhat in their coverage of employment. Conduct that would be found discriminatory if done by an employer within the coverage of a statute is not illegal when the employer lies beyond the scope of a statute's coverage. Thus, not all discrimination by all employers is prohibited.

B.   TITLE VII OF THE CIVIL RIGHTS ACT OF 1964

Section 703(a) makes it an unlawful employment practice for "*an employer* to fail or refuse to hire or discharge any individual or otherwise to discriminate against any individual with respect to his compensation, terms, conditions, or privileges of employment . . . or to limit, segregate, or classify his *employees* or *applicants* . . . because of such individual's race, color, religion, sex, or national origin." Title VII also covers employment agencies and labor organizations.

1.   An Employer Under Title VII

The definition of "employer" includes any person engaged in an industry affecting commerce with 15 or more employees. Section 701(b) further defines an "employer" as a "*person* engaged in an *industry affecting commerce* who has fifteen or more *employees* for each working day in each of twenty or more calendar weeks in the current or preceding calendar year, and any agent of such a person." Bona fide private membership clubs that are tax exempt are exempted from coverage of Title VII.

EXAM TIP

Whenever a fact pattern with Title VII or ADEA substantive issues has anything in it about a small employer, and has numbers of employees described, apply the coverage rules. Title VII coverage reaches employers with 15 employees, while the ADEA reaches only those employers with 20 employees.

---

a. **Counting employees.** In Walters v. Metropolitan Educ. Enter., Inc., 519 U.S. 202 (1997), the Court resolved how to count employees for purposes of determining Title VII coverage. Finding a bright line test most appropriate, the Court adopted the "payroll" method of counting employees. By looking at who is on the employer's payroll, "all one needs to know is whether the employee started or ended employment during that year and, if so, when. He is counted as an employee for each day working after arrival and before departure."

Where a single employer does not have 15 employees, it is sometimes possible to combine two or more entities and count them as a single employer. In Westphal v. Catch Ball Prods. Corp., 953 F. Supp. 475 (S.D.N.Y. 1997), the court found that two entities could be counted as one for purposes of Title VII coverage where there were: (1) interrelated operations; (2) common management; (3) centralized control of labor relations; and (4) common ownership. Agency principles apply when an agent of the employer commits a violation of the Act.

b. **A "person" as "employer."** Put simply, a "person" pursuant to §701(a) comports with our everyday notions of what a person should be: natural persons as well as legal entities acting as individuals. Further, the definition of employer includes individuals, governments, and governmental agencies, political subdivisions, labor unions, partnerships, associations, corporations, legal representatives, mutual companies, joint-stock companies, trusts, unincorporated organizations, trustees, or receivers.

c. **An "industry affecting commerce."** Pursuant to the Constitution, federal legislation must be based on a power enumerated in the Constitution, such as the power to regulate interstate commerce. Although the statute stipulates that the definition of an "industry affecting commerce" derives from the Labor Management Reporting and Disclosure Act and the Railway Labor Act, that definition is more easily understood through the Supreme Court's decisions of Heart of Atlanta Motel v. United States, 379 U.S. 241 (1964), Katzenbach v. McClung, 379 U.S. 294 (1964), and United States v. Lopez, 514 U.S. 549 (1995). In *Heart of Atlanta,* the Court ruled that discrimination at a motel located near two interstate highways discouraged those in the black community from traveling and that had an impact on interstate commerce. The Court, in *Katzenbach,* extended the concept of an "industry affecting commerce" to a restaurant located away from all interstate highways because it bought provisions that had been in interstate commerce. Discrimination on the part of the individual restaurant did not affect commerce very much, but when this restaurant was taken in the aggregate with all other such enterprises, there was an impact on commerce by discouraging travel by those in the black community. In United States v. Lopez, 514 U.S. 549 (1993), however, the Court cut back from the most liberal view of what affects commerce by holding that activity must "substantially" affect commerce before it could be reached by an act of Congress. Allegations that commerce is affected must be supported and cannot be based on inference after inference, according to the majority in *Lopez.*

d.   **State and local government employers.** In the 1972 amendments to Title VII, Congress expanded the coverage of Title VII to include state and local governmental employers. In doing so, Congress relied on its powers enumerated in both the Commerce Clause in Article I of the Constitution as well as §5 of the Fourteenth Amendment. Antidiscrimination legislation that is applicable to state and local governmental employers has been upheld under the Commerce Clause, EEOC v. Wyoming, 460 U.S. 226 (1983), and under §5 of the Fourteenth Amendment, Fitzpatrick v. Bitzer, 427 U.S. 445 (1976). Kimel v. Florida Bd. of Regents, 120 S. Ct. 631 (2000), however, raises a question of the constitutionality of disparate impact analysis as applied to the states.

e.   **Federal employment.** In the 1972 amendments to Title VII, Congress added a new §717, which extended Title VII to most federal employment but established specialized procedures for federal employees to advance their claims of discrimination.

f.   **Individual liability of agents.** Section 701(b) defines "employer" to include "any agent" of the employer. It is clear that "agents" were included in the definition of employer so that the employer was clearly liable for the acts of its agents.

There is a split within the circuits whether the agents themselves are individually liable as employers for the discrimination that they cause. In Miller v. Maxwell's Intl., Inc., 991 F.2d 583 (9th Cir. 1993), the court found that agents are not individually liable for discrimination. In Reinhold v. Commonwealth of Virginia, 135 F.3d 172, *opinion withdrawn & superseded on reh'g by* 151 F.3d 172 (4th Cir. 1998), the court held that an individual is liable as an agent if she serves as a supervisor and exercises significant control over hiring, firing, and other terms and conditions of employment.

g.   **Extraterritorial employment.** Section 701(f), which was added by the Civil Rights Act of 1991, overturned EEOC v. Arabian American Oil Co., 499 U.S. 244 (1991), in defining "employee" to apply Title VII extraterritorially: "With respect to employment in a foreign country, such term includes an individual who is a citizen of the United States."

2.   An "Employee" Under Title VII

Section 701(f) defines an "employee" as simply an individual employed by an employer. "Employee" does not, however, include any person elected to public office in any state or political subdivision of any state, any person chosen by an officer to be on such officer's personal staff, or an appointee on the policy-making level or an immediate advisor with respect to the exercise of the constitutional or legal powers of the office. In Gregory v. Ashcroft, 501 U.S. 452 (1991), the Supreme Court decided that state court judges are excluded from coverage of the ADEA because they are policy-making employees.

a.   **The boundary between employer and employee.** Employees who have an opportunity to become partners and therefore employers are protected against discrimination in partnership decisions.

EXAM TIP

While partners are not employees protected by Title VII, some employees, such as law firm associates, with an expectation of being considered for partnership are protected since that expectation is a term and condition of their employment.

 # EXAMPLE AND ANALYSIS

In Hishon v. King & Spalding, 467 U.S. 69 (1984), plaintiff was an associate in a law firm who claimed she was denied a partnership because of sex discrimination. The court found that "partnership consideration was a term, condition, or privilege of an associate's employment at respondent's firm, and accordingly that partnership consideration must be made without regard to sex."

C.   AGE DISCRIMINATION IN EMPLOYMENT ACT OF 1967

Section 4(a) of the ADEA makes it an unlawful employment practice for an "employer to fail or refuse to hire or to discharge any individual or otherwise discriminate against any individual with respect to compensation, terms, conditions, or privileges of employment because of such individual's age." The Act also covers age-based discrimination by employment agencies and labor organizations.

1. An "Employer" Under the Act

The ADEA coverage provisions mirror Title VII but coverage requires 20 employees, not the 15 that satisfies Title VII. Section 11(b) defines "employer" as any "*person* engaged in an *industry affecting commerce* who has twenty or more *employees* for each working day in each of twenty or more calendar weeks in the current or preceding calendar year." State and local governmental employers are covered by the ADEA as is the federal government.

a. **A "person" as "employer."** Section 11(a) defines "person" under the ADEA to include individuals, partnerships, associations, labor organizations, corporations, business trusts, legal representatives, or any organized groups of persons. Although this definition does not encompass all of the groups enumerated under Title VII's definition of "person," it is equally applicable due to the last phrase, which encompasses all organized groups of persons.

b. **An "industry affecting commerce."** The term an "industry affecting commerce" is a liberally construed term intended to cover any activity that substantially affects commerce.

c. **An "employee" under the act.** Like Title VII, the definition of an "employee" is simply an individual employed by an employer, including United States citizens in foreign countries. In Kline v. Florida Bd. of Regents, 120 S. Ct. 631 (2000), the Supreme Court held that Congress exceeded its authority under §5 of the Fourteenth Amendment by applying the ADEA to state and local government employers.

D. RECONSTRUCTION CIVIL RIGHTS STATUTES

Three civil rights statutes survive from the Reconstruction period following the Civil War and have potential impact on employment discrimination.

1. 42 U.S.C. §1981

42 U.S.C. §1981 prohibits race, ethnic, ancestry, and alienage discrimination in all contracts. Since employment is typically characterized as contractual, §1981 covers all employment except the federal government as employer. Brown v. General Servs. Admin., 426 U.S. 820, 825 (1976). While in Jett v. Dallas Indep. Sch. Dist., 491 U.S. 701 (1989), the Court found that §1981 did not apply to state and local governments, the Civil Rights Act of 1991 overturned *Jett* by adding new subsection (c) to §1981. That subsection also made it clear that §1981 also covers all private contracts. "The rights

protected by this section are protected against impairment by nongovernmental discrimination and impairment under color of state law."

EXAM TIP

When the employer described in a fact pattern is very small, §1981 should be discussed since it applies to prohibit race, ethnic origin and alienage discrimination in all contracts.

---

2. 42 U.S.C. §1983

Section 1983 creates an action for damages for individuals when their constitutional or other federal rights are violated by someone acting under color of state law. While the governmental employers themselves are immune from suit under §1983, this Act reaches the employees of the states as well as local governments and makes them personally liable for violating the constitutional rights of others.

    a. The "every person" defendant under §1983. Liability under §1983 does not actually apply to "every person" because that term is further limited to those persons acting "under color of law." In simple terms, "every person" includes those individuals acting pursuant to state action such as employees of state and local government agencies. There is absolute immunity from liability under §1983 for legislators, prosecutors, and judges acting in their official capacity. Qualified immunity is available to many other officials as long as they do not violate clearly established statutory or constitutional rights of which a reasonable person would have known.

        i. "Under color of law." "Under color of law" includes actions by defendants "who carry a badge of authority of a state and represent it in some capacity whether they act in accordance with their authority or misuse it." Monroe v. Pope, 365 U.S. 167 (1961). In that case, 13 Chicago police officers broke into plaintiffs' bedroom, routed them from bed, made them stand naked in the living room, and ransacked every room, emptying drawers and ripping mattresses. They were acting under color of law even though their actions violated state law.

    b. 42 U.S.C. §1985. Section 1985 provides a remedy when two or more individuals conspire to deprive another of equal protection or equal privileges and immunities under the law. The Court, in Great American Federal Savings & Loan Assn. v. Novotny, 442 U.S. 366 (1979), held that Title VII rights were not among the rights subject to §1985(3) protection. But other constitutional and federal rights involving employment can be the object of conspiracies and §1985 provides a remedy against the conspirators, be they public or private actors.

E.   AMERICANS WITH DISABILITIES ACT

Section 102 (a) of the ADA creates the general rule prohibiting discrimination because of disability. "No *covered entity* shall discriminate against *a qualified individual* with a *disability* because of the disability . . . in regard to . . . employment."

EXAM TIP

While the coverage concepts of the ADA differ from Title VII, the effect is pretty much the same since employers with 15 employees are covered as are employees of public entities.

---

1.   A "Covered Entity" Under the Act

Section 101(2) defines "covered entity" as "any employer, employment agency, labor organization, or joint labor-management committee." The definition of an "employer" under this Act mirrors Title VII, so that a person who employs at least 15 people for each working day for 20 or more weeks per year falls within the purview of the Act. An employer, under this Act, does not include the United States, a corporation of the United States, Indian tribes, or bona fide private membership clubs exempt from paying taxes.

2.   Other "Covered Entit[ies]"

Title II of the ADA expands coverage so that disability discrimination by public entities is prohibited. 42 U.S.C. §12132 provides that "no qualified individual with a disability shall, by reason of such disability, be excluded from participation in or be denied the benefits of the services, programs, or activities of a public entity, or shall be subjected to discrimination by such entity." A "public entity" is defined in 42 U.S.C. §12131 as any state or local government or agency, and Amtrak as well as certain commuter transportation authorities. The discrimination prohibited by 42 U.S.C. §12132 includes discrimination in employment. 28 C.F.R. §35.140(a). After Kimel v. Florida Bd. of Regents, 120 S. Ct. 631 (2000), there is serious question whether Congress has the power to make the ADA applicable to state and local governments.

F.   THE EQUAL PAY ACT

The Equal Pay Act (EPA), 29 U.S.C. §206(d), requires equal pay for equal work without regard to sex. It was enacted as an amendment to the federal wage and hour law, the Fair Labor Standards Act (FLSA), 29 U.S.C. §201 et seq.

1.   An "Employer" Under the EPA

The Equal Pay Act looks to the FLSA to determine who is an employer within its coverage. There are two separate ways to establish coverage.

EXAM TIP

The Equal Pay Act coverage tests look back to the New Deal Fair Labor Standards Act approach, which was subsequently amended to provide several alterantive ways of deciding coverage.

---

   a.   **The individual test.** The first, based on the FLSA as originally enacted, looks to the work of the individual plaintiff. If the plaintiff was "engaged in commerce" or "in the production of goods for commerce," then that person's employer is covered by the Fair Labor Standards Act and the Equal Pay Act.

   b.   **The enterprise test.** In 1961, FLSA was amended to create a new basis for coverage that looks to whether the enterprise is engaged in commerce by doing a particular dollar volume of business or was among a list of specified industries where the enterprise had individual employees who were engaged in commerce or in the production of goods for commerce.

      i.   **Exclusions from coverage.** There are certain employees who are not covered because of specific statutory exceptions for certain small local newspapers, certain fishing and agricultural industries, and small retail and service establishments.

   c.   **Federal and state employees.** In 1974, Congress extended the coverage of the Equal Pay Act to the federal government and to state and local governments. As to federal employees, the Act's coverage parallels the coverage of Title VII and the ADEA, but is explicitly limited to civilians in military departments. In general, anyone employed by a "state political subdivision of a state or an interstate government agency" is covered if in the civil service or if not an elected official, on the personal staff of an elected official, or a policy-making appointee or legal advisor. 29 U.S.C. §203(e)(C).

REVIEW QUESTIONS AND ANSWERS

Question: How many employees must work for an employer for the employer to be covered by Title VII?

Answer: For Title VII coverage the employer must have 15 or more employees for each working day in each of 20 or more calendar weeks in the current or preceding calendar year. A person is an employee as long as she is on the employer's payroll.

Question: Do the ADEA coverage provisions mirror Title VII?

Answer: Yes, but coverage does not begin until the employer has 20 employees.

Question: Does §1981 cover all contracts of employment?

Answer: Since employment is considered to be contractual and since §1981 prohibits all race discrimination in contracts, all employers are within the coverage of §1981.

Question: Do the ADA coverage provisions mirror those in Title VII?

Answer: Yes, entities, which term includes employers, with 15 employees are within the coverage of the ADA.

Question: Does the EPA coverage reach all employees?

Answer: The employers of individuals actually engaged in commerce, employers doing certain dollar levels of business, or employers engaged in specified industries are covered by the EPA.

Question: Do the recent federalism decisions of the Supreme Court affect the coverage of state and local governmental employees under federal antidiscrimination statutes?

Answer: Yes. In Kimel v. Florida Bd. of Regents, 120 S. Ct. 631 (2000), the Court found that Congress lacked the power to apply the ADEA to state and local governments. The ADA and disparate impact analysis under Title VII appear vunerable as well.

PROCEDURES FOR ENFORCING ANTIDISCRIMINATION LAWS

CHAPTER OVERVIEW

- **The Scope of Antidiscrimination Procedures.** The Civil Rights Act of 1964 created a complex enforcement scheme that is generally followed by the federal antidiscrimination statutes subsequently enacted.

- **Reconstruction Era Civil Rights Statutes.** The Reconstruction era civil rights statutes, 42 U.S.C.A. §§1981, 1983, do not have a federal agency charged with their enforcement and have no required procedure specific to their application. These statutes are enforced in much the same way as any private suit in civil litigation.

- **Private Enforcement of Title VII.** Under the Title VII procedures, an individual must meet two preconditions:

  - **Filing a Timely Charge.** An individual must file a charge under oath with the EEOC.

    - **Timeliness.** The general rule is that the charge must be filed within 180 days "after the alleged unlawful employment practice occurred." That 180-day rule is extended where a state or local antidiscrimination agency exists so the charge can be filed with the state or local agency and also with the EEOC within 300 days of the alleged violation.

    - **The Time the Alleged Discrimination Occurred.** Section 706(e)(1) requires that the charge be filed within 180/300 days "after the alleged unlawful employment practice occurred." The filing period starts running when the act of discrimination occurs and the employee receives notice of the employer's decision.

- **Continuing Violation Exception.** A continuing violation can exist because the discrimination is ongoing. It is necessary, however, that what continues is the discrimination and not just its effect.

- **File Lawsuit.** Once the EEOC has had 180 days to act or has acted, the claimant can demand a right-to-sue letter and then has only 90 days to initiate a lawsuit.

- **Private Class Actions.** In order to maintain a Title VII, §1981 or ADA class action suit, Rule 23 of the Federal Rules of Procedure must be satisfied. Courts have borrowed from Title VII decisions applying Rule 23 to ADEA cases.

  - **Requirements of Rule 23(a).** Rule 23(a) sets forth four requirements which all must be met by the party seeking to maintain the suit as a class: (1) *numerosity,* (2) *commonality,* (3) *typicality,* and (4) *adequate representation.* Most of the problems focus on the adequacy of representation. The scope of class actions is limited so that a plaintiff can only represent a class of those similarly situated to herself.

  - **Requirements of Rule 23(b).** Once a suit has met the requirements of Rule 23(a), it still must satisfy either Rule 23(b)(2) or (b)(3).

- **Federal Government Enforcement.** Title VII enforcement by the federal government is largely committed to the EEOC, with the exception of the Attorney General's role with respect to suits against state and local governments. The EEOC, after investigation, may bring suit against the charged defendant.

- **The Relationship Between Public and Private Suit.** Since suits can be brought by the EEOC and by private parties, the following deals with the relationship between the two types of suits.

  - **The Public Suit.** When the EEOC files suit on behalf of an individual, the individual has a right to intervene but loses the right to bring a separate private cause of action.

  - **The Private Suit.** Courts have split on the issue whether a prior private suit bars the EEOC from filing a public suit on behalf of the individual or whether both suits may proceed concurrently.

- **Title VII Suit Against Governmental Employers.** Special enforcement provisions apply to suits against governmental employers.

  - **State and Local Government Employment.** The Department of Justice, not the EEOC, has the power to sue state or local governments under Title VII.

  - **Federal Employment.** Title VII, the ADEA, and the Rehabilitation Act (adopting ADA remedies, procedures, and rights) afford protection to most federal employees against discrimination. The procedures with respect to federal employees differ from the procedures that apply to employees of other employers.

A. THE SCOPE OF ANTIDISCRIMINATION PROCEDURES

The Civil Rights Act of 1964 created a complex enforcement scheme that is generally followed by the subsequently enacted federal antidiscrimination statutes. The Equal Employment Opportunity Commission is a five-person federal commission, appointed by the President and confirmed by the Senate. The EEOC is charged with enforcement of these statutes and it can bring actions to enforce them. Given the enormous caseload of the EEOC, however, the main thrust of actual enforcement rests with private litigation.

1. Modern Antidiscrimination Procedure

Generally, the antidiscrimination laws enacted since 1964 follow the procedural requirements of Title VII, which require a claimant to first file with an administrative agency before being able to file a lawsuit.

The more procedurally complicated antidiscrimination laws include Title VII, 42 U.S.C.A. §§2000e et seq. (1988); the Age Discrimination in Employment Act, 29 U.S.C.A. §§621 et seq. (1985); and the Americans with Disabilities Act, 42 U.S.C.A. §§12101 et seq. (Supp. 1983). These laws all tend to be governed by the special procedures set forth in §706, 42 U.S.C.A. §2000e-5 of Title VII. There are two steps to these procedures.

a. File with an administrative agency. There is reasonably short period— 180 or 300 days depending on whether the state has an appropriate antidiscrimination agency—within which a claimant must file a charge of discrimination with a state antidiscrimination agency and then the EEOC. Once a charge is filed, no statute of limitations operates until the EEOC terminates its proceedings either by dismissing, finding reasonable cause, bringing a lawsuit, or issuing the claimant a right-to-sue letter.

b. File lawsuit. Once the EEOC has acted, the claimant has only 90 days from receipt of notice of that action to initiate a lawsuit.

EXAM TIP

The key difference in procedure in Title VII, the ADEA, and the ADA and what you learned in Civil Procedure is that a threshold requirement to filing a lawsuit is the timely filing of a discrimination charge with the EEOC.

2. Reconstruction Era Civil Rights Statutes

The Reconstruction era civil rights statutes, 42 U.S.C.A. §§1981, 1983, 1985 do not have a federal agency charged with their enforcement and have no required procedure specific to their application. These statutes are enforced in much the same way as any private suit in civil litigation. The primary procedural issue is the appropriate statute of limitations with the rule being that these actions are subject to the state statute applicable to "personal injury" actions or the most analogous state statute. Wilson v. Garcia, 471 U.S. 261 (1981) (§1983); Goodman v. Lukens Steel Co., 482 U.S. 656 (1987) (§1981); Owens v. Okure, 488 U.S. 235 (1989) (covering states without "personal injury" actions).

EXAM TIP

If the fact pattern involves specific dates of events that suggest a problem of timeliness in filing a Title VII charge of race discrimination, discuss §1981 since traditional statute of limitations periods apply.

B. PRIVATE ENFORCEMENT OF TITLE VII

Under the Title VII procedures, an individual must meet two preconditions: (1) the timely filing of an appropriate charge with the EEOC and (2) the timely filing of a court suit after receipt of an EEOC right-to-sue letter (or notice of dismissal). The procedures are identical for Title VII and the ADA, but there is one minor wrinkle in ADEA procedures.

1. Filing a Timely Charge

a. **Filing.** An individual must file a charge under oath with the EEOC. §706(b), 42 U.S.C. §2000e-5(b). Title VII directs that the charge comply with EEOC requirements as to form and content. **Courts have been very liberal as to what constitutes a "charge" and almost any writing received by the EEOC, which identifies the parties and describes the alleged unlawful practices, will suffice.** Waiters v. Robert Bosch Co., 683 F.2d 89, 92 (4th Cir. 1982). For example, the absence of an oath at the time of filing can be subsequently remedied. Weeks v. Southern Bell Tel. & Tel. Co., 408 F.2d 228 (5th Cir. 1969).

b. **Timely.** The general rule is that the charge must be filed within 180 days "after the alleged unlawful employment practice occurred." §706(e), 42 U.S.C. §2000e-5(e); see also the ADEA, §7(d)(1), 29 U.S.C. §636(d)(1). That 180-day rule is extended where a state or local antidiscrimination agency exists so the charge can be filed with the state or local agency and also with the EEOC within 300 days of the alleged violation or "within thirty days after receiving notice that the State or local agency has terminated the proceedings under the State or local law, whichever is earlier." §706(e), 42 U.S.C. §2000e-5(e). **Since most states have local antidiscrimination laws, this exception has in effect become the general rule.**

  i.   The ADEA wrinkle. While the 180/300 day time period applies in ADEA actions, filing with the state deferral agency is not a prerequisite to filing with the EEOC. Thus, filing with the EEOC within 300 days suffices, though at some point filing with the state agency is necessary.

  ii. The time the alleged discrimination occurred. Section 706(e)(1) requires that the charge be filed within 180/300 days "after the alleged unlawful employment practice occurred." The Supreme Court in Delaware State College v. Ricks, 449 U.S. 250 (1980), established a **"notice of decision"** rule for Title VII actions. The filing period starts running when the act of discrimination occurs and the employee receives notice of the employer's decision to take an adverse employment action, such as a projected termination.

EXAMPLE AND ANALYSIS

In *Ricks*, the plaintiff was a professor who was told at the end of a year of teaching that his contract would be terminated after one more year of employment. The Court found that the decision that he claimed was discriminatory had occurred—the decision to give him a terminal contract—and he had received notice of the adverse decision at that point. His time to file commenced running at that point even though he had a job for another year. *Ricks* and subsequent cases based on the "notice of decision" rule indicate first that a "decision" may trigger the beginning of the filing period even if that "decision" may later be reversed on appeal or in a grievance proceeding; second, an agent of the employer must be the person to give notice; and third, the "notice" to the employee must spell out what will happen to the employee.

  (a) Continuing violation exception. A continuing violation can exist because the discrimination is ongoing. For example, discrimination in pay continues for each pay period. A filing will always be timely because it is necessarily within 180/300 days of the point when some discrimination occurred. Policies of the employer that are discriminatory, under either systemic disparate treatment or systemic disparate impact theories, may be challenged if they are applied within 180/300 days of the filing. The filing need not be within 180/300 days of their adoption.

(1) The discrimination must be what continues. For the continuing violation exception to apply, **it is necessary that what continues is the discrimination and not just its effect.**

 # EXAMPLE AND ANALYSIS

In United Air Lines, Inc. v. Evans, 431 U.S. 553 (1977), plaintiff had been terminated from her job as a flight attendant under a rule that prohibited flight attendants to be married. That rule had been struck down as discriminatory by the time she applied to be rehired and was given no seniority credit for her earlier period of work. Evans claimed that the denial of past seniority was a "present effect of past discrimination" and was, therefore, a continuing violation. Finding that such "present effects of past discrimination" was not a theory of discrimination under Title VII, the Court held that there was no continuing violation, only a continuing effect. The time for filing a charge ran 300 days after her discriminatory discharge, and had long since run.

EXAM TIP

If more than 300 days have elapsed between the date the "alleged unlawful employment practice occurred" and the filing of a charge with the EEOC, try to apply the continuing violation exception. That requires, however, showing that the discrimination is ongoing and not just its effect.

---

ii. Timely filing with the EEOC is not jurisdictional. The Supreme Court in Zipes v. Trans World Airlines, Inc., 455 U.S. 385 (1982), decided that timely filing with the EEOC was not a jurisdictional prerequisite to federal court jurisdiction to hear the case. Instead, the period was merely a procedural prerequisite so that it was subject to waiver, estoppel, and equitable tolling.

iii. Grounds to toll the filing of the charge. Equitable doctrines such as waiver and estoppel can toll the running of the filing period.

2. Timely Filing Suit

A precondition to filing a Title VII suit in federal or state court is the filing of an EEOC charge.

a. **The EEOC has 180 days.** The charging party must wait a minimum of 180 days from the filing with the EEOC before bringing suit in court unless EEOC procedures are terminated earlier. After 180 days, the charging party can demand a right-to-sue letter from the EEOC. Once that letter is received, the charging party must file a court suit within 90 days or be barred from bringing action on that charge.

b. **No time period runs while charge is at EEOC.** The charging party may elect to permit the EEOC's procedures to continue after the 180-day period and still retain the power to demand a right-to-sue letter at any time up until the EEOC has made a final determination.

EXAM TIP

While a timely charge must be filed with the EEOC after the occurrence and a timely complaint must be filed in court once the EEOC has finally acted on the charge, there is no limitations period that applies while the charge is in the EEOC's hands.

---

c. **Letting EEOC pursue its process.** If the charging party allows the agency to process the charge to conclusion, the EEOC will either:

1. bring suit itself;

2. find no reasonable cause as to the truth of the charge and issue a notice of dismissal; or

3. find reasonable cause, attempt conciliation, and, if that fails to resolve the matter and if the EEOC does not file suit itself, ultimately issue a right-to-sue letter.

d. **File lawsuit.** Once the EEOC has had 180 days to act or has acted, the claimant can demand a right-to-sue letter and then has only 90 days to initiate a lawsuit.

3. Relationship of the EEOC Charge to Private Suit

Various aspects of the EEOC charge requirement raise questions that arise in subsequent private court actions.

a. **Proper plaintiffs.** Plaintiffs must have standing. The individual must be a party aggrieved by the discrimination. Examples include unsuccessful applicants, and present and former employees. Additionally, a plaintiff who can allege a nexus between damage to herself and discrimination against co-workers will also have standing. See Trafficante v. Metropolitan Life Ins. Co., 409 U.S. 205 (1972); Waters v. Heublein Inc., 547 F.2d 466 (9th Cir. 1979). Furthermore, organizations or associations can be proper plaintiffs if they can allege harm suffered to themselves or to their constituents. See Northeastern Florida Chapter of Associated Gen. Contractors v. City of Jacksonville, Florida, 508 U.S. 656 (1993).

b. **Proper defendants.** Title VII authorizes the bringing of a civil action only "against the respondent named in the charge," §706(f)(1), 42 U.S.C. §2000e-5(f)(1). Courts, however, have construed this language liberally. A general rule has emerged that **a defendant who is sufficiently implicated by the charge on which the action is predicated may be sued under Title VII.** See Mickel v. South Carolina State Employment Serv., 377 F.2d 239 (4th Cir.). Some courts have gone further, allowing suit against a non-charged defendant where no affirmative relief is sought against them or where there is a sufficient nexus with a properly charged party. See EEOC v. MacMillan Bloedel Containers, Inc., 503 F.2d 1086 (6th Cir. 1974); EEOC v. McLean Trucking Co., 525 F.2d 1007 (6th Cir. 1975).

c. **Scope of the suit.** The courts have interpreted the requirement that the scope of the complaint in the lawsuit must be based on the EEOC charge quite broadly. The court, in Sanchez v. Standard Brands, Inc., 431 F.2d 455, 466 (5th Cir. 1970), formulated a standard that is generally followed: **"[T]he allegations in a judicial complaint filed pursuant to Title VII 'may encompass any kind of discrimination like or related to allegations contained in the charge and growing out of such allegations during the pendency of the case before the Commission.'"**

C. PRIVATE CLASS ACTIONS

In order to maintain a Title VII, §1981, or ADA class action suit, Rule 23 of the Federal Rules of Procedure must be satisfied. Moreover, while the ADEA is not technically governed by Rule 23, courts have borrowed from Title VII decisions applying Rule 23 to ADEA cases. However, a recent case, Allison v. Citgo Petroleum Corp., 1998 U.S. App. LEXIS 8773 (5th Cir. 1998), appears to bar class certification in any case where compensatory or punitive damages are sought.

EXAM TIP

Systemic disparate treatment and systemic disparate impact cases would seem to lend themselves to the creation of class actions. The adequacy of representation requirement of Rule 23(a), however, limits the class to people similarly situated to the plaintiff and, for disparate treatment cases involving claims for damages, the requirement of Rule 23(b)(2) that the defendant acts on "grounds generally applicable to the class" requires that the class be limited to the opt-out class provided for in Rule 23(b)(3), which requires notice to all class members.

1. Requirements of Rule 23(a)

Rule 23(a) sets forth four requirements, which all must be met by the party seeking to maintain the suit as a class:

1. *Numerosity:* the class has so many members that joinder of all members individually is impracticable.

2. *Commonality:* there are questions of law or fact common to the members of the class.

3. *Typicality:* the claims or defenses of the representative parties are typical of the claims or defenses of the class.

4. *Adequate Representation:* the representative parties will fairly and adequately protect the interests of the class.

a. **Adequacy of representation.** Generally, because of the nature of employment discrimination claims, numerosity, commonality, and typicality are fairly easy to meet by the claimants. The fourth factor, adequacy of representation, tends to be the focus of most class action questions. This factor focuses on conflicts of interests among named plaintiffs and other class members, the competence of plaintiffs' counsel, and potential collusiveness. The Supreme Court, in General Telephone Co. of the Southwest v. Falcon, 457 U.S. 147 (1982), indicated that a plaintiff can adequately represent a class of individuals who would each have a prima facie case of discrimination made out by plaintiff's proof that she was the victim of the defendant's discrimination. In other words, a plaintiff can represent a class of those similarly situated to herself.

 ## EXAMPLES AND ANALYSIS

1. Jerry Falcon sued General Telephone, claiming that he was discriminated against in two promotions because he is a Mexican-American. He added a class action that claimed General Telephone discriminated "across the board" against Mexican-Americans, including in hiring. The Court found that Falcon, who did not claim to have been the victim of hiring discrimination, could not adequately represent

a class of victims of hiring discrimination. General Telephone Co. of the Southwest v. Falcon, 457 U.S. 147 (1982).

2. If Sam Smith, a plaintiff, can establish that he was not hired by Unicomp Corp. for the position of secretary because of his sex, then a class of all male applicants for the position of secretary could be certified since their individual claims would be established by plaintiff's proof that he was discriminated against.

---

2.   Requirements of Rule 23(b)

Once a suit has met the requirements of Rule 23(a), it still must satisfy either Rule 23(b)(2) or (b)(3).

a. **Rule 23(b)(2)** is satisfied where the defendant employer acts "on the grounds generally applicable to the class, thereby making appropriate final injunctive relief or corresponding relief with the respect to the class as a whole." Thus, Rule 23(b)(2) is satisfied where the employer treated all the members of the class similarly. Because of the general treatment by the employer, the individual members of the class need not be notified nor given the opportunity to opt out of the class.

The most difficult issue is whether a Rule 23(b)(2) certification is appropriate where the relief sought by plaintiffs includes backpay since that is so dependent upon the particular circumstances of each individual. Generally, it has been held that where traditional injunctive relief is the "predominate" remedy and the backpay award is merely incidental, then class certification based on Rule 23(b)(2) is appropriate.

In Allison v. Citgo Petroleum Corp., 1998 U.S. App. LEXIS 8773 (5th Cir. 1998), the court refused to extend what it called the "backpay exception" to class actions seeking compensatory and punitive damages now provided in Title VII actions in addition to injunctive and declaratory relief. Thus, the individual determinations of that legal relief predominate and preclude the certification under Rule 23(b)(2).

When the class is certified under Rule 23(b)(2), class members need not be notified and they do not have the right to opt out of the class. Kyriazi v. Western Elec. Co., 647 F.2d 388 (3d Cir. 1981).

b. **Rule 23(b)(3)** requires that the court find that common issues predominate over individual claims, and that the class action is the superior form to litigate the action. In Allison v. Citgo Petroleum Corp., 1998 U.S. App. LEXIS 8773 (5th Cir. 1998), the court also ruled out a Rule 23(b)(3) class action where compensatory and punitive relief was sought because individual questions predominated over common questions of law or fact. Procedurally, Rule 23(b)(3) requires class members be given notice of the existence of the class and the opportunity to "opt out" of the class.

3. The Preclusive Effect of a Class Action

Typically, when a proper class action is prosecuted, every member who does not opt out is bound by the judgment entered. However, the Supreme Court in Cooper v. Federal Reserve Bank of Richmond, 467 U.S. 867, 869 (1984), held that a determination in a class action suit "that an employer did not engage in a general pattern or practice of racial discrimination against the certified class of employees [does not preclude] a class member from maintaining a subsequent civil action alleging an individual claim of racial discrimination against the employer." However, the determination of no classwide liability might still be relevant on the issue of pretext: if the employer did not discriminate generally, then it is less likely that it discriminated against this particular individual.

Additionally, it is important to note for defendants who oppose class certifications, that the filing of a Title VII class action tolls the applicable statute of limitations and thus allows "all members of the putative class to file individual actions in the event that the class certification is denied." Crown Cork & Seal Co. v. Parker, 462 U.S. 345 (1983). Thus, a denial of a class certification offers class members a choice of seeking intervention in the suit to appeal the denial of a class action or of commencing their own individual actions.

4. Settling Class Actions

Rule 23(e) provides, "[a] class action shall not be dismissed or compromised without the approval of the court, and notice of the proposed dismissal or compromise shall be given to all members of the class in such manner as the court directs." Rule 23(e) has been interpreted to govern class actions, even where the class has not yet been certified. Generally, notice must be given to class members and a hearing should be held so that members can object to the settlement proposal. See Mandujano v. Basic Vegetable Prods., Inc., 541 F.2d 832, 835 (9th Cir. 1976). The general favored status of settlements gives the trial court broad discretion in approving settlements.

D. PUBLIC GOVERNMENT ENFORCEMENT

Title VII enforcement by the federal government is largely committed to the EEOC, with the exception of the Department of Justice's role in bringing suits against state and local governments. The EEOC, after investigation, may bring suit against the charged defendant. The Supreme Court has adopted a liberal approach, so that suit by the EEOC generally will not be barred unless the defendant can show it was prejudiced by any errors of the EEOC. See EEOC v. Shell Oil Co., 466 U.S. 54 (1984).

1.　Sufficiency and Scope of the Investigation

Challenges as to the sufficiency of the EEOC's investigation have not been successful. *EEOC v. Keco Indus., Inc.*, 748 F.2d 1097 (6th Cir. 1984). Furthermore, the EEOC's suit is not limited to the original charge but can be broadened resulting from its investigation of an individual party's charge. The Fourth Circuit held that the sole test for legitimacy of the suit is whether the discrimination was stated in the charge itself or disclosed in the course of a reasonable investigation of that charge. *EEOC v. General Electric Co.*, 532 F.2d 359 (4th Cir. 1976).

 # EXAMPLE AND ANALYSIS

Caroline Baker filed a charge with the EEOC claiming race discrimination but, within the course of the EEOC investigation, the EEOC determined that she was discriminated against because of a disability. The EEOC can bring suit for disability discrimination because the disability discrimination was revealed during the EEOC's investigation of the race discrimination charge.

2.　Statute of Limitations

Time limitations do not apply in suits brought by the EEOC unless the time period is unreasonably long and the defendant can show enough prejudice as to warrant dismissal. *Occidental Life Ins. Co. v. EEOC*, 432 U.S. 355 (1977). The ability of a defendant to show extreme prejudice as to warrant dismissal, coupled with the sympathy of the courts with the EEOC backlog, make unreasonable delay difficult to establish.

3.　EEOC's Duty to Attempt Conciliation

The conciliation requirement of Title VII has provided defendants with one procedural challenge to EEOC suits. The courts have generally held that some sort of conciliation effort is normally required by the EEOC before suit can be brought in federal or state court. *EEOC v. Hickey-Mitchell Co.*, 507 F.2d 944 (8th Cir. 1974).

E.　TITLE VII SUIT AGAINST GOVERNMENTAL EMPLOYERS

Special enforcement provisions apply to suits against governmental employers.

1.　State and Local Government Employment

The Department of Justice, not the EEOC, has the power to sue state or local governments under Title VII.

2.   Federal Employment

Title VII, the ADEA, and the Rehabilitation Act (adopting ADA remedies, procedures, and rights) afford protection to most federal employees against discrimination. The procedures with respect to federal employees differ from the procedures that apply to employees of other employers.

Section 717 of Title VII requires the federal employees or applicants to first file a complaint with the federal agency alleged to have discriminated against them. After final action by that agency on the complaint, the individual then has a choice of either appealing to the EEOC or filing an action in district court. The other differences in procedural requirements for federal employees have to do with time limitations in filing the agency complaint, the EEOC charge, and the private suit.

F.   THE RELATIONSHIP BETWEEN PUBLIC AND PRIVATE SUIT

Since suits can be brought by the EEOC and by private parties, the following deals with the relationship between the two types of suits.

1.   The Public Suit

When the EEOC files suit on behalf of an individual, the individual loses the right to bring a private cause of action. The private individual's interest is represented by the EEOC, with the right to intervene being retained by the charging party, Cooper v. Federal Reserve Bank, 467 U.S. 867 (1984).

2.   The Private Suit

A dispute has arisen, however, when the individual initiates a private cause of action before the EEOC does. Courts have split on the issue of whether the private suit bars the EEOC from filing a public suit on behalf of the individual or whether both suits may proceed concurrently. See McClure v. Mexia Indep. Sch. Dist., 750 F.2d 396 (5th Cir. 1985).

G.   SETTLING AND ARBITRATING DISCRIMINATION SUITS

1.   Knowing Waiver of Discrimination Claims

The Older Workers Benefit Protection Act (OWBPA), 29 U.S.C.A. §626(f), permits a knowledgeable waiver of ADEA claims so long as minimum conditions are met. That statute has served as a guide for courts attempting to interpret waivers of rights under the other antidiscrimination laws.

2.   Settlement by Agreement or by Consent Order

A settlement can be a purely private contract or it can be incorporated into a consent order approved by the court. The Supreme Court has indicated that consent decrees should be interpreted along the same lines as contracts. See Firefighters Local Union No. 1784 v. Stotts, 467 U.S. 561 (1984). Modification of a consent decree requires the movant to establish a sufficient change in factual conditions or the law to warrant modification. See Rufo v. Inmates of Suffolk County Jail, 502 U.S. 367 (1992) and Patterson v. Newspaper & Mail Deliverers' Union, 13 F.3d 33 (2d Cir. 1993).

a. **Binding of non-parties.** Martin v. Wilks, 490 U.S. 755 (1989), involved a group of white firefighters who were affected by but were not parties to a consent order settling a race discrimination suit against the fire department. While these plaintiffs knew of the prior suit and did not take the opportunity to intervene, the Court rejected a rule of mandatory intervention as a way of avoiding conflicts of judgments and suggested Rule 19 of the Federal Rules of Civil Procedure be a solution. Rule 19 permits the joinder of a non-party to the action when not joining would leave an original party "subject to a substantial risk of incurring double, multiple, or other inconsistent obligations by reason of the claimed interest." Thus, under *Martin*, a company that perceives possible conflict in judgments can seek joinder of the parties under Rule 19, but generally non-parties will not be bound by prior judgments.

In attempting to overrule *Martin,* the 1991 Civil Rights Act added §703(n) to Title VII, which binds non-parties when (1) they are adequately represented by a party or (2) they have actual notice of the threat to their interest and an opportunity to protect themselves.

3. Arbitration

Voluntary agreements to submit disputes, including existing discrimination claims, to binding arbitration provide a valuable opportunity for employees and employers to resolve their dispute in a timely and effective manner. But the large question involved is whether executory agreements to arbitrate discrimination claims that may arise in the future ought to bar an employee from bringing a lawsuit claiming discrimination. The law is unclear as to that issue.

The fact that an employee files a grievance and the union takes that grievance to arbitration pursuant to a collective bargaining agreement does not prevent the employee from bringing a Title VII action. See Alexander v. Gardner-Denver Co., 415 U.S. 36 (1974). In contrast, an employee, whose employment as a broker was regulated by the New York Stock Exchange rules that required all future employment disputes be arbitrated, may be forced into arbitration even where there is an alleged violation of an antidiscrimination statute. See Gilmer v. Interstate/Johnson Lane Corp., 500 U.S. 20 (1991).

The lower courts have taken many different positions as to the meaning of *Gilmer.* One court has held that *Gilmer* overruled *Gardner-Denver* so that employers can condition employment on an agreement to take future discrimination claims to arbitration. Austin v. Owens-Broadway Glass Container, Inc., 78 F.3d 875 (4th Cir. 1996). At the other extreme, two courts have held that an employer may not require its employees, as a condition of employment, to waive their right to bring future discrimination claims. Duffield v. Robertson Stephens & Co., 144 F.3d 1182 (9th Cir. 1998); Cole v. Burns, 105 F.3d 1465 (D.C. Cir. 1997). The Seventh Circuit holds that an arbitration clause that was no more than the employee's unilateral promise to submit her claims to arbitration was unenforceable. Gibson v. Neighborhood Health Clinics, Inc., 121 F.3d 1126 (7th Cir. 1997).

EXAM TIP

Any fact pattern with an agreement to arbitrate disputes requires the application of *Alexander*, that arbitration of a statutory claim does not cut off a court action, or *Gilmer*, a provision in a regulatory scheme requiring arbitration does foreclose a court action.

EXAMPLE AND ANALYSIS

Gibson was employed by Neighborhood Health Clinics when she was presented with a contract of employment that reserved the right in the employer to terminate her "at any time, with or without notice, and with or without cause" but that required her to submit any employment discrimination claims to arbitration. Since she was already working, Gibson's employment was not given consideration for her agreement and there was no other consideration flowing to her nor any bargained-for detriment to the employer. The arbitration agreement was unenforceable.

Another court has held that *Gilmer* is limited by the Federal Arbitration Act to only apply to situations such as the registration requirements of the Stock Exchange because §1 of the FAA provides that nothing in the Act "shall apply to contracts of employment of seamen, railroad employees, or any other class of workers engaged in foreign or interstate commerce." Craft v. Campbell Soup Co., 161 F.3d 1199 (9th Cir. 1998). Most courts, however, have limited the exclusion in §1 of the FAA to include only workers directly engaged in the transportation of interstate or foreign commerce. See, e.g., Miller v. Logicon, Inc., 143 F.3d 573 (10th Cir. 1998).

REVIEW QUESTIONS AND ANSWERS

Question: Must claimants under the Reconstruction era civil rights statutes file with any administrative agency before commencing a lawsuit?

Answer: No, those statutes create causes of action that follow the general rules of procedure for civil litigation. The statute of limitations is the most analogous state statute.

Question: Must claimants under Title VII, the ADEA, and the ADA file their claims with an administrative agency before commencing a lawsuit?

Answer: Yes, claims under Title VII and the ADA require that the claimant file charges with the federal EEOC and the appropriate state or local antidiscrimination agency before commencing a lawsuit, while ADEA claims must at some point be filed with an appropriate state or local agency.

Question: What is the time period for filing a discrimination charge with the appropriate administrative agency?

Answer: While the general rule sets the period at 180 days, the exception, which applies in most cases, sets the period at 300 days in jurisdictions that have appropriate state or local antidiscrimination agencies.

Question: What is a continuing violation?

Answer: A continuing violation is one in which the discriminatory conduct of the employer continues so that a claimant may file at any time while the practice persists.

Question: How long does the EEOC have to deal with a charge?

Answer: While there is no time limit for the EEOC to act, the charging party can demand a right-to-sue letter from the EEOC 180 days after the charge was filed.

Question: Once a charging party receives notice that the EEOC has taken final action, how long does the charging party have to file a lawsuit?

Answer: The charging party has 90 days from receipt of the EEOC's final action to commence a lawsuit.

Question: May private plaintiffs bring class actions?

Answer: Private class actions may be brought but must satisfy Rule 23 of the Federal Rules of Civil Procedure. Private class actions must satisfy all four requirements of Rule 23(a)—numerosity, commonality, typicality, and adequacy of representation—and either Rule 23(b)(2) or (b)(3).

Question: Is there public enforcement of Title VII, the ADEA, and the ADA?

Answer: The Department of Justice may bring enforcement actions against state and local governments, while the EEOC may bring actions against all other employers.

16   JUDICIAL RELIEF

CHAPTER OVERVIEW

The Scope of Judicial Relief. Once a violation of an antidiscrimination statute—Title VII of the Civil Rights Act (Title VII), §§1981 and 1983, Title I and Title II of the American with Disabilities Act (ADA), the Rehabilitation Act §501 the Age Discrimination in Employment Act (ADEA), or the Equal Pay Act (EPA)—has been proven, a broad array of relief is available. Equitable relief includes backpay, reinstatement, attorney's fees, and injunctive and declaratory relief. Since the passage of the Civil Rights Act of 1991, compensatory and punitive damages, subject to caps, are also available in Title VII actions for intentional discrimination. Compensatory damages are available in §§1981 and 1983, Title I, and probably Title II of the ADA, but are not available in ADEA or EPA litigation. Liquidated damages are available in ADEA and EPA actions.

- **Presumption of Full Relief.** Under these antidiscrimination statutes, victims of proven discrimination are presumed entitled to full relief for which they qualify. Section 706(g)(2)(B), however, creates a defense to full remedies where the plaintiff proved an impermissible factor was "a motivating factor" of the employer's decision and where the employer proves that it would have made the same decision even in absence of the impermissible motivating factor.

- **Types of Remedies in Individual Cases.** A broad array of remedies is available in discrimination cases.

  - **Backpay.** Antidiscrimination statutes permit a victim of discrimination to recover the income lost due to the employer's unlawful discrimination.

Such an award includes all compensation the victim would have received in the absence of discrimination.

- **Calculation of Backpay.** The beginning date for backpay is generally the date the victim first lost wages due to the unlawful conduct and it normally ends on the date of judgment. Title VII limits backpay to two years prior to the filing of the charge.

- **After-Acquired Evidence.** An employer who acquires evidence after a case is commenced can cut off backpay as of the date of discovery if it carries the burden to establish that the wrongdoing was of such severity that the employee would have been terminated on those grounds alone.

- **The Duty to Mitigate Damages.** The antidiscrimination statutes require the court to reduce backpay by amounts that were or could have been earned with reasonable diligence from other employment. The employer has the burden of proving the existence of comparable employment, the amount the plaintiff would have earned, and that the plaintiff's lack of reasonable diligence resulted in the failure to obtain the position. The victim is not required to "go into another line of work, accept a demotion, or take a demeaning position."

- **Instatement and Reinstatement.** Antidiscrimination statutes create a presumption that the victim of discrimination is entitled to prohibitory and compensatory equitable relief, in the form of an injunction, or order of reinstatement or instatement. The employer has the burden of proving that either of two grounds justify the denial of reinstatement or instatement.

  - **No Bumping of Innocent Incumbent.** When the position plaintiff would have been entitled to is occupied by another employee who is innocent of any involvement in the discrimination against the plaintiff, reinstatement may be denied.

  - **Hostility or Animosity.** Where the employer can prove that there is such hostility and animosity between the plaintiff and the employer that a harmonious working relationship would be impossible, reinstatement or instatement can be denied.

- **Retroactive Seniority.** Victims of hiring discrimination are presumed to be entitled to the grant of retroactive seniority under a "rightful place" right to instatement. "Rightful place" means that a victim is hired when a job opens up and then is granted seniority retroactive to the date she would have been hired but for the employer's discrimination.

- **Front Pay.** An award of front pay compensates a victim of discrimination for the wages and benefits she will lose even after the judgement date until the victim is reinstated or, if not reinstated, as "the difference (after discounting to present value) between what the plaintiff would have earned in the future had he been reinstated at the time of trial and what he would have earned in the future in his next best employment.''

- **Compensatory and Punitive Damages.** The availability of compensatory and punitive damages in employment discrimination varies from statute to statute. Both compensatory and punitive damages are available under §1981 and §1983, with several restrictions when sought from a governmental entity. Title VII and Title I of the ADA allow such damages but place limits on the amount of these awards where (1) disparate treatment is proven, and (2) the claim is not recognized under §1981. Compensatory and punitive damages are capped depending upon the number of employees. The caps are: (1) $50,000 for an employer with 100 or fewer employees, (2) $300,000 for an employer with 500 or more employees. The ADEA and the EPA do not permit either type of damages, which are, although both allow liquidated damages, essentially double damages for willful violations.

- **Liquidated Damages.** The ADEA and the EPA permit recovery of ''liquidated damages'' if the plaintiff can establish a ''willful'' violation. A willful violation is knowledge or reckless disregard of the risk on the part of the employer that its action contravened the statute.

- **Attorney's Fees.** Each antidiscrimination statute, with slight variation, contains a provision allowing an award of attorney's fees and costs to the prevailing party. While a prevailing plaintiff is presumed entitled to attorney's fees, a court may award attorney's fees to a prevailing defendant only upon a finding that the plaintiff's action was frivolous, unreasonable, or without foundation.

  - **Calculating the Fee.** The fee calculation is a two-step process:

    1. Multiply the number of hours the attorney reasonably expended on the litigation by a reasonable rate per hour.

    2. In rare circumstances, where supported by specific evidence and judicial findings, the district court may adjust this ''lodestar'' figure upward or downward to account for other relevant factors.

- **Relief for Systemic Discrimination.** Individuals merely must show they are members of the class to gain the presumption. The employer then carries the burden of persuasion to prove that the individuals were not discriminated against.

- **Affirmative Action Relief.** Judicially imposed affirmative action relief is a form of classwide relief that requires the employer to take positive action to benefit members of the discriminated class. The use of race is justified as a compelling government interest because it remedies the prior discrimination of the defendant, even if some beneficiaries were not themselves the victims of the employer's discrimination.

A. THE SCOPE OF JUDICIAL RELIEF

Once a violation of an antidiscrimination statute—Title VII of the Civil Rights Act (Title VII), §§1981 and 1983, Title I and Title II of the American with Disabilities Act (ADA), the Rehabilitation Act §501, the Age Discrimination in Employment Act (ADEA), or the Equal Pay Act (EPA)—has been proven, a broad array of relief is available. Equitable relief includes backpay, reinstatement, attorney's fees, and injunctive and declaratory relief. Since the passage of the Civil Rights Act of 1991, compensatory and punitive damages, subject to caps, are also available in Title VII actions for intentional discrimination. Compensatory damages are available in §§1981 and 1983, Title I, and probably Title II of the ADA, but are not available in ADEA or EPA litigation. Liquidated damages are available in ADEA and EPA actions.

This chapter will first look at relief in individual discrimination cases and will then turn to relief in systemic cases.

EXAM TIP

Remedies include equitable relief such as backpay, orders of reinstatement, declaratory and injunctive relief, as well as legal relief for intentional discrimination in the form of both compensatory and punitive damages.

B. FULL RELIEF FOR INDIVIDUAL VICTIMS OF DISCRIMINATION

The statutory remedial schemes to redress individual discrimination provide a variety of types of legal and equitable relief, as well as attorney's fees. With this wide array of relief available, courts are to make whole the victims of unlawful discrimination. Additionally, in some circumstances, the court is permitted to assess punitive damages.

1. Section 706(g)(2)(B) Exception to Full Relief

When the employer is found liable, the plaintiff is generally entitled to the whole panoply of remedies for which she qualifies. The Civil Rights Act of 1991, however, added an affirmative defense to most relief when the employer can carry the burden of proving that it would have made the same decision even if it had not discriminated. Section 703(m) establishes that the employer is liable when the plaintiff proves that discrimination was "a motivating factor" in the decision plaintiff challenges even though other factors also motivated the decision. Section 706(g)(2)(B), then, creates an affirmative defense to full remedies if the employer can prove that it would have taken "the same action in the absence of the impermissible motivating factor." If the employer does carry its burden on this same decision defense, then the court "shall not award damages or issue an order requiring any admission, reinstatement, hiring, promotion, or payment" of backpay. But plaintiff is entitled to declaratory relief, injunctive relief (except for orders of admission, reinstatement, hiring, or promotion), and attorney's fees and costs demonstrated to be directly attributable only to the pursuit of a claim under §703(m).

C. TYPES OF REMEDIES IN INDIVIDUAL CASES

A broad array of remedies is available in discrimination cases.

1. Backpay

Antidiscrimination statutes permit a victim of discrimination to recover the income lost due to the employer's unlawful discrimination. Such an award includes all compensation the victim would have received in the absence of discrimination—including lost wages, raises, overtime compensation, bonuses, vacation pay, and such fringe benefits as contributions to a retirement plan.

a. **Backpay is presumptively awarded to victims of discrimination.** In Albemarle Paper Co. v. Moody, 422 U.S. 405 (1975), the Supreme Court held that the trial court has discretion in awarding backpay but that this discretion must be exercised in light of the twin purposes of Title VII—to end discrimination and to make its victims whole. Thus, backpay is presumed available.

   i. **Presumption overcome.** In Los Angeles Dept. of Water & Power v. Manhart, 435 U.S. 702, the Court held that the employer violated Title VII by discriminating in pension plan contributions. Because of the complexity in administering pension programs and the likelihood that harm would come to innocent third-party participants in the pension plan, backpay was not awarded because Congress had not plainly commanded that result.

   ii. **Backpay awards as legal or equitable.** Both §706(g)(1) and the decision in *Albemarle* establish that an award of backpay is discretionary and thus an equitable remedy. In ADEA and other actions, backpay is considered a legal remedy. Until the Civil Rights Act of 1991 added a jury trial right to Title VII, that distinction meant that a jury trial right existed in the ADEA but not in Title VII.

   iii. **Burden on plaintiff to prove damages.** Most courts hold that the plaintiff must establish damages in the form of the difference between her actual earnings and the amount she would have earned in the absence of discrimination.

b. **Calculation of backpay.** The federal antidiscrimination statutes provide little guidance on how to calculate backpay awards. The ADEA and

§§1981 and 1983 have no provisions, while Title VII, Title I, and §501 have two provisions. One limits the period of recovery to two years before the date the charge was filed and the other states that the concept of mitigation of damages applies.

    i.   **The backpay period.** The beginning date for backpay is generally the date the victim first lost wages due to the unlawful conduct, which may or may not be the same date as the discriminatory act, and it normally ends on the date of judgment.

        (a) **Limits on period.** The normal backpay period is limited by §796(g)(1) to a period of two years prior to the date of filing. Although §§1981 and 1983 and Title VII do not contain a limitation on the backpay period, the relevant statute of limitations for bringing the action provides a limitation. Under the ADEA, there appears to be no limitation period on lost wages claims.

        (b) **After-acquired evidence.** In McKennon v. Nashville Banner Publ. Co., 513 U.S. 352 (1995), the Court recognized a possible limit on the time period for backpay if the employer gains access to after-acquired evidence. For an employer to be successful in limiting the remedy afforded a victim of discrimination, the employer has the burden to establish that the employee's wrongdoing was of such severity that she would have been terminated on those grounds alone.

 ## EXAMPLE AND ANALYSIS

In McKennon v. Nashville Banner Publ. Co., 513 U.S. 352 (1995), a newspaper discharged several employees as part of a reduction in workforce. An employee filed suit claiming that her discharge violated the ADEA. During a deposition, she revealed that she had copied several confidential documents she had received in the course of her employment and had showed them to her husband. After the depositions, the employer conceded its discrimination and declared that it would have terminated her had it known of this misconduct. The Supreme Court concluded that the misconduct did not render the ADEA violation irrelevant. If after-acquired evidence was permitted to bar relief for an earlier violation, the goals of Title VII and the ADEA would be frustrated. After-acquired evidence, however, may bear on the remedy awarded. As a general rule, the Court noted, in after-acquired cases, neither reinstatement nor front pay is an appropriate remedy. With regard to the issue of backpay, the district court must give proper recognition of the fact that an ADEA violation occurred. As a result, the calculation of backpay should be from the date of the unlawful discharge to the date the new information was discovered.

---

c. **The duty to mitigate damages.** The antidiscrimination statutes require the court to reduce backpay by amounts that were or could have been earned with reasonable diligence from other employment.

i. **Burden on employer.** The employer has the burden of proving that the backpay should be reduced because the plaintiff could have earned more with reasonable diligence. To do this, the employer must show the existence of comparable employment, the amount the plaintiff would have earned, and that the plaintiff's lack of reasonable diligence resulted in the failure to obtain the position. In any event, the victim is not required to "go into another line of work, accept a demotion, or take a demeaning position."

EXAM TIP

The three ways to cut off backpay are the two-year rule, after-acquired evidence, and the duty of the plaintiff to mitigate.

 # EXAMPLE AND ANALYSIS

In Jurgens v. EEOC, 903 F.2d 386 (5th Cir. 1990), the Fifth Circuit was faced with the problem of calculating backpay where the victim retired from the position after the employer promoted a minority male instead of the plaintiff. At about the same time, the EEOC reorganized its offices to reduce its workforce. As part of the reorganization, the EEOC offered the plaintiff the choice of either a demotion or early retirement. The plaintiff accepted the latter. The district court awarded backpay from the time of the denial of the promotion until the effective date of the plaintiff's retirement. The plaintiff argued that "but for" the denial of the promotion, he would not have been compelled to retire. The Fifth Circuit held that where an employer discriminatorily denies a promotion to an employee, that employee's duty to mitigate damages encompasses remaining on the job. In so holding, the court noted that in order for an employee to recover backpay beyond the date of his retirement or resignation, the evidence must establish that the employer constructively discharged the employee.

ii. **Offering the claimant the previously denied job.** In Ford Motor Co. v. EEOC, 458 U.S. 219 (1982), three women were discriminatorily denied vacant positions. The women eventually returned to their previous positions with another automobile manufacturer. Ford later offered the women the jobs they had wanted but did not offer to grant them seniority. The women declined the offer. The Supreme Court held that the accrual of backpay tolled when the defendant unconditionally offered the claimants the jobs they originally sought. Requiring the offer to include retroactive seniority, however, would adversely affect the employment interests of innocent third parties.

iii. **Fringe benefits.** The duty to mitigate has also been applied to insurance coverage lost when an employee is discharged. In Fariss v. Lynchburg Foundry, 769 F.2d 958 (4th Cir. 1985), a person who had been wrongfully terminated because of his age died before judgment. The Fourth Circuit held that his widow could only recover the value of the insurance premiums, not the face value of the policy, because the plaintiff had not attempted to procure substitute coverage.

d. **Prejudgment interest.** Prevailing plaintiffs may recover prejudgment interest on their backpay awards. The Eleventh Amendment does not bar such an award where a state is the defendant.

i. **Government employers and the eleventh amendment.** In Fitzpatrick v. Bitzer, 427 U.S. 445 (1976), the Court held that the Eleventh Amendment does not preclude a federal court from rendering a backpay award against a state or state official. In so holding, the Supreme Court reasoned that Title VII was enacted pursuant to Congress' enforcement power under the Fourteenth Amendment, which permits Congress to override the state's Eleventh Amendment immunity. In Kimel v. Florida Bd. of Regents, 120 S. Ct. 631 (2000), the Court found that Congress could not abrogate the Eleventh Amendment immunity of the states because it was beyond its enumerated power under the Fourteenth Amendment to apply the ADEA to the state and local governments. In §1983 actions, backpay awards are precluded by both the Eleventh Amendment and statutory interpretation.

2. **Instatement, Reinstatement, Retroactive Seniority and Prohibitory Injunction**

Antidiscrimination statutes permit the courts to grant prohibitory and compensatory equitable relief, in the form of an injunction, reinstatement, or instatement.

a. **Reinstatement and instatement.** The same policy of providing a make-whole remedy underlying the presumption of backpay supports a similar presumption of instatement in a hiring case and reinstatement in a discharge case.

    i. **Rebuttal.** The employer has the burden of proving that special circumstances exist that justify the denial of reinstatement or instatement.

        (a) **No bumping of innocent incumbent.** Reinstatement is denied when the employer proves that the position plaintiff would have been entitled to is occupied by another employee who is innocent in any involvement in the discrimination against the plaintiff.

EXAMPLE AND ANALYSIS

Walters was found to be the victim of discrimination and reinstatement was ordered even though the position was occupied by an "innocent" employee. The reason the court ordered that the incumbent be "bumped" to accommodate the reinstatement of the plaintiff was that the job, museum director, was unique. Walters v. City of Atlanta, 803 F.2d 1135 (11th Cir. 1986).

        (b) **Hostility or animosity.** Where the employer can prove that there is such hostility and animosity between the plaintiff and the employer that a harmonious working relationship would be impossible, reinstatement or instatement can be denied. That typically, however, triggers an award of front pay as an alternative remedy.

b. **Retroactive seniority.** In Franks v. Bowman Transp. Co., 424 U.S. 747 (1976), the Court held the denial of retroactive seniority is permissible "only for reasons which, if applied generally, would not frustrate the central statutory purpose of eliminating discrimination." Victims of hiring discrimination were presumed to be entitled to the grant of retroactive seniority under a "rightful place" right to instatement.

    i. **"Rightful place" instatement or reinstatement.** Where hiring discrimination is proven and incumbent workers hold jobs pursuant to a seniority system in a collective bargaining agreement "rightful place" relief is presumed appropriate. Instead of ordering defendant to hire plaintiffs immediately, which would displace incumbent employees, "rightful place" relief puts the plaintiffs on a priority hiring list. When a job opens, plaintiff is hired and then is granted seniority back to the date she was discriminated against. No incumbent workers are displaced but all incumbent workers with less seniority than the plaintiff become somewhat more vulnerable to layoff.

ii. **Benefits seniority.** In contrast to the competitive seniority that protects the jobs of workers by length of service, which is governed by the "rightful place" approach, benefits seniority determines pension rights, vacations, insurance, and unemployment benefits, and is analogous to backpay in that the burden of such awards is borne by the employer and not innocent incumbent workers. Victims of discrimination are entitled to full make-whole relief regarding benefits seniority.

 # EXAMPLE AND ANALYSIS

In Franks v. Bowman Transp. Co., 424 U.S. 747 (1976), a group of African-American applicants successfully brought a Title VII action alleging racial discrimination in hiring and discharge policies. The Supreme Court found that seniority relief is consistent with the statute's purpose of making victims whole. Such seniority is important in allocating employment benefits, determining order of layoffs, and bidding for jobs. Without the ability to award seniority relief, the court would be unable to satisfy the make-whole objective of Title VII. In this case, the company argued that the award of seniority would adversely affect the employment interest of innocent employees. Accepting this argument would frustrate the purpose of Title VII and there is nothing in Title VII or the legislative history that bars awarding seniority as a remedy. Incumbent and discriminated employees should both share the burden of past discrimination. "Rightful place" seniority means that the court creates a priority hiring list of the victims of discrimination. When there is a job opening, a victim is hired for it and is then granted retroactive competitive seniority back to the date she would have been hired but for discrimination. No innocent incumbents are displaced from their jobs, but, once a victim is hired with retroactive competitive seniority, incumbent workers' seniority protection is to some extent altered.

c. **Injunctive relief.** A defendant found liable of discrimination is subjected to an injunction against further discrimination. The Fifth Circuit has held that "absent clear and convincing proof of no reasonable probability of further noncompliance with the law a grant of injunctive relief is mandatory." James v. Stockham Valves & Fittings Co., 559 F.2d 310, 354 (5th Cir. 1977).

3.   Front Pay

An award of front pay compensates a victim of discrimination for the wages and benefits she will lose even after the judgment date. Such an award complements an award of instatement or reinstatement and runs from the date of the judgment until the date the victim of discrimination obtains the wrongfully denied position. Cassino v. Reichhold Chems., Inc., 817 F.2d 1338 (9th Cir. 1987).

EXAM TIP

Where lost wages arise in a fact situation, address backpay and front pay. Backpay involves lost compensation until judgment and front pay involves future compensation until the plaintiff is reinstated or, if she will not be reinstated, then the difference between what she would have earned if reinstated and what she will earn in her next best employment.

---

a.   **Front pay as alternative to instatement or reinstatement.** Where the employer proves that special circumstances exist that justify denying plaintiff instatement or reinstatement, front pay is awarded. In Avitia v. Metropolitan Club of Chicago, 49 F.3d 1219 (7th Cir. 1995), the court defined front pay as "the difference (after discounting to present value) between what the plaintiff would have earned in the future had he been reinstated at the time of trial and what he would have earned in the future in his next best employment."

4.   Compensatory and Punitive Damages

The availability of compensatory and punitive damages in employment discrimination varies from statute to statute.

EXAM TIP

Legal damages include compensatory and punitive damages that are not subject to caps under §1981 and §1983 but are subject to caps in Title VII actions, which caps depend on the size of the employer.

---

a.   **Sections 1981 and 1983.** Both compensatory and punitive damages are available under §1981 and §1983, with several restrictions when sought from a governmental entity.

b. **ADEA.** The ADEA does not permit either type of damages, although it allows liquidated damages, essentially double damages for willful violations.

c. **Title VII, Title I of the ADA.** Title VII and Title I of the ADA allow such damages but place limits on the amount of these awards. Section 1981a(a)(1) authorizes recovery of compensatory and punitive damages for a Title VII violation where both (1) disparate treatment is proven and (2) the claim is not recognized under §1981.

   i. **Limitations of recovery under Title VII.** Punitive damages can only be recovered if the defendant acted with malice or with reckless indifference, but they cannot be recovered from the government.

   ii. **Compensatory and punitive damages under Title VII.** Compensatory and punitive damages are capped depending upon the number of employees. The caps are: (a) $50,000 for employer with 100 or fewer employees; (b) $300,000 for an employer with 500 or more employees.

d. **Title II of the ADA.** Based on existing precedent, the availability of compensatory and punitive damages under Title II is uncertain.

5. **Liquidated Damages**

The ADEA and the EPA permit recovery of "liquidated damages." To recover liquidated damages, the plaintiff must establish a "willful" violation.

a. **"Willful" defined.** In Trans World Airline, Inc. v. Thurston, 469 U.S. 111 (1985), the Supreme Court had held that a willful violation is acting with knowledge or reckless disregard of the risk that the policy plaintiff challenged contravened the statute.

b. **Prejudgment interest.** Some courts have held that liquidated damages are a substitute for punitive damages, while others have held that such awards are partly compensatory so a plaintiff cannot recover prejudgment interest.

6. **Lost Wages Under the Equal Pay Act**

The FLSA permits the plaintiff to recover the wages lost due to an EPA violation. Lost wages are the difference between the amount of pay the victim received and the higher amount of pay received by the comparable person of the opposite sex.

7. **Attorney's Fees**

Each antidiscrimination statute, with slight variation, contains a provision allowing an award of attorney's fees and costs. Under Title VII, the court may grant the prevailing party (other than the federal government) a reasonable attorney's fee. The ADEA, through the Fair Labor Standards Act, requires the court to award attorney's fees and costs to a prevailing non-federal employee victim of discrimination but does not authorize the court to award fees and costs to either a prevailing federal employee or a prevailing employer. Sections 1981 and 1983, and the ADA generally follow the Title VII pattern. The ADA, in addition to allowing the court to award attorney's fees, permits the EEOC to make a fee award.

a. **Prevailing plaintiffs.** In Christiansburg Garment Co. v. EEOC, 434 U.S. 412 (1978), the Court recognized an exception to the general American rule that litigants must pay their own attorney's fees for antidiscrimination statutes in which Congress has provided for attorney-fee–shifting in favor of the prevailing party. **Only if there are special circumstances of unjustness will the presumption that a prevailing plaintiff is entitled to attorney's fees be defeated.**

b. **Prevailing defendants.** The Court in *Christiansburg Garment Co.* differentiated prevailing plaintiffs from prevailing defendants because the equitable considerations that justify the award of attorney's fees to plaintiffs are absent in the case of a prevailing defendant. Thus, the Supreme Court held that the proper standard is that a **district court may award attorney's fees to a prevailing defendant only upon a finding that the plaintiff's action was frivolous, unreasonable, or without foundation.** In applying this standard, the trial court should avoid engaging in post hoc reasoning by concluding that, because the plaintiff did not prevail, the action must been without foundation when initially brought.

c. **It is not always clear who is a "prevailing party."** Since the statutes provide an award of attorney's fees to the "prevailing party," it is necessary to determine which party prevailed. In Farrar v. Hobby, 506 U.S. 163 (1992), the issue was whether a plaintiff who recovered nominal damages in a §1983 action was the prevailing party. The plurality opinion of the Court stated "to qualify as a prevailing party, a civil rights plaintiff must obtain some relief on the merits of the claim . . . [that] directly benefit[s] him." However, the plurality found that when plaintiff's recovery is limited to nominal damages, a reasonable attorney's fee is "usually no fee at all." Justice O'Connor's concurrence that made a majority applied three factors—the extent of relief, the significance of the issue prevailed on, and the public purpose served—to justify a fee even if plaintiff received only nominal damages.

 # EXAMPLES AND ANALYSIS

1. In Gudenkauf v. Stauffer Communications, Inc., 158 F.3d 1074 (10th Cir. 1998), the court applied Justice O'Connor's public purpose factor that was served by

plaintiff's lawsuit in exposing defendant's ignorance of the need for sexual harassment policies, justifying the award of attorney's fees even though plaintiff was awarded only nominal damages.

2. In contrast, in Sheppard v. Riverview Nursing Ctr., 88 F.3d 1332 (4th Cir. 1996), the court remanded the consideration of attorney's fees where plaintiff proved her pregnancy was "a motivating factor" in her layoff but the employer successfully proved it would have made the same decision even if it had not considered her pregnancy.

---

    d. Calculation of attorney's fee. A prevailing party may be awarded a "reasonable" fee award. The Supreme Court, in several opinions, laid out the formula for calculating an award of attorney's fees.

        i. Calculating the fee. The fee calculation is a two-step process.

            (a) Hours worked times reasonable rate. Multiply the number of hours the attorney reasonably expended on the litigation by a reasonable rate per hour to find a "lodestar" amount.

                (1) The work that counts. A fee award includes the attorney's service for every stage in the enforcement scheme including labor arbitration, proceedings before a state agency, a request for preliminary injunction, the taking of an appeal, post-judgment monitoring of the decree, and even the hearing to establish the propriety and amount of a fee award.

            (b) Special circumstances justifying an adjustment. In rare circumstances, where supported by specific evidence and judicial findings, the district court may adjust the figure upward or downward to account for other relevant factors.

D. RELIEF FOR SYSTEMIC DISCRIMINATION

In a systemic discrimination case, the individual, as well as the class as a whole, is entitled to relief.

1. Retroactive Seniority and Backpay

Awarding individual relief in a systemic case can pose problems. Courts often award seniority and backpay in a way that avoids the need to determine the precise injuries sustained by each class member. For example, in Teamsters v. United States, 431 U.S. 324 (1977), a class of employees were proved to be the victims of a pattern of discrimination excluding them from a job, giving them the lower paying, less desirable city route jobs. The Court held that the court could not grant a seniority award to predate the effective date of enactment of Title VII. As to post-Act discrimination, a prima facie case justifies an award of prospective relief in the form of an injunction or any other order necessary to fulfill the purpose of Title VII.

a. **Individual relief.** Proof of a pattern or practice of discrimination creates a presumption that employment decisions as to individuals were made pursuant to the employer's discriminatory policy. Individual class members need only establish that they unsuccessfully applied for a job or would have applied. That shifts the burden of proof to the employer to prove the defendant's discrimination on a case-by-case basis that the individuals had not been discriminated against.

b. **Retroactive seniority and non-applicants.** The failure to apply for a job does not automatically bar an award of retroactive seniority. In accordance with the goals of Title VII, the district court is given broad equitable powers to fashion complete relief and, in accord with *Franks*, an employee must be awarded seniority unless special circumstances exist. Applied to this case, all minority employees within the class, whether or not they applied for a position, should be entitled to relief. The Court reasoned that a consistently enforced discriminatory policy has the effect of deterring employees, who are aware of the policy, from submitting applications. Non-applicants, however, have the burden of establishing that they were potential victims. Moreover, non-applicants must come forth with evidence that they possessed the threshold qualifications for the job. Once established, the employer bears the burden to prove that lawful reasons existed for the employment decision.

c. **Backpay.** In a systemic discrimination case, the potential class includes those who were actually rejected because of discriminatory reasons and those who were deterred from applying because of the discriminatory criteria. The problem is that not all those who were rejected because of discrimination would have been hired if the employer did not discriminate. In determining backpay, the courts have used two different approaches.

   i. **Individual approach.** First, the court determines how many African Americans would have been hired if the employer did not discriminate. It does this by figuring that the same proportion of African American applicants would have been hired as whites. Then, the court subtracted the actual number of minorities hired to come up with the actual number of African Americans that would have been hired with no discrimination. Once that number was established, the district court identified which persons would most likely have been selected who, therefore, receive full backpay.

   ii. **Class approach.** The first step is to determine the number of applicants who were potentially denied as a result of the discriminatory selection process over the applicable period. Then, the court will select applicants who were admitted and subtract the earnings of the applicants who were denied positions for each period. The total award is then to be distributed on a pro rata basis to all the applicants, without determining which individuals would have been hired if the employer had not discriminated.

 ## EXAMPLE AND ANALYSIS

In Hameed v. Iron Workers, Local 396, 736 F.2d 506 (8th Cir. 1980), the court articulated both approaches but decided to distribute the total amount of backpay among all the applicants because it was too speculative to pick those who would have been hired if the employer had not discriminated.

---

    d. **Choosing between the individual and class approach.** In Pettway v. American Cast Iron Pipe Co., 494 F.2d 211, 260–62 (5th Cir. 1974), the court discussed both methods. The individual approach, the Fifth Circuit wrote, should be utilized where the class is small, the time period short, or where a backpay award can be made with some precision. The class approach, the court added, is more appropriate when the class size is large, the period of conduct extended over a long period, or where multiple effects of the discrimination existed.

2. Affirmative Action Relief

Judicially imposed affirmative action relief is a form of classwide relief that requires the employer to take positive action to benefit members of the discriminated class. In United States v. Paradise, 480 U.S. 149 (1987), the Supreme Court decided that a court order of one-for-one promotions for state police officers survived strict scrutiny as a remedy for past discrimination, even though not all the beneficiaries of the affirmative action had been victims of the defendant's discrimination.

Affirmative action relief, the Supreme Court noted in Local 28, Sheet Metal Workers' Intl. Assn. v. EEOC, 478 U.S. 421 (1986), is not always proper. A district court's judgment should be guided by sound legal principles.

    a. **Factors considered.** In *Local 28*, the Supreme Court found several factors persuasive in concluding that affirmative action relief was appropriate.

        i. **Pervasive discrimination.** The union had a history of pervasive and egregious discrimination.

        ii. **Non-whites discouraged.** The history of discrimination discouraged nonwhites from applying for membership.

iii. **No racial balancing.** The flexible approach taken by the district court supports the proposition that the action was being used as a benchmark, rather than to achieve racial balance.

iv. **Temporary nature.** The affirmative action was a temporary measure to end when the goal of minority membership that matched the labor pool was achieved.

v. **Trammeling of incumbents.** The remedy did not trammel the interests of innocent third parties.

REVIEW QUESTIONS AND ANSWERS

Question: Are the victims of discrimination generally presumed to be entitled to the full remedies provided by antidiscrimination laws?

Answer: Yes.

Question: What is the normal period for backpay?

Answer: Generally, the period begins on the date the victim first lost wages due to discrimination and it continues until the date of judgment.

Question: Are there any grounds to cut off backpay before the date of judgment?

Answer: The employer may be able to cut off, or reduce, backpay by proving one of two grounds:

1. that it acquired evidence of the plaintiff's wrongdoing so severe that it would have discharged the plaintiff on those grounds alone, with the date the evidence was discovered then becoming the end date for backpay; or

2. that the plaintiff earned mitigating earnings or would have earned in comparable employment but for the plaintiff's lack of diligence.

Question: Must the employer always hire or rehire the plaintiff?

Answer: While instatement or reinstatement is presumed, the employer can avoid that remedy by proving that an innocent employee occupies the position plaintiff would have had but for the discrimination or that there is such animosity between the parties that a harmonious working relationship would be impossible.

Question: What is "rightful place" seniority relief?

Answer: Rather than providing full make-whole relief immediately, "rightful place" relief means the plaintiff will be hired into the first job opening and will then be given retroactive seniority back to the date she would have been hired but for the employer's discrimination.

Question: What is front pay?

Answer: Front pay compensates a plaintiff for lost wages from the date of judgment until she is reinstated, or, if she is not to be reinstated, it is an amount to compensate for earning less in the future in her next best employment.

Question: Are compensatory and punitive damages generally available under the antidiscrimination statutes?

Answer: They are available in §§1981 and 1983, Title VII, and Title I of the ADA actions. In Title VII and Title I, these damages are subject to caps determined by the number of employees of the employer.

Question: What are liquidated damages and in which statutes are they available?

Answer: Liquidated damages are essentially double damages available for willful violations of the ADEA and the EPA.

Question: What is a "willful" violation?

Answer: A willful violation is the knowledge or reckless disregard of the risk on the part of the employer that its action violated the ADEA or the EPA.

Question: Is the prevailing party entitled to attorney's fees under the antidiscrimination statutes?

Answer: A prevailing plaintiff is presumed entitled to attorney's fees but a prevailing defendant is entitled to them only upon a finding that the plaintiff's action was frivolous, unreasonable, or without foundation.

Question: Are members of classes of workers who are the victims of systemic discrimination presumed to be entitled to relief?

Answer: By showing they belong to the affected class, victims are presumed entitled to relief in systemic discrimination cases. The employer, however, can rebut the presumption by proving that each individual in fact had not been discriminated against.

Question: Does judicially imposed affirmative action serve a compelling governmental interest?

Answer: Providing a remedy for the discrimination of an employer is a compelling governmental interest justifying affirmative action, even if all its beneficiaries are not themselves the victims of defendant's discrimination.

Sample Exam Questions and Sample Answers

INTRODUCTORY ADVICE

The first rule of law school exam taking is that you should somewhere find and apply in your exam every issue you think your professor thinks is important. Studying for exams is preparing yourself to do that, with your studying planned in light of the particular course and your professor. That being said, employment discrimination exams usually present the test taker with the opportunity to work both deeply within issues and broadly across a variety of areas. Therefore it is important not only to know how each issue works but also how the different issues interrelate as they apply to any particular set of facts.

As an exception to the general rule that you need not cite case names, there is some value in employment discrimination to use case names as shorthand descriptions of the two different approaches to individual disparate treatment law. *McDonnell Douglas/ Burdine* is a good shorthand way to describe the circumstantial evidence or pretext approach to proving individual disparate treatment discrimination, while *Price Waterhouse* is shorthand for the direct or mixed motive method.

CHAPTER TWO: INDIVIDUAL DISPARATE TREATMENT DISCRIMINATION

Question 1: Tom Tyler, age 48 with 26 years of service and consistently good performance evaluations, was a general products salesman assigned to Bethlehem Steel Corporation's Buffalo sales office. When the company told him he was going to be "permanently laid off" because the Buffalo office was being closed, he asked to be transferred to an opening he knew of in the Pittsburgh office. Tyler's supervisor told him they had already decided to fill that opening with Frank Weber, age 47. Instead of assigning Weber to the opening, the company gave it to a 26 year old, David Moules.

In the two years preceding Tyler's layoff, the performance evaluations of employees in the sales department gave "youth" a very positive significance. For example, the latest evaluation of a 26 year old described him as a "young tiger, with much upside future potential." Of the 12 new hires in sales positions in that time period, 10 were right out of college. In a deposition, David Land, the company's sales manager, described why young workers were being recruited. "The demographics of our sales force were shifting upwards, so that over half were age 45 and older. We were providing for a time when they would be eligible for retirement." How would you evaluate Tyler's individual disparate treatment case?

Answer: *Direct versus Circumstantial Evidence Approach*
Since there are two mutually exclusive models for analyzing individual disparate treatment cases, the first question is whether the *Price Waterhouse* direct evidence approach or the default, *McDonnell Douglas/Burdine* circumstantial evidence approach applies.

Direct Evidence Approach
For *Price Waterhouse* to apply, plaintiff must show that the record includes "direct" evidence of the employer's intent to discriminate. Courts have taken several different views of what constitutes direct evidence of intent to discriminate. One view is that direct evidence means evidence that does not require the factfinder to draw an inference to resolve the relevant question of fact, here the state of mind of the employer. While there is evidence in the record that age was in some sense on the minds of the managers in making employment decisions concerning the sales force, there is no direct statement from a decision-maker that Tyler was laid off because he was too old. Thus, there is no evidence that meets this strict definition of direct evidence. Another view treats "circumstantial-plus" evidence as sufficient to trigger the use of *Price Waterhouse,* which evidence has some direct connection with the decision plaintiff challenges. The evidence here that age was on the mind of the sales manager and that being young was a plus may qualify under the circumstantial-plus definition even though it does not focus on the decision to lay off Tyler.

Applying the Direct Method Approach
If the trial judge decides that *Price Waterhouse* applies, plaintiff needs to prove that age was "a substantial factor" in the employer's decision and, if shown, the employer would then have an affirmative defense to liability if it could prove that it would have made the same decision even if it had not considered Tyler's age. The Civil Rights Act of 1991 modified Title VII's approach to *Price Waterhouse* cases but did not similarly amend the ADEA. Nevertheless, there

is strong precedent to treat individual disparate treatment cases uniformly under all the antidiscrimination statutes. Thus, the court could submit the case to the jury using the Title VII approach, which would only require the plaintiff to prove that age was "a motivating factor" in the employer's decision to lay him off permanently. Here the circumstances, that there was an opening that Tyler could transfer to, that that job ultimately went to a much younger worker, and that being young was a positive value in the mind of the manager of this department all could support finding discrimination because of age. If the jury so finds, then the employer has the opportunity to limit full remedies by proving it would have made the same decision even if it had not considered plaintiff's age in deciding to lay him off. There is, however, no evidence to support that defense.

Circumstantial Evidence Approach

If the direct evidence approach is held not to apply, the default position is to analyze the case under *McDonnell Douglas/Burdine*'s three-step approach. The first step is for plaintiff to establish a prima facie case, which Tyler can easily do because (1) he is within the age group protected by the ADEA, (2) he was successfully performing his sales job, (3) he was qualified for an opening that he could have transferred to, and (4) he was denied that transfer and that job ultimately was filled by a much younger person. The second step is defendant's rebuttal, which would be successful, that the job opening to which plaintiff wanted to transfer was not open at the time he asked about it because the decision had been made to assign it to another worker even though that assignment ultimately did not work out. The third step requires plaintiff to prove by a preponderance of the evidence that age played a role and had a determinative influence in the employer's decision to lay him off. At this stage, the jury can base that decision on the facts plaintiff relied on to prove his prima facie case, the evidence that Frank Weber did not get the Pittsburgh opening and it went to a much younger worker and all the evidence including evidence that age was on the mind of the sales manager in making employment decisions. If the jury finds that age was a determinative factor in the decision to lay off Tyler, then plaintiff wins since there is no same decision defense to a circumstantial evidence case of individual disparate treatment discrimination.

Question 2: Sharon Foster, an African-American woman, sued the Navy for failing to promote her to the position of management analyst at the Newport Naval Hospital, claiming race and sex discrimination. Foster had been working as the hospital's professional affairs coordinator when the management analyst job opened up. The management analyst job essentially supervises Foster and a number of other civilian administrative employees at the hospital. It is typical in the Navy for internal candidates such as Foster to be promoted where possible. When the management analyst slot opened up, the hospital's director of administration, Commander Bill Travis, asked his staff for a list of potential candidates. Foster stood out on this list of five as the only person presently working at the hospital, as the only woman, and as the only African American. Travis rejected the list because it did not include his fishing buddy, James Berry, and told the staff to rewrite the job description to focus on Berry's credentials. The staff then gave Travis only Berry's name and he was hired to fill the management analyst job. In his deposition, Travis stalwartly maintained that he hired Berry because Berry was the best qualified person for the job. How would you decide Foster's case?

Answer: *Race or Sex Claim*
Where Foster can claim race or sex discrimination (or the "intersectional" claim that focuses on her as an African-American woman), special problems arise. If she picks only one of the two bases, say race, the employer may be able to escape liability by pointing to the other, here sex, as the actual explanation for its decision. Since virtually any reason (even an illegal or patently silly reason) other than a reason the plaintiff can still challenge legally suffices to rebut plaintiff's prima facie circumstantial evidence case, that pushes the plaintiff to assert as many bases as possible. But, by asserting many bases for the discrimination, plaintiff may be diluting the power of the evidence as to any one of the claims. Perhaps that is why the "intersectional" approach would be the best, though that has yet to be recognized by the courts.

Direct versus Circumstantial Evidence Approaches
Based on the discussion in Question 1, it is clear that there is no direct or circumstantial-plus evidence in the record that would justify the use of the *Price Waterhouse* direct evidence approach. Nothing in the record points to Commander Travis having gender or race on his mind in his decision to pick Berry rather than Foster for the management analyst job.

Applying the Circumstantial Evidence Approach
Again, based on the discussion answering Question 1, it is clear that plaintiff easily established a prima facie case of both race and sex discrimination using the *McDonnell Douglas/Burdine* model: she is an African-American woman, who is qualified for the job, the management analyst job was open but she was not promoted into it, and the job went to a white male. The Navy can easily rebut plaintiff's prima facie case by relying on Commander Travis' claim

that he picked the most qualified person. That leaves the focus on the third step, requiring plaintiff to prove that her race or sex was the determinative factor in the Navy's decision. Given the fact that the evidence in the record supports the conclusion that Travis did not pick Berry because he was the most qualified, the factfinder could conclude that the rebuttal reason advanced by the Navy is not true. While that helps support the inference that Foster was not promoted because of her race or sex, a finding that the employer's stated reason for its decision is not true does not justify plaintiff winning as a matter of law. Here, however, it may be possible that the jury would find for the plaintiff since she was the only candidate who satisfied the general rule that internal candidates get the promotions but she did not get it because she was an African-American woman. But if the jury believes that Travis was going to hire only his fishing buddy, Berry, no matter who the other candidates were or what the general practice was, then Foster will lose.

CHAPTER THREE: SYSTEMIC DISPARATE TREATMENT DISCRIMINATION

Question 1: AmericaFirst Taxi Company operates a large fleet of cabs throughout the city of Chicago. After receiving many complaints that the company discriminated against Latinos, the EEOC conducted an investigation that showed that, of the company's 500 taxi drivers, only 5 are Latino. The general population of the city is about 24 percent Latino. Almost 15 percent of Latinos in the city have driver's licenses but only 1 percent have the chauffeur's licenses necessary to drive a cab. There is much turnover among employees. While the company does require applicants to have driver's licenses to be hired, it has hired many drivers and then helped them get their chauffeur's license. AmericaFirst has no written employment policies and it does not keep records of applicants who are not hired. How would you analyze the EEOC's case against AmericaFirst and any rebuttals or defenses of the employer?

Answer: *Race or National Origin Discrimination*
Discrimination against Latinos is race discrimination because Latinos are generally people of color who come from a number of different Spanish-speaking countries. National origin discrimination may also be asserted where the discrimination is focused on people who come from a particular Hispanic country, such as Mexico. Since there is no indication that the employer fails to hire because of the country of origin of applicants, the claim should proceed as a race discrimination claim.

Formal Policy or General Practice of Discrimination
Systemic disparate treatment discrimination can be shown by either a formal policy of discrimination or by proof that a general practice

of discrimination exists. Since the employer appears not to have any employment policies of any kind, much less formal policies of discrimination, this case should be analyzed as a general practices case.

Applying the Practices Approach

Because it is a cumulation of what the employer does rather than just what it says it does, statistical evidence is used to establish whether an employer engages in a practice of systemic disparate treatment discrimination. The underpinning of statistical evidence is the probability assumption that over time the employer's workforce should resemble the pool from which it would draw its workers absent discrimination. The employer's workforce of 500 cabbies includes only 5, or 1 percent, Latino drivers. Since there is much turnover among drivers and the employer has been covered by Title VII since it became effective in 1965, there are probably no pre-Act hires to subtract from the employer's workforce. The basis for the comparison with the employer's workforce is the qualified labor pool. The EEOC would argue that the city's general population, which would set the probability figure (the "P") at 24 percent, is an appropriate proxy for the qualified labor pool since driving a cab is a skill that most people could readily acquire. Alternatively, the 15 percent of the city's Latino population with driver's licenses could be used as well. Under either one, the comparison with the 1 percent workforce representation of Latinos would likely support a finding of "gross and longlasting" disparity that establishes a prima facie case of systemic disparate treatment discrimination. To avoid that, the employer might try to argue for a labor pool with a smaller representation of Latinos. While the 1 percent figure of Latinos with chauffeur's licences would effectively rebut the EEOC's case, a court is unlikely to accept that figure since the employer has a practice of hiring drivers who do not have chauffeur's licenses. The employer could look for some way to avoid using the entire city of Chicago as the geographical labor market by showing that it actually hires applicants from a different geographic area with a lower percentage of Latino population than the whole city. That may not be accepted, since the geographic pool used for comparison is the pool the employer would use absent discrimination, which is not necessarily the pool it actually uses. Given residential segregation by race, it would be wrong to always rely on the geographic area the employer uses since that may simply correlate with the fact that it only hires white drivers. Finally, there does not appear to be a way for the cab company to argue that it does its hiring "in spite of" rather than "because of" its racial impact. Since the cab company did not keep any records of applicants, it would be difficult for the cab company to undermine the EEOC's statistical showing with evidence that Latinos lack the qualifications for, or interest in, cab driving jobs. The best hope for the company would be to argue that the lack of anecdotal evidence of individual Latinos who applied but were not hired by AmericaFirst undermines the EEOC case by showing a lack of interest in cab driving jobs by Latinos. The chances are quite good that the EEOC's action will be successful since the exclusion of Latinos despite their availability reveals the employer's intent to discriminate.

Question 2: Many inmates at the Fellstone Prison for Women have been the victims of physical and sexual abuse by their fathers, husbands, lovers, and even their sons. As a result of many complaints by inmates that male guards were abusing them and invading their privacy, the prison decided to require that all guards assigned to duty observing inmates in showers and toilet areas should be the same sex as the inmates. To schedule guards to meet that requirement, the prison decided that 6 of 41 guard jobs needed to be assigned to women. Malcolm Miller applied for but was denied a job as a guard because the only opening was reserved for a woman. How will his Title VII suit be decided?

Answer: *Formal Policy of Systemic Discrimination*
There is no question that reserving 6 of 41 guard jobs for women is a formal policy of sex discrimination that is prohibited as systemic disparate treatment unless it is saved by the bona fide occupational qualification (BFOQ) defense.

Bona Fide Occupational Qualification
The prison bears the burden of persuasion to prove that reserving 6 of 41 prison guard jobs for women is justified by the BFOQ defense. The first step is to prove that the guard job goes to the essence of the operation of the prison. Since security is key to the successful operation of a prison, it is clear that the job of prison guard is essential. The next step is for the employer to prove one of two possibilities. First, it could try to prove that no men could successfully perform the job of maintaining order in the shower and toilet areas of a woman's prison while taking account of inmate privacy. The prison may be successful on this wing of the BFOQ test if the court accepts the concern about inmate privacy: women inmates would feel that their privacy was invaded as long as any man observed them in the shower or in the toilet. If, however, the focus was on abuse, the prison would not be able to prove that no men could do the job without abusing inmates. The second possible showing is that so few men could do the job that it is impractical for the employer to choose them. The prison would not likely be successful under this wing of the BFOQ as to abusive guards since few men would be abusive even though it would be hard to pick

who those would be. In sum, the privacy-based claim may well succeed as the basis of upholding the prison rule as a BFOQ.

CHAPTER FOUR: SYSTEMIC DISPARATE IMPACT DISCRIMINATION

Question 1:   William Barkman, an African American, was first hired as an accountant in the Mayor of Los Angeles' Office of Job Development after an interview and some checking of his references. He had served effectively in that position for three years when the Job Development Office was transferred to the Community Development Department, which department was subject to civil service. To keep his job, Barkman was required to take a civil service exam and to score high enough to be selected for the job. Barkman passed the test but did not score highly enough to retain his job. While 20 of the 100 test takers were African Americans, only 5 passed the accountant test and only 2 were appointed to accountant jobs. Of the 80 test takers who were not African Americans, 35 passed the test and 16 were appointed. The civil service test for the accountant job was constructed as follows: A group of city accountants analyzed the accountant jobs for which the test would be used and determined the type of accountant work involved in that work. They then took some of the actual books and records involved and used them as samples of the job to make up the test. Barkman sues, claiming systemic disparate impact discrimination. What result?

Answer: *Prima Facie Disparate Impact Case*
Barkman easily establishes a prima facie disparate impact case by showing that the city used the accountant test, which was an employment practice; it had an impact on African Americans since 10 percent of the African American test takers were appointed versus 20 percent of the test takers who were not African American; and the impact was adverse to a group that historically has been victimized by discrimination, and was of sufficient amount to conclude that the impact was disparate.

Defendant's Rebuttal
The city can defend by proving that the test was validated pursuant to professional test standards. The validation technique that the city would argue applies is content validation. Here the test was constructed after a job analysis was undertaken to determine what kind of accountant skills and knowledge were involved in the jobs for which the test would be used. Since the actual books and records involved in the accountant jobs at issue were used to develop the test, there is a strong argument that this test is content valid. The

test is in essence a sample of the jobs for which the test will be used. Unless the plaintiff can show that the sample used did not reflect the actual content of the accountant jobs, it is likely that the test will be found to have been validated and therefore to be job related.

Plaintiff's Surrebuttal

Plaintiff can try two arguments in surrebuttal. The first is to argue that new §703(k) requires that an employment practice that causes a disparate impact be proven to be both job related and justified by business necessity. Even if the test is job related, it is not justified by business necessity since Barkman had been successfully performing the job for three years without having taken the test. The city's answer is that the professionally developed test exception in §703(h) applies instead of the job related and business necessity defense in §703(k). The second argument of the plaintiff would be that an alternative employment practice exists without similar racial impact that the employer refuses to use. Here, plaintiff can point to his own background as the alternative: he was initially hired by an interview and by a check of his references, and he then performed the job successfully. An interview and reference check is an alternative employment practice, it has less disparate impact, and the employer refuses to use it. It may be that plaintiff will be successful on his alternative employment practice argument and thus may win his disparate impact case, despite the city's legal requirement that the civil service test rules apply.

Question 2: Faced with an increasing number of robberies, the Brinxs Armored Car Company decided to impose new hiring requirements that all operators of armored cars be at least 5 feet 5 inches tall. The idea is that tall drivers will scare off potential robbers. Bonnie Small is 5 feet 4 inches tall and so is ineligible to drive a Brinxs truck. Relying on national data, the 5 feet 5 inches height requirement excludes about 13 percent of men but over 40 percent of women. How does systemic disparate impact law apply to Small's case against Brinxs?

Answer: *Plaintiff's Prima Facie Disparate Impact Case*

A height prerequisite for a job is a particular employment practice subject to disparate impact attack. Here the amount of impact on women is certainly significant, and it is adverse to women, who have historically been the victims of employment discrimination. National data has been accepted to show that an employer uses an employment practice that causes a disparate impact.

Defendant's Rebuttal Case

Brinxs has a number of possible responses. First, Brinxs can try to rebut the national statistics Small relies on or, alternatively, can undertake to carry the burden of persuasion of proving that its own use of the height requirement does not cause an impact. Such a showing would be dependent on Brinxs having mostly tall women applicants and employees, which is possible but not probable without some proof that tall women are particularly attracted to driving armored cars. Second, Brinxs could try to show that the height requirement was job related and necessary for business. While Brinxs would try to argue that tall people scare off potential robbers, to be successful it would have to introduce actual evidence, probably by expert testimony, that this is so. The height and weight requirement in Dothard v. Rawlinson was overturned because the Court required empirical evidence supporting the employer's argument, which evidence was not forthcoming.

Plaintiff's Surrebuttal

Assuming Brinxs could find such evidence that convinced the court that the height requirement was job related and justified by business necessity, Small could still try to prove that an alternative employment practice exists that serves the employer's interests but has less impact, which practice Brinxs refuses to use. Perhaps Small could show that other armored car companies have increased the armament the crews of armored cars carry and that worked as well as having tall guards to scare off potential robbers. That would be an alternative employment practice and Small would win her disparate impact claim as long as Brinxs refused to increase its armament.

CHAPTER FIVE: THE INTERRELATIONSHIP OF THE THEORIES OF DISCRIMINATION

Question 1: A salmon packing company each summer operates a canning factory in an area of Alaska remote from any towns and cities. The jobs and the workers are divided in two groups—cannery jobs and non-cannery jobs—with separate living quarters, cafeterias, etc. All the cannery jobs involve hard, physical labor, as do some of non-cannery jobs. Most of the non-cannery jobs involve office work but 10 percent involve physical labor around the canning factory but not in the cannery itself. The cannery workers are mostly Aleuts and Eskimos and they are hired through a union hiring hall in Fairbanks. The non-cannery workers, who are mostly white, are all hired at the Portland, Oregon, headquarters of the company. Sam Nogant, an Aleut who has worked in the cannery in the summer since high school, tried to apply with the company representative at the union hiring hall for a non-cannery job in the accounting department after he received a business degree. Nogant was told that the company only recruited non-cannery workers in Portland.

Answer: *The Three Theories of Discrimination*

All three major theories of discrimination law potentially apply to these facts.

Systemic Disparate Treatment Discrimination

Lacking a formal policy of discrimination, the question is whether the employer engaged in a practice of systemic disparate treatment discrimination by hiring mostly white employees for its non-cannery jobs. The hard question is what is the appropriate labor pool from which the employer would draw its non-cannery employees absent discrimination. The Supreme Court in *Wards Cove* held that the pool of incumbent cannery jobs was inappropriate because the non-cannery jobs were so different from the cannery jobs. Without evidence showing the applicant pool for the employer's jobs, the plaintiff would have to look elsewhere for a labor market pool with the workers having the qualities needed for the non-cannery jobs, which were basically white collar office work. An added quality is the ability and willingness to take a job just for the summer in an isolated place. Absent a showing of that pool to establish the basis for comparison with the minority representation in the employer's non-cannery workforce, plaintiff's systemic disparate treatment case will fail.

Systemic Disparate Impact Discrimination

The particular employment practice plaintiff can challenge using the disparate impact theory is its practice of not accepting applications for non-cannery jobs at the union hiring hall when it is recruiting cannery workers. Plaintiff can argue that refusing to accept any non-cannery applications at the hiring hall causes impact on Aleuts and Eskimos because it is a barrier to them applying for the 10 percent of non-cannery jobs that involve physical labor plus those white collar non-cannery jobs for which at least some of them are qualified. Since the hiring hall applicants are virtually all minority group members and the non-cannery applicants and workers are virtually all white, the employer policy minimizes the chances of Native Americans to work in non-cannery jobs from over 10 percent to close to zero. That impact should be found to be disparate and adverse. Thus, a prima facie case of disparate impact discrimination can be made out. Defendant would then have the opportunity to rebut plaintiff's disparate impact case by undermining plaintiff's showing of impact, which appears unlikely, or to carry the burden of proving that its rule precluding applying for non-cannery jobs at the union hiring hall is "job related for the position in question and consistent with business necessity." On the assumption that at least some of the applicants at the hiring hall can be shown to be qualified for some of the non-cannery jobs, the rule preventing anyone at the hiring hall from applying for those jobs can hardly be found to be job related. And, since company recruiters are at the hiring hall anyway, there is no added cost to accept these applications so it would be difficult to conclude that this rule is consistent with business necessity. Hiring for non-cannery jobs at the union hiring hall might also be an alternative employment practice that the employer refuses to use. Thus, plaintiff is likely to be successful with his systemic disparate impact claim.

Individual Disparate Treatment Discrimination
Because plaintiff has been successful in proving systemic disparate impact discrimination that affected him, he is presumed entitled to a remedy. Since it was discriminatory not to accept applications for non-cannery jobs at the union hiring hall, plaintiff is presumed to be entitled to full equitable relief provided for the victims of disparate impact discrimination. To avoid providing plaintiff with a remedy, the employer has the burden of persuasion to prove that it did not discriminate against Nogant.

CHAPTER SIX: GENDER DISCRIMINATION

Question 1:   Willow Fragante was a pathbreaker. The daughter of a firefighter in Manilla, Willow came to Dallas with a passion to follow in her father's footsteps and become a firefighter. Willow trained very hard and passed the written and physical firefighter exam for the Dallas Fire Department, placing twenty-ninth on the recruit list of 500. After being the first woman to successfully complete training, she was assigned to Fire Station No. 9. She was not welcomed. Black shrouds were hung above the station entrances when she arrived. Inside, several pornographic posters were hung in the lounge with scrawled writing that said, "Welcome home to Manilla!" The locker she was assigned had a sign on the inside of the door that said, "We are going to have your c— for breakfast, lunch and dinner, you Filipino whore." When she complained to the captain on duty, he said, "Lighten up, they will back off if you don't let it get to you." After several weeks of continued torment, including more pornographic photos, statements that Filipino women only had sex with animals, and more complaints by her to the captain in charge of the fire station as well as to the headquarters downtown that all got nowhere, Fragante sued the fire department, claiming sexual and national origin harassment. How will her case be decided?

Answer: Both sexual harassment and harassment because of national origin violate Title VII. Since no demand for sexual relations was made to Fragante, this is not a quid pro quo case. Thus, it is analyzed as a hostile environment case, both as to sex and as to national origin. To prove hostile environment, plaintiff needs to show that the workplace was permeated with discriminatory intimidation, ridicule, and insult that was so severe or pervasive that it changed the conditions of her employment. The pornographic posters and signs would be objectively abusive to a reasonable person in Fragante's position as well as subjectively abusive to her. Based on the evidence in the record, a finder of fact would likely conclude that the harassers were motivated by general hostility to the presence of women and Filipinos in the workplace. That proves the harassment was because of her sex and her Philippine national origin. Finally, the fire department is likely to be found liable for the harassment by her co-workers. While there is no indication that supervisors were perpetrators of the harassment, Fragante made frequent complaints about the harassment to her superior at the fire station as well as with higher officials. The public display made the harassment obvious to all at the firehouse, including supervisors. Thus, the fire department was negligent since it knew about the harassment and failed to stop it. The fire department is, therefore, liable to Fragante for the sexual and national origin harassment that she suffered.

CHAPTER SEVEN: RELIGIOUS DISCRIMINATION

Question 1: Khahil Al-Abrahim works on the Ford assembly line at a plant that produces Ford Explorers. As a Moslem, Al-Abrahim is required to stop all activity five times a day and bow to Mecca in prayer for about 15 minutes each time. Because the Ford Explorer is very popular, Ford has scheduled all workers to work 12-hour days and it changed the way breaks are given. Formerly roving relief workers would take over when a worker signaled he needed a break. Now the relief workers follow a strict schedule of providing workers a break. These changes means that Al-Abrahim is in the plant for four of the five prayer times per day and the new relief system means that he cannot get a relief worker to take his place in the assembly line at his prayer times. Al-Abrahim requested that Ford accommodate his religious needs but Ford says the relief system it provides is as much accommodation as it is willing to do. Using the system of scheduled relief means that Ford needs to schedule several fewer relief workers for each shift, which saves money. Does Al-Abrahim have a good reasonable accommodation case?

Answer: Al-Abrahim can easily establish that his need for time to pray to Mecca during the workday is a religious practice and his testimony that he is sincere about it is pretty much determinative on that issue. The main focus of the case will be, first, on whether Ford has provided an accommodation that is reasonable, and, second, if not, would an effective accommodation of plaintiff's practice needs cause an undue hardship on Ford's business. First, the previous system just happened to work out to accommodate Al-Abrahim but it was not undertaken to accommodate anyone's religion. The new system of providing relief workers is also not an accommodation of the religious needs of the plaintiff. If what Ford does would be considered an accommodation that is reasonable, that would end Al-Abrahim's case. Since it is not an accommodation, the second step of undue hardship is reached. The Supreme Court has defined undue hardship as being shown whenever more than a de minimis cost is imposed on the employer. Since Ford would have to pay for several more relief workers to go back to the old system, that cost would be more than de minimis and therefore Ford would have shown undue hardship. The Supreme Court has even ruled that having a supervisor undertake some additional duties in order to accommodate a worker involves real and, therefore, more than de minimis costs. Plaintiff is likely, therefore, to lose his reasonable accommodation case.

CHAPTER EIGHT: NATIONAL ORIGIN AND ALIENAGE DISCRIMINATION

Question 1: All American Magazine Distributors is involved in soliciting house-to-house, selling subscriptions for magazines that focus on pride in the United States, American history, and the like. It has a rule that all employees must be citizens of the United States. Else Moeller, a citizen of Denmark but a lawfully admitted authorized resident of the United States, was denied employment because she is not a U.S. citizen. Does she have any way to challenge the refusal of All American to hire her?

Answer: While Title VII does not protect people from alienage discrimination, there is authority that 42 U.S.C §1981 prohibits alienage discrimination in both public and private employment. Further, the Immigration and Reform and Control Act of 1986 (IRCA) makes it an unfair immigration-related employment practice to discriminate because of a person's "protected status." Aliens authorized to work in the United States have protected status.

IRCA claimants, however, give up their right to proceed on any alternative basis. Although Moeller cannot proceed against All American under Title VII, she can choose to bring either a §1981 action or to file an IRCA claim.

CHAPTER NINE: AGE DISCRIMINATION

Question 1: Wildness Law School has a practice of only hiring as professors lawyers who have been out of school less than five years. Since older lawyers tend to be out of law school longer than younger lawyers, the practice of hiring only relatively recent graduates as professors has a disparate impact on older lawyers. Is that illegal under the ADEA?

Answer: The Supreme Court has yet to decide whether the disparate impact theory is available in ADEA actions. There are differences between the two statutes that bear on the question. First, the Civil Rights Act of 1991 amended Title VII, but not the ADEA, to include an explicit adoption of the disparate impact concept which, up until that time, had been a common law creation of the courts. While Congress did not amend the ADEA to include disparate impact analysis, it is also pretty clear that Congress did not do anything to forbid the courts to continue the development of antidiscrimination law by finding that the disparate impact theory was available in ADEA actions. There are also two provisions in the ADEA—that good cause and actions based on a reasonable factor other than age are not age discrimination—that may focus the thrust of the statute on only intentional age discrimination and not on practices that merely cause an impact on older workers. Nevertheless, it may be argued that a practice that causes a disparate impact on older workers may be a factor other than age but it is not reasonable. The present Supreme Court has been loathe to expand the scope of antidiscrimination statutes, so the best guess is that the present Court will not find that the ADEA includes the disparate impact theory of discrimination.

CHAPTER TEN: RETALIATION

Question 1: Cynthia Kim, a Korean American, worked as a cashier at a WalMart store in Columbus, Georgia. While the store employed a number of Asian Pacific Americans, several of whom had applied for promotions to supervisory positions, none of the supervisors or other managers were Asian Pacific Americans even though most supervisors had been promoted from clerk positions. While Kim was on an economic layoff during a slow period at the store, she undertook a campaign protesting Walmart's employment discrimination against Asian Pacific Americans. Several days a week Kim would picket on the public sidewalk surrounding the store, carrying a placard that said, "Uncle Sam Says No More Employment Discrimination. He Means You, WalMart." When WalMart started to recall workers on layoff, Kim tried to reapply but was told that she would not be rehired because there were no openings. She then filed a retaliation charge with the EEOC. What will happen in her case?

Answer: Since she had not yet filed a charge with the EEOC when WalMart refused to recall her and since there is no indication that Kim had up to that point participated in any legal proceedings involving claims of discrimination against WalMart, it is clear that no free access claim is involved here. Instead, the case is an opposition clause case. Whether a person on layoff is characterized as a present or former employee, Kim is a person protected by §704(a). The second question is whether Kim had an honest and reasonable belief that WalMart had discriminated. Given that WalMart generally promoted supervisors from the pool of clerks but had never promoted an Asian Pacific American, Kim's belief that WalMart discriminated against Asian Pacific Americans is honest and is probably reasonable. The final question is whether Kim's opposition conduct is reasonable. Unlike the illegal stall-in protest activity involved in *McDonnell Douglas,* WalMart has not shown that Kim's opposition conduct was illegal or otherwise unreasonable. Given the fact that shortly after she engaged in opposition conduct, other workers on layoff were being recalled but Kim was not, Kim has proven that WalMart did not rehire her because of her protected conduct.

CHAPTER ELEVEN: RECONSTRUCTION CIVIL RIGHTS ACTS

Question 1:   Lisa Lanovich comes to your office and tells you that slightly over a year ago her employer, the Croatian Club, a tax-exempt, nonprofit private membership club, refused to promote her permanently to the job that she had been doing on an interim basis. A young woman of Croatian background was hired from the outside to fill the job. Lanovich was born in the part of the former Yugoslavia that is now Bosnia. Her family is Serbian by background. She worked for the club for many years with no problem, but, with all the recent troubles in the former Yugoslavia, the work environment has become more stressful. Lanovich has asked you if there is any legal action she can take.

Answer: *Title VII is Not Available*
Title VII is unavailable for two reasons. First, the failure to promote occurred over a year ago, so the time period for filing a Title VII

charge with the appropriate administrative agency has run under either the 180-day or the 300-day rule. Second, the Croatian Club, as a tax-exempt, nonprofit private membership club, is not an employer for Title VII purposes.

42 U.S.C. §1981

Section 1981 applies to all contracts. So the fact that the Croatian Club is exempt from Title VII does not mean that its employment contracts are not covered by §1981. Also, there is no requirement that a claim be filed with an administrative agency in order to initiate a §1981 action. Further, the statute of limitations for §1981 actions is set by looking at the most analogous state statute, which typically is longer than a year. The substantive scope of §1981 prohibits discrimination in employment contracts because of a person's ancestry or ethnic characteristics, but not solely because of her place of birth. Thus, Lanovich can make a §1981 claim if she can prove that she was denied the promotion because of her Serbian ancestry. The club, however, can try to rebut that by showing that it acted solely because she was born in Yugoslavia. Given that the former Yugoslavia is the ancestral home to both Serbs and Croats, it is difficult to believe that the club's action was based on Lanovich's place of birth, rather than her ancestry or ethnic characteristic as a Serb. Lanovich has a good chance to win if she brings a §1981 action against the Croatian Club.

CHAPTER TWELVE: DISABILITY DISCRIMINATION

Question 1:   Dr. Gene Wilson is an orthopedic surgeon working as an employee of Mercy Orthopedic Hospital. His specialty has been knee replacement surgery. When Wilson informed the medical staff that he was infected with the HIV virus, but that he suffers none of the symptoms of AIDS, the hospital transferred Wilson from the surgical department to the recovery department, in which physicians make rounds checking the status of patients recovering from surgery. There are a variety of types of orthopedic surgery, from orthoscopic surgery, which involves tiny wounds and does not require the surgeon to place his hands inside the body of the patient, to such major invasive surgery as hip or knee replacement. The risk of transmission of the HIV virus comes from the possibility that the surgeon would cut himself while operating and that his blood would be able to mingle with the blood of the patient in the patient's wound. The Centers for Disease Control (CDC) Guidelines report that there is no recorded incidence of physician-to-patient transmission of HIV, but the guidelines do recommend that surgeons with HIV consult with their medical staff to develop a plan that safely focuses the practice of the physician. Wilson is willing to stop performing knee replacement surgery but he would like to continue in the surgery department, performing non-invasive surgery such as orthoscopic surgery. The hospital has refused because, in the words of Dr. Candice Neilson, the hospital's medical director, "the only way to eliminate the risk of HIV infection in patients is for Wilson to stop doing surgery." Wilson wants to know if an ADA action would be successful.

Answer: Two different concepts of discrimination that violate the ADA appear to be involved in Wilson's case. First, the transfer of Wilson out of the surgery department may be individual disparate treatment discrimination under the general rule of §102(a) prohibiting disability discrimination. Second, the failure to reasonably accommodate a known disability may violate the separate reasonable accommodation theory of discrimination prohibited by §102(b)(5). Both theories, however, first focus on whether plaintiff can establish that he is a "qualified individual with a disability," which involves a set of multi-layered statutory definitions.

An Individual with a Disability
The first question is whether plaintiff is an individual with a disability, a question that looks to three different definitions of disability in the ADA. The first, and basic, definition is that the individual has a physical or mental impairment that substantially limits one or more major life activities. In *Bragdon v. Abbott,* the Supreme Court decided that an individual infected with HIV had a physical impairment, even though she was asymptomatic. In that same case, the Court found that HIV infection implicates the major life activity of reproduction, while also acknowledging that other major life activities were also likely to be implicated. Finally, the Court also found that plaintiff's physical impairment from the HIV infection substantially limited her major life activity of reproduction. Since Wilson established that he is an individual with a disability under the first definition, it is not necessary to decide whether he had a record of impairment or was regarded as having an impairment, the other two definitions of disability.

Qualified Individual
The second step is for plaintiff to establish that he is qualified, which is defined as an "individual who, with or without reasonable accommodation, can perform the essential functions of the employment position that such individual holds or desires." His infection with HIV does not change Wilson's ability to perform surgery, which is the essential function of the job he desires. To take account of the risk of transmitting the HIV infection, Wilson here seeks an accommodation that would allow him to continue work as a sur-

geon but that would have him perform orthoscopic and other surgery that does not involve either open wounds or the need for the surgeon to place his hands in the body cavity of patients. Such job restructuring is recognized by §101(9)'s definition of reasonable accommodation. The restructuring Wilson proposes would even appear to satisfy the cost-benefit test of reasonableness that some lower courts apply.

The Hospital Acted Because of Plaintiff's Disability
This final element of an individual disparate treatment case of disability discrimination is established because the hospital admitted that the reason it decided to transfer Wilson was his HIV infection.

The Hospital's Defenses
The hospital has two possible affirmative defenses. Because Wilson requests an accommodation, the hospital can escape liability by proving that the accommodation is an undue hardship. Undue hardship means "an action requiring significant difficulty or expense." Here there appears to be no direct increase in expenses for the hospital to accommodate Wilson's desire to continue doing a different type of surgery. There may be some difficulty in accommodating Wilson because it may entail the need to have other surgeons change their mix of types of surgery but, without more, that difficulty is unlikely to be found significant. Thus, the hospital is not likely to prevail on the undue hardship defense to the need to reasonably accommodate Wilson. The second defense is the direct threat to others. Section 103(b) creates the direct threat defense and §101(3) defines it as "a significant risk to the health or safety of others that cannot be eliminated by reasonable accommodation." The key question is whether the accommodation that Wilson requests would still be a "significant risk to the health or safety of others." All agree that the risk that HIV would be transmitted to any one patient if Dr. Wilson is allowed to do orthoscopic and other non-invasive surgery is very small. All agree that if the risk occurs, the resulting infection of a patient would be terrible since there is no cure for HIV and so far no way ultimately to prevent the development of AIDS. The health care professional standards as expressed in the CDC Guidelines do not require an HIV-infected surgeon to stop all surgery but the hospital's medical director's view is that he should. The Court in *Arline* said that the courts should defer to health care professionals, which would mean that the CDC Guidelines would apply. They do not view HIV infection as creating a direct threat to the patients of surgeons. In *Bragdon,* the Court said that "a health care professional [such as medical director Neilson] who disagrees with the prevailing medical consen-

sus may refute it by citing a credible scientific basis for deviating from the accepted norm." The present record does not include any evidence that Neilson had a scientific basis for her position and so the hospital would fail in attempting to prove that Wilson would be a direct threat to others if he performed surgery according to the accommodation he requests.

CHAPTER THIRTEEN: EQUAL PAY FOR EQUAL WORK

Question 1:   Sharon Tisdale worked her way up from an accounts payable clerk eventually to be the coordinator of the raw materials department of Fort Apache Paper Company. Her pay as coordinator was less than Michael Sullivan, her male predecessor in the job, was paid. While Sullivan had held the Coordinator position in the raw materials department for four years, he had been classified by the company as "temporary." That temporary status allowed him to retain seniority and the higher pay that he had received in his prior department. Tisdale brought both Equal Pay Act and Title VII claims.

Answer: *Equal Pay Act Claims*

Tisdale needs to prove four elements to establish a prima facie Equal Pay Act case. Choosing Sullivan as her comparator, Tisdale has to prove that they worked in the same establishment, that they received unequal pay, on the basis of sex, for work that is substantially equal in content. There is no question Tisdale and Sullivan worked in the same establishment and received unequal pay. In most EPA cases, proving the work of the two workers is substantially equal in content is the most difficult issue. Here, in absence of evidence that the content of the job changed when Tisdale took over from Sullivan, it is clear that the two performed equal work. The fourth element of a prima facie EPA case, "on the basis of sex," is shown by the proof that a man and woman received unequal pay for equal work. It does not require proof of the employer's intent to discriminate. Proof of a prima facie case shifts the burden of persuasion to the employer to prove the wages were paid pursuant to a seniority system, a merit system, a system that measures earnings by quality or quantity of production, or a differential based on "any other factor other than sex." None of the first three defenses appear to be applicable, so the entire case turns on whether the employer can prove that the pay difference was based on "any other factor other than sex." While the EEOC recognizes that a temporary reassignment is a factor other than sex that justifies the employee being paid the rate of his previous position, there is some doubt whether the reassignment here can be considered "temporary" when Sullivan held the job for four years. Alternatively, if Sullivan came from a department that was predominantly male, it may be argued, based on *Corning Glass*, that the sex-segregated departments render Sullivan's status as a permanent employee in that department to be "on the basis of sex." Tisdale will likely win her EPA claim.

Title VII

Since Title VII bans sex discrimination and discrimination in compensation, Tisdale can proceed against the employer with a Title VII action. Since there is no direct evidence that the employer paid Tisdale less than her predecessor because of sex discrimination, she will have to proceed using the *McDonnell Douglas/Burdine* approach, with the key issue being whether the employer discriminated against her in pay because of her sex. She can easily prove a prima facie case by showing she is a woman and she was paid less salary for doing the same job than her male predecessor was paid. Defendant can also rebut the prima facie case by introducing evidence that the salary difference between Tisdale and Sullivan was the product of his classification as "temporary" while he served as coordinator of the raw materials department and not because Tisdale was a woman. That leaves the plaintiff's surrebuttal stage. It may be difficult for Tisdale to carry her burden of persuasion to prove that, but for her sex, she would have been paid the same as Sullivan. Absent some more evidence that the "temporary" classification was a sham, the factfinder is likely to conclude that Sullivan was paid more than he otherwise would have been paid, and more than Tisdale was paid, because the company allowed him to maintain his higher pay from his prior department. That would mean Tisdale would lose her Title VII claim because she would not be able to prove the employer's intent to discriminate.

CHAPTER FOURTEEN: COVERAGE OF THE ANTIDISCRIMINATION STATUTES

Question: The law firm partnership of Whipp, Savage & Fleece has three partners, five associates, an office manager, a computer specialist, a bookkeeper, four secretaries, and two file clerks who all work full time. Sara Whipp, the daughter of partner Tom Whipp, is a law student but she does part-time work throughout the year as a law clerk for the firm. One of the associates, Dean Levinson, was considered for but denied partnership. He claims that it was because he is Jewish since none of the other lawyers at the firm are Jewish. The partners of the firm ask you to tell them if the firm is an employer under Title VII and whether the decision to consider an associate for partnership involves employment.

Answer: Title VII defines an employer as "any person engaged in commerce in an industry affecting commerce who has fifteen or more employees for each working day in each of twenty or more calendar weeks in the current year." Further, "person" is defined to include partnerships, such as Whipp, Savage & Fleece. A firm the size of this partnership will undoubtedly be found to be in "an industry affecting commerce." The key question for coverage is whether the firm has 15 employees. In the firm, the three partners are employers and are not employees. The test used to count employees is whether the employee is on the employer's payroll. Since they work full time, the five associates, office manager, computer specialist, bookkeeper, four secretaries, and two file clerks are no doubt on the firm's payroll. As such they count as 14 employees. So the question of coverage of the law firm will depend on whether the law clerk, Sara Whipp, is on the payroll. If she is on the payroll, she counts as the fifteenth employee even if she works part time. Thus Whipp, Savage & Fleece is an employer covered by Title VII. Since partners are not employees for purposes of Title VII, the decision to bring in someone from the outside as a partner is not an employment decision covered by Title VII. However, the decision to make an employee, such as associate Levinson, a partner is a term and condition of his employment. Thus, the law firm will be considered an employer if Sara Whipp is on the payroll and the decision concerning the partnership of Dean Levinson is an employment decision within the coverage of Title VII.

CHAPTER FIFTEEN: PROCEDURES FOR ENFORCING DISCRIMINATION LAWS

Question 1: In 1997, Austin McHenry, an African American, had been an assistant professor of English at Coalhurst College for six years when he applied for tenure. In April 1998, McHenry was told by Susan Lockhart, the Dean of Arts and Sciences, that his application had been denied and that he would be given a terminal contract for the 1998–1999 academic year. After receiving the terminal contract, McHenry appealed his denial of tenure to the college president and the board of trustees. In January 1999, the president and board of trustees vacated the decision denying McHenry tenure and sent the decision back for reconsideration by the faculty of Arts and Sciences. The terminal contract was retracted and replaced with a contract for 1998–1999 that was renewable according to the college's general rules. In May 1999, Dean Lockhart told McHenry that, while he had not been granted tenure, the faculty had decided to give him a contract for two academic years, 1999–2001, with the expectation that he would reapply for tenure in the fall of 2000. While McHenry is happy to have the contract, he would still like to challenge the original denial of tenure because he thinks it was discriminatory. Can he timely file a discrimination charge against the college in May 1999?

Answer: When in April 1998 McHenry received notice that the college had denied him tenure and given him a terminal contract for the following year, he had 180/300 days "after the alleged unlawful employment practice occurred" in which to file a Title VII charge of discrimination with the appropriate antidiscrimination agency. Even in a deferral jurisdiction, which triggers the 300-day rule, that time, which began in April 1998, was long since passed by May 1999. Thus, his claim that the original decision to deny him tenure was discriminatory is barred even though he had a right of appeal within the college and even though that appeal was to some extent successful. Once the decision to deny him tenure had been made, the alleged discriminatory event occurred. There is no continuing violation because all that continues here is the effect of the college's decision, not the discrimination itself. McHenry does, however, have 180/300 days to file a charge of discrimination starting from his receipt of notice in May 1999 that he had not been granted tenure, though he had been granted two more years to work towards tenure. Since the state statutes of limitation that apply to §1981 actions are typically longer than one year, McHenry may be able to file a timely §1981 lawsuit challenging his April 1998 denial of tenure.

CHAPTER SIXTEEN: JUDICIAL RELIEF

Question 1: Zoe Zellman applied for and was the only woman finalist for the job of principal of Peaceful Place High School. At the school board meeting considering the four finalists, two of the five board members were quoted as saying that "we don't need the trouble of having a woman as principal," "no woman could keep those students in check," etc. Wayne Myers was appointed principal. He has a Ph.D., 10 years of high school teaching experience, 15 year's experience as principal at another high school, and has received the "Principal of the Year" award from the state board of education. Zellman has a master's degree and has served as the assistant principal of the Peaceful Place Middle School for three years. Before that she taught in the Peaceful Place Elementary School for five years. Zellman's sex discrimination case was sent to the jury with instructions framed under §§703(m) of Title VII and 706(g)(2)(B). The jury returned a verdict finding that plaintiff proved that sex was "a motivating factor" in the school board's decision not to choose her as principal but that the defendant had carried its burden of proving that the school board "would have taken the same action in the absence of the impermissible motivating factor" of sex. What remedies are available for Zellman?

Answer: Title VII provides a wide array of legal and equitable relief to the victims of employment discrimination. When, however, an employer is successful in proving the same decision defense in §706(g)(2)(B), the relief provided the plaintiff is quite limited. Section 706(g)(2)(B) says that the court "shall not award damages or issue an order requiring any admission, hiring, promotion, or payment [of backpay]." Thus, Zellman is not eligible for compensatory or punitive damages or general equitable relief, including reinstatement and backpay. The relief available to Zellman is limited to "declaratory relief, injunctive relief [except injunctive relief concerning admission, hiring, or promotion], and attorney's fees and costs demonstrated to be directly attributable only to the pursuit of a claim under section 703(m)." Thus, Zellman is presumptively entitled to a declaratory order that the defendant had discriminated against her and an injunction prohibiting the defendant from discriminating in the future. Zellman is a prevailing plaintiff since she obtained some relief on the merits of her claim. Thus, she is presumptively entitled to attorney's fees attributable to her §703(m) claim. According to Farrar v. Hobby, the reasonable fee award would be "no fee at all" if plaintiff only was entitled to nominal damages. Zellman's action, however, did serve a public purpose because of the declaratory order that the defendant discriminated against Zellman because of her sex and the injunction against discriminating in the future. Thus, Zellman should be paid attorney's fees for all the work attributable to her §703 (m) claim. Since her whole case focused on her claim that sex was a motivating factor in the defendant's decision not to appoint her principal, the fees for every stage in the enforcement scheme should be paid to her. The fee will be calculated by multiplying the number of hours her attorneys spent on her case times a reasonable rate per hour. The court may modify the award either upward or downward in those rare circumstances where a party proves that special circumstances justify such a modification.

GLOSSARY

Affirmative action. The use of race, gender, or other characteristic by an employer to remedy barriers to the employment of women and minority group men, which does not violate Title VII as long as it does not trammel the interests of the majority and is not permanent. A public employer faces a more difficult standard under equal protection where, for race, strict scrutiny applies, so that the use of race needs to be justified by the compelling governmental interest test. While an employer may voluntarily undertake the use of affirmative action, it may be imposed by a court to remedy discrimination.

After-acquired evidence. Evidence of employee wrongdoing that the employer acquires at some point after the employee has claimed discrimination, which evidence may cut off remedies for the employee if the employer can prove the wrongdoing was of such severity that the employee would have been terminated on those grounds alone.

Alienage. One's citizenship.

Alternative employment practice. The third, surrebuttal step in a disparate impact case where the plaintiff proves that an alternative exists to the practice she challenges that would serve the employer's interests but which the employer refuses to adopt.

At-will employment. The rule at common law was that employment was at will, that is, that either party could terminate the relationship at any time for good reason, bad reason, or no reason at all.

Backpay. Amount of earnings an employee lost because of the employer's discrimination, which may be recovered as equitable relief.

Binomial distribution. The sophisticated statistical technique discussed in *Hazelwood* used to compare two groups of data, such as the employer's workforce and the labor pool from which the employer chooses its employees in order to make out a systemic disparate treatment case.

Bona fide occupational qualification (BFOQ). A "bona fide occupational qualification" is a defense to systemic disparate treatment discrimination where it can be shown that religion, national origin, sex, or age goes to the essence of the job and either no one of the excluded group can do the job or the difficulty of picking the few qualified members in the excluded group make that impractical. The BFOQ does not apply to race, color, or disability.

Bona fide merit system. An exception to the application of disparate impact law for a system that sets compensation by quantity or quality of production.

Bona fide seniority system. An exception to the application of disparate impact law for a collectively bargained system involving the traditional components of a seniority system that has not been adopted or applied out of an intent to discriminate.

Business necessity. One element of the defense to a disparate impact case, which requires the **employer** to prove that its challenged practice is justified by business necessity and is related to the job for which it is used.

Content validation. A technique developed by test professionals to validate a test by showing that the test is a fair sample of the job for which the test will be used.

Circumstantial evidence. This is the most typically used method of analyzing individual disparate treatment cases. Based on *McDonnell Douglas* and its progeny, a circumstantial evidence case is based on three steps. First, the employee must prove a simple prima facie case. Second, the employer must then undertake a simple burden of introducing evidence of a reason for its action other than discrimination. The third step becomes the focus of the case, with the factfinder having to decide whether the reason the employer advances is true or not and then whether the employee has proved that the decision she challenges was taken because of discrimination. The test is called the circumstantial evidence test because the factfinder, looking at the evidence, must draw the inference that the decision was taken because of discrimination.

Continuing violation. Where the defendant's action that is discriminatory continues so that it is always timely to file a charge of discrimination.

Criterion-related validation. A method test professionals use to validate a test by statistically comparing the performance of a sample of applicants on tests with their subsequent performance on the job.

Direct evidence. Based on *Price Waterhouse,* this is an alternative method of proving individual disparate treatment discrimination from the *McDonnell Douglas* circumstantial evidence method. Direct evidence is evidence that proves something without having to draw an inference. An employer telling an employee, "You are fired because you are an African American," is direct evidence that the employer fired the worker because of her race. Some courts have stretched the definition to cover some circumstantial evidence, which requires that an inference be drawn based on the fact found as to the fact at issue.

Employment at will. At common law, the employment relation was characterized as one of contract, with the presumption that it was "at will." At will means that either the employer or the employee could terminate the relationship at any time for good reason, bad reason, or no reason. Antidiscrimination law adds an exception to the at-will rule: the employer may terminate an at-will employment relation at any time for good reason, bad reason, or no reason but not because of discrimination.

Formal policy of discrimination. A written or otherwise admitted policy of an employer that discriminates on its face. This is one form of proof of systemic disparate treatment.

Front pay. Compensation to a victim of discrimination for earnings she will lose after judgment until reinstatement or, in lieu of reinstatement, as the difference between what she would have earned in the future if she had been reinstated and what she will earn in the future in her next best employment.

Hostile environment harassment. Claims of harassment where the work environment is permeated with discriminatory intimidation, ridicule, and insult so severe as to alter the employment conditions of the employee.

Individual disparate treatment discrimination. The most typical discrimination claim that the employer acted against an employee because of an intent to discriminate.

Individual with a disability. Plaintiff in an ADA action must prove she suffers a physical or mental impairment that substantially limits a major life activity.

Intentional discrimination. Either individual or systemic disparate treatment discrimination in which the key question is the state of mind of the employer in taking the action that the employee challenges.

Job related. One of two elements in the affirmative defense to a prima facie case of disparate impact discrimination. Thus, the challenged practice must be related to the actual needs of a particular job and also necessary for the business.

Liquidated damages. Double of the basic backpay award where plaintiff can establish that defendant's violation of the ADEA or EPA was "willful."

Mixed motives. When more than one motive was in the mind of the employer when it took the action that the plaintiff challenges as discriminatory. This is one description of *Price Waterhouse* cases.

Multiple regression. The sophisticated statistical technique used in *Bazemore* to analyze a number of variables against a continuous variable like salary.

National origin. The country where you or your forebears came from. It does not include your citizenship.

Null hypothesis. The starting point of all sophisticated statistical techniques, which states the proposition to be disproved. Thus, in employment, the null hypothesis is that race is not connected with the employer's employment decisions.

Practice of discrimination. Systemic disparate treatment discrimination established by statistical and anecdotal evidence that it is the general practice of the employer to discriminate.

Pretext. The third step in a *McDonnell Douglas* case where the plaintiff tries to prove that the nondiscriminatory reason the employer claims it based its action upon is not true and is a cover to hide its discriminatory intent.

Probability theory. The basis for use of statistical evidence to prove discrimination. It is that over time the employer's workforce will be more or less representative of the qualified labor pool from which the employer hires its employees.

Professionally developed test. An exception to the application of disparate impact law where the employer has validated the test that plaintiff challenges using test validation standards developed by test professionals.

Qualified individual. A term of art in the ADA, which means an individual with a disability, who, with or without reasonable accommodation, can perform the essential functions of the job she wants.

Qualified labor pool. In using statistical evidence to prove a practice of systemic disparate treatment discrimination, the employer's workforce is compared with the qualified labor pool, the potential people who could be hired for the type of job involved, to determine whether there is a gross and longlasting disparity between the two.

Quid pro quo harassment. Sexual harassment where the employee consents to sexual relations in order to save her job or where the employee is punished with an adverse employment decision for refusing to have sex with a supervisor.

Reasonable accommodation. Reasonable accommodation requires an employer to take account of the religious practices and beliefs of employees or applicants under Title VII and to modify its workplace requirements to meet their needs unless that accommodation would cause an undue hardship. Similarly, the Americans with Disabilities Act requires employers to take account of the needs of individuals with disabilities in order that they may be qualified to work. Unlike Title VII, the ADA defines some accommodations that are reasonable.

Retaliation. Adverse action taken by an employer against a past or present employee who has opposed the employer's discrimination or who has participated in proceedings involving discrimination.

Right-to-sue letter. Letter from the EEOC to a charging party indicating that the agency has had the charge for the mandatory 180-day period and that the charging party is entitled to file a claim of discrimination in court.

Rightful place reinstatement. Instead of displacing incumbent employees by providing immediate relief to victims of discrimination in a classwide case, "rightful place" relief puts plaintiffs on a priority hiring list for job openings. When hired off the list, the individual is granted seniority and other benefits back to the date she was discriminated against.

Same decision defense. In a *Price Waterhouse* case, once a plaintiff has used direct evidence to prove that a protected characteristic was "a motivating factor" in the employer's decision, the burden of persuasion shifts to the defendant to prove that it would have made the same decision even if it had not had the impermissible motivation. If the defendant proves the same decision defense plaintiff is limited to declaratory relief that the employer had discriminated against him, an injunction against future discrimination, and attorney's fees and costs.

Stereotyping. Using stereotypes means that an employer acts as to a particular woman based on the expectation that this woman is like all other women in having traits that are generally unfavorable.

Systemic disparate impact discrimination. A theory that can be used to attack policies of employers that weigh more heavily on groups, such as women or minority groups, than on the majority even where there is no proof that the employer acted with an intent to discriminate.

Systemic disparate treatment discrimination. The broadest theory of intentional discrimination in which the employer has a policy established in writing or otherwise or a general practice of discriminating on the basis of race, sex, or other characteristic prohibited by an antidiscrimination law.

Unequal treatment. One of the ways of showing discrimination is to show that African American or women workers were treated unequally with white male workers. Based on that unequal treatment by the employer, it is possible to draw an inference that the employer acted with an intent to discriminate.

TABLE OF CASES

TABLE OF STATUTES

TABLE OF FEDERAL RULES

INDEX

311